KU-524-880

To Be Mayor of New York

TO BE
MAYOR
OF
NEW
YORK

Ethnic Politics
in the City

CHRIS McNICKLE

Columbia University Press
New York

Columbia University Press
New York   Chichester, West Sussex
Copyright © 1993 Columbia University Press
All rights reserved

Library of Congress Cataloging-in-Publication Data

McNickle, Chris.
    To be mayor of New York / Chris McNickle.
        p.   cm.
    Includes bibliographical references and index.
    ISBN 0–231–07636–3
    1. New York (N.Y.)—Politics and government—1898–1950.   2. New
York (N.Y.)—Politics and government—1951–   3. Mayors—New York
(N.Y.)—History.   4. New York (N.Y.)—Ethnic relations.   I. Title.
F128.5.M39   1992
974.7′ 104—dc20   92–32583
                                                                              CIP

Casebound editions of Columbia University Press books are
printed on permanent and durable acid-free paper.

Printed in the United States of America

c   10   9   8   7   6   5   4   3   2

For Dad, for launching me,
For Arthur Mann, for helping launch this book,
and
For Fred Walters, just 'cause.

Contents

Acknowledgments

I am a lucky man. So many special people took such an active interest in this book that the lonely and demanding tasks of research and writing turned out to be fun almost all the time.

Mom read each chapter as I completed them, footnotes included, with the care and love that only a mother knows. When she finished, she issued her verdict: "It's better than Mayor Koch's books!" Apologies to Hizzoner, but a politician as successful as he knows better than to argue with a mother about her son. While I was working on the manuscript in the Bronx my eldest brother, Nick, and my sister-in-law, Litna, were busy making babies in Queens. First Danny, then Katie, and then Becky was born. They have been a source of joy for every member of the family from the moment they arrived, and they are remarkably well behaved when uncle Chris babysits. (At least, that is what I tell their parents.) Through no choice of their own all of my family became partners in my book and listened to endless stories about New York's political history with apparent interest and infinite patience. And they cheered me on to the end.

Acknowledgments

I owe a special debt to Neal Garelik, a friend who shares my passion for New York and who has been a ready companion for discussions about the city's politics—past, present, and future. In no small way he contributed to the completion of the book by gathering enormous stacks of newspaper and magazine articles that allowed me to write the final chapters while I was working at a job with demanding hours and an unrelenting travel schedule that made access to libraries impossible. Neal's help was terrific (and Judi Sherman's as well) but it is the friendship that counts the most.

Joe Lynch is a wonderful source of encouragement and support—and a great drinking buddy to boot. Many were the nights that he and I solved all the troubles of the world at Connaughton's Steak House in Riverdale only to discover that they had reappeared the next morning. Not to worry, we will stick with it as long as it takes. There were times when Tim Gilfoyle joined us, and the nights lasted even longer. Then Tim met Mary Rose Alexander and we saw him much less. It is my good fortune that I travel to Chicago frequently so I can still see Tim and Mary Rose Gilfoyle, even though we miss them in New York.

When I decided to take a multiyear pause from a career in finance to pursue a very impractical degree in American history, only Mark Gallogly among my friends in business understood. He approved wholeheartedly and helped me throughout the endeavor in every way he could. That is only one of the reasons that he has a special place in my heart, as do Lise Strickler Gallogly and Katharine, and my God daughter, Grace. It was through Mark that I met Kevin Caspersen, a transplanted Texan determined to do good in the South Bronx. I am a better man for knowing him, and New York is a better city for his presence.

Rick Grimes and Linda Walters Grimes invited me frequently to dine in Manhattan and to sail on Long Island Sound, and along with Fred Walters were part of the best vacation ever, spent floating around the Caribbean. Alex was there too, in formation. It was a great way for an author to recharge at the end of a long winter of research and writing. I liked it so much I went back the next year to visit Jamie Calvo and Jennifer O'Neill in St. Croix, a fitting place for a couple that belongs in paradise. That same year Robert Stein, a friend since not long after birth, honored me by asking me to be best man at his marriage to Karen Monash. It was a simple and delightful ceremony that I will always treasure. Writing a history about the city I grew up in made me think often of my childhood friends. In a curious way Charlie and Billy Federman, Billy Reifer, Jonathan and Philip Rhodes, Douglas Panero, Steven Rolnik, Robert Herschenfeld, Rich Friedman, Ricky Rubin, David Fallick, Jerry Sotsky, Jeffrey Danzig, Joseph Donohue, and Peter Paul Cunningham all played a part in this book.

New Yorkers are famed for fighting with their landlords, but my experience is different. After completing my course work in Chicago I returned home to the Bronx to do my research and moved in to the top floor of a two-family house that I lived in as a child. The house had been bought by Florence Porter and Veronica Ladenburg, who insisted from the start on inviting me in for dinner, offering me cookies, and easing my work in countless small ways. When they brought Jenny home I even had a dog to play with without an obligation to walk it. What more could a tenant ask for? And the house is next door to the home of Naomi Cohen whose insights into the Jewish experience in the United States added measurably to my understanding of the Jewish political experience in New York City. In a very different way two more neighbors, Marcia Allina and Sol Zeichner, added to my understanding of local politics.

For two of the summers during which the dissertation that turned into this book was in progress I worked on projects arranged by Mark Wheeler. I learned about banking in Germany and Switzerland during one summer, and about public finance during the other. And I made enough money to keep me going through the autumns that followed. I am grateful to Mark for those opportunities. Another summer I worked for the U.S. Department of State in Mali, West Africa where I met Vicki Huddleston, and Bob and Robert and Alexandra. They treated me like a member of their family, and that same summer, Ambassador Robert Ryan took a special interest in my work. I have fond memories of them all.

While I was doing my course work and preparing for my Ph.D. exams at the University of Chicago, Harriet McCullough hired me as an intern in the Mayor's Office. That experience gave me a window onto the particular brand of politics practiced in America's second city and a valuable point of comparison with New York. I learned much from Harriet and Michael Holewinksi and Leslie Jacobs, and from watching Harold Washington wrestle with Chicago's City Council. Closer to home, while researching in the archives around New York, Harvey Robins hired me at the New York City Human Resources Administration to work on projects housing the homeless. The experience helped me to understand how New York's large bureaucracies work, and I learned a great deal from Caren Ponty, Joan Malin, Greg Kaladjian, Jeremy Ben-Ami, Jeremy Feigenbaum, Stephanie Kretchmer, Marty Ackerman, Barbara Chutroo, Barbara Knecht, and Bill Cohen.

Acknowledgments

At the University of Chicago I learned much about history from my fellow students—Emie Aronson, Matt Berg, Dan Beaver, Dan Gordon, Greg Eghigian, Antoinette Burton, Bill Kunz, Fred Bruner, Robin Einhorn, Peter Gorecki, Chris Kimball, David Shapinsky, Steve Johnson, and a host of others. I benefited from more formal training in scholarship from Akira Iriye, John Coatsworth, Kathleen Conzen, Neil Harris, and Barry Karl. James Grossman and Terry Nichols Clark read my dissertation with great care and offered provocative insights that allowed me to make more of my research than I first realized. And at a moment when my personal finances bore a striking resemblance to New York's during the 1975 fiscal crisis, Dean Anne Ch'ien made available a stipend that helped see me through.

Indirectly, Professor Alvin Rubinstein of the University of Pennsylvania played an important role in the writing of this book. I was among the many undergraduates taken in by his penetrating analysis of international politics and the inspirational force of his personality. One day in the library I came across his doctoral dissertation, written years before. When I saw it in typewritten form in my senior year, while working on my undergraduate thesis, I determined that I was capable of such work (in no small measure because of what Professor Rubinstein had taught me). It was a meaningful moment in my intellectual development, and I am grateful to Professor Rubinstein for it. I am grateful also to other friends from Penn—Rose Chu, Barbara Thompson O'Connor, Bryan Freedman, Robert Gensler, and Grace Chapin.

I have been a happy beneficiary of the City Seminar, one of the University Seminars at Columbia University. Many of the sessions have dealt with topics that, directly or indirectly, have sharpened my thinking on New York politics. At Clifton Hood's suggestion I presented the insights from my dissertation to the seminar and received valuable comments from Tom Kessner, Frank Vos and others. I also received an invitation from Professor Ken Jackson to submit the manuscript to Columbia University Press. This book is the outcome, and I am indebted to Ken for his support. Later, Clifton Hood and Marc Weiss suggested that I apply to the University Seminar for a prepublication grant. I appreciate the assistance from the University Seminars which helped me to prepare this manuscript for publication.

Working with Kate Wittenberg at Columbia University Press was a pleasure. All the world should be so competent and supportive. Her assistant, Chad Kia, helped the process to run smoothly. Leslie Bialler edited the manuscript with great personal interest and good humor. I am indebted to them all.

Acknowledgments

Richard Lieberman, Director of the LaGuardia and Wagner Archives, made access simple to the unique documents, oral history interviews, photographs and memorabilia of an outstanding collection. I am also grateful to Monica Blank for her good spirited help. David Seideman offered generous assistance and impassioned analysis of city affairs. At the New York City Municipal Archives Ken Cobb, Evelyn Gonzalez and others made my task easy. The Municipal Reference and Research Library staff helped willingly, as did the staff at the New York Public Library, at Columbia University's oral history collection, at the Herbert H. Lehman collection at Columbia University and at the archives of the International Ladies Garment Workers Union.

The last three chapters were written while working at Greenwich Associates. Rick Greene, Karen Dehmel Chapman, and Jamie Kalamarides helped me to stay organized so I could complete my work and have time for my manuscript as well. Wendy Crawford, Shirley Davis, and Gardie Nee kept me in touch with the world no matter where I called them from and Irene Mendecino kept my schedule straight no matter how confusing it seemed to become. When my computer ate several solid weeks of editing and revisions just days before the initial deadline for submitting it, Mike Karlin tried valiantly to uncrypt the information from the mangled disk. When that failed John Farley encouraged me to believe that the redone version would be even better than the devoured one. I tried to believe. Since even before I joined Greenwich Associates Jay Bennett has been an insightful confidant, a source of sound advice, and a true friend to whom I am indebted.

During my frequent trips to London for Greenwich Associates I found myself periodically in need of a New York fix. Fortunately, Peter Lighte, a Bronx native and old friend, works there. It is a rare London resident who can swap stories about the Grand Concourse in its glory days, adolescence at the Bronx High School of Science, and the joy of corned beef on rye—but Peter is a rare person, as well as a fine artist, an excellent banker, and a sometime scholar of Chinese philosophy and literature. It is a wonder he missed the renaissance. I frequently saw Bruce Bettencourt in London as well. Bruce was a momentary New Yorker originally from Rhode Island, transplanted to London, and then to Paris. I was with him and Helene Attuyt on their first date, and later at their wedding. I feel lucky to have been in the right place at two special moments to share in the joy.

Toward the final stages of finishing the manuscript a meeting with Robert F. Wagner, Jr. turned into a two hour long conversation about New York politics. We had so much fun we followed up with lunch, and several dinners. We have become good friends since, and I am grateful to Bob for his interest in the book, and his help in some of the final details of publication.

The thanks I owe to the three men to whom the book is dedicated does not lend itself easily to prose. I was just fourteen when my Dad died, but in the short time that I knew him he gave me a sense of right and wrong that has steered me true since. Arthur Mann promised that he would work on my dissertation as hard as I would—an unusual commitment as well as a test of my energies. Along the way he suffered a horrible series of illnesses. He recovered from each, never let me down despite his afflictions, and proved a gentle editor of enormous impact. I cannot say if I admire his dedication to scholarship more than his courage and dignity, or if it is the other way around. I know I am lucky to have studied with him. Fred Walters is the most loyal friend a person could ever have, and terrific fun. He makes sure I do not forget that life is for living as well as for doing—a valuable reminder that I need often, and for which I am deeply grateful.

To Be Mayor of New York

Introduction

From the earliest days of European settlement New York has boasted a
mixed population. As a New World trading port it attracted sailors from
dozens of lands—Dutch and Portuguese, French and Spanish, British,
German, African—and on and on. By 1660 one observer noted that no
fewer than eighteen languages could be heard in the streets of lower
Manhattan. There have not been fewer since. New York has been, and
remains, the world's most cosmopolitan city. Its success has depended
on the ability of its diverse population to compete on terms of relative
harmony.

The major ancestral groups to settle New York were the Irish and
the Germans in the mid-nineteenth century. They were followed by
the Jews and the Italians, who arrived in large numbers between 1880
and 1915. Then the blacks and the Puerto Ricans arrived, principally in
the years after 1940. Each group brought a distinct cultural heritage
with it to New York, and each responded differently to the environment
it found, creating a unique ethnic identity in the process. Among the
things that distinguished these groups from each other were their dif-

ferent approaches to politics, and the tendency of each to vote in a coherent pattern according to ethnic affiliation. As a consequence, the numbers of each group casting ballots in an election, and the nature of their voting patterns, explain electoral results in New York City with more power and consistency than any other form of analysis.[1]

No single group has ever dominated New York in sufficient numbers to control a citywide contest—an election for mayor—itself. Success has required coalitions. The strongest in the city's history was dominated by the Irish and supported by the Jews. It began to emerge as early as 1886, peaked between 1902 and 1932, and endured in weakened form until 1961. The two groups had different political priorities. The Irish wanted patronage and prestige from politics. The Jews wanted protection from discrimination, government programs to help the poorest members of society, and a basic standard of honesty upheld by public officials. The differences in practice were less neat than a simple statement makes it sound, but the two groups' political centers of gravity were in different places. Each could get what it wanted out of politics by working together.

The pact broke down when the formula became obsolete. By 1961 the ability of political leaders to dispense attractive government jobs had been badly crippled. The Irish, who had achieved great success in other arenas, had less need for the patronage and prestige government office afforded. Many had left the city altogether. Jews still wanted protection from discrimination and government programs to help the poor, and still had a lower tolerance for corruption than other groups. But a post–World War II generation of Jews—American born, educated, and raised—wanted to hold the formal reigns of power that an earlier generation of Jews had ceded to others as long as they received the benefits they sought.

During the 1960s, when the Jews replaced the Irish as the dominant group in the city's politics, for a time it appeared that Jewish liberals, working with the city's minorities, would create a multiracial coalition to govern the city. The racial tumult of the era, however, destroyed that much romanticized possibility. A political alliance emerged in the wake of that decade led by not-so-liberal Jews, supported by Irish Catholics, Italian Catholics, and other whites. Racial tension held it together.

By 1989 New York's ethnic arithmetic had changed again and a new political constellation brought to power a black mayor. His coalition is anchored by black voters, supported by Puerto Ricans and other Hispanics, and includes a small but critical number of white liberals—principally Jews. Its endurance has yet to be tested, but early indications are that it is fragile indeed.

When New Yorkers elect a mayor they reduce the diversity of countless neighborhoods and millions of people to a single human point. To be mayor of New York requires an ability to reconcile the competing visions that the city's ethnic groups hold of the metropolis, at least in sufficient measure to earn the confidence of a majority. The political identity of the leader who does that is a telling barometer of New York's political climate. Thus, the story of the quest to win the mayoralty—the city's most powerful office and its greatest political prize—traces the broad outline of the political history of New York City. That is the story this book tells.

In and of itself the tale is important. It explains how the people of the city that has been called the capital of the world have chosen their most important political leader. It is also a story of ethnic succession that explains much about the ways ethnic groups compete with each other and resolve conflicts in the political arena in the United States—something a multicultural democracy can never know too much about.

The organization is chronological, moving from one mayoralty campaign to the next. Often, to illustrate important conceptual points about the political behavior of the principal groups, it ranges far beyond the mayoralty campaigns themselves (this is especially true of the first two chapters).

The book is about politics—Who got elected, how and why? It contends with governance of the city only in so far as politicians' records influenced elections, which is very different from a thorough assessment of how each of the mayors governed the city. While the book's focus is on the years after 1945—the period when the key transitions in the city's politics took place—understanding the recent events requires knowing what came before, so the story begins with the Irish and the Jews during the last century.

Ethnic Arithmetic

1 8 8 1 – 1 9 0 1

When the Irish Ruled

The special role the Irish have played in American urban politics and specifically in New York City has been told before, but it bears repeating to provide the proper context for what followed.

The Irish were the first of New York's principal ethnic groups to arrive in large enough numbers to establish themselves as a coherent political force. Searching for an economic stability that escaped them at home, Irish Catholics emigrated to the United States in growing numbers during the first four decades of the nineteenth century. Then came the blight. From 1845 through the early 1850s every harvest of potatoes in Ireland rotted. More than one million people, perhaps a million-and-a-half, died from starvation. Disease, destitution, and panic followed famine, until Ireland seemed to offer only misery and death. By 1880 nearly three million Irish had sailed to America, the vast majority to New York City, where many stayed. With their American born children the Irish constituted more than a third of the city's population at that time.[1]

For the Famine Irish, as the wave of immigrants that began arriving in America in 1845 became known, the wretched conditions that forced them to leave their native country was a final act of treachery perpetrated by their English rulers. Though the blight was an act of God, English and Scottish landlords, with government sanction, continued to export cattle and grain from the Emerald Island while farmers and their families shriveled to death from lack of food. During several centuries the English had forbidden the Irish to own property, to speak their native language, to educate themselves, or to practice the Catholic religion. Sometimes landlords financed the ocean crossing to America because it was cheaper to send their charges overseas than to comply with the British Poor Laws. Sometimes the voyagers crossed the frigid waters of the North Atlantic in the open hulls of lumber ships whose captains discovered that the Irish made good ballast to stabilize their vessels for the return trip to North America. The migration was the logical culmination of centuries of hideous oppression during which the English used their power to subjugate the people of Ireland.[2]

Such had been the Irish Catholic experience with government when they disembarked in a New York whose politics were divided between the Whigs and the Democrats. In the early years of the nineteenth century the Whigs, who ultimately served as the nucleus of the Republican party, were sensitive to the wishes of a moralistic and self-righteous leadership, composed overwhelmingly of Protestants of English descent. These men sought support among people who shared their cultural habits and outlook. They balked at the illiterate, hard-drinking, Irish Catholic masses who were crowding into lower Manhattan. The men who led the Democratic party were Protestant as well, but many of them were Dutch or German in ancestry, and more tolerant than the Whigs were of Catholics. Moreover, by the 1820s, the Democrats understood more clearly than the Whigs that Irish immigrants were becoming a powerful political force, and that the party that earned their loyalty would win elections. Thus, by the time of the famine migration, a Democratic political identity awaited the Irish at the docks.[3]

Convincing Irish Catholics to vote against the Whigs who so resembled the English took little art. Getting them to cooperate with each other was something else again. Into the 1850s battles among competing factions often led to political fratricide, until the Democratic party and the Society of St. Tammany combined to create an organization that would remain at the center of the city's political life for a hundred years.

The Society of St. Tammany began as a social club in 1789. At first the organization limited membership to native born Americans, but in time accepted immigrants searching for the warmth of friendship and the comforts of a community in a new world. It held grand celebrations at its headquarters—Tammany Hall—sponsored parties and picnics, and developed a loyal following that numbered in the thousands. As early as 1798 Aaron Burr realized that an organized group of men like Tammany could serve political purposes, and he used the Society to further his career within the Democratic party. In 1854 the club helped elect Fernando Wood mayor, and the link between the Society and the Democrats intensified. In 1863 William M. Tweed, Chairman of the Democratic party's central committee for New York County, became Tammany chief, bringing the two institutions closer together still. By the 1880s Tammany had consolidated its control over the Democratic party in New York City so completely that the two organizations were indistinguishable.[4]

Wood was a native born Quaker, Tweed a Brooklyn Protestant of Scottish ancestry; but both owed their power to Irish Catholics, whose great numbers and loyalty to Tammany voted them into the mayor's office. After Tweed's spectacular thievery landed him in jail, control of Tammany passed for the first time to an Irish Catholic, "Honest" John Kelly. From 1872 until 1948 leaders of Irish Catholic heritage controlled the organization. They gave it a style of rule identifiably their own, the product of bitter experience under English government, recast to suit life in New York's slums.[5]

American political parties were geographically organized, hierarchical in structure and democratic in theory by the mid-nineteenth century. Registered party members in New York voted in primaries for district leaders from each city ward (later from each assembly district). The district leaders served on the executive committee that chose the County Chairman, or "boss," to whom the leaders answered. Each district leader was in turn the boss of his domain. He appointed captains to each electoral district within it, a unit that was usually just a few blocks large. At each level the objective of the politician was the same—to win the votes of the people who lived in the area for which he was responsible.[6]

The great numbers of Irish Catholics and their initial geographic concentration aided the efforts of Irish politicians to organize the people of a district. The hierarchical nature of party affairs resembled the disciplined order of things in the Catholic Church with which the Irish were so familiar and comfortable; political districts looked just like a network of parishes. Many of the Irish had at least some knowledge of English, so they did not have to struggle with the meaning of words the way other immigrants did. But the most important advantage the Irish had in American politics was a long, if perverse, acquaintance with the Anglo-Saxon political system.[7]

Centuries of English electoral fraud, judicial chicanery, and religious intolerance had taught the Irish that government was the instrument one group used to secure privilege for itself and dominate another. Morality had nothing to do it, nor did any grand ideology. The objective of politics was to secure power by all conceivable means, hold onto it and exploit it. In practical terms that required discipline and trust among supporters, and called for shrewd deception of the opposition. The Irish had learned never to rely on the formal institutions of state that the English used to oppress them, and created in their stead secret societies to protect themselves. When in 1823 Irish nationalist leader Daniel O'Connell forged the Catholic Association out of the disparate societies fighting for Irish emancipation, it resembled nothing so much as a national political party. One member of British Parliament commented of the organization a few years after its founding, "I did not conceive any system of government could be so complete in carrying on communication from heads to inferiors." A century later O'Connell's biographer wondered, "whether the true parentage of Tammany Hall might not be traced to British law in Ireland." To New York's Irish, the Democratic party was an informal, local link to an unofficial citywide (and state and national) government of the kind they had relied on in Ireland, and its purpose was to help loyal members contend with the often hostile world of the immigrant slums.[8]

The need to-eat—the desperate need for a job that would put bread on the table—was the most pressing reality confronting America's newcomers. Yet the sign "No Irish Need Apply" often accompanied advertisements for employment. The Irish proved masters at providing political patronage positions that solved the immigrants' fundamental problem and made loyal voters at the same time. In New York City in 1888, one estimate placed 12,000 jobs in the hands of the Irish Catholic politicians who controlled City Hall. During the late nineteenth century New York City grew rapidly and the government built bridges, tunnels, streets, subways, sewers, parks, and schools, requiring thousands of laborers. All the while Tammany served as the employment agency for the city's working class. By 1898, after consolidation of Greater New York, about 60,000 posts with salaries totaling ninety million dollars were in the hands of New York's Democratic party officials. The political professionals spoke bluntly about their use of these jobs: "Tammany is for the spoils system, and when we go in we fire every anti-Tammany man from office that can be fired under the law," George Washington Plunkitt, Irish American leader of the Fifteenth assembly district, explained to the journalist who chronicled his political philosophy in 1905. "It's an elastic sort of law," he continued, "and you can bet it will be stretched to the limit."[9]

Always more voters existed than jobs, so professional politicians used other tools to build support. District leaders saw to it that the judges they helped elect dealt kindly with the human indiscretions of loyal Democrats (one prominent jurist was impressed with the ability of machine magistrates to "dispense *with* justice"). Frequently a district leader made it to the local police station in time to intercede directly with the Irish dominated police force and help a voter in trouble avoid the courts altogether. A family facing eviction for lack of rent, or put into the street by fire, could turn to a district leader for a loan, or to find it a place to stay. In the winter a pail of coal could be had, and usually a Christmas basket as well. Tammany sponsored athletic teams and glee clubs, and in the hot, sweltering city summer, many thousands came to Tammany picnics held in Central Park, Long Island, or upstate New York.[10]

To strengthen the personal relationships on which their power rested many district leaders socialized in local saloons—meeting places where men told jokes, created friendships, and conducted business while sharing a few whiskies. But the political professionals kept sober minds when it came to running the affairs of Tammany Hall. Their livelihood depended on the organization's success. So when delivering jobs, offering social welfare benefits, providing recreation and companionship, and creating cultural solidarity were insufficient to keep the machine running, Tammany resorted to fraud.[11]

Opponents frustrated by Tammany's success exaggerated the importance of electoral thievery. Yet, there was a firm foundation on which to build their hyped-up accusations. Machine backed judges improved voter turnout to their party's advantage by granting citizenship to immigrants before their five year naturalization period ended. Boxes of marked election ballots floated in the East River the day after the 1886 mayoralty contest, launched on their voyages by machine workers who knew those votes would not help the Democratic cause. The adage "vote

9

early and often" applied to machine "repeaters," who cast as many ballots as necessary to ensure a favorable outcome, while burly "poll watchers" discouraged the opposition from exercising voting rights. Richard Croker, Tammany boss from 1886 to 1902, almost literally fought his way to the top. In the early part of his career Croker's successor, Charles Francis Murphy, also relied on physical prowess to establish his place as leader. Perhaps it is not coincidence that at the time Tammany consolidated its control over New York an Irish American was making himself famous as "boxing champion of the world" with the boast, "My name's John L. Sullivan, and I can lick any sonofabitch alive!" The arts of boxing and politics had something in common among the Irish.[12]

The kind of brains that could work through the city payroll and invent jobs, or outwit election monitors, went far in Tammany; philosophy counted for little. Plunkitt explained that young men looking for political careers who "cram their heads with all sorts of college rot" raised the odds against success to one hundred to one. He guessed such fellows were "not to blame for their misfortune," but Tammany had no use for them, or for orators who "traveled on their tongues." The ability of Charles Francis Murphy to avoid taking stands on the controversial issues of his time became legendary. Once, at a function that included the playing of the "Star Spangled Banner," a reporter remarked that Murphy did not sing. "Maybe he didn't want to commit himself," a supporter offered.[13]

A Tammany boss was a worker. To know the people of a district, find them jobs, be there to help in emergencies, establish the personal trust and loyalty on which the machine depended, and deliver votes by whatever means necessary on election day demanded an extraordinary commitment. In return, the leader expected to profit. Just as the Tammany faithful wanted something tangible for their votes, so the bosses expected compensation for their efforts. Neither leaders nor followers had any apologies for this view of politics. When a New York State legislator investigating corruption in New York City accused Richard Croker of working for his own pocket, the Tammany chief growled in response: "All the time—just like you." Plunkitt wanted his epitaph to read: "George Washington Plunkitt—He seen his opportunities and he took 'em," and unabashedly referred to himself as a statesman.[14]

Tammany's governments were corrupt, but typically they were not inept. The bosses knew that they risked being chased from office if the sewers backed up, or if water did not flow in the tenements, or if blazes raged beyond the control of municipal firemen. A practice evolved of placing competent technicians in the deputy's post in important city departments even if the commissioner was chosen strictly on the basis of party loyalty. To many that did not matter. In the minds of moralizing Protestants the Catholic immigrants were the source of all the vulgarity, vice, and urban wretchedness of New York City, and Tammany was the creature that helped the foreign masses ravage the metropolis. When cartoonist Thomas Nast drew pictures of Tammany as a rapacious tiger devouring a fair maiden named "Republic," he captured the sentiments of New York's elite.[15]

Many upper-crust businessmen reached accommodations with political powers when it served their economic interests, but the cultural cleavage between Irish Catholics and other immigrants and old-stock Protestants hardened political loyalties. Self-proclaimed reformers seeking morality and efficiency in government excoriated the Democratic machine and sought to unseat Tammany politicians. They used the Republican party as the nucleus of these efforts, but to distinguish themselves from the often tawdry practices of New York's Grand Old Party, and to broaden their appeal, they periodically organized Fusion campaigns to reach beyond the formal party structure and attract all voters unhappy with Tammany.[16]

To the reformers, government was an instrument to be used to improve society; the practice of politics a noble calling to serve the public. For the Irish, politics differed from other professions only in detail. It was practical and profitable, devoid of intellectual drapings; holding power was a way to earn a living. Elections were not exercises in moral judgement, simply contests between the "ins" and the "outs" for the spoils that went to the victor. Tweed once explained it this way: "The money . . . was distributed around in everyway, to everybody, and paid for everything." Boss Croker made clear who "everybody" was when the Irish ruled New York: "All there is in life is loyalty to one's family and friends," he once said.[17]

In 1880, William R. Grace, a native New Yorker whose success as a shipping magnate brought him great wealth, became the first New York mayor of Irish Catholic ancestry. At the time of his election immigrants from Ireland and their children made up about one third of the city. Alone their numbers could not win a citywide contest, so Irish political bosses plied their trade with slum dwellers of all nationalities. More than eighty percent of New York's citizens were of foreign stock the year Grace won election as mayor. Germans, comprising about thirty percent of the city, were second only to the Irish as a portion of the population. The machine techniques that bound the Irish to Tammany attracted many Germans, and other immigrants as well.[18]

A solid Irish base, and reliable support from German and other foreign stock voters, primarily Catholics, resulted in Democratic victory in every mayoral election in New York City from 1874 until reformer William L. Strong won office two decades later. Three years after that, in 1897, Tammany took back control in the first election of the greater metropolis. Four years later reformer Seth Low won. In 1903 Tammany returned, and held on until 1913 when it lost to a Fusion movement backing John Purroy Mitchel. Victorious in 1917, Tammany Democrats then held power until 1933. Such domination of the politics of a city the size and complexity of New York was extraordinary, but why the defeats? Who voted for Tammany one election, reformers the next? The answers lay in the shifting population of the Lower East Side.[19]

The Jewish Vote

Tammany first learned that a Jewish vote existed in the mayoral election of 1886. That year Republican candidate Theodore Roosevelt opposed Democrat Abram Hewitt, but the life of the campaign came from third party candidate Henry George, a radical economist who generated a curious cross-class, multiethnic appeal. Hewitt won the election, but returns showed that, among other strongholds, George ran especially well in Jewish districts on the Lower East Side. In one speech he compared his efforts to liberate workers to the deliverance of the Jews from the Pharoah 3,500 years before. An 1880 estimate that New York had only 11,000 Jewish voters scattered throughout the city was already out of date as lower Manhattan shook from the consequences of an explosion in Russia.[20]

On March 13, 1881 a band of revolutionaries threw a bomb that killed Czar Alexander II. Alexander III proved less tolerant than his father and a pogrom swept Russia. Jewish property was plundered, Jewish women raped, and Jewish children mutilated. Some 20,000 families lost their homes, 100,000 suffered financial ruin. By the time this murderous wave struck, economic conditions had already begun to deteriorate in the Pale of Settlement, a great ghetto stretching from the Baltic to the Black Sea where nearly all of Russia's Jews lived. As the country stumbled toward modernity the economy discarded those who could not compete, and legal restrictions on Jews crippled their ability

TABLE 1.1

Jewish Population of New York City and Percent of Total

	1880	1900	1920	1940
NYC Population	1,206,289	3,437,202	5,620,048	7,454,995
Number of Jews	60,000	597,674	1,643,012	1,950,000
% of NYC	5.0	17.4	29.2	26.2

SOURCE: Ira Rosenwaike, *Population History of New York* (Syracuse, New York: Syracuse University Press, 1972), page 77 for 1880, 58 for 1900 and 188 for 1920 and 1940. The Jewish population figure for 1880 is an estimate from 1878 and includes only old New York, principally Manhattan. Approximately 600,000 people and 13,000 Jews lived in Brooklyn in 1880.

to adapt to the changing circumstances. When official anti-Semitism intensified the numbers of Jews who fled enforced deprivation, periodic attack and potential death accelerated. Life for Jews in Poland, Romania, and the Austro-Hungarian Empire was better, but not much.[21]

In the half-century following 1820 about 7,500 Eastern European Jews trickled into the United States. An outburst of anti-Semitism in Odessa in 1871 generated a Jewish exodus that numbered about 40,000 in the decade that followed. By the time of the 1881 pogrom the suffocating conditions within Russia contrasted sharply with the news filtering back from sons and daughters abroad. America was a magic land where Jews could succeed at business, know freedom—live. Over the next fifty years the push to leave, the news that pulled, led some 2.5 million East European Jews, more than a third of their numbers, to cross a continent on land, then brave the Atlantic. Almost all flooded into New York City. Most stayed.[22]

The effect on New York's population was dramatic, as table 1.1 shows.

It did not take long for the massive influx of Jews to affect the city's politics. Twice during Tammany boss Richard Croker's reign—in 1894 and again in 1901—the Democrats lost control of the mayor's office. Both times the principal reason was that the machine lost the support of large numbers of Jewish voters.

Normally, Jewish immigrants voted for Tammany. Like other newcomers, Jews benefited from the help of the local boss in adjusting to their new surroundings, and like Catholics they resented the often evangelical tone of the city's Protestant reformers. Moreover, there was a certain prudence to staying on the good side of the institution that controlled the police, and the streets where people lived and work ed.

Yet, for a number of reasons, Jewish loyalty to Tammany did not

13

approach the visceral support that the Irish gave to the organization that they created and ruled. First, Jews had alternate sources of employment. In the 1890s, between fifty and sixty percent of the city's gainfully employed Jews worked in the needle trades. About seven percent worked in other industries and ten percent were peddlers. To such a group the jobs that came with control of City Hall had less meaning than they did to those without alternatives.

Just as patronage jobs meant less to the East Europeans than to the Irish, so the welfare benefits of the machine bound the Jews less strongly. Like other immigrant groups, perhaps a little more so, the Jews set up self-help organizations. *Landsmanshafts* assisted families in need of education for children, medical care for the sick, loans for the impoverished, burial plots for the least fortunate of all. The Workmen's Circle preached socialism, but mostly offered help to needy immigrant Jews.

Jews also benefited from the influence of New York's German Jews, who were at once part of the city's wealthy elite and its Jewish community. German Jews had been part of the migration that brought so many of their countrymen to America in the second and third quarters of the nineteenth century. By the time the East European wave began to cross the Atlantic many German Jews had achieved substantial commercial success and commensurate social status. Most practiced Reform Judaism, a much reworked version of the traditional religion that was heavy in ethical values, respectful of logic and man's rationality, and that all but dispensed with ancient rituals. In the United States much was changed to conform to local Protestant custom. By the start of the twentieth century Rabbi Judah Magnes of Temple Emanuel, the prestigious Fifth Avenue home of New York's wealthiest Reform congregation, recounted the story of a "prominent Christian lawyer of another city . . . [who] entered this building at the beginning of a service on Sunday morning and did not discover that he was in a synagogue until a chance remark of the preacher betrayed it." By mutual consent, New York's Protestant and Jewish economic elites kept their social functions separate, but they transacted business with each other, and the cultural gulf between them was rather shallow.[23]

Paradoxically, the gulf between the German Jews and the East European Jews was in many respects great. The impoverished foreigners spoke little English, knew nothing of American customs, and abided by a Judaism more different in some ways from the religion of the Reform Jews than was the Episcopalianism of New York's wealthiest Protestant sect. Nonetheless, New York's German Jews felt a compelling obligation to help the East European immigrants pouring into the wretched slums of the Lower East Side. Some German Jews did not entirely welcome the burden of caring for their coreligionists, but recognized that all American Jews, "should be sensible of what we owe not only these . . . coreligionists, but to ourselves, who will be looked upon by our gentile neighbors as the natural sponsors for . . . our brethren." Yet more important than the fear of an anti-Jewish reaction by native Americans against the East European immigrants and all who shared their faith was a sense of collective responsibility. Differences in language, economic class, cultural upbringing, and even religious practices were insufficient to overwhelm the sense of a common religious heritage, the notion that fundamentally all Jews were a single people. That understanding revealed itself in ways consistent with American philanthropic impulses and the Jewish tradition of *zedakah*, a blend of the ideas of charity and justice.[24]

Settlement Houses were the most potent instruments of these impulses. Privately sponsored social welfare agencies located in the heart of the slums, Settlement Houses provided lodging and medical care, meals and educational services, and often an employment bureau that rivaled the most competent political machine. They were started by the likes of Lillian Wald, a Cincinnati born nurse of German Jewish descent, and funded by the likes of Jacob Schiff, the senior partner of the Kuhn Loeb investment house and one of the wealthiest and most generous of the city's German Jews. The Settlement Houses attracted members of the Protestant elite as well, and linked the ghettos in a tangible way to the people who spearheaded the city's political reform movements.[25]

One such movement was launched in 1894 when the Reverend Charles Parkhurst made the remarkable discovery that prostitution existed in New York City. From the pulpit he denounced the Tammany politicians he held responsible for the decadent life of the slums. State Senator Clarence Lexow initiated an investigating committee that exposed Tammany's feeding at the public trough. Testimony featured evidence of profitable collusion between politicians and law enforcement officials that permitted vice to thrive in the poor areas of the city. Outraged, New York's better citizens coalesced into an anti-Tammany force known as the Committee of Seventy. It consisted of three score and ten of Gotham's bluest blooded crusaders for good government, prominent German Jews among them. With Republican backing, it launched William L. Strong, a successful merchant, on a quest for the mayoralty.

In a city where more than eighty percent of the inhabitants were immigrants or their children reformers could defeat Tammany only if they cut into machine domination of foreign stock voters. Since the

Irish were sure to stand by the political machine they had created, the battle took place in the non-Irish foreign quarters, which in 1894 were inhabited primarily by Germans of various religions, and East European Jews.[26]

Boss Croker and his inner circle understood that the threat to their rule came from reform efforts to siphon off non-Irish supporters. In self-defense they gave the Democratic nomination to Nathan Straus, a German Jew who was a rich and respectable scion of the family of the Abraham & Straus and Macy's retail chains. With a single stroke the pros found a way to refute accusations that they ran dirty candidates and to make a gesture to the two most uncertain elements of their coalition. Never mind that Straus had a conscience, was not a Tammany regular, or that his commitment to the Democratic party was based on national issues, not local boodle. There would be time enough to contend with all that when the election ballots were counted; the first rule of professional politics is staying in power.

Straus's peers, dismayed at his affiliation with so corrupt a crew, put heavy pressure on him to disassociate himself from Tammany. German Jews were particularly concerned about the potential consequences of having one of their own serve as a Tammany tool to attract Jewish voters so that vice could continue to thrive. Late in the campaign, Straus resigned in order to preserve his reputation. With few options available Tammany turned to a former mayor, Hugh J. Grant, but the Irishman could not carry the ticket in German and Jewish neighborhoods and lost the election.

By 1894 it was becoming clear that taking the non-Irish immigrant vote was the key to winning citywide elections in New York. It was also clear that the Jewish population was growing by the day, while the German population was falling sharply as a proportion of the city and increasingly blending into old-stock society. In a sign of how the political times were changing a German Jewish politician named Edwin Einstein, who had proudly boasted his German heritage when he ran for Congress in 1878, identified himself as a Jew when he ran for mayor on the Republican ticket in 1892.[27]

Tammany's failure to hold the Jewish vote in 1894 was not due to a misunderstanding of its importance or an unwillingness to appeal to it. The evening before the 1894 mayoralty election all of Tammany's Jewish politicians appeared on a platform on the Lower East Side to address the crowd. "The speeches were all in Yiddish," one voter remembered, "Tammany did not have to worry about the Irish voters: [the Irish district leader] would tend to them." It was the Jews they needed to convince to stand with the machine. That was why, George Washington Plunkitt explained, a Tammany pro "eats corned beef and kosher meat with equal nonchalance, and it's all the same to him whether he takes off his hat in the church or pulls it down over his ears in the synagogue." By the turn of the century Tammany publications stopped printing offensive jokes in the pidgin-English of East European immigrants, and instead advertised in the Yiddish press to reach the readership and to provide a form of patronage for the publishers. By 1900 the Tammany leader of the Fourth assembly district gave the Democratic Congressional nomination to Henry Goldfogle, an East European Jew, leading a machine lieutenant to announce that, "the Yiddish-speaking community knew it had come of political age."[28]

He was not quite right. The relationship of Jewish voters to Tammany Hall was still evolving, and Jews had already demonstrated at least one distinctive trait that Boss Croker did not understand: a willingness to respond to moral arguments in greater numbers than most other immigrants. The lack of a moral weapon in Tammany's arsenal is what allowed the reformers to win Jewish votes away from the machine in 1894. It would do so again in 1901, costing Richard Croker his job just as New York was settling into the new century in greatly expanded form.

Until 1898 New York City consisted of Manhattan and part of the present-day Bronx and Westchester. With formation of the consolidated metropolis the city became organized into five boroughs. Brooklyn, Queens, and Staten Island each became its own county with its own party leadership. The Bronx would remain part of Manhattan-dominated New York County until 1914, when it too became a separate county with separate political leadership. Although Brooklyn was growing most rapidly, Manhattan held the largest population at the turn of the century and remained the economic nucleus of the city. Moreover, the Democratic party there was older, stronger, and better organized than in the other boroughs. Tammany was therefore first among equals in the greatly expanded city. Negotiation and accommodation were important elements in party decision-making, particularly between the Manhattan and Brooklyn organizations, but in citywide contests Tammany played the greatest role and generally got its way.[29]

The new metropolis, in addition to the mayor, chose a comptroller and president of the board of alderman in citywide elections, and the population of each county elected a borough president. From 1901 until 1989 these eight officials constituted the Board of Estimate, which held power over all budget decisions. By extension, as it worked out, they also had effective control over most legislation. The Board of Aldermen, later the City Council, until 1989 was a weak participant in New York City government.[30]

Republicans expected the 1898 merger to strengthen their position because Brooklyn, more heavily populated by native born Americans than Manhattan, had voted Democratic less regularly than old New York. Still, at the time of the 1900 census, less than a quarter of the eligible voters in the enlarged city were children of American born mothers. Beating the machine still meant taking foreign stock ballots, and in 1897, the first election for a five borough government of the greater metropolis, the reformers came up short.[31] Their candidate, former Brooklyn Mayor Seth Low, ran badly among poor immigrants of all backgrounds. Low's Protestant supporters made strident demands throughout the campaign for Sunday blue laws. This alienated Germans, who viewed the day as a time for recreation, and Jews who observed the sabbath on Saturday and faced economic hardship if deprived of a second day's work. Jacob Schiff had explained to Protestant philanthropists in 1896 that if they evangelized while dispensing charity on the Lower East Side they would alienate the Jews. He might have added that the practice would hurt them on election day too. Tammany-ite Robert Van Wyck and his ticket entered City Hall amidst rejoicing at the enhanced patronage opportunities the newly expanded government offered.[32]

Two years later New York's Episcopal Bishop Henry C. Potter, working with other Protestant and German Jewish civic leaders, established the Committee of Fifteen to once again expose and denounce Tammany complicity in police corruption. The State Legislature appointed the Mazet Committee to investigate the allegations and, as in 1894, evidence of Tammany's links to prostitution and vice filled the newspapers, including the Yiddish press.[33]

As the 1901 municipal election approached, reformers again nominated Seth Low, and added political strategy to their moral campaign by launching a concerted effort to win the votes of the East European Jews. A number of politically active Settlement House workers, Henry Moskowitz in particular, undertook political organizing in the neighborhoods where they worked—becoming, in effect, reform district leaders. (A Tammany politician who later compared his work to Lillian Wald's concluded: "Its the same thing, only *we* keep books.") The anti-Tammany forces nominated a Jew for Manhattan borough president, and added to their appeal among the poor East European immigrants by calling for expanded municipal services. The *American Hebrew* told its

Jewish readership that, "The opportunity now exists [to rid the Jewish community of political 'wretches'] in actively joining the campaign against the Tammany horde, which has corrupted the Police and used its political power for money considerations, in polluting the virtuous Jewish home." Campaigners spoke more softly of Sunday closings, and instead, cast their moral arguments in terms most likely to have effect. Jerome Travis, reform candidate for Manhattan district attorney, speaking to Jews about Tammany collusion in prostitution, said, "If there is one ounce of manhood in you . . . you will stop the police growing rich off the shame of fallen women. Is the honor of Jewish women sold for brass checks nothing to you?" Contemporary journalists and scholars confirmed the strategy. One newspaperman wrote that, "the vital question in reform politics was as to how the 'East Side' vote can be won." In 1905 a political scientist explained that: "It is almost incredible, but is nevertheless a fact, that the entire machinery of the fusion campaign [of 1901] was largely directed to that portion of the city mostly inhabited by the Russian Jewish citizens."[34]

Seth Low and his entire ticket, save the candidate for Bronx borough president, won. The victory, available reports assert, occurred because the densely populated, heavily Jewish, "second, fourth, eighth, tenth, twelfth and sixteenth Assembly Districts, which in former years ran up insurmountable Tammany majorities, showed such a remarkable change that the other districts in the city normally in favor of reform movements had an easy task."[35]

Fundamentally, the 1901 campaign on the Lower East Side was an ethnic appeal to Jewish voters cast in moral terms. Clever speeches made ridding the Jewish ghetto of politicians linked to vice an issue of Jewish self-respect. The 1894 and 1901 elections proved that reform notions of politics could unbolt large numbers of Jewish voters from the machine and determine the outcome of a municipal election in New York City. But in spite of heroic efforts by Henry Moskowitz, Lillian Wald, and a handful of others to organize the immigrant Jews of the Lower East Side into an enduring political force, the emotions of 1901 faded without leaving a solid structure behind. By the turn of the century politicians knew that the Jewish vote existed. Organizing it to hold on to power was another matter, one that would preoccupy New York politicians for the rest of the century.[36]

TWO

Organized Religion

1901–1941

Following the reform victory of 1901 Richard Croker faded from Tammany leadership. His control had been slipping for some time and he had developed a preoccupation with racing horses in England, a sure sign that he was no longer the man to lead the Democratic party through the rough-and-tumble politics of New York City. After a brief interregnum, Charles Francis Murphy consolidated his position as the new boss in 1902. For more than two decades he reigned over the most successful period in Tammany's history.

Under Murphy, Tammany solidified the allegiance of the city's Jews, added it to the traditional electoral strength of the Democratic party's Irish base, and won an impressive string of victories. To bring Jewish voters into their coalition Tammany politicians removed the moral taint that cost them the mayoralty in 1901, used their political power to defend Jews against anti-Semitism, and defused the philosophical appeal to Jewish voters of the Socialist party, and of the Republican party, which possessed a strong progressive wing in New York early in the century.

Beginning shortly before Murphy became Tammany chief, and continuing into the 1940s, Jewish New Yorkers went through a period of intense political organizing. The efforts took place both within America's traditional two party system and without. Murphy's ability to recognize the power of this newly organized political strength and to harness it was the genius that made him unusually successful. After his death in 1924 inept leaders rose to power in Tammany. They understood neither the importance of keeping the Jews in the coalition, nor the tactics required. By 1933, the lost confidence of Jewish voters weakened the Democratic coalition and allowed Fiorello LaGuardia to oust the Democrats from the mayor's office for a dozen years.

Puritan Boss

Born in a lower Manhattan tenement in 1858, the son of Irish immigrants, Murphy grew up in the streets of the slums. Physically tough, a natural leader, he commanded respect and built a following based on the personal loyalties of men who knew him. About 1880 he opened a saloon, began delivering votes with the kind of monotony that excited the machine and moved up through the ranks a pure organization man. He was part of a triumvirate that ran the Democratic party's affairs after boss Croker lost interest following Tammany's 1901 defeat, and then became the undisputed leader.[1]

Murphy recognized that removing the moral taint on Tammany was the starting point for restoring the coalition of immigrant voters that could keep him and his Irish compatriots in power. That suited him just fine. Although he was a gutter hardened bar keeper, he was also a "thoroughgoing puritan," according to his biographer. He barely drank at all. One crony said of him, "I would have just as soon thought of telling an off-color story to a lady as I would to Murphy." The boss was a man of religious conviction who found prostitution deeply offensive. By the time the 1903 mayoralty campaign began he had already purged his party of the men most infected with vice.

Meanwhile, reform mayor Seth Low was chasing thousands of immigrants back toward the Democrats by strictly enforcing Sunday blue laws. Murphy convinced the very respectable George B. McClellan to run as Tammany's candidate for mayor and cleverly lured the incumbent comptroller and president of the Board of Alderman, whom the reformers had elected in 1901, onto the Democratic ticket. For borough president of Manhattan he selected John Ahearn. A Lower East Side district leader second only to Murphy in organization clout, Ahearn was pragmatically solicitous of his Jewish constituents. Just the year before, some gentile factory workers with a gift for hatred had thrown objects onto a crowded Jewish funeral procession following the remains of Jacob Joseph, the city's most prominent rabbi, to his grave. To demonstrate his disgust Ahearn ordered party workers to break all the factory's windows. "The Jews loved him for that," reported a contemporary. Tammany swept the city elections in 1903.[2]

Guardians of the Jews

Impatience with anti-Semitism became a hallmark of Tammany politicians. While some Irish bosses treated Jewish political workers unkindly, and cultural antagonisms between Catholics and Jews flared periodically, Tammany pros understood they could not alienate Jewish voters and stay in power. Events at home and abroad in the first decade of the twentieth century stimulated Jewish organizing to protect members of the faith against anti-Semitism. These efforts ensured that conscious and explicit opposition to anti-Jewish bigotry became an enduring part of New York's political landscape.

For example, in response to the 1903 massacre of Jews in Kishinev, Russia, and the persecution of Jews that followed the failed Russian revolution of 1905, a group of prominent Jews led by Jacob Schiff, New York attorney Louis Marshall, former United States Ambassador to Turkey Oscar Straus, and others established the American Jewish Committee. The organization's purpose was to coordinate American efforts to lend support to European Jews and to raise money to help refugees. Its leaders were influential men. By institutionalizing their concern for their fellow Jews they made the importance of the topic clear to political leaders.[3]

Closer to home, the Anglo-Saxon-on-the-brain among old stock Americans convinced themselves that the immigrants arriving in numbers of up to a million a year came from undesirable races. Jews were far from exempt from the general nativist rancor. In 1908 New York Police Commissioner Theodore Bingham created an uproar when he asserted without evidence that fifty percent of the city's criminals were Jewish. The hapless official retracted the unsubstantiated statement, but in its aftermath uptown and downtown Jewish leaders created the New York *Kehillah*. A mega-imitation of an East European village council, the institution sought to coordinate the philanthropic activities intended to improve the deplorable living conditions that led to crime on the Lower East Side. The *kehillah* also hoped to speak for all members of the faith on affairs that concerned Jews. The diversity of the Jewish community prevented the organization from achieving this ambitious goal before disbanding in 1922. Yet, its founding emphasized that by the first decade of the twentieth century New York City Jews had developed an awareness that certain issues affected them all, and they were prepared to act in forceful unison to protect themselves.[4]

Tammany responded to Jewish fears. The Irish, who of course had known their fair share of discrimination as newcomers, sympathized. More important, battling anti-Semitism was a way to win Jewish support without giving up the offices or jobs that the Irish wanted. One demonstration of the machine's effectiveness on the issue occurred after the fashionable Marlborough Hotel in Atlantic City, New Jersey, refused to allow a leading Jewish citizen to stay as a guest in 1908 because of her religion. Prominent members of New York's Jewish community took bitter offense to the action but had little means of influencing matters on the far side of the Hudson River. In symbolic response they rallied a Republican assemblyman from Manhattan's elegant West Side, where many of New York's prosperous German Jews lived, to draft legislation to "protect all citizens in their civil and religious rights," in New York State. But the upstate Republican who headed the Codes and Judiciary Committee responsible for the bill's disposition refused to release it from committee. Although Louis Marshall saw fit to mention "in passing" to Governor Charles Evans Hughes that, "850,000 New York State Jews were watching with interest the outcome of the current legislative session," bigotry and control of the legislative machinery proved powerful enough to block the law for several years.

Then the 1912 elections swept Democratic majorities into both houses of the legislature. Two Tammany politicians, State Senator Robert F. Wagner, majority leader in the upper house, and Al Smith, Speaker of the lower house, had a Jewish assemblyman draft a new version of the anti-discrimination bill. With Tammany efficiency they then rammed the bill through the legislature in a unanimous vote. As a result, they won the respect and gratitude of New York's Jews, including prominent German Jews who normally opposed the Democratic machine.[5]

Thus, under Murphy's guidance, Tammany rapidly overcame two challenges to maintaining favor with Jewish voters. Democratic politicians learned to steer clear of moral crimes and blatant corruption, and to respond vigorously to Jewish concerns about discrimination. Both tactics solidified Jewish support for Irish politicians without surrendering much of the spoils the Irish sought for themselves. A third, more threatening, challenge emerged—an independent political party of Jewish workers.

The Socialist Threat

By the time large scale Jewish emigration to America began, Marxian thought had permeated the heavily Jewish worker movements of Russia and Eastern Europe. In 1897 militant Jewish labor leaders had gathered a number of emerging unions into an organization called the General League of Jewish Workers in Russia, Poland, and Lithuania, popularly known as the *Bund.* Historian Moses Rischin has described the organization as a combination of the "resentment against the suppression of elementary civil rights, the longing [for] political freedom, the aspirations of factory workers for higher wages, and a widespread yearning for social justice," that came together to create a "hotbed of revolutionary work." Not all Jewish workers participated in the League, or agreed with all of its programs, but few were untouched by it in some way. Anti-Semitic pogroms in 1903 and 1905 sent many of the Bund's most ardent believers to America.[6]

A fledgling Jewish union movement with socialist sympathies already existed on the Lower East Side when the Bund radicals infused it with new blood. As early as 1888 the United Hebrew Trades loosely linked together unions dominated by Jewish employees, most important in the garment industry. Yet typically, after brief periods of organizing accompanied by strikes and modest wage gains, the locals waned lethargic. Then, in 1909, New York's shirtwaist workers struck successfully. The group was 20,000 strong and overwhelmingly female. About one quarter of its membership was Italian and almost all the rest Jewish. The strike began when an unassuming teenage seamstress named Clara Lemlich stood during a crowded union meeting, and in Yiddish, pleaded with her colleagues to refuse to work until their demands had been met. The following year the city's cloakmakers, perhaps eighty percent of them Jews, walked off the job and won an agreement called the Protocol of Peace that opened new ground in labor relations and boosted unionizing efforts.[7]

Labor organizing on the Lower East Side was intensely political. It was an effort by Jewish workers to win the power to exert control over their lives. "In brief, what politics accomplished for the Irish, trade unionism promised New York's Jews," historian Melvyn Dubofsky has concluded of the movement. It was the ethnic fiber of its Jewish leaders and members that tied the movement together. In the late nineteenth century Lower East Side radicals denied (in Yiddish, of course, Irving Howe has pointed out) the Jewishness of the drive to organize the workers of the needle trades. By the end of the first decade of the twentieth century, with much of its leadership drawn from the East European Bund that found strength in its ability to link socialist thought to Yiddish culture, the Jewish labor movement accepted its role as an effort to serve as the voice of working-class Jews. Others were welcome and participated, most notably Italians. But the movement, its leadership and politics, were all dominated by Jews and Jewish thought.[8]

The Socialist party was the electoral instrument of the Jewish workers movement in New York City. In the late nineteenth century and in the earliest days of the twentieth century the party presented its proposals for a new relationship between workers and owners in a somewhat radical form that limited its appeal. By about 1910 the Socialists had learned to support incremental reforms to accomplish such goals as improved working conditions and increased wages, restrictions on child labor, and municipal ownership of utilities. The party's long-term objectives did not change, but the short-term rewards for workers became far more tangible.

The Socialists also learned to marry their call for social justice and incremental improvement with ethnic pride. A series of congressional elections on the Lower East Side illustrates the point. Tammany's Henry Mayer Goldfogle, a Jew, held the ninth congressional district during the early years of the twentieth century. He was standard Tammany fare and paid careful attention to his constituents' ethnic concerns. Socialist Morris Hillquit ran against Goldfogle in 1904, 1906, and again in 1908, in a series of spirited efforts. Hillquit was his party's principal theorist, and he remained faithful to all of its stated positions during his campaigns. Some, including one that called for immigration restriction to limit the number of low-wage workers allowed in the country, was very unpopular with Jewish immigrants who had relatives abroad at risk of persecution. Hillquit vowed that, if elected, he would put Socialist ideals before the special interests of any particular ethnic group. The Jews believed him and returned Goldfogle to Washington.

In 1910 the Socialists ran Meyer London, like Hillquit a committed Socialist, but also an ethnically conscious Jew. He rejected the party's stand on immigration, offered free legal advice to local union organizers and anyone else in need, and labored tirelessly in the streets of the Lower East Side to improve living and working conditions. He fell short

25

of victory in his first attempt, came closer in 1912, and finally went over the top in 1914 to become the first Socialist congressman elected from New York. He announced with pride that he planned to show Washington "what the east side of New York is and what the east side Jew is."[9] London succeeded where Hillquit failed because he combined the ideals of social justice with concern for the immediate needs of the immigrants and respect for their ethnic identity. The Jews were not willing to sacrifice their right to a political spokesman to defend their particular interests, but when they had the chance to choose a representative who would speak on their behalf and seek social justice as well, large numbers could be convinced to abandon the Democratic machine.[10]

Here was a threat to Tammany Hall. Younger Democratic politicians, including Robert F. Wagner, Al Smith, and Jimmy Walker, convinced Boss Murphy that the number of voters who favored the kinds of policies that the Socialists espoused was too great to ignore. The Democrats had to respond if they expected to maintain the loyalty of Jewish voters. The boss determined that to keep his party in power his men should "give the people what they want," and support social welfare legislation, provided it did not weaken the political prerogatives of the machine. A shift toward progressive policies, the greasing of the Tammany machine with liberal ideas, began in earnest about 1909 and endured through the next two decades. It appealed to all of the laborers in the polyglot immigrant districts of New York, as well as to many upper-crust reformers. But it was the relative ease with which large numbers of Jewish voters abandoned Democrats for philosophically alluring candidates from other parties, especially Socialists, that pushed the machine to adopt the strategy.[11]

By the end of the first decade of the twentieth century Murphy had arrived at a clear formula for keeping Tammany in power. The Democrats held onto Irish votes with standard machine tactics, which usually included an Irish candidate at the head of a citywide ticket. And they won Jewish votes by making sure that the candidate was perceived as honest, deeply concerned about discrimination and anti-Semitism, and liberal in political outlook. With solid Irish and Jewish votes a candidate was almost guaranteed victory in New York City.

In six contests for mayor Murphy followed the strategy. His candidates won five. George McClellan was elected mayor in 1903 and 1905, William Jay Gaynor in 1909, and John Hylan in 1917 and again in 1921. In 1913 Tammany candidate Ed McCall lost to John Purroy Mitchel, an Irish Catholic Democrat running on a Fusion ticket who managed to seize the image of the more honest and more liberal politician. The voting pattern in that election was familiar. The Irish voted most faithfully for Tammany—Jews abandoned the machine in the greatest numbers.[12]

The Decline of the Socialists

The 1917 election that returned Tammany to office marked a turning point in Socialist strength. The campaign took place against the backdrop of World War I, which the United States had finally entered in April of that year. Pacifist sentiment among the city's Jews ran high. Morris Hillquit was the Socialist standard bearer, and at first he emphasized his party's municipal platform. In the course of the campaign, however, he discovered that the crowds he spoke to responded vigorously to the notion that "a Socialist victory in the New York City elections will be a clear mandate to our government to open immediate negotiations for a general peace."

According to the best evidence available, Hillquit won a majority of the city's Jewish ballots, and more than twenty percent of the total vote. It was the strongest citywide race the Socialist party had ever run. Eleven Socialists won seats in the New York State Assembly in 1917, and seven members of the party were elected to the Board of Alderman as well. A significant part of the success came from the party's pacifist stand, but the Socialists seemed to be solidifying their position as the political party of choice among Jewish workers. The success did not last.

The American government reacted harshly against critics of its war policy and attacked organized dissidents. The Socialists continued their protests throughout World War I and provided authorities with a justification for arresting its leadership when it sent antiwar literature through the mails. In New York elections in 1918, 1919, and 1920, Tammany strong arm tactics in Socialist bastions increased as respectable elements had little quarrel with tough treatment of a party perceived as disloyal. More subtly, but with great effect, Murphy and his Republican counterpart agreed to run a single candidate on both the Republican and Democratic tickets in districts where the Socialists held power, negotiating between themselves which district would go to the one boss, which to the other. The combined effort almost invariably toppled the Socialist.[13]

In 1919 the State Assembly refused to seat five Socialists (three Jewish) duly elected to that body, and threw them out again in 1920 after the districts reconfirmed their choices. About the same time, the Jewish labor unions so important to the Socialist party entered into a period of debilitating internal battles. The Bolshevik revolution of 1917 inspired some union organizers to seek links with Moscow and an international Communist party, while others favored continued loyalty to homegrown Socialism. With its house divided, labor could not come to the aid of the Socialists.[14]

Battered by the federal government, persecuted by the state legislature, outmaneuvered by opponents, suffering from bitter dissension within its ranks, and having alienated patriots with its policy of pacifism, the Socialist party was a badly weakened force in New York politics at the start of the 1920s.

The End of Jewish Republicans

The Republican party also suffered setbacks in the city after 1920. Theodore Roosevelt's rise to prominence, first as Governor of New York State and then as President, boosted GOP fortunes in New York early in the century. His forward looking policies suited the cautious liberalism of the urban upper class that dominated the Republican party in the city, including the many influential German Jews active in GOP politics. Charles Evans Hughes's election as governor in 1906 consolidated the power of Republican progressives in New York, and the fortunes of the liberal wing of the party, constantly at odds with the diehard conservatives from upstate, surged for a time.[15]

Sam Koenig was the Republican district leader in the tenth assembly district on Manhattan's Lower East Side at the time of Hughes's election. A Hungarian Jew who was an equal match for the cagiest of Tammany's troops, Koenig shrewdly combined street smart politics with progressive candidates. In 1906 and 1908, with his party in power in Albany and the White House, he managed to win some electoral victories in his neighborhood, which typically voted for Democrats and Socialists. Koenig became Republican county leader of New York in 1911, and that year delivered twenty of forty-one aldermen, and ten of twenty-nine Assembly spots. Most victories came from uptown districts hospitable to Republicans, but some from Jewish areas downtown.[16]

Just when it appeared that liberal Republicanism had a chance to make a potentially lasting dent in Jewish voting patterns, Theodore Roosevelt launched his 1912 Progressive campaign for President. His candidacy forced Republicans to choose between the liberal and conservative wings of their party. The former President ran better in Jewish districts than the Republican candidate, William Howard Taft, and in at least one district outpolled Woodrow Wilson running on the Democratic line. Oscar Straus, also a liberal Republican, ran for Governor of New York State on Roosevelt's Progressive ticket. Straus was of course the object of special ethnic pride among his coreligionists, and he won every Jewish district where the results have been documented. But the effect of the failed third party bid was to grant control of the GOP to its conservative faction, and Jewish Republicans committed to social reform shifted away from the increasingly illiberal party toward the Democrats.[17]

In 1920 Woodrow Wilson's failed Versailles peace treaty so discredited his party that Jews split their presidential votes almost equally between Republican Warren G. Harding and Socialist Eugene V. Debs. That same year Harding's coattails pulled eleven Republican assemblymen from Manhattan into office, but that number fell to seven a year later. As the 1920s progressed bigotry and nativism, anti-Catholicism and anti-Semitism rose across the country. North of the Mason-Dixon line the Republican party housed the worst of the Anglo-Saxon supremacists. GOP fortunes declined in all of the urban centers where large numbers of immigrants lived. Jews no less than other religious minorities turned away from what seemed to be the party of meanness. In 1924 Jews gave the Democrats a majority of their presidential vote, and the next year only three Republican assemblymen could hold onto seats in Manhattan. By the time Al Smith ran for President in 1928 Jewish movement away from the Republican party in national elections was almost complete, and its allegiance to the Democratic party in local elections in New York City had become increasingly consistent.[18]

Al Smith and the Jews

Al Smith learned politics on the streets of the Lower East Side where his father died young and his mother struggled to keep the family intact. He left school at thirteen to work as a newspaper boy, graduated to a job with a trucking firm, and then hauled barrels at the Fulton Fish Market where he would later claim he got his education—an FFM degree. He met some Tammany regulars at District Leader Tom Foley's saloon, and developed a reputation as a tactful fellow who could accomplish the little tasks that eased the lives of tenement dwellers and helped them make it to election day. Just before his thirtieth birthday, in 1903, Smith won a seat in the State Assembly.

Like other political professionals Smith disdained reformers and good government advocates—"Goo-Goos" he called them—who thought up plans that never got used. He believed in party discipline, patronage, and personal loyalty, and understood the Tammany tools of his trade. But Smith had a keen sense of responsibility too, and he worked tenaciously to make himself an effective legislator earning respect as an expert in matters of government organization. He also developed a reputation as a man who owned a social conscience, a professional politician unafraid to use his considerable cunning to steer bills through the torturous path of the New York State Legislature if they would make life easier for the poor who lived in the city's slums. When the disastrous Triangle Factory Fire struck in 1911 killing 141 Lower East Side working women, it was Smith, then Speaker of the Assembly, and State Senate leader Robert Wagner who wrote new codes into New York State law to protect the factory workers.[19]

Although his ancestry was mixed and not quite clear (perhaps part English, part German, and part Italian), in upbringing and outlook Smith was pure Irish Catholic and the Irish loved him as one of their own. The Jews saw a fellow Lower East Sider, an *Irisher mensch*, responsive to the constellation of considerations that determined Jewish voting patterns. He was untainted by scandal, liberal on matters of social policy, and a defender of minorities of all nationalities and faiths, including Jews.[20]

A remarkable campaigner whose razor sharp memory allowed him to deliver speeches in an inimitable off-the-cuff style, Smith won election citywide in 1917 when he became president of the Board of Alderman. The next year, with machine backing and an impressive reputation as a reform minded politician, Smith was elected governor. Turned out of office in the 1920 national Republican onslaught, he regained the position in 1922 and won reelection in successive landslides until he ran for President in 1928. Comedian Will Rogers once remarked that the man Smith ran against for governor of New York, "ain't a candidate. He is just a victim."[21]

More than anything else, it was Smith's commitment to far-reaching social legislation that distinguished him from the typical machine politician and made him so much more successful than the average Tammany regular. To an extraordinary degree, the progressive policies he wrote into law were drafted for him by Jewish advisers whose principles and priorities emerged from the settlement houses of the Lower East Side and the Jewish labor movement.

Attorney Abram I. Elkus, an active supporter of the Educational Alliance, served as counsel to the New York Factory Commission that Smith helped lead following the Triangle Factory Fire. Elkus eventually managed Smith's 1918 campaign and remained an important adviser to the governor throughout his Albany years, as did Elkus's assistant from the Factory Commission, Bernard Shientag. Elkus brought prominent Jewish attorney Samuel Untermayer into Smith's advisory circle as well. Attorney Joseph Proskauer, who like Elkus had run an Educational Alliance club as a young man, became an indispensable member of Smith's staff who helped to run the State government, draft legislation, and manage Smith's political campaigns, including the 1928 bid for the presidency. Herbert Lehman, whose social conscience was also forged in part in the settlement houses of the Lower East Side, was finance chairman for Smith's 1928 presidential campaign.

Lillian Wald, and to a lesser degree Rose Schneiderman of the Women's Union Trade League, influenced Smith's attitudes toward legislation involving working women and children, and Smith relied on Julius Henry Cohen, an attorney heavily involved in the early development of the needle trade unions, for advice on labor, housing, and other matters. During the days of the Factory Commission Smith met Henry Moskowitz, one of the most political members of the settlement house movement and a committed labor activist. The two men worked together again on municipal matters after Smith's election to the Board of Alderman. Smith met Moskowitz's wife, Belle, during the 1918 race for governor, the first that allowed women to vote in New York State. Like her husband, Belle Moskowitz was a product of the settlement house movement and the efforts to unionize the needle trades. She taught Smith how to campaign among ladies, and Smith learned that Moskowitz possessed a shrewd and powerful mind. She became his most trusted assistant, never holding formal power but exercising more influence over Smith's policies than anyone in New York State. Some thought her the most powerful woman in the country. Through Belle Moskowitz other Jewish professionals joined Smith's staff. Among them were Robert Moses, a young civil service expert and parks advocate, and Aaron Rabinowitz, who on Moskowitz's recommendation became the first chairman of the New York State Board of Housing, and Samuel Rosenman, and on and on.[22]

The Irish bosses never stopped liking Al Smith, or the way the coattails of his huge electoral majorities brought victory to their local candidates. Yet, Smith's biographers, Matthew and Hannah Josephson, concluded that Tammany's pros resented Smith's "inclination to choose descendants of Kings of Israel, rather than Kings of Erin, as his counselors." And sometimes late at night, after a whiskey too many, the regulars would sing a dirge with the bitter-sweet refrain:

And now the brains of Tammany Hall

Are Moskie and Proskie and Mo-o-o-ses.

Al Smith indisputably ruled over the most liberal period in Irish Tammany's history, but Jewish social reformers directed it.[23]

After the disastrous failure of Smith's presidential bid, the man soured. He saw his loss as a triumph of anti-Catholic bigotry. It took him years to admit how little he understood America beyond Manhattan, and to acknowledge that his loss had as much to do with the country's prosperity in 1928 as it did with hate. As he sat on the outside of power looking in, Smith turned increasingly bitter and conservative. According to one close friend, "It was Belle Moskowitz who had kept Smith on the liberal side until 1928." If so, she was responsible for much. While Smith ruled Albany, Tammany reigned supreme in New York City. The machine not only delivered its goods to needy immigrants and addressed ethnic concerns, but also passed forward reaching legislation that reformers, liberals of all stripes, even Socialists supported. The combination proved powerful because it kept the Irish and the Jews voting for Tammany's candidates. During the 1920s and into the 1930s the Democrats piled up election victories one after the other. When the machine's handsomest dandy, former song writer and crooner James J. (Beau James) Walker ran for mayor in 1925, the Irishman took the city, Jewish vote included, in a landslide. He won reelection easily in 1929. Full of style and grace, with a wit that charmed, he "wore New York in his button hole" until 1932. Then, in an abrupt change of fortune, he resigned in disgrace.[24]

The LaGuardia Coalition

Political scandals in 1929 prompted Governor Franklin Roosevelt to direct the Appellate Division of the New York State Supreme Court to appoint a special investigator. Between 1930 and 1932 Judge Samuel Seabury, a patrician reformer of stock so old it could be traced to the Mayflower, conducted a series of public investigations into Tammany's affairs. With extraordinary competence and endurance Seabury questioned four thousand witnesses whose testimony revealed a depth and breadth of corruption shocking even to New Yorkers. While Charles F. Murphy ran Tammany Hall plenty of profits poured into political pockets—Murphy died a millionaire—but limits on connections to crime and vice obtained. After Murphy died in 1924, a series of intellectual and moral weaklings held the New York County Democratic Party Chairman's post. "The brains of Tammany Hall lie buried in Calvary Cemetery," Jimmy Walker himself once lamented. Informally, Al Smith dominated the nominating functions of the machine, but he did not monitor the organization's daily activities from Albany, or later from his Fifth Avenue apartment. The boys went wild.

Seabury and his researchers uncovered Tammany connections to gambling and prostitution, bid-fixing and office-selling, contract-rigging and extortion, that led to bank transactions and brokerage accounts in the names of New York's Irish ruling class. All this was above and beyond the call of cronyism, nepotism, and favoritism that went with the territory. On May 25, 1932 Seabury called Mayor James J. Walker himself to the stand. The judge showed that the city's chief executive, even though very busy conducting an extramarital love affair in illegal speakeasies, honkytonks, and gambling joints around the city, found time to collect several hundred thousand dollars of boodle. The judge filed charges with the governor and Walker stepped down on September 1, 1932. Joseph V. McKee, President of the Board of Alderman, assumed the city's top office pending a special election that same fall.[25]

The short interval between Walker's unseating and the election of an interim mayor to serve out the remaining year of the term left reformers unprepared to wage battle. Tammany gave the bid to an unknown and uninspiring regular, John P. O'Brien, who buried his Republican counterpart, Lewis H. Pounds. Machine bosses ridiculed the Seabury commission while they celebrated on election night, but an intelligent reading of the returns would have generated a different mood. O'Brien ran nearly 400,000 votes behind Democratic party presidential candidate Franklin D. Roosevelt, and even further behind Herbert H. Lehman who replaced FDR in the Governor's Mansion. McKee eliminated himself from the contest, but still received almost 235,000 unsolicited write-in votes. Morris Hillquit carried the Socialist banner to the field again, and took 250,000 ballots, more than double the take of his party's presidential candidate that year. A lot of New Yorkers were disgusted with Tammany.[26]

Fiorello LaGuardia was one of them. Through hard work, shrewd politicking, an impressive liberal record, the crucial support of Judge

Seabury, and sheer luck LaGuardia became the candidate of the reformers in 1933 running on a Republican/City Fusion ticket. A short, squat, firecracker of a man whose rumpled suits and big fedora seemed to explode through the city's streets, LaGuardia brought a new style to the demand for good government, normally the province of genteel patricians in New York. He was a political professional, a tribute to the philosopher who once said: "Choose your enemies wisely, for in time you will be like them." After two decades of battle with Tammany he knew all their tricks, used most himself, and threw his five feet four inches of fury into battling the ones that stood between him and power.[27]

LaGuardia was undeniably the son of Italian immigrants, but raised Episcopalian, born of a Jewish mother, and married to an American of German-Lutheran descent, he was a balanced ticket all by himself and he campaigned in the city's polyglot neighborhoods in a half-dozen languages. His opponents were the lackluster O'Brien and Joseph V. McKee. McKee returned to politics as the candidate of the Recovery party, a vehicle of political convenience that Bronx Democratic boss Edward J. Flynn and New York State Democratic Party Chairman James Farley created at the insistence of FDR. The President saw in the mayoralty race a chance to weaken the Tammany Democrats with whom he was feuding.[28]

LaGuardia beat the split opposition easily, taking more than 40 percent of the vote, while Neither O'Brien nor McKee won the confidence of even 30 percent of New York's voters. With a man who shared their heritage at the head of a major party ticket, Italians went to the polling booths in greater numbers than usual. They probably cast more than 15 percent of the city's vote in 1933, and instead of strongly backing the Tammany candidate as they typically did, delivered an overwhelming majority of their ballots to LaGuardia. Jewish voters accounted for about 27 percent of the electorate. LaGuardia took a slim plurality, 36 percent of the total, compared to 32 percent for O'Brien and 23 percent for McKee. Jews who lived in the poorest districts and needed the help of the machine most desperately voted for Tammany. The rest cast ballots against corruption and scandal.[29]

McKee, a respectable candidate, linked to FDR, who had won nearly three-quarters of the Jewish vote in the presidential election the year before, might have run better if he had not lost a mudslinging contest with LaGuardia. The Irish-American tried to portray remarks that some of the Italian-American's backers made about Governor Herbert Lehman as anti-Semitic. The two-fisted reformer (LaGuardia once bragged that he had invented the low blow) responded by circulating an article McKee had written years earlier in which the Irishman warned that the disproportionate success of Jewish students in New York City was threatening the ability of Catholic students to get ahead in the world. McKee was no Jew-hater. The piece was simply meant to encourage Catholic students to work harder, but the tactless words he had penned a decade-and-a-half earlier no doubt left many Jewish voters suspicious.[30]

Just under half of LaGuardia's total vote came on the City Fusion ticket. Significant numbers of New Yorkers, although outraged by Tammany, cared little for the conservative Republican party even with the unorthodox LaGuardia at its head. These voters were looking for an organization respectable in practice and liberal in outlook. The Fusion party served the purpose in 1933. As usual, however, it was something less than a coherent organization that could endure beyond a single election. In 1936 the exigencies of presidential politics created an ethnically based party that could.

The American Labor Party

As planning for FDR's reelection began early in 1936, American union leaders, realizing that the nation's workers solidly supported Roosevelt, vied with each other for the right to serve as labor's link to the White House. A split between the AFL and CIO had occurred in 1935, intensifying the competition. The head of the latter coalition, United Mine Workers president John L. Lewis, along with Sidney Hillman of the Amalgamated Clothing Workers, launched a political lobby for union members called Labor's Non-Partisan League. The organization worked closely with the Democratic party to reelect President Roosevelt and his New Deal policies.[31]

In New York City the Socialist party was undergoing a resurgence as a result of the depression. Capturing the votes of its members was the key to bolstering FDR's already strong working-class support in New York. Roosevelt refused to consider accepting the Socialist endorsement for fear that in most parts of the country the affiliation would hurt him more than it would help. In an effort to find a solution to the dilemma Sidney Hillman met with David Dubinsky, the leader of the 210,000 member International Ladies Garment Workers Union, and Max Zaritsky, president of the United Hatters, Cap and Millinery Workers, with membership of about 25,000. Hillman's own union represented more

35

than 160,000 members. The trio devised a plan to create a new and independent political party to support the President and his policies in New York City. They tested the idea with the President's wife, Eleanor Roosevelt, who liked it, and they presented it to Fiorello LaGuardia as well.[32]

LaGuardia found the idea intriguing. A one time labor lawyer and co-author of the Norris-LaGuardia Act, his sincere interest in improved conditions for workers made it easy for him to favor development of a political party rooted in the city's needle trade unions. As a political professional, the mayor knew that to stay in power in 1937 he would have to cut into the traditional Democratic loyalties of New York's voters, as he had in 1933. The organization that the three Jewish union leaders proposed to create promised to help him do just that. The mayor heartily endorsed the plan.[33]

On July 16, 1936, Hillman, Dubinsky, and Zaritsky, joined by other New York union leaders, created the American Labor party (ALP). They announced their support for Roosevelt and the New Deal, placed on their ticket Herbert H. Lehman, who was running for reelection as governor, and selected their own officers. ILGWU vice president Luigi Antonini became chairman, Rose Schneiderman of the Women's Union Trade League, vice chairman. United Hatter vice president Alex Rose was made party secretary, and Jacob Potofsky, vice president of the Amalgamated, headed the executive committee.[34]

Dubinsky and Hillman, Alex Rose, Russian born Max Zaritsky and Jacob Potofsky, and Russian Polish Rose Schneiderman were all Jewish immigrants raised in the social context that had given meaning to the worker's Bund in Eastern Europe and that permeated the political consciousness of thousands of garment industry laborers in New York City. The new party's titular chairman, Luigi Antonini, was Italian, but as a member of the ILGWU he was closely tied to the Jewish labor movement. His appointment to the top post appears to have been a deliberate effort to avoid drawing attention to the Jewishness of the organization. The ALP received some support from unions not dominated by Jews, notably Mike Quill's heavily Irish Transport Workers Union. Because the New Deal and Franklin Roosevelt had inspired its creation, the ALP generated some enthusiasm among liberal intellectuals of the kind in FDR's brain trust. Still, Jewish labor leaders and the heavily Jewish membership of their unions dominated the new political organization. They set its tone, its priorities, and its style.[35]

Like New York's Socialist party two decades earlier, the American

Labor party was a movement of working-class Jews. Its purpose, beyond helping reelect President Roosevelt, was to reject the corruption of Tammany Hall and to support progressive social legislation that would help workers in particular, the poor in general. It gave voice to the demands of Jewish laborers, and it was their ethnic solidarity that glued the party together. It delivered 237,000 votes for Roosevelt in his 1936 landslide, including Fiorello LaGuardia's. "I am going to vote the American Labor ticket and I hope it will not be the last time that we will have the opportunity to vote under that label," the nominally Republican mayor announced just days before the Presidential election. He had already sent word to the new party that he planned to seek its support for his own bid for reelection.[36]

LaGuardia and the Jews

In 1937 the Procrustean vanguard of New York's Republican party tried to deny the GOP nomination for mayor to the squat, irreverent, much-too-liberal-for-them son of Italian immigrants who campaigned for "that man" in the White House and befriended the city's workers. LaGuardia, however, managed to hold onto sufficient support to win the Republican primary, and he also headed the ALP ticket. He buried his Democratic opponent, Jeremiah Mahoney, by 454,425 votes. On the ALP line he took 487,128 votes, more than one fifth of the total ballots cast and more than his margin of victory. Moreover, the combined ALP/Republican forces of 1937 gave LaGuardia backed candidates a majority on the Board of Estimate—every spot except Bronx borough president—something the Fusion campaign of 1933 had not accomplished. The *New York Times* concluded that the ALP "held the balance of power" in the city. *Newsweek* asserted that the party could "swing any closely contested New York City election."[37]

Jewish voters cast just under half of the total ALP ballots in 1937. The mayor took nearly 70 percent of the total Jewish vote that year, up dramatically from 36 percent in 1933. More than 40 percent of Jewish votes were cast on the ALP line, more than on either of the major party tickets. Italian-American support for LaGuardia in 1937 was almost the same as in 1933, but with about a third of the votes cast on the ALP ticket. The Jewish vote, larger than the Italian vote, and more solidly for LaGuardia, became the most important component of the mayor's electoral base. The ALP had no appeal for the Irish, who continued to back Tammany overwhelmingly, and little for the Germans. Many Germans voted for Mayor LaGuardia, but they did so on the Republican ticket.[38]

LaGuardia was popular with Jewish voters for several reasons. Jewish professionals were prominent among the city's political reformers. It was natural for the mayor to offer high profile appointments to people who had helped him to get elected and who agreed with his policies. As a result, during his Administration the number of Jews in top city posts rose substantially, and, no doubt, the mayor's standing in the Jewish community along with it. Perhaps more importantly, to a greater degree than any previous mayor, LaGuardia insisted on strict application of civil service codes when hiring municipal workers. The intent of the reforms he implemented was to improve and professionalize government employment, but the strong cultural emphasis Jews placed on education smoothed their entry into civil service jobs that were based on exams, often at the expense of the Irish. During the depression Jews, who in better times favored business, the professions, and positions requiring skilled labor, turned to government jobs more than ever before. This gave LaGuardia's policies greater impact than they might have had under other circumstances.[39]

Emotions bound Jews to Mayor LaGuardia as strongly as jobs, perhaps more so. The anti-Semitic horrors of Nazi Germany had begun by the late 1930s, greatly alarming New York's Jews. Members of local pro-Nazi groups, like the German-American Bund, and the Christian Front, marched the streets of the city hurling hate rhetoric at their Jewish neighbors. Demonstrations sometimes escalated into violence. The mayor sat astride his intolerance for bigotry and his support for free speech. Despite some delicate moments and periodic criticisms, Jewish voters knew where LaGuardia's sympathies lay. With typical flair he once assigned an all Jewish contingent of policemen to protect anti-Semitic speakers. At the same time, LaGuardia's perception of Mussolini's fascism was unclouded by the ethnic romanticism so many Italian-Americans held for Il Duce. Until 1940 the mayor kept his own counsel to avoid alienating his backers, but finally began to speak out against the rising dangers of right-wing fanaticism abroad. This, coupled with charges that LaGuardia was not providing patronage and favors for his fellow paesans in the depths of depression, cut sharply his support from the group that was so instrumental to his 1933 election.[40]

In 1941 New Yorkers elected LaGuardia for the third time. His 132,000 vote margin was down sharply from his performance four years before. The ALP again provided his margin of victory. The mayor's fellow Italians gave him fewer than half their votes, and Germans abandoned him in response to his criticisms of their fatherland with which America was not yet at war. A few months before the election LaGuardia accepted appointment by President Roosevelt to the post of Civilian Defense Coordinator, a full-time job for a country at risk of being pulled into the conflict already raging in Europe. Many New Yorkers resented their mayor's decision to assume a post that took him to Washington three days a week, and still stand for reelection. But nearly three Jews of four, a higher proportion than ever before, cast ballots for LaGuardia in 1941. Nearly 40 percent of all Jewish votes were cast on the ALP line.[41]

Never before had a reform mayor succeeded in getting himself re-elected in New York City. LaGuardia did it twice. In a city that even in the 1930s was three-quarters foreign stock, only by capturing solid blocs of votes from the city's large ethnic groups could a politician persevere. In 1933 Italians voted for ethnic pride and sent LaGuardia to City Hall based on common blood, while significant numbers of Jewish voters rejected Tammany's candidate because of corruption in the Democratic party. In 1937, after four years to assess the man, a solid force of Italian and Jewish voters gave LaGuardia a landslide. In 1941, Jewish commitment to the mayor, based on his liberal policies and his responsiveness to their ethnic concerns, kept him in office. The American Labor party was instrumental to LaGuardia's success. It offered the city's working class Jews a way to support the mayor without appearing to favor the Republican party, which they disliked, just as it provided them a means of voting for Franklin Roosevelt and Herbert Lehman without appearing to approve of Tammany Hall, which they distrusted.

Like the Socialist party a generation earlier, the ALP gave coherent voice to New York City's Jewish workers. Neither party ever achieved much standing with any other group. While their numbers were large, there were never enough working-class Jews to win a citywide contest on their own. The ALP succeeded to a degree that the Socialists did not by supporting attractive candidates nominated by the major parties. This tactic, one the Socialists did not use, allowed the ALP to expand electoral support for its candidates beyond its own base, and therefore to be on the winning side. By 1941 it seemed that the large number of Jewish workers in New York City morally uncomfortable with Tammany, philosophically uncomfortable with the Republican party, and culturally uncomfortable with both, had finally created an effective political organization to represent themselves.

LaGuardia and the ALP reminded New York's Democrats in no

uncertain terms that holding the allegiance of Jewish voters was essential to success in citywide campaigns. To do this the Democrats had to run liberal candidates, untainted by scandal and sensitive to Jewish ethnic concerns. In short, to keep control of their party and the mayor's office, the Irish had to adopt the Jewish political agenda.

THREE

The Machine Overhauled

1942–1945

To win back City Hall Democratic party leaders needed to reconstitute their ethnic coalition. Yet, political tensions among Irish and Jews on several levels posed challenges. By and large the Jews who belonged to the Democratic party were more liberal than the Irish who ruled the organization. These philosophical differences periodically created struggles that threatened party unity. Winning the votes of the Jewish workers who supported the American Labor party posed a second obstacle. Then the ALP suffered internal conflicts and another splinter party, the Liberal party, emerged. This made maintaining the allegiance of Jewish workers more complicated still.

The rising importance of New York's Italian population added another dimension of complexity. If solid Irish and Jewish support could be won the Italians were not crucial. But a coalition that included them would be stronger than one that did not, and LaGuardia had already proven the political danger of ignoring the Italians. The years between 1942 and 1945 were filled with challenges for New York's Democratic party leaders. Some responded more skillfully than others.

Ed Flynn, Sophisticated Boss

"For more than a quarter of a century Bronx County has elected only Democratic officials," Bronx boss Edward J. Flynn bragged in a 1947 article that appeared in the *Atlantic Monthly*. "It has become, on percentage, the greatest Democratic County north of the Mason Dixon line." The boast was not idle. While local Democratic candidates around New York fell victim to Fusion, Fiorello LaGuardia's coattails, and the American Labor party, Flynn kept control of his borough. In the process he became the most powerful Democrat in the city, one of the most powerful in the entire country.[1]

Flynn was an unusual boss. He was the son of Irish immigrants, but his father, who had been educated at Trinity College, Dublin, possessed a degree of culture and sophistication rare for the emigrants who left the emerald isle in the mid-nineteenth century. Flynn's mother too had a strong appreciation for education, and she saw her five children through college, and beyond. Her youngest son, Edward, born in 1892, graduated from Fordham University law school in the Bronx. When the Democratic district leader in the neighborhood where Flynn grew up needed an attractive candidate for assembly in 1914, he asked the young attorney to make the race. While on the surface it was just another case of an Irish American launching a political career, Flynn's background, education, and bearing made him a standout from the start. He was elected Sheriff of Bronx County, a job rich with patronage power, in 1922. When Bronx county leader Arthur Murphy (no relation to the Tammany leader of the same last name) died later that year, Flynn became part of a triumvirate selected to rule the borough's Democrats. Within a short time Charles Murphy decided that Flynn was the most capable of the three and saw to his appointment as Bronx county leader.[2]

About the same time Flynn rose to power a mass exodus of Jews from the Lower East Side was transforming the population of the Bronx. Subway lines that reached from Manhattan's tenements to the still bucolic borough to its north had been completed fifteen years earlier. New apartment houses went up alongside them that offered clean, cheap housing to slum packed city workers. By the tens of thousands garment laborers rode the new subways out of their ghettos towards parks, trees, cleaner air, and a healthier life. By 1930 almost six out of ten Bronx residents were Jewish compared to fewer than two of ten just a decade earlier. By 1940 it had settled down to just over half.

Like Jewish workers elsewhere around the city, many of those who moved to the Bronx found that the ALP's politics suited them. They voted for President Roosevelt, Governor Lehman, and Mayor LaGuardia on the American Labor party line. But Ed Flynn's organization had more success holding the loyalty of Jewish voters in local contests than the Democratic machines in Manhattan or Brooklyn, the other boroughs with large concentrations of Jewish voters.[3]

Part of the reason was Flynn's personal integrity. He himself was meticulously honest, and insisted on the same from the men he supported. Judge Seabury's staff reviewed every aspect of the Bronx boss's finances during the investigations into political corruption that so damaged Tammany, but filed no charges against the politician. "Nothing wrong was found. There was nothing wrong to find," was Flynn's summary of the inquiry. No one had any evidence to the contrary. His law practice, in partnership with an able Jewish attorney named Monroe Goldwater, certainly benefited from the Irishman's connections, but by all accounts their business was strictly legitimate.[4]

In 1933 the other bosses nominated party hack John O'Brien for reelection as mayor in spite of public disillusionment with Tammany incompetence and corruption. Flynn, at FDR's urging, launched Joseph McKee's independent campaign on the Recovery party. The strategy allowed Flynn to disassociate his organization from Tammany's malfeasance and gave the Bronx Democrats a strong New Deal image. McKee lost to LaGuardia, of course, but Flynn's other candidates won. They won again in 1937 when LaGuardia's combined Republican/ALP ticket allowed him to win all the spots on the Board of Estimate except Bronx borough president. Flynn's sound reputation and strong support for President Roosevelt gave Bronx Democrats an honest and liberal image that won the loyalty of Jewish voters. And Flynn's success won him the right to distribute much of the federal patronage in New York City, strengthening his position with his fellow Irish and others looking for jobs. Until the 1950s Flynn would practice in the Bronx the same strategy that Charles Murphy adopted successfully in Manhattan and citywide in the first two decades of the twentieth century. It remained the way to win elections in New York City.[5]

A Rift Between Irish and Jewish Democrats

When FDR launched his presidential candidacy in 1932 he asked Edward Flynn to coordinate the effort to line up support from Democratic organizations across the nation. The Bronx boss had little interest in mixing with unknown politicians around the country. After some discussion the two men agreed that Jim Farley, the Democratic leader from Rockland County New York, would be a good man for the job. Farley, like Flynn, was of Irish descent. Although not as refined as the Bronx boss, he had a smooth style and an unusually confident manner that inspired trust. He did his job well and when Roosevelt became President, Farley became Chairman of the New York State Democratic Party, National Chairman of the Democratic Party, and the Postmaster General, then the greatest source of patronage jobs in the country.

In 1936 Farley delivered again. He alone among the President's political advisors predicted the extent of FDR's reelection landslide. Yet, in spite of the mutual dependence and respect, Roosevelt and Farley never developed a close personal friendship. In some ways the two men were philosophically incompatible; Farley shared Roosevelt's love of power but lacked his liberal convictions. In 1940 Farley, who had never held elective office before, thought he could use his position as Democratic national chairman to win his party's nomination for President. He had been thinking about it for years, and had assumed that Roosevelt would abide by the tradition (that later became law) of not serving for more than two terms. Even after it became clear that FDR would be a candidate again, Farley persisted in his unrealistic quest. At the Democratic convention in Chicago he had his name placed in nomination. Roosevelt overwhelmed him and the inevitable purge followed. Farley lost his position as national party chairman, but managed to maintain his post as New York State leader. He would have a last hurrah.[6]

In 1942 Governor Herbert Lehman announced that he would not seek reelection again after ten years in office. Farley sought to deliver the Democratic nomination to John J. Bennett, Jr., the New York State attorney general. Bennett, who had once participated in a Catholic fundraising event for General Francisco Franco's forces in Spain, rightly or wrongly had an antilabor reputation. The ALP made it clear that it would not make common cause with the Democrats for such a candidate, which would ensure his defeat. The President wanted his party to retain control of New York's chief executive office and used his influence with all of the top elected officials in the state to try to shift the nomination to Senator James M. Mead, who was acceptable to the ALP.

In a bitter battle at the nominating convention held in Brooklyn that year, Farley led his bloc of Democratic delegates committed to Bennet against those pledged to Mead. It broke down very much into a factional fight between a conservative wing, substantially Irish Catholic in composition, against a liberal wing, heavily populated by Jewish Democrats. The center of gravity of the formal party structure still lay with the Irish in 1942, and Farley's men carried the vote. "That was a great tribute to me, as state leader," Farley felt. "We nominated our man against the President of the United States, against the governor of the state, against two United States Senators, Mead and Wagner . . . [and against] Flynn. We beat the hell out of them." Yet he had to concede, "We won the battle, but lost the war." The ALP nominated Mead on their own and the Jewish workers party took over 400,000 votes away from Bennett. Republican gubernatorial candidate Thomas Dewey won election easily. The sharp tensions between the liberal and conservative wings of the Democratic party, which to a great extent were the Irish and the Jewish wings of the party, did not bode well for restoring the coalition that could win back the mayor's office. The election also made clear how weak the Democrats were when they lost the support of the many Jewish working- class voters who cast their ballots on the ALP line.[7]

A Split Among Jewish Workers

By 1942 the American Labor party was itself suffering from bitter internal strife. Four years before, the Communist party's candidate for governor failed to win the minimum support necessary to remain on a statewide ballot in New York without the onerous burden of gathering petition signatures in every county. As a result, the Communists instructed their followers to join the ALP in a plan to take control by "boring from within." After a series of backroom maneuvers and bitter primary contests the Communists succeeded. In 1944, with President Roosevelt up for reelection to a fourth term, Sidney Hillman sought party unity and he urged the original leadership of the ALP to seek an accommodation with the Communists. Hillman pledged the considerable political resources of the Amalgamated Clothing Workers Union to the cause. David Dubinsky and Alex Rose refused. They withdrew from the ALP and formed the Liberal party.[8]

Dubinsky and Rose were fierce anti-Communists who had purged their unions of party cells in the 1920s. Their objections were philosophical, emotional, and practical. Neither one believed the Communists were committed to democracy, and neither one trusted the party members who sought close ties with the Soviet government that seemed in some ways more similar than different to the Russian autocracies that had launched so many anti-Jewish pogroms. Moreover, the political instincts of the two men told them that a party of extremists would fail. Their own political commitments were rooted in a pragmatic desire to improve the lot of the workers they represented, and a deep belief in social justice inextricably linked to their sense of identity as Jews.

David Dubinsky was born David Dobnievski in Brest-Litovsk in 1892. His family moved to Lodz, Russian Poland, when he was a small child. At the age of eleven he left school to work in his father's bakery, and in 1905 he joined the local union of master bakers organized by the Bund. He participated in Socialist workers meetings, joined in protests, was arrested twice, and exiled to Siberia in 1908. He escaped, made his way back across Russia, and soon afterward left his native land for New York, arriving on Manhattan's Lower East Side in 1911. Dubinsky resumed his labor organizing efforts and in the late 1920s and early 1930s helped rescue the International Ladies Garment Workers from impending extinction. Catapulted forward by a whirlwind series of successful strikes in 1933, the ILGWU grew in size and importance, and Dubinsky's reputation along with it.

His Socialist beliefs in the universal brotherhood of man led Dubinsky to reject Jewish ritual and "dogma" as he called it, but his religious heritage was a fundamental part of his identity. "I am not a professional Jew, I am a Jewish worker, and I am proud of it," he once declared at a meeting of the Jewish Labor Committee, of which he was a founding member. At the same time Dubinsky balanced his Socialist convictions with a pragmatic sense of how to get things done. In 1936 he resigned from the Socialist party announcing that, "pending the establishment in this country of an effective and constructive labor party it is imperative . . . to defeat the reactionary forces, now trying to regain supremacy in this country, by supporting President Roosevelt's reelection." He eagerly backed the creation of the ALP in 1936 as a way of attracting voters like himself who favored the New Deal but who could not bear to cast a ballot in favor of the party of Tammany Hall because of its corrupt practices. But when the Communists took control of the ALP Dubinsky cut his ties unequivocally and helped to launch the Liberal party. The new organization was yet another phase in the quest by Jewish workers to find a philosophically and morally comfortable vehicle for pursuing social justice.[9]

Alex Rose was born Olesh Royz in Warsaw in 1898 to a family of modest wealth. In his youth Rose wanted to be a doctor, but the Russian regime that ruled Poland forbade Jews to attend college. In 1913 the would-be physician traveled to America in search of a medical education, but the next year war broke out in Europe and Rose's family could no longer send him money. The young man went to work in the garment industry where he became caught up for a time in the excitement of the Jewish labor movement.[10]

In 1918 Rose joined the Jewish Foreign Legion of the British Army fighting to free Palestine from Turkish control. The crucible of war affected the young soldier's outlook on life. "Personally, I have undergone a change lately," he wrote in a private diary in January 1919, shortly after arriving in Egypt on his way to the front. "From materialism and skepticism in the life in New York I turn to idealism and hopefulness for a life in Palestine." He thought he might find a place for himself in a Jewish homeland. During long nights of guard duty Rose found strength in the realization that he was fighting "to assure the proper treatment of jewish [sic] affairs at the Peace Conference."[11]

A Jewish homeland was not to be in 1919, but Rose returned to New York with a renewed sense of purpose in life, and some valuable lessons as well. British soldiers in a military hospital where Rose received treatment for a minor wound had harassed and ridiculed him. "It is no use to hide the fact, that the men have a dislike for me, although obviously there is no reason for it, except that I am a Jew," he wrote in his diary. He could not fathom the contradiction of the men "suppose [sic] to fight for, democracy, liberty and justice, things which are entirely strange to them by knowledge and practice." Yet, Rose's anger and frustration at his confrontation with anti-Semitism failed to embitter him; it made him more sensitive. When he arrived in Egypt a short time later he discovered that the "British treat the Egyptians like dogs. . . They [the Egyptians] have been introduced to us a very dangerous and treacherous people. To speak to them humanly was forbidden. We were always told to guard well, for they are thieves. My present impression is that all this is a lie." He concluded that the "policy of rough treatment towards them is dictated by selfish interests of certain people," who convince others to "blindly practice it."[12]

The sense of justice Rose learned in those years, and the resentment toward those who abused their power, was apparent a long time later when he explained his role in the creation of the American Labor party in New York City: "In the thirties I shared . . . [a] feeling of distrust in the politics of the day, together with many independent and progressive minded individuals. We saw the Republican Party primarily as a party for the privileged, and the Democratic Party in New York as a Tammany Hall with men entrenched in power, helped by shady elements for the purpose of self-enrichment and widespread corruption."[13]

To Rose, who rededicated himself to the labor movement upon returning to New York, his union organizing and political activism were efforts to make the world more just. His commitment to both causes was intimately bound to his understanding of what it meant to be a Jew. He knew he was a member of a race of people who had long experienced the kind of discrimination that could force a young man who wanted to study medicine to leave his family and native country and end up as a garment maker. Years later, with a dry smile, he would comment of his career: "The medical world lost a doctor." But the political world gained a master. Not long after the creation of the American Labor party Alex Rose became its chief political strategist. He assumed that role for the Liberal party upon its founding. Rose's decision, and Dubinsky's, to reject the ALP and to channel their unions' organizational muscle into another political party meant that winning the solid support of New York's large population of Jewish workers, never easy, had become even more complicated.[14]

Enter the Italians

The rising influence of New York's Italians added yet another dimension of complexity to the city's political landscape by the 1940s. The Italian presence in New York had been growing since the 1880s. At first, most Italian immigrants were single men who came to the United States intent on making money and returning home to their ancestral villages. For the most part they were peasants who had no experience with formal democracy and little understanding of the electoral process. They tended to be unconcerned with citizenship and indifferent about the right to vote. As late as 1911 only 15,000 Italians were registered voters in New York City according to one estimate, even though more than a half million of the city's people were of Italian stock by then. Tammany responded predictably. The same George Washington Plunkitt who spoke fondly of his district's Jewish voters referred to Italians as "dagoes" without a second thought. Tim Campbell, a late-nineteenth-century Tammany congressman, once campaigned for reelection against his Republican opponent by claiming that "the local issue is the Dago Rinaldo. He is from Italy, I am from Ireland. Are you in favor of Italy or Ireland?"

As the decades passed greater numbers of Italian wives and children crossed the Atlantic. An American born generation linked the parents, whose hearts and minds remained in the old country, to the new one. By the early 1930s the city's Italian population had surged over one million, more than one New Yorker in five, and slowly they began to assert themselves in the city's political life.[15]

In 1931, almost a quarter of a century after the first Jew won election as a Tammany leader, Albert Marinelli became the first Italian district leader. He had an unusual style of campaigning. Rather than trying to out-politic the incumbent Irish American, Harry Perry, he sent two henchman to visit the leader and explain that it was time the Italians had one of their own to represent them in a district where they made up the largest bloc of votes. Blatantly gesturing to the guns under their coats they suggested that Perry step down. He did, and Marinelli's victory followed.

By the time of Marinelli's victory Jews made up nearly fifteen percent of the Democratic party hierarchy in Manhattan. Their proportion was about the same in the Bronx, but somewhat higher in Brooklyn, where Republican strength made it prudent for Democrats to make extra efforts to bind Jewish supporters to their organization. Some Jews complained that their participation in party leadership positions was less than it should have been based on the proportion of party enrollment that was Jewish—about thirty percent of the total according to one estimate—but the Jewish presence in the Democratic organization's leadership was second only to the Irish. Throughout the 1930s Italians remained a distant and unimportant third.[16]

In his 1933 campaign for mayor LaGuardia awoke a strong sense of pride among his fellow Italians and he attracted them to the polls in greater numbers than in the past. Italians voted for LaGuardia on the Republican line during his first victory and on the Republican and ALP tickets in 1937. By 1941, after LaGuardia spoke out against Mussolini, a majority of Italians voted for the Democrat in the mayoral election. The shift was not complete—many Italians would continue to support Republicans—but the group had finally achieved a measure of electoral significance in the city's Democratic politics by the early 1940s.[17]

Italians exerted influence on the Democratic party in another way by the 1940s. The group had come to dominate organized crime in New York by then. In many respects Italian success in illegal businesses mimicked the earlier achievements of Irish, Jewish, and other gangsters. In the late nineteenth century Irishmen ran the numbers racket on the Lower East Side and oversaw houses of prostitution. In one of the more ironic episodes of the city's politics some went into the business as a result of a law inspired by the moralizing of New York's gentry. A group of zealous reformers succeeded in passing a law that forbade establishments to serve alcohol on Sundays, but they exempted lodging houses because many upper crust New Yorkers had adopted the custom of finishing their Sunday afternoon walks by sipping sherry in the fancy hotels that lined Central Park. To comply with the law without closing down saloon owners rented apartments in the tenements above their stores and then let them to transients. Whores were ready customers for the rooms, and so the desire to improve immigrant morals turned a small coterie of Irish barmen into pimps. But the people who lived in New York's ghettos never really needed inspiration from others to engage in vice. Their poverty had a way of making a virtue of profits from any source.[18]

Jews figured prominently in the white slave trade in the early twentieth century, and in gambling and other rackets as well. The victims of Arthur Flegenheimer, better known as Dutch Schultz, Arthur Rothstein, Louis "Lepke" Buchalter, Jacob "Gurrah" Shapiro, Tootsie Herbert, and the Diamondstone and Frankel gangs died just as violently as the many men murdered by a rising band of mobsters from Italy. However, just about the time New York's Italians began entering the city's underworld America passed a constitutional amendment forbidding the sale of alcohol. Prohibition forced a multi-billion-dollar industry from the hands of small businessmen into the criminal realm. The huge profits laid the foundations for an enduring Italian dynasty over organized crime. Beginning in the 1920s collaboration between the men who made a living by systematically violating the law and the politicians who could influence the city's judges and the police force increasingly linked the respective urban fortresses of the Italians and the Irish. Jews participated in both activities, but dominated neither.[19]

Italian mobsters accepted Irish control of the Democratic party as long as the leadership used its power to permit vice to thrive, but LaGuardia's election reduced Tammany's ability to provide protection. Increasingly, the criminals bankrolling the party wanted to run it and they forced their men in. By 1945 a half dozen Italian district leaders had replaced Irish politicians in Manhattan. Tammany's Irish boss, Edward Loughlin, often followed the orders of an immigrant from Italy named Francisco Costiglia, known in America as Frank Costello. The police knew him as the prime minister of the underworld for the eastern United States. The public learned of the power he wielded in 1943. The day after being nominated by the Democrats for a spot on the New

York State Supreme Court, City Magistrate Thomas A. Aurelio called Costello to thank him. "When I tell you something is in the bag you can rest assured," the gangster bragged, unaware that Manhattan District Attorney Frank Hogan had tapped his telephone and was recording the conversation. To hold onto power the Democratic party's Irish bosses were learning to accommodate the Italians on several levels it seemed.[20]

A Looser Grip

New York's shifting ethnic mosaic made its politics more complex, and responding coherently on a citywide basis had become more difficult for the Democratic machine by LaGuardia's third term in office. When Manhattan held the greater part of New York's population the Tammany machine dominated Democratic politics in citywide elections. As the other boroughs grew, their political influence increased. By the time LaGuardia won office for the third time 2,700,000 people lived on the far side of the Brooklyn Bridge compared to fewer than 2,000,000 on its near shore. When Ed Flynn became Bronx county leader in 1922 about one third as many New Yorkers lived in his borough as in Manhattan. Twenty years later Flynn ruled over more than three quarters as many voters as Tammany. Queens, though much more heavily populated with third and fourth generation Americans, and less strongly Democratic than the other three boroughs, was home to 1,300,000 of New York's nearly 8,000,000 people by 1940. Only Staten Island continued to have a small role in citywide contests. Manhattan, as the economic and cultural center of the metropolis, as the communications hub that linked the other boroughs together, and as the site of City Hall, continued to hold the most important place among the five organizations. But maintaining the unity of the many headed Democratic party was more difficult than ever.[21]

At the beginning of the century, when immigrants crowded into Lower East Side tenements until they were more densely packed than the slums of Calcutta, a single block captain could reach hundreds of potential voters. In neighborhoods in northern Manhattan, and in other boroughs where air and light separated the bodies of the men and women whom Democrats relied on to cast the ballots that kept them in power, the task became harder. By the 1930s politicians discovered that they could talk to more voters by radio in fifteen minutes than they could greet in person in weeks of grueling campaigning. The little box

that by 1940 sat in almost every living room in New York City competed with the district leader as the means of communication between
candidate and people. During the 1945 mayoralty campaign a Holly-
wood producer created newsreel press releases for the Democratic candidate that played before the feature movies in the city's theaters during
the final weeks of the election contest. The age of mass media had
begun, while some time earlier the age of mass immigration had ended.[22]

In 1924 America destroyed a long tradition of virtually unrestricted
entry for foreigners. The Johnson-Reed Act turned the floodtide of
humanity that peopled the country in the century between 1820 and
1920 into a trickle. Fulfilling the basic needs of immigrants had been
one of the most important ways big city political organizations secured
support. By the 1940s this source of machine strength had been virtually shut for a generation.

The immigrants who did come, and the city's poor who once relied
on the local party leader to help them because no one else would, had
new options. The New Deal era had fostered federal work programs
that replaced the patronage jobs of city governments when the depression left municipalities in financial crisis. Then the nation shifted to a
wartime economy and there were plenty of jobs to be had. In the
postwar prosperity wages in industry would rise until government jobs,
where pay scales did not keep pace, were less attractive than they had
been before. The demand for patronage did not end suddenly, but its
strength as a means of holding a party together began to decline.
Municipal jobs appealed most to unskilled workers, but civil service
restrictions, and the increasing complexity of city government, limited
the ability of the machine to place these supporters. To a great degree
federal programs displaced the welfare functions that the machines once
performed. The Social Security Act of 1935 established a national commitment to the needy. The aged, widows and orphans, the unemployed,
the disabled, all received help from the government whether they were
registered with the local party or not. The implicit contract between
district leader and voter, a ballot in return for bread, became harder for
the politicians to maintain, especially in New York City.[23]

When a strong political organization ran City Hall during the expan-
sion of government welfare functions, the local district leader often
became the vehicle for access to federal programs. In Chicago, under
Democratic mayor Ed Kelly, the easiest way to qualify for public assistance in the 1930s and 1940s was to see the ward boss. The same was
true in Albany where Dan O'Connell ran a tough Democratic organization. In New York, however, with the exception of a few chosen favor-

ites like East Harlem congressman Vito Marcantonio, Fiorello La-Guardia relied on neither his Republican cohorts nor his Democratic opponents as the keepers of the welfare gate. By implementing New Deal initiatives professionally he weakened the Democratic machine without replacing it. In the Bronx, Ed Flynn relied on federal patronage to keep his machine greased. Tammany and the Brooklyn Democratic organization relied principally on local elected offices to maintain their base of support. The result was that by 1945, although the Democratic party remained the most powerful political organization in the city, it was significantly weaker than it once had been. In a telling symbol of Tammany's relative decline, by 1943 the party could not meet the mortgage payments on its large headquarters building completed in 1929. They sold it—to David Dubinsky's ILGWU.[24]

William O'Dwyer, A Candidate for Coalition

By the time politicians began contemplating the 1945 mayoralty campaign Fiorello LaGuardia's fortunes had reached bottom. He had managed to win Republican party endorsements in three successive elections, but many of the GOP's staunchest stalwarts had hated him with a special passion through every minute of his twelve year rule. Traditional Republicans found new strength after Thomas E. Dewey's election as governor in 1942, and they refused to nominate LaGuardia for a fourth term as mayor. The American Labor party, so important to LaGuardia's past two victories, now was split. The unconventional boost the non-Democratic mayor had received from a Democratic White House in 1937 and 1941 died with Franklin Roosevelt in 1944. Early in 1945 a *New York Daily News* straw poll confirmed for LaGuardia the unfriendly roll of the political landscape—only a quarter of the people interviewed favored his reelection.[25]

Personal factors too weighed heavily against another run for office. By his third term LaGuardia the performer sought a larger stage than the one he commanded at City Hall. In 1940 he had harbored presidential ambitions, but when Roosevelt ran again it ended his hopes. In the years from 1941 to 1945 the eyes of the world were watching the battlefields of Asia and Europe, and the mayor wanted to be a general. He petitioned the President to place him in command of allied forces in Italy, a post he desired so intensely that he commissioned a tailor to cut his uniforms. The appointment never came and LaGuardia had to settle for his assignment as head of Civil Defense, a post that he held while he continued to run the biggest city in the United States, a job he no longer enjoyed. Shortly after the 1945 election LaGuardia's successor paid a courtesy visit. "Sit down in that chair," LaGuardia told the mayor-elect pointing to the seat behind his own desk—"Now you'll have a perpetual headache," he shrieked. At sixty-two the once limitless energy of the Little Flower was drained, and his associates noticed that he often suffered from sharp pains in his lower back. Always, a small bottle of white pills now sat on his desk. LaGuardia declined to run for a fourth term. Less than two years after he drove away from City Hall for the last time as mayor, the most colorful politician in the city's history died of cancer.[26]

LaGuardia's political demise boosted the Democrats' chances to reclaim City Hall, but they needed a candidate who could reconstitute an ethnic coalition of Irish and Jewish voters, and appeal to Italians as well. The man they had nominated in 1941, William O'Dwyer, seemed perfect for the job.

Born in Bohola, County Mayo, Ireland in 1890, O'Dwyer traveled to a Jesuit seminary in Salamanca, Spain to study for the priesthood in 1909. After a year of spiritual self-assessment the twenty year old youth left the religious school and sailed to New York where he worked as a construction hand, a plasterer's apprentice, a coal fireman aboard a freighter on the South American run, and a bartender at the elegant Vanderbilt Hotel. In 1916 he became a citizen, and a year later began walking a beat as a Brooklyn cop. He enrolled in Fordham law school at night, and by 1926 had a small private practice.

Like other fledgling attorneys, O'Dwyer joined local organizations to meet people who might need a lawyer, and he made contact with the local Democratic party as well. He once helped organize the visit of an Irish football team to the United States and had it play a benefit game on behalf of Mrs. William Randolph Hearst's favorite charity, the Free Milk Fund for Babies. In 1932 when acting Mayor Joseph V. McKee needed a respectable choice for city magistrate in Brooklyn, the Hearst connection led to O'Dwyer. He handled himself intelligently and humanely, and in 1938 Governor Herbert Lehman appointed him to a vacant judgeship on the Kings County Court. In 1939 Brooklyn Democratic chief Frank V. Kelly ran O'Dwyer for district attorney. Once elected, the former cop launched a series of skillful criminal prosecutions of notorious dock yard mobsters. The press dubbed the gang of killers for hire that O'Dwyer's detectives investigated "Murder, Incorporated," and in the kinds of headlines that sell newspapers praised the hardworking DA whose office solved more than eighty murders in less than two years.[27]

Democratic leaders watched the fast rising fortunes of Manhattan's Republican district attorney, Thomas E. Dewey. His success in prosecuting criminals had earned him the Republican nomination for governor in 1938, and serious if premature consideration as a presidential contender in 1940. With a crime buster of their own the Democrats hoped to launch one of their stars into higher office and to defuse accusations that they conspired with lawless men to keep their party coffers full. They made O'Dwyer the Democratic candidate for mayor in 1941. He lost to LaGuardia, but ran several hundred thousand votes better than Democratic nominee Jeremiah Mahoney had in 1937. When World War II broke out O'Dwyer volunteered and held a series of high level administrative posts in the United States Army, ultimately reaching the rank of brigadier general. He returned to New York in 1945, and after some interborough jostling his party again chose him to run for mayor.[28]

O'Dwyer's selection showed that the Irish still controlled the Democratic party in New York. It was the eleventh time in succession—an unbroken string dating back to 1909—that the Democrats had chosen a candidate of Irish descent to head their ticket. But the hold was weakening. Typically party leaders had chosen Irish candidates for the other citywide offices of comptroller and City Council president as well. Some ethnic balancing had started as early as 1909 with the nomination for borough president of Manhattan typically (though not always) going to a Jew, but rarely had the Democrats offered a citywide office to a Jewish candidate. They had never run an Italian for even a borough presidency.

LaGuardia created the first balanced ticket in the city's political history in 1933. With his Italian self at its head, an Irish Catholic for comptroller, and a Jew for President of the Board of Alderman (predecessor to the City Council), LaGuardia showed that he recognized the political composition of the city better than the inept bosses running Tammany at the time. By 1945 the Democrats had learned, and they sought to round out their slate for maximum ethnic and geographic effect. O'Dwyer was a Brooklyn Irishman, so the leaders announced that a Manhattan Jew named Irwin Davidson would stand for City Council president, and Lawrence Gerosa, a Bronx Italian, for comptroller. O'Dwyer understood the reasoning behind the selections that reflected the ethnic reality of the city's politics, but he understood some other things as well.

O'Dwyer knew that his heritage and impressive background stood him in good stead with his fellow Irish New Yorkers. Combined with the backing of the Democratic county leaders his image would win him the votes of the Irish as it had before. He won a majority of the ballots of the city's Italians too in 1941, and his work during World War II included a well publicized stint in a humanitarian capacity with the Allied Commission in Italy. He could expect his electoral performance among Italians to be even better in 1945 than it had been four years before running against LaGuardia. Of the city's three major voting blocs, only Jews had not cast a majority of their votes for O'Dwyer in 1941.

Despite the split in the ranks of the ALP, many Jewish workers were still loyal to the party, so O'Dwyer wanted its backing. The Democratic county leaders counseled him to stay away from it because of its Communist affiliation, but O'Dwyer appeared unconcerned. He understood not only that winning the party's backing would bring him the support of its members, but also that many of New York's Jewish Democrats objected to the tactics of the local party. The more he asserted his independence from the bosses and portrayed himself as a "New Deal" rather than machine Democrat, the better he would run with Jewish voters. Besides, by temperament O'Dwyer was fiercely independent and it suited him to maintain some distance from the county leaders.[29]

Forty-eight hours after their selection, O'Dwyer rejected Gerosa and Davidson, declaring that he would not let the bosses dictate his ticket. His choice for City Council president was Vincent Impellitteri, and for comptroller State Senator Lazarus Joseph. The latter was a well known and well respected grandson of one of the city's most prominent rabbis—a smart political choice. Impellitteri, on the other hand, was an anonymous political hack who held a minor patronage job as legal secretary to a city magistrate. When someone asked Tammany Secretary Bert Stand how the unlikely candidate had been chosen he replied, "We flipped through the Green Book [the directory of City Government Employees] for the longest Italian name we could find." The truth was more complicated.[30]

Vito Marcantonio had become the American Labor party's most powerful official by 1945 even though Sidney Hillman remained its public spokesman. Marcantonio's political career began in 1921 when Fiorello LaGuardia heard him deliver a rousing speech to his DeWitt Clinton High School senior class. Impressed with the oratory that would eventually earn Marcantonio a reputation as New York's greatest demagogue, LaGuardia, then President of the Board of Alderman, took the young fellow Italian into his confidence. In 1934 LaGuardia helped Marcantonio win the East Harlem Congressional seat that the Little Flower himself once held. Like his mentor, Marcantonio was nominally Republican but a tireless laborite and champion of the underdog. He battled GOP leaders continuously, and he kept strong ties to Communists and to Italian underworld figures influential in his district. He joined the American Labor party at its inception in 1936, and found that it suited his left-wing tastes more than the traditional organizations. With LaGuardia's active support Marcantonio built up a tough political machine in East Harlem and he became the *de facto* leader of the ALP after David Dubinsky, Alex Rose, and other party founders left.[31]

Shortly after O'Dwyer won the Democratic nomination for mayor in 1945, Marcantonio called him from his Washington congressional office where a visitor overheard the conversation. "Bill-O," Marcantonio began, calling O'Dwyer by his well known nickname, "you have to rearrange the ticket. I have my own *guinzo* for City Council president, Vince Impellitteri." Marcantonio pushed the unknown Italian at the urging of Tommy "Three Finger Brown" Lucchese, a rising mobster who wanted to challenge Costello as both underworld king and political power in New York City, and who was a boyhood friend of the fellow with the long Italian name. With an Italian replacing a Jew as candidate for president of the City Council, the Irishman restored balance to his team by choosing a Jewish running mate, Lazarus Joseph, for comptroller, and dropping the Italian the Democrats had selected. The ALP, and Marcantonio individually, then endorsed the entire ticket.[32]

Although O'Dwyer's motives were hidden in political shadows, the public perceived a man independent of the Democratic bosses, and the ALP backing boosted his image as a liberal and as a friend of the working class. A few days later when the Democrats tried to drop Frank Hogan as their candidate for Manhattan district attorney, perhaps in retribution for releasing the 1943 tape proving Frank Costello's influence in selecting judges, O'Dwyer again broke with the party leaders and insisted that they nominate the well respected incumbent. They did. The more O'Dwyer fought with the Democratic party leaders who backed him, the higher his standing rose with the public.[33]

The Republicans Court the Jews

The Republicans watched O'Dwyer adeptly position himself as an independent minded politician and the voice of liberalism. The combination, they concluded, would attract the support of the Jewish voters so important to the coalition that had sustained LaGuardia. Running a Jewish candidate offered the only chance to keep a Republican in City Hall reasoned GOP state party leader J. Russell Sprague and Paul Lockwood, Governor Dewey's secretary. Dewey approved of the strategy wholeheartedly. He thought the Democrats would win anyway, but wanted to make a gesture to the Jewish ethnic group that had voted so heavily against him when he ran for president in 1944 against FDR. He hoped the maneuver would encourage some Jews to consider voting for the Republican ticket for governor in 1946.[34]

With their strategy set, the Republicans offered their nomination to Jonah Goldstein. Goldstein was the son of East European Jews who made their way to Manhattan's Lower East Side via Canada when Jonah was six. He joined Tammany as a young man and earned a reputation as a competent lawyer, serving briefly as counsel to Al Smith when he was still a fledgling assemblyman. In 1931 Mayor Jimmy Walker rewarded Goldstein for many years service to the party by appointing him to a city magistrate's position, and in 1936 Governor Lehman promoted him to a vacancy on the Court of General Sessions. When his seat came up for election in 1939 Goldstein expected the party to back him. But Tammany had an agreement with the Republicans to split the nominations for judgeships between them. To keep their end of the bargain the Democratic leaders planned to drop Goldstein. For the first time the loyal Tammany soldier bolted the party, ran on his own, and won.[35]

At heart Goldstein remained a Tammanyite, and the man hoped someday to be mayor. In 1945 he sought the backing of the Democratic bosses for the city's top spot. The leaders dismissed him out of hand, leaving Goldstein angry and with no obvious outlet for his ambitions. When the Republicans came along with an offer, he willingly seized the opportunity. There was a certain logic to Goldstein's candidacy on the Republican line. At the top of the GOP ticket Goldstein would win the support of loyal Republican voters. At the same time, as a former Democrat, he could appeal to the anti-Tammany wing of that party, especially Jewish Democrats. To solidify Jewish support, Republican strategists sought to boost Goldstein's image as a political independent and a man committed to progressive social policies. Goldstein had been active in Jewish circles that supported the settlement houses on the Lower East Side, especially the Grand Street Boys Club, but his involvement was limited, and he had no particular standing with Jewish labor unions. The nomination of the newly created Liberal party could help compensate for these weaknesses.[36]

Political circumstances more than philosophical commitment led the Liberals to agree to back Goldstein. The Liberal party laid out its urban political agenda in 1945 in a seventy page document. The program was a call to complete the unfinished business of the New Deal, supplemented by important matters of local interest. It urged New York City to undertake slum clearance and to build better housing; to improve education for children and adults, to provide more funding for libraries, and to offer special programs for juvenile delinquents. It called on the city government to sponsor health services and medical care for the indigent, and for poorly paid workers; to prevent discrimination against minorities, especially blacks, and to ensure freedom of speech and assembly. The plan called for a revamped civil service system with improved salaries, better career options, and the right of collective bargaining, and it encouraged the city to adopt special measures to help returning war veterans readjust to life at home. It suggested that the city consider running its own utilities, insisted on special protections for consumers, and also endorsed the system of proportional representation on the City Council, an experiment that the major parties were in the process of dismantling precisely to limit the power of minor parties like the Liberals.[37]

The candidate most likely to move the major aspects of that agenda forward was William O'Dwyer. He was the only man in the race who had himself been a worker and union member. He had an excellent reputation on civil rights, and had instituted innovative policies for dealing with juvenile delinquents when he sat on the bench. O'Dwyer had pledged to build more housing, hospitals, schools, parks and playgrounds, and publicly asked Robert Moses, the city's master builder and a hero of good government groups at the time, to stay on in a Democratic administration and oversee an ambitious construction plan.[38]

O'Dwyer was indisputably the New Deal candidate in 1945, yet the Liberal party's leaders distrusted the local machine that sponsored him: "It is tortured logic which holds we must suffer corrupt Tammany government in New York City in order to have progressive government in our state and nation," David Dubinsky wrote in reply to critics who thought the Liberals should automatically endorse the Democrat. Besides, the Liberals had launched their independent effort to distinguish themselves from the Communist tainted ALP and refused to back any candidate that accepted the Labor party's endorsement. As a result, they felt compelled to back the Republican nominee.[39]

Goldstein's candidacy choked good government advocates. Instead of one Tammany candidate, Judge Seabury announced, now two were in the race. LaGuardia, continuing his long standing feud with the GOP leadership, rejected Goldstein and ran his City Council president, Newbold Morris, as an independent candidate for mayor on the No Deal ticket. "This organization looks like a worthy charity," an observer wrote, "one that should provide a refuge for innumerable homeless New York Republicans." Other than that, it was running on "a pun and a prayer." The Republicans accused LaGuardia of acting out of spite, deliberately splitting his former party to prevent it from winning without him. When Lester Stone, LaGuardia's former press aide, joined O'Dwyer's campaign team, apparently with the mayor's blessing, it gave credence to the claim.[40]

Campaigning for Jewish Votes

The three candidates, O'Dwyer, Goldstein, and Morris, shared a single campaign strategy. Each portrayed himself as the most liberal minded in the race and the man most likely to govern New York honestly. To a great extent, the rhetoric was aimed at the city's Jews.

Morris's approach was simple. For eight years he had been La-Guardia's City Council president. He told New Yorkers that voting for him would extend LaGuardia's liberal-reform style rule. The partyless candidate, a descendant of a signer of the declaration of independence in a city where the parents of three quarters of the voters were born on foreign soil, never had a chance. But at LaGuardia's urging he was determined to take as many votes as possible away from the GOP. In addition to professions of liberalism and honesty Morris emphasized that the Republican "bosses" had nominated Goldstein in a cynical effort to win Jewish votes, and he urged the group to show defiant independence in response.[41]

Goldstein of course denied the charge. He reminded voters that he had once run for judge against a Tammany backed nominee offering that as proof that he was not a political stooge. But the public knew that he had sought the Democratic nomination for mayor first and accepted the Republican line on the ballot as his best bet for victory only after

Tammany rejected him. Without serious credentials as a fighter against machine rule, when he crusaded against corruption his words had a hollow ring. *The New Yorker* subtly lampooned him: "Judge Goldstein says the issue in the New York mayoralty campaign is greed. His own position is admirably clear. He is against it."[42]

By the end of the campaign the Tammany trained candidate running on a Republican/Liberal ticket realized that he had been unable to seize the philosophical ground needed to attract his fellow Jews to his cause. Out of desperation he sought to create a straw man that would be easier to knock down than the politically rugged Irishman he opposed. "Despite provocation, despite the efforts of others to inject such issues," he declared in a radio broadcast, "I have scrupulously adhered to my stated policy that 'religion has no place in politics—and politics no place in religion.'" He then went on to charge that posters of O'Dwyer that appeared in Jewish neighborhoods, purportedly sponsored by the Kosher Butchers Union, were actually paid for by the Democratic party. The Kosher Butchers Union, Goldstein insisted, was not a bonafide labor organization at all, and he then went on to imply that O'Dwyer was an anti-Semite. There is a certain irony to Goldstein's use of the tactic. Years earlier he had written a letter to the *American Hebrew* warning Jews to be suspicious of "the Mortimer of old [who] becomes the Moishe of the moment," in an effort to win Jewish support.[43]

The city's Jews yawned at Goldstein's charges. Nothing that O'Dwyer said even hinted at an anti-Jewish attitude. To the contrary, the World War II general spoke eloquently about the plight of the people in the devastating aftermath of the Holocaust: "This year there are five million fewer Jews left in the world to make their accounting before God," he said in a radio address on the eve of Rosh Hashanah, "and the world is poorer in an untold number of ways for that." As a member of the War Refugee Board he had tried to ease Jewish entry into America, and he urged United States support for a Jewish homeland. O'Dwyer pledged that as mayor he would cooperate with and for "the Jew, the Catholic and the Protestant in the exercise of all their civil and civic rights."[44]

A widely circulated story told of the time an Irish policeman hauled forty Jewish peddlers into O'Dwyer's court for selling wares on the streets of Brooklyn without a license. The vendors, afraid of facing an Irish magistrate to respond to charges levied by an Irish cop, refused to come forward when their names were called. They hoped that the cases would be held over so that they could reappear before an ethnically neutral judge. When O'Dwyer realized the source of the delay he announced that he would see to it that any defendants not tried that day would reappear before him. One by one the frightened sellers came forward, and forty times in succession O'Dwyer suspended sentence. The stunned Jewish merchants returned to their trade thinking kindly of the robed Irishman. The city's true anti-Semites, the Christian Fronters, had little good to say about the fair minded Democratic candidate. They called him a "Jewish Irishman" in an effort to insult that ironically could only help O'Dwyer at the polls. Eleanor Roosevelt, Herbert Lehman, and prominent members of FDR's administration who were well regarded by Jews endorsed the Democrat, so that his opponent had no way of making a charge of anti-Semitism stick.[45]

The only moment of doubt in the campaign's outcome came just days before the election. Throughout the race whispers circulated that in spite of O'Dwyer's record as a criminal prosecutor he had close ties to the underworld. One source of the charges was a single trip O'Dwyer had made to the Central Park West apartment of Frank Costello during World War II while investigating racketeering abuses of military contracts. The former DA was looking for information of the kind men like Costello often had. Unsubstantiated stories accused him of frequent visits to the politically powerful mobster's home, and rumors persisted that he had uncovered ample evidence to convict Murder, Inc. top man Albert Anastasia, but never did. During most of the campaign people dismissed the charges as political claptrap. Then, George Beldock, a loyal Republican whom Governor Dewey had appointed to fill O'Dwyer's Brooklyn DA seat while the Democrat ran for mayor, released a grand jury report offering powerful evidence that at least some of the assertions were true. For eighteen months, while O'Dwyer was district attorney, Brooklyn police held a witness named Abe Reles who had information that linked Anastasia to a murder. The night before legal action against the Murder, Inc. chief was finally planned, Reles plunged fourteen stories from the hotel room where six police officers were guarding him. Unconvincing evidence pointed to a failed attempt to escape, and some thought the death a suicide. The only reasonable conclusion was that some or all of the cops on duty conspired to murder him.

With the witness dead Anastasia could not be tried. The police guards received only superficial reprimands, and O'Dwyer never could explain why he never used Reles's testimony against Murder Inc.'s most powerful boss, although during a period of eighteen months he used the witness to help jail many lesser figures. The former DA barely responded to the charges as election day approached, and his campaign

chairman, Henry Epstein, dismissed the publicity as politically motivated. Most of the city seemed to believe him.[46]

Nearly six New Yorkers in ten voted for O'Dwyer in 1945. He
gathered 44 percent of the vote on the Democratic line, down slightly
from the 47 percent he took when he ran against LaGuardia in 1941.
He won another 13 percent on the ALP line. His base was largely the
same in the two elections. O'Dwyer won the solid support of Irish and
Italian voters in both. In 1945 black voters who had backed LaGuardia
four years earlier shifted strongly to the Democratic candidate, but
O'Dwyer lost votes in old-stock Republican areas where he had run well
before. The old guard that could not stomach Fiorello LaGuardia and
had opted for O'Dwyer four years earlier cast ballots for Goldstein or
Morris in 1945.[47]

Jewish voters registered the largest shift. In more than 80 percent of
Jewish working class districts around the city, O'Dwyer ran stronger on
the Democratic ticket in 1945 than he had in 1941. In addition to the
greater Jewish vote he took on the Democratic line, O'Dwyer ran well
with the ethnic group on the ALP ticket. Four years earlier, LaGuardia
had been the most liberal candidate, and the one most sensitive to
Jewish concerns. In 1945, O'Dwyer was. The shift in Jewish votes is the
principal reason O'Dwyer lost in 1941 and won in 1945.

Of the American Labor party's ballots, some 35 to 45 percent came
from Jewish districts in 1945. The split with the Liberals that took the
ILGWU and the Hatters union out of the ALP lessened the proportion
of Jews backing the Labor party. Still, to a great degree it remained an
ethnic, not a working class organization. With two opponents in the
race, O'Dwyer would have won easily on the Democratic line alone.
With the heavy Jewish support of the Labor party as well, he took every
assembly district save the "silk stocking" neighborhood on New York's
Upper East Side.[48]

Morris won about 21 percent of the vote, principally from areas
where New York's remaining Protestants lived, and from some elegant
German Jewish neighborhoods as well. Fifteen percent of Goldstein's
vote came on the Republican ticket, six percent on the Liberal party
line. About half of the ballots cast for the Liberal party came from
Jewish voters making it even more strongly an ethnic organization than
the ALP. Six percent of the vote was an inauspicious beginning, but
with the ALP becoming more and more heavily associated with Communism, the Liberal party was becoming the heir to the Jewish working
class quest for a political voice. Against a fair minded, humane, and
ethnically sensitive Democrat like O'Dwyer, the party had little to

offer. Yet, Dubinsky and Rose were determined to keep their new organization together to try to keep Tammany in check, and to battle the ALP.[49]

O'Dwyer reconstituted and modified the ethnic coalition that had brought the Democrats victory when Charles Murphy ruled Tammany. It was still rooted in an alliance of Irish and Jewish voters, and O'Dwyer had made modest room for Italians as well. The Irish immigrant's victory seemed to reaffirm the role of the Irish as New York's ruling class. All five of the city's Democratic county leaders were Irish in 1945, as were four of the eight incoming members of the Board of Estimate, including the mayor-elect. It was an impressive performance at a time when only one New Yorker in fourteen was of identifiably Irish stock, but it was deceptive. The creation of an ethnically balanced Democratic ticket for the first time in 1945 indicated that the future of the city's politics would be colored less emerald than its past. In spite of the ease of the Democratic victory in 1945 ethnic tensions building within the party would soon leave it badly weakened.[50]

FOUR

The Machine Breaks Down

1945–1952

"Joy at Tammany," read the headlines the day following O'Dwyer's election. After twelve long years out of power the party faithful looked forward to the usual rewards for helping put their candidate in City Hall. In spite of civil service regulations that protected almost eighty-five per cent of the city's workers, the mayor still controlled 28,000 municipal jobs. There were contracts to be had, there was influence to be peddled, and there was money to be made.[1]

O'Dwyer owed his nomination to the five Democratic party county leaders and was prepared to recognize their loyal soldiers. Yet, he possessed a powerful independent streak and he was determined to control the party rather than have things the other way around while he was mayor. The task would prove difficult. Italians seeking greater influence in Democratic party affairs directly threatened the standing of the Irish, and a group of younger Jewish Democrats began to call for reform of the party rules. O'Dwyer found contending with the Democratic party's ethnic cleavages a demanding job that strained him to his limits. After he left office, the party threatened to spin out of control.

William O'Dwyer: Practical Mayor

Postwar New York required a leader of unusual ability to return it to a peacetime economy. O'Dwyer proved up to the task. He did not approach the job with a grand vision, but tackled problems one by one. As chief executive he was more comfortable responding to crises than rearranging organizational charts, and there were plenty of crises to occupy his time.

It was a rare week during O'Dwyer's first year in office that the city did not cringe before a threatened job action, as workers who had patriotically avoided striking during World War II unleashed pent up frustrations. Returning war veterans needed housing and their children needed classrooms. The subways had been neglected, and the hospitals could not accommodate all who required them. The outflow of able bodied men to the armed forces had decimated the police force, and on and on.[2]

The mayor responded to the endless challenges with practical good sense. He established a Division of Labor Relations that worked with private sector unions to settle conflicts without walkouts. In a showdown with transit workers he earned the city's respect when he announced unequivocally that as long as he ran City Hall public employees would not be allowed to strike. Armed with this principle, he then implemented a fair settlement and maintained his reputation as a friend of the working man. "O'Dwyer could hardly have done more for the unions' cause had he been a labor or socialist mayor on the European model," concluded one observer of the administration's policies.[3]

Pursuing a program of public construction required expanded sources of funding. O'Dwyer supported Governor Dewey's prized program to develop the New York State Thruway, and as result won approval from the state to increase the city's borrowing and taxing authority. The mayor used the additional money to build more than 42,000 apartments. It was only a dent in the 360,000 units that his own staff estimated the city needed, but the federal government refused to provide funding for housing limiting what could be done. O'Dwyer's program was a sensible response to the city's needs and in proportion to the city's resources. New schools and playgrounds began to appear around the city as well.

The subway fare in New York had been five cents since the system began operating in 1904. Pledging to maintain it had become a political rite, but the deficits the low fee caused drained the city treasury.

O'Dwyer led the uncomfortable battle to end the nickel ride. "You may have 5¢ fare for transportation but what you get in return are 5¢ hospitals and a 5¢ health system," he explained. The fee for service finally doubled to a dime, relieving some of the strain on municipal coffers. The mayor consistently made the tough decisions the city needed to stay on track. Presiding over New York's first billion dollar budget in 1947–48, O'Dwyer proved that he was both responsible and sensitive as he balanced the endless needs of eight million people with the fiscal imperatives of a sound budget.[4]

In the aftermath of World War II the Allied governments established the United Nations in the hope that international cooperation would replace armed conflict among nations. The United States was the most powerful country in the world and New York its premier metropolis. O'Dwyer wanted the new organization's headquarters located there. Working with Nelson Rockefeller, Robert Moses, and other New Yorkers, O'Dwyer led the effort to bring the new institution to his town. He succeeded, and anchored New York's position as the "capital of the world" in the process. After a rocky start, he also helped expand the city's links to the rest of the world as he oversaw the completion of Idlewild Airport, which later became John F. Kennedy International Airport.

O'Dwyer kept some of LaGuardia's staff on board in his administration, and he hired the competent among those recommended by the Democratic party leadership while rejecting the hacks who did not measure up. On the whole, he appointed able men to important jobs. Near the end of his first year in office the Citizens Union, a good government group that usually bashed the Democrats who ran New York, honored the mayor. Their award noted that: "A series of major problems has been grappled with an obvious sincerity. . . . The O'Dwyer administration ends its first year with some mistakes, but the town's respect. . . . Politics has not dominated [his] appointments or policies nearly as much as was feared, [and] . . . the capitol of the City, so far, is still in City Hall." Keeping it there would not be easy.[5]

The Irish Battle the Italians and Victory Goes to the Jews

During Vito Marcantonio's congressional reelection campaign in 1946, Democratic thugs attacked and killed a Republican poll watcher named Joseph Scottoriggio. It was the first campaign death in the city in decades, and it caused quite a scandal. In response, O'Dwyer asserted his control over party politics. Early in 1947 he replaced Tammany chief Edward Loughlin, the Irish figurehead atop the party's Italian wing, with Frank Sampson, a district leader of Irish heritage more to the mayor's liking. Newspaper editors praised the move as an effort to clean up affairs, but machine workers saw it as an ethnic power play. The city's Irish chief executive was reestablishing his tribe's command over the Democratic party in Manhattan.[6]

Then in 1948 New York County Surrogate Louis Valente retired. The Italian wing sought to nominate the judge's nephew in his place. The surrogate is responsible for selecting court appointed executors for estates that need them. In Manhattan that translates into the power to decide which attorneys receive hundreds of thousands of dollars in fees. O'Dwyer did not want the Italian faction to maintain control of the post and the patronage that went with it. He launched a battle.[7]

The mayor publicly accused Tammany of "gutter politics," for trying to treat the post as a family sinecure. At the mayor's request, Manhattan District Attorney Frank Hogan subpoenaed twenty-five machine district leaders to answer charges that they had nominated the junior Valente in return for bribes. To defuse the potential accusation that the struggle was just a battle between Irish and Italian politicians, which largely it was, O'Dwyer proposed Italian City Council President Vincent Impellitteri for the spot on the bench. The mayor was confident he would be able to control Impellitteri in the post. Then O'Dwyer punctuated his position in a way that was sure to get Tammany's attention. He fired city employees the machine had sponsored for jobs.

The public praised the mayor for his "anti-boss" stand, but within weeks O'Dwyer negotiated a truce. Tammany dropped Valente in favor of John A. Mullen, an O'Dwyer man more able than Impellitteri. The Democrats also gave O'Dwyer's brother, Paul, their party's nomination for Congress in northern Manhattan's twenty-first congressional district where he ran (and lost) against Republican-Liberal Jacob Javits. In return, however, the mayor agreed to allow Manhattan Borough President Hugo Rogers to replace his man, Frank Sampson, as head of Tammany Hall. Rogers was a Jew, but thoroughly controlled by the Italian wing of the party. He became the first leader of non-Irish descent to head the New York County Democratic organization since 1872.[8]

While the Irish and Italian factions of Tammany battled each other, the Liberal party quietly made common cause with the Republicans behind a Jewish candidate named George Frankentheuler for the Surrogate's seat. The Liberals delivered 63,000 votes, and Frankentheuler won by 1,150 ballots. It was the first time that the Liberal party had determined the outcome of a borough-wide race. Something else surfaced during that campaign. On Manhattan's Upper West Side the election captains of a renegade Democratic district leader named Robert Blaikie did little work for their party's candidate for Surrogate. The neighborhoods that Blaikie's club served included important pockets of liberal Jewish voters. These New Yorkers viewed Tammany's unseemly internal battles with disdain and found a Jewish candidate like Frankentheuler, endorsed by the Liberal party, attractive. Rather than risk alienating the long-term support of local voters by trying to convince them to cast their ballots for a tarnished Democrat, Blaikie's men sat out the contest. Thus, a local Democratic club in Manhattan rebelled against its own party's candidate in response to the pressures of liberal Jewish voting patterns.[9]

That same year O'Dwyer found himself faced with a second political conflict. The 1948 presidential contest pitted Democrat Harry Truman against New York's Republican governor, Thomas E. Dewey, with a third party bid by Henry Wallace on the extreme left. In New York, the ALP backed Wallace's bid for the presidency. O'Dwyer's support for Truman was luke warm, but he had little sympathy for Wallace. As America entered the cold war with the Soviet Union, any connection to the Communist-influenced ALP was becoming a heavy liability. This was especially true during a national campaign that featured foreign affairs. Closer to home, New York's Catholic leader, Francis Cardinal Spellman, intensified his Church's opposition to affiliation with the ALP. In August, O'Dwyer split publicly with the American Labor party and Vito Marcantonio.[10]

The city's politics were developing an air of confusion when early in 1949 Sol Bloom, congressman from the twentieth district on Manhattan's Upper West Side, died. A special election was scheduled for May. Franklin Roosevelt, Jr. sought to launch his political career by capturing the spot, and he approached the Tammany bosses in the hope of securing the Democratic nomination. They refused, and selected instead Judge Benjamin Shalleck, a local regular. Alone among the Democratic district leaders, Lower East Side Jew Bert Stand understood the dangers of casting off the fellow who bore the name of the party's popular hero: "Look fellows, it is none of my business outside my district, but why don't you take Roosevelt? You might need a character witness some day," he suggested in one meeting. The dry advice fell on deaf ears.[11]

The Liberal party took up the battle for the son of FDR, and Robert Blaikie and other insurgents broke with the regulars to back the attractive candidate. At first O'Dwyer refused to take sides in the contest, but a few weeks before the election the mayor declined to attend Tammany's annual dinner. That same evening he went instead to an affair sponsored by the Fair Deal Democrats. The group consisted of young reform minded political activists led by a number of Jewish and Protestant attorneys who strongly backed Roosevelt. The night before the special election the mayor endorsed FDR, Jr., who proceeded to beat his Democratic, Republican and ALP opponents in a landslide. The heavily Jewish Liberal party was developing into a potent organizational force in New York City elections, with its backing providing a seal of approval that allowed liberal minded voters, principally Jews and to a lesser extent Protestants in Manhattan, to abandon the Democratic party in good conscience.[12]

During FDR, Jr.'s 1949 campaign it became apparent that a new generation of Democrats had begun to filter into the party. They were younger and better educated than the men who ran the Democratic party's affairs, and in some respects they were heirs to New York's good government reform tradition. But the political consciousness of the newcomers had been forged in the age of Franklin Roosevelt. Many had fought and risked their lives in World War II for FDR's Four Freedoms, and they belonged to his party. They entered politics not to rid the city of the corrupt Democrats, but to rid the Democratic party of corruption, and to get on with a liberal agenda that they believed in.[13]

At first many entered local political clubs and tried to work from within, but they soon realized that the old-timers did not appreciate their ideas. For a time, the newcomers organized weak citywide organizations, like the Fair Deal Democrats. In 1949, however, the Lexington Democratic Club appeared on the Upper East Side of Manhattan. It was the first reform club. Others soon followed. Catholic members were rare in the new clubs, and although a fair number of Protestants joined them, Jewish members dominated them. Cultural collision between young, well educated, Jewish political activists, and predominantly Catholic, working-class, professional politicians would only intensify the ethnic schisms within the Democratic party.[14]

Schizoid Candidate

Not long after FDR, Jr.'s election to Congress the Democrats had to choose a candidate for mayor. In spite of O'Dwyer's feuding with party leaders the nomination was his for the asking based on a solid record of accomplishment during a demanding term. What remained unclear was whether or not he wanted it. On May 26, 1949, O'Dwyer announced he would not run again. Yet, just days after he bowed out of the race, he sent a telegram to Edward C. Maguire, a trusted political supporter, that read: "If published reports are accurate, the response to various movements to draft me for Mayor are most gratifying and heart-warming. I am very anxious to meet personally all those identified with you and your associates in the leadership and direction of these various movements. . . ." Two days later he held a meeting with the men who wanted him to run for reelection. As a political move initiating a draft was a shrewd means of keeping his distance from the political bosses and maintaining an independent image. But his ambivalence seemed real, and O'Dwyer was more unpredictable than ever during the weeks that followed.[15]

After the mayor's initial announcement that he would not run a movement to draft Robert F. Wagner, Jr. developed. The potential candidate was the son of the New Deal Senator from New York who had written the nation's labor laws, in great measure the Social Security Act and the federal housing statutes as well. The younger Wagner had graduated from Yale University College and law school, and had also taken a year at Harvard to study business and a year in Geneva to study foreign affairs. He was an unusually cultured man, but the course of his father's career had left him equally at home with Tammany district leaders as with university professors. When Bob was just nine his mother, Mary Margaret McTague, "a typical Irish beauty, a twinkle in her eyes, a ready smile, and an equally ready tear," according to Wagner, Sr., died. Afterward, the father included the son in every aspect of his life. Tammany leaders and labor leaders had played poker in young Bob Wagner's living room while he was growing up, and he had met and dined with governors, mayors, senators, and Presidents.[16]

Shortly after graduating from law school in 1937 the young Wagner won election to the New York State Assembly. When World War II broke out he enlisted in the Army Air Corps and served in North Africa. Shortly after his return he accepted a post in O'Dwyer's administration as chairman of the City Tax Commission, later as Commissioner of Housing and Buildings, and then as Chairman of the City Planning Commission. With impressive credentials, a proud Democratic name and ambition, Wagner had a significant following. O'Dwyer knew it, and he used to tease Wagner about it good naturedly. "Here comes young Bob Wagner wearing his father's trousers," the mayor was heard to say on occasion.

One day, in June of 1949, Wagner came down to City Hall to review some work from the Planning Commission with the mayor. O'Dwyer got up from his seat to look at the oversized plans, then turned to Wagner:

"Sit here, Bob. Sit in my chair." Wagner did.

"How do you like it?" O'Dwyer asked.

"It's very comfortable," came the innocent response.

"I mean, how do you like the Mayor's chair?" O'Dwyer insisted.

"Fine," Wagner deadpanned.

"Bob, I'm going to put you there—I'm going to put you right there. I'll run your campaign for you, and I'm going to elect you Mayor."

Ten days later Wagner was again in the Mayor's office, along with staff members, to review some proposals. O'Dwyer spoke as they looked at the papers:

"Well, now, really there is no point in taking these things up with me. You really ought to take them up with the fellow that is going to be the next Mayor of New York—John Cashmore," he said, referring to the borough president of Brooklyn. Wagner, however, was not surprised. He had already heard that O'Dwyer had invited Cashmore to Gracie Mansion to select new curtains. Then, a short while later, O'Dwyer publicly endorsed Manhattan District Attorney Frank Hogan for the Democratic nomination for mayor confusing political insiders even more.[17]

Yet, all the while O'Dwyer's office actively promoted a draft, even though the mayor repeated pronouncements that he was not a candidate and undertook negotiations for a lucrative corporate job. One reporter who covered O'Dwyer concluded, "he could look straight in the mirror and lie . . . he would lie to himself . . . he was schizoid." A long time political rival also figured the man was irrational. Perhaps he was. Five hours after the Democratic leaders finally accepted Hogan, O'Dwyer declared he would run after all. One rumor circulated that he was drunk at the time and had simply been "unable to take the inevitable bump that comes from leaving power." Another said he had been angling for the nomination for Senate that opened when Robert F. Wagner, Sr., resigned because of ill health on June 28, 1949, but that by then the mayor's erratic behavior had so offended the party leaders that they refused to nominate him. Out of spite, O'Dwyer then decided to run for reelection to the job he had. Whatever the reason, the popular Irishman was in the race on the Democratic line.[18]

Liberals in Demand

Many members of the Liberal party wanted to join forces behind the likable former working man, but the leadership did not trust him. Although O'Dwyer made a few overtures to the Liberals after his split with the ALP, Dubinsky and others were genuinely wary of the mayor's reported ties to Frank Costello. They felt that backing him would require "too many apologies." More than anything else, though, political strategy led the leaders to refuse to endorse the Democrat. They were unsure of their base and feared that many voters would cast ballots for O'Dwyer on the Democratic line without a second thought if the Liberals backed him. This would mask the power of their appeal and weaken their ability to negotiate in future elections. If instead, the Liberals could deliver votes that a GOP candidate could not normally win, namely Jewish votes, they would strengthen their standing. In order to adopt the tactic the Liberals had to force the Republicans to nominate someone acceptable.[19]

Early in July Governor Dewey telephoned David Dubinsky to find out if the Liberals would support Edward Corsi, a loyal Republican. Dubinsky informed the Governor that Newbold Morris was the leading non-Democratic candidate for mayor among his party's members. Dewey did not want the man who bolted from the Republicans in 1945 to get the party's nomination four years later, but in a series of negotiations the Liberals refused to budge. Dewey relented. He did not want to run a New York City campaign in 1949 without the Liberal party's endorsement.[20]

Vito Marcantonio decided to run for mayor as the candidate of the ALP. Even his closest advisors admitted that he had no chance for success. His goal was to prevent his party's supporters from developing the habit of backing other tickets. It was the only way to keep the party together, and Marcantonio hoped that his candidacy would take votes away from both the Democratic and the Republican organizations, encouraging them to show the ALP more respect in the future.[21]

While the mayoral race was taking form the Democrats were also preparing to launch a campaign to regain the United States Senate seat vacated by Robert F. Wagner, Sr. Governor Dewey had appointed John Foster Dulles, a Republican, to fill the post. Herbert Lehman agreed to run in a special election to fill out the last year of the term in progress. After retiring as governor in 1942, Lehman had spent four years helping the displaced masses of wartorn Europe as chief of the United Nations

Relief and Rehabilitation Administration. In 1946 he ran for Senate in New York State, but in that year of GOP landslide lost out to the incumbent Republican Senator, Irving Ives, even while finishing 400,000 votes ahead of the Democratic candidate for governor. Lehman remained active in philanthropic activities afterward, and began to assume the position of elder statesman. Deeply respected by the liberal community and revered by the city's Jews, Lehman was the obvious Democratic choice for Senate in 1949. Some minor resistance actually developed among conservative Democrats, but Bronx boss Ed Flynn strongly supported Lehman, and the Liberal party made it clear that the former governor was their choice as well. The opposition faded before a serious rift developed.[22]

In cosmopolitan New York many considered the Senate seat with its national stature far more important than the mayor's office. Tammany's leaders, however, were most concerned with who would win the borough presidency of Manhattan. Hugo Rogers, Tammany's figurehead chief, hoped to run for reelection to the post. But O'Dwyer wanted the man who had displaced his ally, Frank Sampson, removed. Tammany saw little gain in fighting with the popular incumbent mayor running for reelection, so its leaders dutifully denied Rogers the nomination for borough president. In July, 1949, Carmine DeSapio replaced Rogers as Tammany chief.

DeSapio was the tall, dark, and handsome son of Italian immigrants. He possessed the street smarts typical of the young men who grew up in the Italian neighborhood of Greenwich Village, and he added to that an easy confidence and a gracious manner that stood him apart from others. He wore expensive suits, and an incurable case of iritis forced him to wear dark glasses at all times. That should have been a minor matter, but the spectacles gave him a sinister appearance unhelpful to a career in public life. Nevertheless, he became the leader of lower Manhattan's First Assembly District by beating out long-time incumbent "Battery" Dan Finn. The Irish American was the third generation of his clan to hold the spot, and he had not given it up easily. In 1939, when many of the area's Italians remained registered in LaGuardia's Republican party and could not vote in a Democratic primary, Finn had held on. DeSapio won a close election in 1941 in a runoff after voting irregularities nullified the first round of balloting, but Finn's friend, Tammany boss Christie Sullivan, refused to recognize the victory. Finally, in 1943, DeSapio won unequivocally and assumed his place in the machine hierarchy. He soon proved among the most able of the Democratic party's emerging Italian wing. His reputation, coupled with a benign nod from Frank Costello, won him Tammany's top post in 1949.[23]

FDR, Jr.'s victory in Tammany's backyard earlier that same year, and the Democratic defeat in the borough-wide Surrogate's race the year before, signaled the degree to which the machine that DeSapio had inherited was under siege. The new boss knew that to establish his credibility as leader his party had to win the borough president's office. The way to ensure victory was to run a candidate acceptable to Manhattan's liberal and reform minded voters, and the surest means of doing that was to get the Liberal party's endorsement for the Democratic candidate. The boss began talking with Alex Rose to find someone who would work with Tammany, but whom the Liberals would back as well. Robert F. Wagner, Jr. wanted the post, and was the only Democrat that the Liberals would accept.

Wagner had contemplated running for the Manhattan borough president's office in 1941, and Alex Rose had promoted him for the spot then. To help his son, Senator Wagner had arranged for a meeting between the young man and President Roosevelt. The would-be candidate asked FDR to intervene on his behalf with Tammany boss Christie Sullivan, who was also a congressman and always in need of the kind of federal favors that the President could provide. Roosevelt sent an assistant to tell Sullivan that he would be pleased if young Wagner got the nod, but the cantankerous boss, in search of a *quid pro quo*, growled in response: "If the President's so damn concerned let him ask me himself." FDR never did, so Wagner's ambitions had to wait until the political conditions brought the Democrats around in 1949. Once selected, Wagner announced that he would run as a nominee of both the Democratic and Liberal parties, "with the understanding that when elected I shall have a free hand in organizing the office of borough president and in discharging the duties of that office." Although he agreed to reserve one slot for the Liberals, and to accept recommendations for jobs from DeSapio, Wagner insisted that he would reject unqualified candidates. With those modest conditions accepted, Wagner became a candidate for municipal office because he was the one viable Democratic candidate that the Liberals would support.[24]

Campaigning for Jewish Votes

A single theme dominated the election campaign for all offices in New York City in 1949. "This country is in the midst of a titanic struggle between progressive Democracy and reaction, between those who believe in the people's welfare and those who believe in big business and special privilege," O'Dwyer said in a speech heard over radio. He told a crowd at Carnegie Hall that a "Democratic defeat in this city would be hailed by the forces of reaction throughout the country as a repudiation of the Fair Deal—of its program of progressive legislation."

Lehman put it even more simply: "the main issue . . . is that of liberalism versus reaction," he declared. The theme was aimed at Jewish voters.[25]

Newbold Morris also understood he would have to present a liberal image to run well among Jews, and once again he tried to cast himself as the progressive heir to Fiorello LaGuardia. The Democrats ridiculed the strategy. On the cover of an O'Dwyer campaign brochure they pictured a skinny little cartoon caricature of Morris underneath a gigantic black sombrero with the obvious initials "LaG." in the headband. "Newbold, It just won't fit," read the caption. Inside, another drawing featured the mayoral candidate dressed as a woman figure skater. While president of the City Council Morris had won the Middle-Atlantic figure skating championship, hardly the ideal credential for a New York City mayoral candidate. In contrast, the back page listed "The O'Dwyer Record":[26]

"1 New School built every month"
"1 public housing project completed every month"
"$48,000,000 hospital construction"
"18 child day care centers"
"89 Social centers"
"11 health stations"
"28 acres of parks and playground"

The mayor tried hard to prevent Morris from developing a progressive image. Beneath "the liberal mask he is wearing during the election . . . [Morris is] just a Republican stooge," the mayor said in a television speech. And in a joint broadcast with Eleanor Roosevelt, he reminded listeners that Morris had voted against the popular woman's late husband in four consecutive elections. "He is to the last a Republican," and for "reaction," O'Dwyer warned hyperbolically.[27]

For the mayor, insisting on his liberal credentials was even more important in 1949 than it had been four years earlier. In 1945 the American Labor party still held the allegiance of many Jewish workers and O'Dwyer had carried its endorsement. Running without that support he had to take other measures to ensure his strength with the group. Tammany insider George S. Combs, who chaired the committee that prepared speeches for the O'Dwyer campaign in 1949, insisted that, "it is undoubtedly true that the Mayor had found it necessary to identify himself, more and more closely with liberal elements—liberal thought. If he in anyway permitted himself to be divorced from Lehman and what Lehman exemplifies in this campaign, he'd be licked unquestionably."[28]

The target of the effort was clear. One campaign brochure showed a picture of the mayor with Herbert Lehman. The bold print read, "When the Jewish People Needed Action, Who Was There?" The text recounted O'Dwyer's persistent efforts to convince President Harry Truman to support the creation of a Jewish homeland in 1948. One opponent called the piece "ridiculous. . . . [It] states that O'Dwyer is responsible for Israel." No one believed that, of course, but a number of influential Jewish leaders knew that O'Dwyer's commitment to Israel was real. One night, at a time when the Jewish factions fighting against continued British occupation of Palestine still had no official support, the mayor had quietly arranged for the police department to pull its officers off of a dock patrol to allow a surreptitious shipment of arms destined for Palestine to pass unmolested. One can only speculate about the personal satisfaction an Irishman might have felt in helping run guns to a people fighting the English. The political results are easier to assess. Forty years later a former ALP member recalled switching parties to support O'Dwyer in spite of concern about the mayor's purported ties to gangsters. "He was good for the Jews. A bit of a gonif, but good for the Jews," the man explained.[29]

During the campaign an incident occurred that threatened to hurt the mayor's standing with Jewish voters. Congressman Graham Barden proposed a law to block any federal expenditures from going to nonpublic schools. New York's Catholic archdiocese ran a huge parochial school system and therefore felt threatened by the proposed legislation. On June 23, 1949, writing in her column in the *New York World Telegram*, Eleanor Roosevelt declared herself in support of the measure. In the long term, she wrote, separation of Church and State was more important than the temporary benefits that might result from distributing money to schools with religious affiliations. The former First Lady had a nasty reputation as an anti-Catholic, and her stand antagonized Francis Cardinal Spellman, archbishop of New York. A few weeks after Eleanor Roosevelt's letter appeared the Catholic prelate issued a vicious response that said in part, "your record of anti-Catholicism stands for all to see—a record which you yourself wrote on the pages of history . . . documents of discrimination unworthy of an American mother."

Such invective was bound to inflame, and it did. The Catholic hierarchy defended Spellman's stand. Jews, on the other hand, were exceedingly wary of any level of government support for religion. The practice risked opening the door to state sponsorship of a particular faith in an overwhelmingly Christian nation. Consequently, Jewish leaders spoke out in support of the Barden bill. The clamor forced politicians to confront the issue. Herbert Lehman defended Eleanor Roosevelt, and the reaction against him was sharp. "The Irish have decided, many of them, that they are not going to vote for Lehman," Tammany insider George S. Combs reported. They chose their Cardinal over the Jewish statesman. O'Dwyer sought to straddle the emotional matter. He quietly declared himself opposed to the bill, but publicly stated his "high regard for Mrs. Roosevelt," and continued to campaign with Herbert Lehman. Some of his own Irish Catholics found even that compromise too difficult to accept, and his standing with them weakened. Ultimately, President Harry Truman, worried about Lehman's chances to win the New York State Senate seat for the Democrats, dispatched Ed Flynn to Rome where he met with the Pope and explained the problem. Shortly afterward Cardinal Spellman met publicly with Eleanor Roosevelt for tea, and a badly strained peace returned to the Democratic party.[30]

While Cardinal Spellman's comments generated political hostility within the Catholic community, John Foster Dulles, campaigning against Lehman, managed to antagonize New York's Jews. The austere, moralizing Protestant told a crowd of upstate New York supporters that, "if you could see the kind of people in New York City making up this bloc that is voting for my opponent, if you could see it with your own eyes, I know that you would be out, every last man and woman of you, on Election Day."[31]

Jews reacted bitterly to the appeal to bigotry directed against Herbert Lehman, and the senate campaign overflowed into the mayoral contest. O'Dwyer backers reminded voters that Morris and Dulles were from the same Republican party. Morris knew that he had no chance of victory without Jewish support, so he refused to endorse Dulles publicly, and tried to emphasize not his Republican affiliation but the backing he received from the Liberal party. Yet, he did not go so far as to endorse Herbert Lehman, with whom he shared the Liberal ticket. O'Dwyer constantly reminded the city's voters of that.[32]

O'Dwyer also took some steps to defuse the campaign of Vito Marcantonio, who had strong support among Italians, and who was popular with the large Puerto Rican population that lived in his congressional district. One pamphlet, printed in Italian and English, listed the names of Italian Americans the mayor had appointed to important posts. In a campaign flier written in Spanish, the governor of Puerto Rico praised O'Dwyer, and the popular mayor of San Juan flew to New York during the contest to speak well of her New York City counterpart. While O'Dwyer himself avoided slinging mud at Marcantonio for fear the tactic would cause resentment among Italians, the mayor sent his Italian City Council president, Vincent Impellitteri, into East Harlem to do the work he could not. The mayor's reelection campaign also emphasized O'Dwyer's strong support for civil rights for blacks.[33]

On election day O'Dwyer won nearly half of all the votes cast for mayor, an impressive performance in a three way contest but almost ten points lower than he had managed four years earlier. Although political professionals reasoned that his pre-election vacillating hurt his credibility with voters, and opponents even tried to wage what one called a "Dr. Freud campaign," focusing on the Irishman's unstable "psyche," the difference resulted substantially from two sources: the loss of Jewish votes that the mayor had won on the ALP line in 1945 and a decline in Italian votes because of Vito Marcantonio's success in pulling Italians away from the Democrats.[34]

Four of ten Jews voted for O'Dwyer on the Democratic ticket in 1949. This was much better than his 1941 performance when he ran against LaGuardia on the Democratic line alone and attracted only one Jewish vote in four. But without either of the city's heavily Jewish political parties supporting him, O'Dwyer could not hold a majority of the Jewish vote. The Liberal party garnered more than one quarter of the city's Jewish ballots for Newbold Morris, making it second only to the Democrats as a political home to members of the faith. By gathering more than fourteen percent of the total vote, it replaced the ALP as the city's most important splinter party. Moreover, Senator Lehman beat his opponent by fewer than 200,000 ballots with the Liberals delivering more than 425,000 votes to provide the margin of victory. Lehman himself acknowledged that it was the spirited effort by the third party that put him into office. No one was surprised that more than nine out of ten New York City Jews voted for the preeminent Jewish statesman with unimpeachable liberal credentials. None anticipated that a third of them would do so on the Liberal ticket. Jewish loyalty to the Liberal party as an institution was high. Newbold Morris fared almost as well as Lehman on the Liberal line, although many Republicans who voted for Dulles declined to vote for their party's candidate for mayor. Robert Wagner, running with Democratic and Liberal party support in Manhattan, won the borough president's office in a landslide.[35]

The Maturing of Jewish Politics

In both the 1945 and the 1949 mayoral elections the ALP polled about 13 percent of the electorate. But in the earlier one the votes had come mostly from Jews whereas in the later contest more than 40 percent of the city's Italians cast their ballots on that line because one of their own, Vito Marcantonio, headed it. Modest pockets of support for Marcantonio's urban populism existed in black and Puerto Rican communities as well. It was the sheer force of Vito Marcantonio's personality that kept the ALP together in 1949. But by then the Labor party's Communist ties had led politicians from other parties to refuse to work with it at all. When Marcantonio ran for reelection to Congress in 1950, the Democrats, the Republicans, and the Liberals gathered all their support around a single candidate to defeat the ALP's most important leader.[36]

The demise of its leading politician was a blow the ALP could not withstand because the Jewish support that had given the party its coherence had all but faded. The decision of David Dubinsky and Alex Rose to withdraw from the party in 1942 had separated two of the most visible Jewish leaders from the organization, and the support of their heavily Jewish unions went with them. In 1946 Sidney Hillman, the last high level Jewish leader in the ALP, died, severing the groups personal ties to the party decisionmakers.[37]

By the end of the 1940s a small but influential group of Jewish intellectuals who had engaged in radical politics in the 1920s and 1930s had become disillusioned with Marxism. One of the most prominent, Will Herberg, wrote an article in *Commentary* magazine in 1947 with the revealing title, "From Marxism to Judaism." To Herberg, and to others like him, Communism was, "a religion, an ethic, and a theology." But with the passage of time, ". . . the disastrous corrosion and corruptions of the Marxist movement in politics seemed to me clearly a reflection of its lack, or rather its rejection, of an ethic transcending the relativities of power." One Jewish intellectual called Stalin's brand of Communism, an "international Tammany Hall." In abandoning the false religion of Communism, Herberg found his way back to Judaism.

His interpretation of his faith made clear that he remained committed to a more just world: "If there is one strain that has run through Judaism from the earliest codes to the present day, it is the passion for social justice," he wrote. But his understanding of how to achieve the goal and his political outlook changed. A Labor party with Communist links no longer suited Herberg's generation of intellectuals, or those who listened to them.[38]

Other Jews had more visceral reasons for shifting away from the Communist dominated organization that maintained strong links to Moscow. In 1948 the Soviet Union revived anti-Semitic purges that had halted for a time. Intense postwar Soviet nationalism translated into a brutal movement to end Jewish culture because in the minds of paranoid bureaucrats the religion competed with the government for the loyalty of the country's people. For five "black years" Stalin's agents rounded up Jews and exiled them into the vast interior of Russia where they disappeared by the thousands. In January 1953, *Pravda* announced the "Doctor's Plot," accusing nine physicians, six "alleged to have been connected with the international Jewish bourgeois nationalist organization" (whatever that meant), of conspiring to kill public officials. The Soviet Union was the same Russia that had killed Jews by the thousands with cruel pogroms. The appeal of an organization tied to Moscow disintegrated. Large numbers of politically active Jews left the ALP for the Liberal party or the Democratic party in the years after 1948.[39]

The pogroms evoked the painful image of the Holocaust which, coupled with the creation of Israel in 1948, intensified Jewish group consciousness. Different strains of thought over establishment of a Jewish state had divided leaders of the faith before World War II, but these differences melted in the horrors of Nazi furnaces. America became the center of world Judaism, and the five million Jews who lived in the United States spoke with rare unanimity of the need for a homeland for their people. Cooperation on that matter enhanced communication between the group's many members and made working together on other political issues easier.[40]

Jewish movement into the mainstream of American middle-class life also facilitated political activity. By 1950, Jews as a group were well educated, economically successful, and in a strong position to assert themselves on issues of common concern. Even as the income levels of the group rose, however, dedication to liberal causes remained firm. Surveys documented that the Jewish commitment to using government policy in order to achieve economic security remained stronger than that of any other religious faith, even though the group was near the top of the nation's economic scale. Jews also supported giving more political power to the working class even though the number of workers among them was lower than it was in other religions. Such findings differed markedly from survey results of Catholics or Protestants. And, of course, New York remained home to a greater number and a greater proportion of Jews than any other city. As their economic and social position in New York society rose, the ability of the group to influence the city's politics increased.[41]

O'Dwyer's 1949 campaign showed once again that New York's successful politicians understood the importance of attracting the Jewish vote, and that they understood how to do it. The mayor had a liberal record on matters of substance, and made much of it during his race. He kept close to Herbert Lehman and Eleanor Roosevelt. He also injected the issue of Israel into the 1949 contest, a matter irrelevant to the functions of a mayor but rich in symbolic value to the city's Jewish voters. Rumors that tied O'Dwyer to organized criminals probably weakened his standing with the group, and were an important factor in the Liberal party's decision not to endorse him. But in 1949 few New Yorkers gave the claims, by then years old, much credence. For anyone looking for reassurance, O'Dwyer's record as Brooklyn District Attorney provided ample reason to believe he was an honest man.

Hasta La Vista, Bill

New Yorkers in general, and Jews in particular, could feel confident that O'Dwyer's victory gave them a mayor who would govern them fairly and effectively for another four years. Then, just after his reelection, the mayor checked into the hospital. His doctor indicated that the city's chief executive, nearly sixty years old, had suffered a heart attack. According to one story, the physicians told the mayor that he would not survive another term, so he decided to call it quits and filed for retirement. Jim Moran, his chief of staff, retrieved the ailing politician's forms from bureaucratic hands, brought them to the hospital, and burned them. Officially, O'Dwyer remained mayor, but in fact he ceased to govern the city.[42]

O'Dwyer's job had taken its toll. After just a few months in office journalists had already begun to notice that the mayor's hair had turned grayer, he had lines under his eyes, he looked "careworn and preoccupied." O'Dwyer told one reporter that "there are moments when I get scared to death" confronting the city's problems. "In this job . . . you never escape." One night, at a reception at the Waldorf Astoria, a lady who met him was taken aback by the presence of the city's most important figure. "Oh my, what do I do when I meet the Mayor of the City of New York? Do I kiss his ring or what?" she asked. "In New York, lady, you heave a cuspidor at him," the besieged mayor responded. During that tough first year in office, O'Dwyer's wife of nearly thirty years died of Parkinson's disease. Six months afterward, speaking at a ceremony honoring him with an award, he began to speak of her. His usually casual speaking style declined into a stutter, tears came instead of words, and he could not continue. He simply sat down. The lonely office became more lonely.[43]

As early as 1947 the mayor insisted that one term would be enough. In February of 1948 the mayor checked into the hospital with pneumonia, and the press reported rumors that he had suffered a heart attack. He spent several weeks recuperating before returning to his awesome burdens and the tiring political chaos of 1948 and 1949. In December of 1949 he left the hospital for a Florida vacation where he married a young model named Sloane Simpson, a stunning beauty a quarter century his junior. They met two years after the death of O'Dwyer's wife, and the mayor fell instantly in love with the attractive woman whose exuberance enlivened him. The man who from immigrant construction worker, to bartender, to shiphand, from policeman, to district attorney, and on to the mayor's office had known only work discovered there was more to life than that. O'Dwyer honeymooned until February 1950, and by March rumors circulated that he was planning to resign, perhaps to run for another post, perhaps to work in a lucrative private job, perhaps to retire. The mayor dutifully denied the reports until August when the story finally broke. Then O'Dwyer announced that he would leave his office on September 1, and accept the post of United States Ambassador to Mexico.[44]

At the time, scandals were brewing in the Police Department. Some speculated that the ex-cop who bore ultimate responsibility for enforcing the law in New York was getting out of town while he could. In 1951, when Estes Kefauver's Senate Special Investigating Committee on Organized Crime toured the country exposing the extent to which criminal activities permeated life in America, the ambitious senator called the former mayor to testify. The Committee dug up O'Dwyer's past contacts with the mob. A few new details surfaced, and some of O'Dwyer's staff ultimately went to jail; but in spite of the great publicity the inquiry revealed little new information about the mayor. The public would forever link O'Dwyer's resignation to the televised hearings on his ties to criminals, but there is little evidence that the man ran from office in an effort to avoid embarrassing questions. He returned to the United States to answer the charges he had answered before, and no indictment was ever returned, let alone a conviction. More than anything else, it seems O'Dwyer really no longer wanted to be mayor when he ran for reelection in 1949.[45]

An Italian Moment

With O'Dwyer's resignation City Council president Vincent Impellitteri became acting mayor. A loyal Democrat, the accidental incumbent should have been the obvious choice for his party's nomination to run in the special election to fill out O'Dwyer's term. Unfortunately, he was thoroughly unqualified for the job.

Unknown when O'Dwyer selected him, Impellitteri did little to distinguish himself during five years as the city's second ranking elected official. His name was not associated with a single issue confronting the metropolis, and he had not used his visible post to create an independent base of support. The pros who knew him did not respect him. "I would not say that Impellitteri is an astute politician," one remarked. "He was courteous," was the best another could muster when assessing the man's career. He "*barely* scales the standards of literacy," recalled a third, acerbically. "He was stupid," concluded an even blunter man who later worked with him on the Board of Estimate. "I got no ideas, any of you guys got any?" Impellitteri used to say when a complicated issue came before the city's most important governing body. Without ability or political standing, there was no reason for the Democrats to offer him the nomination.[46]

DeSapio tried to negotiate Impellitteri's exit by offering him a judgeship. But Frank Sampson, O'Dwyer's one time Tammany chief, saw an opportunity to regain his stature by allying himself with the dim witted occupant of the mayor's office. He encouraged Impellitteri to fight to keep his job. The acting mayor told DeSapio that he would step aside for the good of the party if the Democrats decided that an Italian should not head the ticket, but otherwise he felt entitled to run. Meanwhile, the Tammany chief searched for his own candidate. The first place he looked was the Liberal party.[47]

DeSapio understood that a boss-selected Tammany man would carry heavy baggage to the polls because of the rumors surrounding O'Dwyer's departure. The Tammany chief's success in backing a joint

Democratic-Liberal candidate for Manhattan borough president the year before led him to follow the same strategy in choosing someone to run for the city's top job in 1950. In 1945 and 1949 David Dubinsky had favored his gin rummy partner, an Italian named Ferdinand Pecora, for the Democratic nomination. O'Dywer's claim to the Democratic slot precluded consideration of other candidates those years. The Liberal leader promoted Pecora again, and the Democrats, in need of the respectability and support among Jewish voters that the Liberal endorsement brought with it, accepted the choice. In addition, by selecting an Italian, none could claim that anti-Italian bigotry had played a role in Impellitteri's replacement.

Pecora, a thoroughly honorable man, had made his reputation investigating the stock market crash for the Securities Exchange Commission in the early 1930s. He exposed the financial sleight of hand that exacerbated the effect of the collapse and went on to become a judge of some distinction. He was a Democrat of the New Deal vintage, and substantially independent from machine control.[48]

The decision to dump Impellitteri for one of his own countrymen singed the acting mayor's ethnic pride. He decided to stay in the battle, and a curious coalition formed behind him. One of Tammany's old-time Irish district leaders, Harry Brickman, resentful of DeSapio's willingness to allow the Liberals to dictate the Democratic nominee, along with other disaffected members of Tammany's Irish wing joined Frank Sampson in support of the renegade Italian candidate. Robert Blaikie and his insurgents saw an opportunity to challenge the party leadership they disliked, so they too abandoned the Democrats for Impellitteri. The group created the Experience party, and the acting mayor was in the race with some of Tammany's most capable pros and committed opponents on his side.[49]

Governor Dewey concentrated on his own reelection in 1950, and on the statewide race for Senate. The large majorities that the Republicans normally captured upstate offered some hope that their candidate, Lieutenant Governor Joseph Hanley, could defeat Herbert Lehman who was running for reelection to a full term. Dewey, however, had little confidence that a Republican nominee for mayor of New York City could win against an opponent holding the Democratic and Liberal endorsements. He delivered his party's nomination for mayor to Edward Corsi, the wealthy Italian businessman Dewey had wanted to run in 1949, and he did not give the race much more thought.[50]

By quirk of fate, all three candidates for mayor had been born in Italy. But Impellitteri was an accidental incumbent, dependent on the

Irish element of the political machine and some insurgents in predominantly Jewish districts who resisted Tammany's discipline. Pecora had been picked by the Jewish leader of the Liberal party because Tammany felt it needed that organization's Jewish support and seal of approval to win. Corsi got the nod from the Republican party because no one else really wanted it. The Italian trio was not evidence that their group had come to dominate New York's politics, but rather an indication of the confused state of affairs in the wake of O'Dwyer's resignation.

In a whirlwind contest less than two months long Impellitteri's team emphasized that above all their man was independent. "I *am* a candidate *against* the wishes of political bosses who pull the puppet strings," he announced. To derail DeSapio's plan to give Tammany a fresh appearance by associating with the Liberals, his campaign chairman asked the public: are ". . . the Liberal Party philosophy and ideals to be prostituted by a few of its bosses?" He also quoted the Liberal party's 1949 campaign rhetoric when they called Tammany Democrats an "unregenerate and vicious pack of community vipers." Impellitteri contrasted the criticisms the Democrats levied against him in 1950 with the praise they had showered on him in 1945 and 1949: "Impellitteri's brilliant reputation in the cause of public welfare [was] gained through long and arduous work. His sense of fair play is strict and admirable," his opponents had written of him just a few years before.[51]

Searching for a way to fit the candidate's name into a headline, the *Daily News* dubbed him "IMPY." The nickname added to his image as a political David taking on the Goliath of the established political parties. Some New Yorkers felt that the mayoralty belonged to Impellitteri by virtue of his right of succession, and they suspected the motives of those who would deny him the office. As a matter of personal style Impellitteri "spoke in a direct, down-to-earth way, no firebrand, but a serious man making important talk," that appealed to the average citizen. "I should prefer . . . to talk to you tonight as a neighbor," the candidate emphasized in his last radio address of the contest, "as another citizen of our city, one who has attended our public schools; one who has for the past 16 years lived in a four-room apartment and who is just as anxious as anyone to have adequate rent control; one who has worked here and grew up here . . . ," and on and on in an effort to show New Yorkers that he was one of them, and that he understood their concerns.[52]

When the balloting ended, Impellitteri had attracted more than forty-three percent of the vote in the three way race to finish out O'Dwyer's term. Although each of the candidates had been born in Italy, Impellitteri was the only one that New York's Italian community perceived as an authentic representative. He won nearly half the Italian votes in the city while his opponents split the other half. Edward Corsi's wealth and upstate connections made him unfamiliar to his urban, working class countrymen, and Pecora was Episcopalian and a cultural high brow. He too was far removed from the city's average Italian and could not bridge the gap. In Carmine DeSapio's own heavily Democratic district, Italian nuns encouraged voters to cast their ballots for Impellitteri, the Catholic, instead of Pecora, the Protestant.[53]

Large numbers of Republicans of various ethnic backgrounds also voted for Impellitteri. During the course of the campaign the GOP leadership, realizing that the renegade had a chance to win and thus deny the Democratic machine the powers of the mayoralty, helped to finance Impellitteri's effort and gave it organizational support. Governor Dewey himself encouraged the tactic and left his own party's candidate without the means to wage a strong campaign. As a consequence, Corsi attracted nearly two hundred thousand votes fewer than Newbold Morris had taken on the Republican line the year before.[54]

More than six out of ten of the city's Jewish voters supported Pecora, who held the Democratic and Liberal party endorsements, but even that was significantly lower than the seven of ten who voted for James Lynch running for governor that year with the same party backing. Impellitteri's successful effort to portray himself as independent of the machine had some impact among Jews, even against a respectable candidate like Pecora. Blacks also voted less solidly for the Democratic candidate for mayor than they did for the gubernatorial nominee. Governor Dewey won reelection easily thanks to a huge upstate majority, and Herbert Lehman won reelection by about the same margin as the year before, with the Liberals again providing his margin of success.

Tammany Under Siege

Impellitteri's victory was a serious blow to the Democratic organization and revealed how badly split it had become. The acting mayor, in spite of his independent image, had been able to keep the support of almost as much of the machine as Pecora, the party's formal candidate. Immediately after the election Frank Sampson and Robert Blaikie called a meeting of Manhattan's district leaders in an effort to oust DeSapio and take control of Tammany, which nearly succeeded. DeSapio would soon receive another blow.[55]

Impellitteri's promotion vacated his seat as City Council president and mandated a citywide election for the spot in 1951. The Republicans tried to get the Liberals to join them behind the candidacy of Congressman Jacob Javits. Both parties had supported Javits before, and he was contemplating a 1953 bid for the mayoralty. But the Liberals were sensitive to accusations that when they had joined with Tammany in 1950 they lost their standing as an independent force for good government. They also hesitated to scheme with the Republican organization for fear of being accused of cutting backroom deals. Besides, they had received little help of any kind from the Republicans in return for their support for the party's candidates in the past.[56]

In Rudolph Halley the Liberals found an attractive candidate of their own. He had been chief counsel to Senator Kefauver's investigating committee, and had achieved public prominence earlier that year when in front of hundreds of thousands of New York City television viewers he questioned Mayor O'Dwyer and his staff about their underworld acquaintances. Ultimately, Javits withdrew and the GOP supported Harold Reigelman, a respected attorney who had served on a number of important government commissions. The Democrats sponsored a machine regular from Brooklyn named Joseph Sharkey. Both Halley and Reigelman were Jewish. Sharkey was Irish.[57]

In a campaign that generated little enthusiasm each candidate accused the others of ties to organized crime and subservience to party bosses. Each claimed to be more liberal than his opponents and tried to seize the good government banner. The climax of the campaign came when Sharkey accused Halley of anti-Semitism. The Liberal party candidate's law firm had once accepted a freedom of speech case for a radio station being sued for broadcasting malicious remarks about Jews. Halley denied the charge of anti-Semitism as ludicrous, which it was. Only about one quarter of New York's eligible voters went to the polls, but those who did elected Rudolph Halley City Council president by a slim margin. For the first time the Liberals defeated the two major parties in a citywide election. In a telegram the next day David Dubinsky wrote to the party's leaders: "WE HAVE HAD SEVEN YEARS OF HARD PLUGGING, BESET WITH DISCOURAGEMENT AND DISAPPOINTMENTS, BUT IT WAS ALL WORTHWHILE TO HEAR LAST NIGHT THAT THE LIBERAL PARTY HAS NOW BECOME THE NUMBER ONE PARTY IN THE GREATEST CITY IN THE WORLD." Hyperbole aside, the event was extraordinary.[58]

The same election that boosted Rudolph Halley to the city's number two office saw a young attorney named Jack Baltzell beat out a DeSapio sponsored candidate for a district leadership spot. Baltzell had been one of the founders of the Fair Deal Democrats, and his campaign had been backed by the reformers of the Lexington Democratic Club in the "silk stocking" district on Manhattan's Upper East Side. Just two years earlier the assembly district had been split into two Democratic party units to accommodate a pair of regulars battling for a place in Tammany's hierarchy. Following Baltzell's victory, DeSapio reduced it to one and sat only the regular candidate, who had won in the northern portion, and who had taken the largest plurality in the overall district.[59]

The next year, the 1952 presidential contest further exacerbated the tensions between the liberal reform wing of the Democratic party and the more conservative regular faction. The party's candidate, Adlai Stevenson, was the paragon of the intellectual politician—thoughtful and sensitive, witty and urbane, humble and committed. New York's liberal community found his eloquence inspiring, his passionate explanation of the complexity of world affairs reassuring that he was a leader who understood the issues confronting the nation. Thousands of young men and women who never before participated actively in electoral politics entered the arena for the first time that year. Most did not join the local Democratic party, but rather affiliated with a citywide organization, Volunteers for Stevenson.

The men whose political educations took place on the streets of New York City instead of college classrooms had little use for Stevenson's rhetoric. They found his aloof style disconcerting. "How in hell can you run a man that don't even want to run and says so for Christ's sake?" an Irish politician once lamented of Stevenson, who insisted he would accept his party's nomination only in response to a draft. To political professionals who fought tough battles, who won their jobs with sweat and work, Stevenson was an oddball. The regular organization liked his independent volunteer organization even less than the candidate. Relations between the professionals and the amateurs were strained throughout the campaign. When Stevenson lost, the young, energetic liberals who idolized him blamed the machine for not delivering the votes.[60]

The regulars had complaints too. They nominated John Cashmore, a loyal Democrat from Brooklyn, to run for United States Senate against Republican incumbent Irving Ives. The Liberal party refused to make common cause and ran its own candidate, educator George Counts. The Liberals took more than 489,000 votes away from Cashmore, even more than they attracted for Adlai Stevenson. In a year of Republican landslide it made no more difference to the outcome than the regulars' incivility to the Stevenson volunteers, but the sense of betrayal was no less keen because of that. On the local level, the reformers in the Lexington Democratic Club won the two Democratic State Committee positions up for election in the neighborhood in 1952. The two party posts, less significant to Tammany than district leader spots, were unimportant in themselves. Yet, they reminded Carmine DeSapio that reform clubbers sought control of his party from within, while the Liberals attacked his organization from without. And a mayoralty race approached. If DeSapio could not find a candidate who could restore harmony to the Democratic party's ethnic coalition and win the mayoralty, his term as Tammany chief was through.[61]

FIVE

Robert F. Wagner and the Political Melting Pot

1953–1957

A Coalitionless Mayor

By early 1953 the average New Yorker realized what political professionals already knew in 1950: Vincent Impellitteri did not know how to
be mayor. More than anything else, he did nothing. He proposed no
housing initiative in a city still filled with slums, and he developed no
plan to improve a transit system straining to meet the needs of a
metropolis growing in its outer boroughs while shrinking at its core.
More automobiles than ever before crowded into midtown Manhattan
creating worse congestion than New Yorkers had ever experienced, and
City Hall announced no strategy to control traffic. The number of
children entering schools grew rapidly, but no program to accommodate
them appeared. Crime rose, or so it seemed, and the city's chief executive prepared no response. The Mayor's Committee on Management, a
blue ribbon panel William O'Dwyer had created to review how the city
ran its government, completed its survey in 1953. The report's assessment of the Impellitteri administration was so negative that mayoral
aides tried to prevent it from becoming public.[1]

Early in 1953 the State Legislature held hearings in Albany to consider raising the rent on apartments subject to mandatory controls in New York City. Nearly nine New Yorkers out of ten leased their dwellings, making resistance to the planned increase almost unanimous within the five boroughs. Instead of traveling to the capital to defend his city's renters the mayor stayed home, and the lack of leadership earned him the blame for a fifteen percent rent hike passed by upstate Republicans. Not long afterward, Governor Dewey forced a bill through the State Legislature that transferred control of the city's transit system from the mayor to a state dominated authority. Then fares went up from a dime to fifteen cents, and New Yorkers held Impellitteri responsible for letting it happen. The Republicans reworked the distribution formula for money collected at state run horse tracks and cut $13 million from the city's share. The citizens who would end up paying for the decision blamed their mayor for not protecting them.[2]

Impellitteri was virtually silent about the mistreatment from Albany, while the governor repeatedly blasted the mayor's administration as "mismanaged and wasteful." The municipal budget deficit approached $175 million, and the city's chief executive had no program to fill the gap. When asked what he would do he responded plaintively, "I'm right behind the eight ball." Few disagreed.[3]

A journalist who lived across the street from the mayor's official residence at Gracie Mansion entertained his fellow New Yorkers periodically with amusing anecdotes about the comings and goings of the town's incumbent top official. Of Impellitteri he wrote, apologetically, "There isn't much to say . . . [He] is an almost non-existent figure. . . . The lights aren't on much. Sometimes I think that nobody has been living there regularly." The one distinguishing sign of Impellitteri's presence in the house was a rubdown table in the bedroom, similar to another kept in a basement hideaway at City Hall. While New Yorkers worked, their chief executive enjoyed massages, sometimes several on a single day.[4]

The mayor's staff worked harder, but more often for themselves than for the city. Impellitteri made Frank Sampson his chief deputy, and the ex-Tammany boss distributed jobs to his cronies with little regard for their ability. The editorial boards of New York's newspapers complained of the mediocrity of the administration's appointments, and enough proof of influence peddling surfaced to convict one of Sampson's top assistants. Moreover, the sense that underworld king Tommy Lucchese helped make the mayor's decisions permeated City Hall.[5]

Impellitteri achieved nearly universal unpopularity. Early in 1953,

Mike Quill, leader of the Transit Workers Union, agreed to end a bus slowdown only on the condition that Impellitteri not receive any credit for breaking the impasse. The powerful CIO council of New York made it clear that it would not support the mayor for reelection. A survey taken of five hundred prominent civic leaders failed to yield a single endorsement for the incumbent, and the City Club, a good government group, reported a great influx of new young members because, "the Impellitteri administration's faults have aroused young businessmen and lawyers as nothing else has in recent years." In March, the mayor appeared at a sporting event in Madison Square Garden, and the crowd booed him with a zeal normally reserved for the referee. Only among organizations composed of fellow Italians did Impellitteri enjoy cordial greetings, and he needed more support than that if he wanted to remain mayor.[6]

Impellitteri could expect no help from Tammany Hall. Personal hostility, and the desire of some of the mayor's closest confidants to displace Carmine DeSapio for their own gain, made reconciliation between the two Italian politicians impossible. But Impellitteri's anti-boss stand had been fiction from the start, and the 1950 electoral returns had barely been counted when the mayor's advisers reached out to the party leaders in the four counties outside Manhattan. They had little trouble convincing the weak organizations in Queens and Staten Island of the value of a good relationship with the patronage rich incumbent. Moreover, both those organizations sided with the conservative wing of the Democratic party, with which Impellitteri and his crew were most comfortable. In Brooklyn, a new and uncommitted leader, Ken Sutherland, came to power late in 1952. In the Bronx, where Ed Flynn had no illusions about the caliber of the man in City Hall, Impellitteri made little progress. In an effort to curry favor with the Bronx boss the mayor appointed two Flynn sponsored lawyers to municipal judgeships in May 1953. "How can the Democratic leaders take Impy's patronage and then toss him overboard?" one City Hall hack asked rhetorically. The answer came days later when the mayor, at the Bronx Democrats' annual dinner, "sang the praises of Edward J. Flynn, . . . but his song fell on deaf ears because Flynn was not around to hear it. . . . [he] did not even wait to listen to the campaigning Mayor, explaining he had to go to bed early."[7]

The Quiet Candidacy of Robert F. Wagner

Flynn had not yet chosen his candidate, but he had adopted a strategy. Late in 1952, and early in 1953, representatives of Manhattan Borough President Robert F. Wagner held separate meetings with Flynn, De-Sapio, and Ken Sutherland. All three county leaders agreed that Impel-litteri was a disaster as mayor, and that he should not, and could not, be reelected. Each boss also agreed to back any liberal, honest Democrat who emerged as a viable candidate. Wagner pledged to do the same. The borough president was of course angling for the nomination him-self, but to avoid the burden of appearing boss controlled, he declined to solicit early support.[8]

While Wagner moved quietly, other ambitious men who sensed the incumbent's vulnerability made noises. In February, 1953, Congress-man Jacob K. Javits announced he was available to run for mayor if "the forces of Good Government really wanted" him. The popular, liberal Jewish politician was exploring the chances of winning both the Republican and the Liberal endorsements. Both parties had backed him when he first ran for Congress, and if he could mount a Fusion cam-paign against a candidate like Impellitteri, he reasoned, he would stand a good chance of winning. But the rent increase, transit fare hike, and other state fiscal programs in 1953 made Governor Thomas Dewey, leader of New York's Republicans, almost as unpopular among the people of New York City as their inept mayor. The Liberals told Javits that they might support him, but only if he agreed to disassociate himself publicly from the governor. A Democratic-Liberal ticket seemed to offer greater philosophic harmony. Sam Leibowitz, a well known Democratic judge from Brooklyn, sought the joint nomination of those two parties. He heavily emphasized the advantages of a Jewish candidate in his conversations with Liberal leaders. But the Liberals had a poten-tial Jewish candidate of their own for mayor, City Council president Rudolph Halley. He had proven less than two years before that he could win a citywide election running on the Liberal ticket alone, and during the interim he had maintained a high profile. He had a reputation for honesty, and his intelligence as a city spokesman contrasted sharply with Impellitteri's blunders.[9]

The most ambitious man to seek the mayoralty that year was Man-hattan District Attorney Frank Hogan. He wanted both the Democratic and the Republican nominations. As district attorney he had run on a joint "non-political" ticket, and Governor Dewey favored him, tantamount to selection for the Republican spot. Both Flynn and DeSapio thought well of Hogan, a registered Democrat, and considered him seriously, but they saw little advantage in supporting anyone who might appear on the ballot as the Republican candidate for mayor.[10]

Averell Harriman, former diplomat and international plenipotentiary under President Roosevelt, and mutual security adviser under President Harry Truman, wanted to be the Democratic candidate for governor of New York in 1954. So did Franklin D. Roosevelt, Jr. The supporters of each urged the other to run for mayor to eliminate him from the gubernatorial race the following year. The two well known names appeared prominently on the lists of candidates, even though neither took the thought of running for city office seriously.[11]

As the candidates jockeyed for position the field narrowed. The Republicans tried to force the Liberals into accepting a conservative candidate. The Liberals refused and decided to go it alone with their own nominee, Rudolph Halley. Javits, who at one point seemed poised to capture the nominations of two parties, won neither. He was too dependent on conservative Republicans for the Liberals, and too cozy with the Liberals to suit the Republicans. Hogan's bid to win the backing of both major parties foundered on the suspicions of Democratic leaders that he would be more loyal to Governor Dewey than to them. Campaigning on the Republican ticket alone, in a city where seven voters out of ten registered Democratic, held little appeal for the incumbent district attorney. He decided to keep the job he had.[12]

Without other support, Dewey knew that his party had little chance to prevail in the mayoralty contest. He therefore threw the nomination to a Jewish candidate as a gesture to the ethnic group where the governor and his party always ran weakest. It was the same thing he had done in 1945. Harold Reigleman, Republican candidate for City Council president in 1951, and by 1953 the New York City postmaster, a job he held as a reward for his loyal service to the New York Republican cause, became his party's nominee for mayor.[13]

Meanwhile, the Democrats feuded publicly. DeSapio did not want his rivalry with Impellitteri to allow the mayor to claim that the Tammany boss was trying to control City Hall against the wishes of the public. DeSapio cleverly announced that he would poll his borough's Democrats to see if they wanted the incumbent as their candidate, and that he would abide by the results no matter what the outcome. Early in June, postcards went out from county headquarters to a sampling of 41,000 party members, one-tenth of the total registered in Manhattan. It asked a simple question:

"Do you want Vincent R. Impellitteri as your candidate for Mayor of the City of New York?"

Yes__ No__

Eight of every ten cards that came back were marked no. DeSapio had damaged the mayor publicly while presenting himself as an enlightened leader who listened to his party's voters.[14]

While the Democrats fought, Robert Wagner kept a low profile. In March, 1953, when he answered questions on a radio program sponsored by the good government advocates of the Citizens Union, he went so far as to say that he did not object to having his name mentioned as a candidate for mayor, but that he had done nothing to encourage it. The polls that the city's newspapers delighted in taking to measure the standing of prospective candidates sometimes failed to include his name at all, and when they did it was far down the list. Political leaders referred to him as a man with a background that met the standards for the city's top job, but none firmly backed him. The reserved posture allowed Wagner to avoid any accusations that he discharged his duties as Manhattan borough president with his own ambitions in mind.[15]

Early in May, Wagner's father died after a long illness, and the would-be mayor virtually dropped out of public sight for some weeks. Then, at the end of June, with Impellitteri determined to run, and major figures within the Democratic party equally committed to defeating him, Wagner announced during a radio interview that if the many civic groups with which he had worked, and "independents, and my party want me to run for Mayor, I shall be happy to undertake that responsibility. As a native New Yorker, who loves his city, I could do no less under these circumstances." He emphasized that as a loyal Democrat he would back any candidate his party chose who met "certain standards," but also made it clear that he was prepared to battle Impellitteri in a primary if necessary because he judged the incumbent unfit for the job.[16]

In theory, ever since 1913, political parties in New York State chose candidates for local offices in primary votes of the party's registered members. To enter a contest a candidate needed to collect a specified number of signatures from the party members who lived in the unit of representation concerned; 5,000 would qualify him to run in the primary for mayor of New York City in 1953. The victor won the right to appear on the ballot as the party's candidate in the general election. In practice, New York City's five Democratic county leaders chose their party's candidate for mayor, and only when they disagreed among themselves did a primary occur. Since the law had gone into effect that had happened only twice, in 1925 and in 1937. It threatened again in 1953.[17]

Impellitteri was sure the county leaders from Queens and Staten Island would support him in a primary if necessary, but neither one commanded an organization as powerful as those in the other boroughs. DeSapio and Flynn were clearly against the mayor, though formally uncommitted to any particular candidate. Brooklyn leader Ken Sutherland remained neutral through June. In an effort to help the boss make up his mind, Impellitteri withheld judicial appointments normally reserved for Brooklyn Democrats. More important perhaps, during prohibition Sutherland had overseen the political protection afforded to bootleggers in his borough, and more than a few associates of the mayor's friend Tommy Lucchese knew it. What conversations they had with the Brooklyn leader is unknown.[18]

On July 20 the city's five Democratic leaders met to try to choose a candidate for mayor. In spite of his earlier commitment to work with Flynn, DeSapio, and Wagner, Sutherland came out in favor of Impellitteri, as did the county leaders from Queens and Staten Island. DeSapio, and Bronx Congressman Charles Buckley, speaking on behalf of Edward Flynn, who was suffering from serious heart trouble by then, refused to abide by the decision. The dispute immediately spilled out of the smoke filled hotel room where the bosses met and into the corridor where reporters waited. Buckley lacked Flynn's sophistication, and in front of television cameras he engaged in a verbal and physical bout with James Roe, a vulgar man who ruled the Democrats in Queens. "If you want to break up the Democratic party in New York City, this is the way to start," Buckley yelled. "This city is made up of New Dealers and Fair Dealers. The voters of the city and state elect men like Lehman, Roosevelt and Al Smith and they will not stand for [Impellitteri]." Roe could hardly be outdone. Of his opponents, he said: "They are a mixture of pinkos, leftists, . . . and political mix breeds that want to exploit our wonderful city. Some of them form a fifth column in the Democratic party." The philosophical battle between the liberal and conservative wings of the party was coming to a head once more.[19]

The next day DeSapio and Buckley asked Robert Wagner to meet them for lunch at Longchamps restaurant in lower Manhattan. The two men pledged that Tammany and the Bronx Democratic organization would back Wagner if he ran in a primary for his party's nomination for mayor. "They came to me," Wagner recalled, emphasizing that he made no commitments to the two men, "and I did not want to be

97

borough president my whole life, so I decided to run." His low key plan had worked. By the time of his selection he was the logical choice. Just days earlier James Hagerty, the respected political reporter of *The New York Times*, analyzed New York's mayoralty politics and concluded that the, "Bronx and Tammany leaders look on the prospective primary contest . . . as one between conservative Democrats [backing Impellitteri] . . . and liberal New Deal-Fair Deal Democrats represented by Mr. Wagner, Senator H. Lehman, [and] Averell Harriman . . . ." Flynn and DeSapio understood that holding onto the liberal image was the key to holding onto Jewish voters, so often the determining factor in New York City elections. None of the available candidates could match Robert Wagner as a symbol of the New Deal.[20]

From the very beginning of the campaign Wagner himself stressed the ideological distance between himself and his opponent. "I do not want the party of Franklin D. Roosevelt, Alfred E. Smith, Robert F. Wagner, Sr. and Herbert Lehman to fall into lesser hands, to slide back to lesser ideals and goals," he said the day after his decision to run. Averell Harriman praised Wagner's progressive credentials calling him a man who "has shown effective administrative ability in the important positions he has held, and brought to them integrity and liberal conviction, worthy of the highest traditions of the Democratic party." Senator Lehman announced, "I am glad to indicate my unqualified support of [Wagner] for the democratic nomination in the coming primary. Bob Wagner is the worthy heir of a great father and represents those fine traditions of liberal progressive and forward looking government with which New Yorkers proudly identify themselves."[21]

The Coalition Adds Color

With the battle lines firmly drawn, the two camps set out to create ethnically balanced tickets to satisfy the Democratic party's ethnic factions and to appeal to the city's polyglot public.

Wagner himself had diverse appeal. His name was German, and his father, who was born a Lutheran, converted to the Methodist Church as a young man, and to Catholicism late in life, so he could be buried with his wife. The senior Wagner was remembered as a great man of liberal conviction and humane instincts, and during the 1930s he had been one of the first of New York City's public officials to condemn the Nazis and the city's anti-Semitic hatemongers. Jews recognized the name as one that belonged to a man who had helped protect them and who had passed far reaching legislation in support of workers, the poor, and the little man. Quite a few thought the Wagners were actually German Jews. The son benefited from the reputation of the father, and had the added political advantage of an Irish mother and a Catholic upbringing. He appealed to Irish Catholics as one of their own, more or less. "They didn't know what to make of me," the younger Wagner once said about his ethnicity, but it all worked to his advantage. He was a likable and well respected man, so any group that could find a way to tie themselves to him, did.[22]

For the purposes of balancing a ticket, he qualified as an Irish Catholic from Manhattan. Abe Stark, a Jewish businessman from Brooklyn became his running mate for City Council president, and Bronx Italian Lawrence Gerosa, booted off O'Dwyer's ticket in 1945, joined Wagner's in 1953 as the candidate for comptroller. Impellitteri's ticket included a Bronx Irish Catholic named Charles E. Keegan for comptroller and Julius Helfand, a Brooklyn Jew, for City Council president. And in 1953, for the first time in a municipal election, blacks entered New York City's ethnic political equation.[23]

Governor Dewey keenly understood the power of ethnic voting, and he suffered no illusions about his party's weak standing with the many national, religious, and racial minorities that made up New York City. Unwilling to offer policies that would attract these urban voters to Republican candidates, he often relied on symbolic gestures to try to achieve electoral success. By 1953 the number of blacks living and voting in Harlem had grown large enough to attract the governor's attention. In an effort to win their support, Dewey picked Elmer A. Carter as his party's candidate for Manhattan borough president. The editor of *Opportunity*, a journal of black life published by the National Urban League, Carter was the first black man nominated for so high a city post.[24]

Blacks had once been loyal to the Republican party. Effectively disfranchised between 1821 and 1870 in New York, blacks cast their ballots solidly for Republicans after Lincoln's slave-freeing party passed the fifteenth amendment to the Constitution and secured them the right to vote. Even before they developed an attachment to the GOP, the group felt little love for the ruling Democratic organization that had administered the denial of black political rights for nearly half a century. Moreover, the blacks and the Irish often competed for manual labor during the nineteenth century, creating antagonism between the outsiders seeking recognition and the people who controlled the city's dominant party.[25]

Coldly calculating politicians saw little reason to pay much attention to the sixty thousand blacks scattered throughout the five boroughs at the turn of the century. Just a few drops in the city's sea of nearly three and a half million people, and without a neighborhood of great concentration to focus the mind of a local candidate, the race counted for little in the ethnic arithmetic of New York City politics. During Seth Low's mayoralty bid in 1897, a group of ambitious black men decided that the Republicans took their people's vote for granted and established the United Colored Democracy, a citywide unit intended to give blacks some political clout. Richard Croker recognized the organization according to Tammany's unwritten rules: "We can treat the colored people in proportion to their work, and give them patronage in accordance with their merit and representation," he informed the UCD. He kept his word, but with so few blacks in New York, and most remaining loyal to Tammany's opposition, the group did not go far.[26]

Blacks began migrating north in large numbers after 1890, when a post-slave generation fleeing the brutality of Jim Crow and the poverty of the South looked for work in America's major economic centers. The process accelerated during World War I, which generated a great demand for labor. The influx of black men and women into New York coincided with a real estate bust in Harlem, then a decidedly upper-crust quarter, but one with a noticeable minority of blacks living on its periphery. Unrented apartments built for the city's elite became homes for the migrants, who could afford to live in them only by piling an extraordinary number of paying tenants into each. More and more, Harlem became a black neighborhood, and as waves of blacks continued to arrive, its size grew.[27]

Harlem gave blacks an identifiable political base, and during the first three decades of the twentieth century party professionals begrudgingly made room for a few of their numbers in elected and appointed offices. But the clubhouses stayed segregated in keeping with the bigotry of the times, and Democratic machine workers did little to attract blacks to their organization. As late as 1932, when the nation rejected the party of the Great Depression in favor of Franklin D. Roosevelt, blacks still voted overwhelmingly for the Republican candidate. Then came the New Deal with its alphabet soup of job programs, relief assistance, and other tangible benefits. Starving even worse than their neighbors as a consequence of the nation's economic catastrophe, blacks developed an unshakeable loyalty to the man in the White House who offered them work, food, and hope. Eleanor Roosevelt's tireless and uncompromising commitment to civil rights strongly reinforced the devotion of the black community to the President. In 1936 there occurred a political migration of profound import as blacks, for six decades solidly Republican voters, moved into the Democratic party with the force of an earthquake. They remain there to this day.[28]

In New York City, blacks perceived Fiorello LaGuardia as the voice of the New Deal and their protector. They continued to cast their ballots for him even as they developed an allegiance to the party that opposed him. When LaGuardia passed from the scene, black votes landed on the Democratic line in local as well as national elections. In 1930, 327,000 blacks lived in New York, less than five percent of the population. Ten years later, with more than 458,000, the group inched its way to over six percent of the expanding city's people. By 1950, three quarters of a million members of the race lived within the five boroughs, nearly one of every ten inhabitants. Black communities existed in Brooklyn, and were developing in the Bronx, but one-fifth of the people who lived in Manhattan, Harlem's home, were black. Almost all voted Democratic. This simple arithmetic led Governor Dewey to name a black man as his party's candidate for Manhattan borough president in 1953.[29]

The Liberals had selected a Jewish politician to run for the Manhattan spot, but after the Republicans announced their candidate they switched in favor of a black man. Impellitteri's crew also dropped a Jew they had selected and named a black candidate for the post. Carmine DeSapio had promised the position to a Jewish Tammany loyalist, but knew even before announcing the nominee that the commitment could not be kept. In an effort to disarm his opponents, DeSapio set out to attract a more distinguished black to his ticket than his adversaries had found for theirs.[30]

Several embarrassing weeks ensued as the boss tried to convince Ralph Bunche of the NAACP, A. Philip Randolph, President of the International Brotherhood of Sleeping Car Porters, and a long list of distinguished Harlem leaders to accept the designation. None cared to enter the rough-and-tumble of New York City politics as the candidate of Tammany Hall. "We've tried the high road," an exasperated DeSapio finally told Wagner, and Warren Moscow, a top political aide to the mayoral candidate, "now let's get down to practical politics." A quick review of Harlem politicians led the men to select Hulan Jack, a former assemblyman. Every ticket had a black candidate for Manhattan borough president to complement the Irish, Italian and Jewish candidates running for citywide offices.[31]

Candidate Wagner: Competent, Practical, Liberal and Honest

Impellitteri saw himself as champion of the underdog. He thought he would run well among blacks, and campaigned heavily in black neighborhoods, but when he did he took with him his remarkable ability to say dumb things. Referring to his rivalry with Tammany's Italian chief, Impellitteri announced to an East Harlem crowd that, "the Negro people are a lot like the Italians—my own stock. DeSapio is from my own stock and he is against me. As soon as a man gets away up, his own people try to knock him down." Whether the mayor thought blacks would be pleased to be compared to Italians, or that Italians would enjoy the comparison to blacks, is unclear. It is unlikely that either group was proud to learn the mayor thought betrayal to be a prominent characteristic of its people.[32]

The mayor's appeal to race offended many New Yorkers, especially Jews, and the ideological struggle between liberals and conservatives taking place inside the Democratic party had already created special resistance to Impellitteri among New York's most liberal ethnic group. Wagner, on the other hand, was popular with the city's Jews. Not only did he wear his father's proud name with its unmistakable New Deal association, but as an assemblyman, and as Manhattan borough president, he had shown ample commitment to liberal social policies. The longer the campaign went on, the more apparent the differences between the two candidates became.[33]

City employees heard Wagner declare that Impellitteri had failed to give them an effective labor policy, and then pledge that as mayor he would recognize their right to bargain collectively. He urged adoption of "the enlightened labor relations policies of private industry, leaving every employee free to join any union or association of his own choosing." The proposal was a bold departure from the prevailing practice in American municipalities that forbade public employees from such organizing. Emphasizing that his attitude toward workers was part of an overall philosophy, he told one labor committee that their choice in the mayoral campaign was "whether to carry on the tradition that made the party great or . . . retreat into reaction. We must see to it that the liberal movement in the Democratic party be continued." All of the major labor organizations of the city, save those tied to the Liberal party that backed Rudolph Halley, and the Columbia Association, an affiliation of Italian workers that backed Impellitteri, supported Wagner, the son of the man who wrote the nation's labor laws.[34]

Wagner's liberal image had a clear effect. In many neighborhoods of Brooklyn, the only borough with a large Jewish population whose Democratic boss had backed the incumbent mayor, Democratic party officials bolted to Wagner in spite of the potential consequences of defying their county leader. Early in the campaign, district captains in Jewish areas encountered trouble getting signatures on designating petitions to put Impellitteri on the primary ballot. Talk spread among party workers that the mayor would run badly in "New Deal" neighborhoods, meaning areas with large Jewish populations. Before the campaign ended Franklin Roosevelt, Jr., speaking in support of Wagner, accused the mayor's political sponsors of sending "out word to district leaders to keep a certain element from voting in the September 15 primary." Journalists reported that, "while the Manhattan Congressman did not explain this remark about a 'certain element' further, observers took it to mean generally voters with strong New Deal tendencies, and . . . particularly Jewish voters."[35]

Emphasis on his liberalism served Wagner well in Jewish districts. When talking with Democratic party workers of all faiths, Wagner took a different tack. At political clubs around the city, where men thought more about their own employment than about issues and rhetoric, the challenger emphasized Impellitteri's unpopularity. Even if he won the Democratic nomination, the mayor would never win re-election against the Liberal party's Rudolph Halley, Wagner implied. To the Democratic faithful, whose jobs depended on keeping a benevolent leader in City Hall, the meaning of this pitch was clear. If Wagner's liberalism made him electable, they would be for it.[36]

In general terms, the public viewed Wagner as a competent defender of the common man. In sharp contrast to Mayor Impellitteri's complaisance, Wagner had protested strongly the 1953 rent increase that hurt the city's working class, and he had opposed the Republican transit plan and the fare hike that went along with it. The fifteen cent fee meant that for the first time since the subway system opened in 1905 the riders who relied on it could not drop a single coin from their pockets into the turnstile to gain access. Instead, they had to wait on line to buy special tokens. The Wagner campaign barraged New York's subway cars with posters that read, "New York Needs More Than a Token Mayor," reminding straphangers whom to blame for the higher price of a ride. Wagner also had a consistent record of opposition to Governor Dewey's biased fiscal policies that cost the average New York City resident hard-earned tax dollars and gave little in return.[37]

Unable to find a winning campaign issue, Impellitteri adopted the red-baiting tactics of Senator Joseph McCarthy, then at the peak of his notoriety. Of his supposedly leftist detractors, the mayor said with venom, "I have worked hard to earn [their] hatred and I cherish it." His backers insisted that their man was the only "American candidate." In one of the more bizarre episodes of the cold war, some of the mayor's assistants schemed to arrange for New York's dwindling Communist party to endorse Wagner in an effort to deliver a political kiss of death. Wagner's staff learned of the plan and, before it could be implemented, publicly detailed Marcantonio's role in selecting Impellitteri as a candidate for City Council president in 1945. When newspaper headlines read, "Marcantonio Called Impy's First Sponsor," the mayor, not Wagner, spent his time explaining his ties to extremists.[38]

Some of the mayor's advisers, realizing the damage their candidate's conservative image was causing, belatedly tried to win back some support by insisting that Impellitteri was a New Dealer. After all, they argued, he had backed FDR, Herbert Lehman, and Harry Truman. The mayor himself asserted that he was a "genuine liberal," and tried to dismiss his opponent, and Wagner's supporter young Franklin Roosevelt, as nothing more than "two juniors." But when the son of the man who invented the New Deal told an audience at a Brooklyn synagogue that, "Bob and I are proud of the fact we stand for the same thing our fathers stood for," the audience broke into loud and sustained applause.[39]

Wagner outclassed Impellitteri in every respect. More well spoken to a listener's ear, more competent in spite of the mayor's incumbency, better respected for his integrity than the man who lunched regularly with Tommy Lucchese and whose staff gave city jobs to dolts with impunity, few aspects of the contest seemed fair. Impellitteri's greatest political asset, perhaps, was his wife, Betty. Simple and sincere, she gave the mayor's campaign a touch of kindness when she appeared by her husband's side.[40]

Even so, the quiet charm of Robert Wagner's wife, Susan, could only help a man running for political office, and their marriage was blessed with two children. The enthusiastic boys, Duncan, aged seven, and Bobby, nine, crayoned cardboard boxes into "Wagner for Mayor" posters. One day they connected two signs with string to create a makeshift billboard that they swung over their cocker spaniel, Trey. Marching up and down the block where they lived on East 86th Street, they urged passers-by to "vote for my dad." The Impellitteri campaign had no weapon that compared. When the Wagners all appeared on television on the Sunday before the primary vote, the candidate declared that "the city should be so operated that it will be a fit place to raise a family," while his adorable children and pretty spouse looked on.[41]

Wagner trounced Impellitteri in the primary by a margin of two to one. In spite of a low voter turnout expected to favor the mayor, Wagner took every borough, save heavily Italian Staten Island where the two men ran neck and neck for the few percent of the total vote that resided there. So completely did the challenger out-poll the incumbent that breaking the results down into parts becomes an exercise in triviality, except to note that Impellitteri ran well among his fellow Italians. In all other neighborhoods Wagner ran strongly; almost eight voters of ten in the Bronx cast their ballots for him, nearly seven of ten in Manhattan, six of ten in Brooklyn against the local machine, and even in Queens, where Impellitteri had done so well in 1950, Wagner won a clear majority.[42]

Impellitteri promptly announced that he would run in the November election as an independent candidate. His "battalion of incompetents," as one detractor referred to his staff, tried desperately to qualify the source of their jobs for a place on the ballot. They failed. A short time afterward, a journalist without a story to file for the day passed by City Hall searching for copy and asked one of Impellitteri's Jewish party hacks, "What's new?" Came the melancholy reply, "What should be new? We're all sitting *shiva*." The accidental administration of Vincent R. Impellitteri was over.[43]

Wagner emerged from his battle with the mayor as the municipal spokesman for the city's liberal Democrats, precisely the position he wanted to confront Rudolph Halley, who had been perceived as the favorite before the Democratic primary. The Liberal party candidate would have run well against Impellitteri by attacking the mayor's conservative views, assailing his competence, and questioning his underworld ties. Against Wagner it was not so easy. The Manhattan borough president was a tough politician to out-liberal, and Halley and Wagner had taken similar positions as colleagues on the Board of Estimate. Wagner also had the longer and more substantive city government career. Newspapers reported the "almost complete loss of support for Liberal party candidate Rudolph Halley, following the primary victory of Mr. Wagner." In some Liberal party strongholds, members asserted their independence: "Mr. Wagner has a long record of fighting for the right things in city government," declared Irving Getnick, the Liberal leader in the second assembly district in Brooklyn. "The Liberal Party has endorsed Mr. Wagner before for public office. It should have done so again," he announced.[44]

Searching for a way to get back in the race, Halley sought to tie his opponent to past Democratic scandals and Tammany's negative image. It was a tough task because Wagner personally had never been tainted by corruption. Still, the Liberals tried. One harsh toned Halley spokesman, a young and ambitious politician named Edward I. Koch, told a forum sponsored by the Jewish Community Center at Avenue I and East 13th Street in Brooklyn, that the Liberal candidate would follow in the LaGuardia good government tradition, and that Wagner was, "a tool of the Democratic leaders and racketeers."[45]

In response to such intemperate attacks, Wagner revealed that Halley had chased the Democratic nomination early in the year. Only after DeSapio turned him down did Halley consent to run on the Liberal ticket alone. Halley denied it, but the gobetween confessed. If all Democrats were thieves, then so too was Halley, who had sought the party's support. Furthermore, before Wagner's own candidacy for mayor bloomed, the Liberals had offered him the chance to run on Halley's ticket as City Council president. And of course, the Liberals had supported Wagner for Manhattan borough president four years before. If all Liberals were virtuous, then so too was Wagner.[46]

The Citizen's Union, the elite arm of New York's good government activists, endorsed Wagner over Impellitteri during the 1953 Democratic primary. They stressed that they were only selecting between the two Democrats in an effort to ensure that the best choice appeared on the ballot in November, but once the seal of approval had been bestowed it could not be erased. The City Fusion party, once a powerful coalition that helped elect Fiorello LaGuardia, by 1953 was little more than a symbol of honest and efficient government, but it also backed Wagner. It was the first time ever that the group endorsed a Democrat. New Yorkers simply did not believe Wagner was corrupt.[47]

Wagner received endorsements from his party's national figures, including Harry Truman and Adlai Stevenson. The popularity of America's top Democrats in New York City contrasted sharply with the prevailing negative opinion that the city's people had of Governor Dewey and his Republicans in 1953. GOP mayoral candidate Harold Reigleman was saddled with his party's damaged image, and was himself a conservative in liberal territory. His call for extensive cuts in the municipal budget, and proposals to limit Puerto Rican migration to New York City, frightened his listeners. He also made an inept bid for the

Jewish vote. Late in the mayoral campaign the United States suspended aid to Israel when the young nation ran into a dispute with Syria that displeased Secretary of State John Foster Dulles. The Republicans arranged for Reigleman to meet with Dulles and then announce that a resolution of the problem was imminent. The Israeli Embassy promptly charged that Reigleman had misrepresented the facts, and New York's Jews saw the cynical act to win their votes for what it was.[48]

The only surprise on election day was the strength of Wagner's victory. Just a few points shy of a majority, he won more than forty-six percent of the recorded ballots, an impressive plurality in a three way race. The German-Irish Catholic candidate took a slight majority of Jewish votes, even though both his opponents were Jewish. Halley, liberal and respectable, took more than one-third of his coreligionist's ballots. The Liberal party held its committed core, but confronted with an attractive Democratic opponent who was liberal in outlook, honest, and considered sensitive to matters of discrimination, the Liberals could not broaden their appeal. Not even one Jewish voter in a dozen had any use for Reigleman, a conservative opportunist in their minds.[49]

The available evidence shows that Irish Catholics voted gladly for Wagner, more or less one of their own, and Italians cast six votes of ten for the Democratic candidate. Fears that Italians would punish Wagner for unseating Impellitteri were overblown, and Reigleman's performance earned him just one vote out of four from the group. Halley could not garner even one out of ten. Only the most conservative Italians voted for the Republican candidate. The less conservative among them preferred the Catholic family man running on the Democratic ticket over the nominee of the Liberal party, who had divorced his wife some years before, a practice not readily accepted by Catholics in the 1950s.

Seven of ten blacks cast their ballots for Wagner, president of the borough where the largest concentration of the group lived. Wagner had earned a reputation as a fair man who favored greater civil rights for minorities, and who tried to help his constituents. Reigleman ran poorly among blacks; Halley, worse still. The Liberal party had no standing with blacks. Puerto Ricans constituted a small but growing proportion of the city's voters and, like blacks, were concentrated in Manhattan in 1953. Wagner's staff had been so responsive to the needs of the Caribbean newcomers that when his father died in May, the Spanish language daily, *La Prensa*, ran a headline that translated, "Borough President's Dad Dies," implicitly placing the kindness of the son above the greatness of the father.[50]

Wagner's coalition, like Al Smith's, Fiorello LaGuardia's, and William O'Dwyer's, reached across ethnic barriers. The Irish took pride in Wagner's achievements, and Democratic party workers of all backgrounds knew that the new mayor, while honest and committed to sound government, would be no prude when dispensing city jobs to Democratic regulars who supported him. The increasing numbers of black and Puerto Rican New Yorkers made these two groups more important to Wagner than to earlier candidates, and both groups seemed to believe that promoting the sensitive Manhattan borough president to mayor would help them to get the attention they needed from government.

For Jews, in addition to his general competence and sound reputation, Wagner's liberalism held special attraction. It seemed to matter little that both his opponents were Jewish and that he was Catholic. Perhaps it helped that Wagner's staff, like Al Smith's, was dominated by Jewish liberals. Twelve of eighteen speech writers working under the direction of a young Protestant attorney named Jonathan Bingham, husband of a grandniece of Herbert Lehman, were Jewish. Shortly after his election, Wagner reviewed the names of top campaign staffers, competent men whom he planned to appoint to powerful policy making positions within his administration. Nearly every one, he realized, was Jewish. In order to avoid public comment the personally unbiased but ethnically shrewd politician held off announcing the decisions until appointments of non-Jewish commissioners and assistants had also been arranged. Still, throughout his administration, Jews would move into important posts in New York City government in greater numbers than ever before.[51]

DeSapio On Top

Just after he helped select Wagner to oppose Impellitteri in the Democratic primary, Edward J. Flynn sailed with his family to Ireland. The long reigning boss of Bronx politics, suffering from a serious heart ailment, died peacefully in the land of his ancestors shortly before his candidate's victory. Congressman Charles Buckley, like Flynn the son of Irish immigrants, assumed the Bronx county leader's post. With Flynn's demise, and Wagner's election as mayor, Carmine DeSapio became the city's top Democratic party official.

By 1953 DeSapio had made much progress in improving the image of Tammany. Good government groups greatly preferred Wagner over Impellitteri, so that during the primary they found themselves allied with the Manhattan Democratic party leader, an unusual occurrence. The intraparty dispute among the Democrats reached down to the district leader level where DeSapio ran a number of candidates against party office holders backing the incompetent incumbent mayor. The Citizens Union, which had never before taken a stand in district leader races, endorsed a number of DeSapio's candidates. In Wagner's landslide almost all of DeSapio's people won. An important exception was in the ninth assembly district, home of the Lexington Democratic Club, where the good government group endorsed the reformers' nominee, Jack Baltzell, who was elected. It was the first time a reform clubber held the right to sit at the table with the men who ran the affairs of Tammany Hall.[52]

DeSapio seemed unconcerned. When asked how he felt about the well-educated Baltzell's entry into his organization, the boss quipped, "hell of a place for a Princeton man," and turned his attention to the other boroughs. He used the power that flowed to him from City Hall to consolidate his citywide position by deposing the county leaders in Queens and Brooklyn who had fought Wagner. Then he began to consider the 1954 campaign for governor.[53]

Some Democrats thought that after his impressive showing Wagner should try for the Governor's Mansion right away, but the idea did not interest the new mayor. Averell Harriman and Franklin Roosevelt, Jr., both prominently linked to the New Deal, well known and popular, sought the job. Neither really had much desire to be governor, but rather saw the position as a necessary stepping stone on the way to the White House.[54]

Averell Harriman had inherited a fortune estimated at forty million dollars as a young man. He grew up a Republican, but in 1928 abandoned the party of the rich to support Al Smith, a friend. He remained active in Democratic politics thereafter, hooked up with FDR in the days of the New Deal, and compiled an unequaled record as a diplomat during the perpetual crisis of World War II and the years that followed. At one time or another he had been Ambassador to London, Ambassador to Moscow, and Secretary of Commerce. Impressive credentials for a world statesman, they showed little awareness of domestic issues, so Harriman needed the governor's post to give himself political credibility.[55]

Franklin Roosevelt, Jr. owned a magic name, had won a seat in Congress, and hoped to move upward to greatness from there. But he had accomplished little as a legislator, and lacked his father's skill at creating a coalition. New York's Democratic organization disliked the boy who had grown up with every advantage imaginable, and who talked down to them. He once offered, without being asked, to stop by Gracie Mansion and explain politics to Mayor William O'Dwyer. The tough, determined Irish immigrant who became the chief executive of America's greatest city through the sheer force of his hard political work, responded in "sulfurous" language indicative of the way many of Gotham's political pros felt about FDR, Jr. In the opinion of one long time Democratic party worker, the man was a carefree "peripatetic aphrodisiac," who owed his political standing to the power of his name and his good looks.[56]

Adolf Berle, one of President Roosevelt's New Deal brain trusters who added highbrow prestige to the Liberal party as its state chairman from 1947 to 1954, thought FDR, Jr. "a young man in a hurry," filled more with ambition than ability or ideas. Alex Rose thought the young Roosevelt a playboy, but he knew that FDR, Jr. wanted to run for governor, so he tested the political waters to assess the potential candidate's chance for victory in 1954. His conclusion was that Roosevelt could not win because the Democratic party's conservative wing would not back him. Upstate New York typically returned strong Republican majorities so that recapturing Albany from the GOP required a solidly united effort. Averell Harriman was acceptable to both wings of the party, a New Dealer by philosophy but a party regular by temperament. He was ready and willing to run. In search of victory, Rose worked closely with DeSapio to block support for FDR, Jr. and to see to it that Harriman won the nominations of both the Liberal and Democratic parties. Franklin Roosevelt, Jr. agreed somewhat reluctantly to accept the nomination for attorney general on the joint Democratic-Liberal ticket.[57]

After twelve years in office Governor Thomas E. Dewey decided not to stand for reelection. He chose respected Republican Senator Irving Ives to run on his party's ticket to replace him. After some maneuvering Jacob K. Javits, tired of the House of Representatives but possessed of a driving ambition, became the Republican candidate for attorney general. As a New York City Jew he added geographic and ethnic balance to the party's ticket, and as a liberal he could run a strong race against FDR, Jr.[58]

The election pitted Harriman, talking in traditional New Deal terms, against Ives, defending the GOP's pro-business policies. Early assessments predicted a Democratic victory, but Harriman was "not a handshaker," and gave the impression that he was "autocratic and somewhat enigmatic." Men who knew him commented on his striking, "impersonality." He was "widely acclaimed . . . as an orator of egregious ineptitude." Speakers told anecdotes to try to humanize the candidate in the public mind, but the stories they recounted took place in Moscow and North Africa, not the Bronx, or Albany, or Erie County. Harriman was as distant from the people whose votes he needed as the places where he had traveled, and his uninspiring campaign allowed the race to narrow. On election night an early Democratic-Liberal lead in New York City began to dwindle as upstate returns flowed in. Governor Dewey, talked out of conceding on behalf of his party by Jacob Javits at 10:00 P.M., determined at 2:00 A.M. that the contest would be so close that a recount would be in order, and he impounded ballot boxes around the state.[59]

Harriman won by a majority of just 11,125 votes of more than 3.4 million cast, 264,093 of them on the Liberal party line. He would have lost without the third party's support. The rest of his ticket won in spite of the narrowness of the gubernatorial candidate's victory, with the surprising exception of Franklin Roosevelt, Jr. The young would-be president did not really aspire to the attorney general's job, nor did he have any special claim to it, while Jacob Javits politicked tirelessly throughout the state in pursuit of the post. Javits ran effective television commercials emphasizing that FDR, Jr. had missed many votes in Congress and had no relevant experience to act as the state's top attorney. Javits, on the other hand, had been a trial lawyer for a number of years before entering politics. He ran about as well as other Republicans upstate, and much better in New York City, to defeat Roosevelt by 173,000 votes. The Democratic organization failed to deliver votes for FDR, Jr. in its urban stronghold.[60]

The Liberals received some credit for their role in electing the governor, but it was Carmine DeSapio who led the Democratic effort that delivered over eighty-five percent of Harriman's votes. Shortly after the election the Tammany boss outmaneuvered Rose to ensure that his party, and not the Liberals, got the bulk of New York State patronage, a matter that caused Rose some resentment. Back to back, the New York County Democratic party leader had chosen winning candidates for mayor of New York City and governor of New York State. In both instances DeSapio carefully built coalitions around honest, progressive political figures. Such men had a philosophical attraction for the predominantly Jewish, liberal wing of the party that would readily revolt if a candidate did not meet their standards. The promise of victory and the jobs that would follow kept the loyalty of the party's traditional Irish

Catholic workers, and Italian and Jewish regulars as well. The hope of greater government sensitivity to their needs secured poor minorities to the cause.[61]

DeSapio was least confident of the commitment of the liberal wing of his party, so he made a series of gestures to them. Tammany's county committee, the organization's general membership, was theoretically empowered to make policy decisions, but consisted of more than 11,000 people. The anachronistic structure, a throwback to the days when every block captain had a say in the affairs of Tammany Hall, was so unwieldy that it did not function. Power had gravitated to the executive committee, which consisted of the district leaders, and reformers claimed the result was an autocratic party of machine regulars. In 1954 DeSapio accepted changes that reduced the county committee to about 4,000. There was no practical effect, but plenty of positive publicity; when the leader of Tammany Hall agreed to a more open party system, it was news.

Also in 1954, DeSapio accepted direct election of district leaders. Until then, the local members of the county committee ran for election in the primary to represent a tiny geographic unit, and the winners of these contests then chose the district leader. The system, by placing many names on the ballot in a given district, favored the traditional party organization that was so good at reaching people block by block, and weakened the effects of media campaigns that could reach larger numbers of people on behalf of more prominent candidates. This reform, somewhat more significant than the reduction in the size of the county committee, added to the boss's image as a politician committed to an open Democratic party.[62]

DeSapio also adopted a fresh style. He assumed Edward Flynn's place as New York representative to the Democratic National Committee and, urged on by a public relations consultant named Sidney Baron, spoke out on political issues in forums in New York and elsewhere. That he addressed the public at all contrasted sharply with the dour taciturnity of earlier bosses like Richard Croker and Charles Francis Murphy. The theme that underlay most of DeSapio's talks was especially striking: "The Democratic party will be ruled only by the voters," he declared wherever he went, a novel noise coming from the head of America's oldest, toughest, traditionally most closely controlled political machine. The new style boss appeared on the cover of *Time*, and was featured in the pages of *Newsweek, Life, US News & World Report, The Saturday Evening Post*, and The Sunday *New York Times Magazine*. On radio and television he became, de facto, a national party spokesman. Newspapers in Chicago, Cleveland, Kansas City, Atlanta and Los Angeles printed articles about him.[63]

Fundamentally, the machine had not changed. It still distributed jobs, helped its friends, and punished its enemies. Its base had been weakened by civil service reform, by an enduring prosperity that was making government jobs less desirable, by a shift over the control of social welfare programs from local district leaders to city bureaucrats, and more professional municipal contracting procedures. Yet, these were differences of degree. DeSapio used the same techniques that brought Charles Murphy success, including a keen awareness that winning elections in New York City required due deference to the special concerns of Jewish voters. Candidates had to be liberal, opposed to discrimination and scandals had to be avoided. Under DeSapio, the Democratic ties to organized criminals, so prominent in the 1940s, faded. Judgeships were still sold, but the sales were quiet, and typically went to well-qualified lawyers willing to pay a price, not the highest bidder. And DeSapio supplemented his understanding of the classic ingredients for political success in New York City with a sound instinct for the rising importance of the media. He managed to give the machine a public facelift that added to his prestige. DeSapio's success in electing the mayor of the nation's largest city, and the governor of its most populous state, emboldened him, and in 1956 he began to contemplate the election for president.[64]

In late 1955 President Eisenhower suffered a heart attack. The Democrats suddenly seemed to have a real chance to recapture the White House the following year. Adlai Stevenson and Tennessee Senator Estes Kefauver sought the nomination in a series of primaries, while Averell Harriman sat on the sideline hoping for a deadlocked convention. The New York governor who campaigned so awkwardly preferred to take his chances on a deal cut in the back room where he would have the support of his former boss Harry Truman, and Carmine DeSapio. The two political pros, Harriman reasoned intelligently, could corner the support of the big city machines for him and throw him the nomination. The strategy depended on the two frontrunners ending up in a stalemate, but they did not. Stevenson remained his party's spokesman. When the Democrats reached a compromise on a civil rights plank, the last chance of a tangled convention looking for a fresh candidate faded, and Harriman's potential along with it.[65]

The rugged general living in the White House recovered from his coronary, and by the time the 1956 contest began in earnest political professionals realized that the prospering country was not about to force his retirement. With Adlai Stevenson again their party's nominee and a sure loser, the Democratic machines around the country found scant energy for his campaign.

Stevenson understood the predicament. In New York he tried to improve his fortunes by convincing the popular mayor Wagner to run for the Senate seat Herbert Lehman no longer wanted. By then seventy-eight, the nation's most prominent Jewish statesman had decided to retire from elective office. Stevenson knew the local party would deliver votes for Wagner, so he wanted him on the ticket. One staff aide confronted the mayor with the reality that 1956 would be a Republican year no matter what. "The best you can hope for is to lose by a little," he said. But Wagner had a political itch. He had gone to the Chicago convention harboring the secret hope that just maybe Lyndon Johnson would emerge as a compromise candidate, and that the calculating Texan would need an eastern Catholic, like the mayor of New York, to run with him. When that did not happen Wagner would have been content to return home. But in response to strong pleas from Stevenson and Lehman that he make the Senate race for the good of the party, Wagner agreed to campaign for the seat once held by his father.[66]

The regular Democratic organization in New York worked hard for Wagner in 1956, but shared little of its effort with Stevenson's forces. The young reform minded men and women who had volunteered to help the liberal, intellectual voice of the Democratic party in 1952, however, rallied to his cause again in 1956. Four years had passed, and the numbers of youthful idealists old enough to vote had swelled. They were eager to campaign, ready to fight for principle, and willing to face defeat on behalf of a man who spoke to them in terms they understood and that inspired them. Their dedication seemed without limits. One Stevensonian wrote to the Executive Director of the Liberal party a month before the election: "My husband and I are honeymooning here in Florida, and in the midst of our wonderful time remembered that this coming week is Registration Week in New York City. This will be my first experience," wrote the woman on her wedding trip, "in actually voting and I look forward to putting all possible support behind Mr. Stevenson. We would greatly appreciate your sending us . . . Absentee Registration Blanks. . . ." Another veteran of the campaign later recalled, "We would never have grown up without Adlai Stevenson. He, so far as I am concerned, is the spiritual and intellectual father of the reform movement."[67]

In neighborhoods around the city where young, well-educated men and women lived, Stevenson campaign clubs developed; the Riverside on Manhattan's Upper West Side, and the Lenox Hill Club just east of the territory claimed by the reformers of the Lexington Club, whose membership expanded during the 1956 campaign. The Village Independent Democrats formed in DeSapio's home district, the FDR-Woodrow Wilson Club emerged on the lower West Side, and others developed around Manhattan, as they did to a lesser degree in the Bronx, Brooklyn, and Queens. Wherever it can be documented, Jews were the dominant ethnic group in the reform clubs, with a significant number of Protestants, and very few Catholics.[68]

Two decades earlier, Jewish activists dissatisfied with Tammany Hall but inspired by the Democratic party's presidential candidate had created the American Labor party to support Franklin Roosevelt and the New Deal. Similarly, in 1956, the sons and daughters of those Jews disapproved of the men who ran the Democratic party in their neighborhoods, but were energetically committed to the nationally sponsored presidential nominee. The members of the earlier movement, uncomfortable with the institution that dominated local political affairs, created their own outside of the Democratic organization. It evolved from the ALP into the Liberal party and gave a voice to the hopes and aspirations of a large segment of a generation of Jewish working-class immigrants. They wielded important influence, but operated at the edges of the political system. The younger group, more thoroughly integrated into American life, did not contemplate leaving the Democratic party, but rather tried to achieve its goals by competing from within.

The reform Democrats, like the regulars, backed Wagner for Senate. So did the Liberal party. Despite discomfort among some party leaders with the mayor's close affiliation to the Democratic machine, Wagner had already developed an impressive record as the city's chief executive, and had worked closely with the Liberals during Harriman's 1954 campaign. On national matters of the kind that concern a United States Senator, the Democrats were philosophically far more congenial to the Liberals than the Republicans, even when the GOP presented a reasonably liberal candidate, like Wagner's opponent Jacob Javits. Thus, all factions of the Liberal-Democratic coalition were on Wagner's side for his Senate race.

Eisenhower crushed Stevenson by more than 1,590,000 votes in New York State, typical of the general's performance nationwide. Riding on the President's coattails Javits beat Wagner by 460,000 votes, more than a million votes fewer than Eisenhower's margin of victory. Within the city's five boroughs Wagner kept his coalition together and actually defeated Javits by 400,000 votes. Virtually eight Jewish voters in ten cast ballots for Wagner, a Catholic candidate running on the Democratic and Liberal tickets rather than for Jacob Javits, a fellow Jew. In part Javits's weak showing with members of his faith stemmed from his position on an international crisis that occurred just days before the election. In the fall of 1956 Egypt's mercurial president, Gamal Abdal Nasser, seized the Suez canal from international control. In response, on October 29, Israel invaded Egypt. President Eisenhower, however, insisted that the Israelis withdraw, and Javits, long a fervent supporter of Israel, decided to stand with his party's President. Wagner took Israel's side and reaped the political benefits. Even Jacob Javits, a well-respected, liberal, Jewish politician could not take New York's Jewish voters for granted.[69]

After the excitement of the 1956 campaign died down, the reform political clubs that helped Adlai Stevenson to spread his message in New York City met to decide what to do next. As in 1952, they blamed Stevenson's bad performance in New York on boss inspired treachery. After all, DeSapio had backed Harriman, not Stevenson, at the Chicago convention. In their idealistic zeal the reform clubbers could not see with the Tammany chief's clarity that Stevenson, admirable as a man, was a lost cause as a candidate. Their hero had fallen, perhaps for four years, perhaps forever, and some simply went home. Most decided to stay around. They appointed themselves defenders of the liberal faith, and pledged to fight on the local level for the high ideals the Democratic presidential candidate had proposed for the nation and the world. The growing number of reform clubs had no countywide system of organization, but the different groups came to the common conclusion that to achieve their goals they needed to elect local public and party officials of their own to replace the officeholders aligned with the traditional Democratic organization. These new clubs, as well as the old, began to consider the municipal elections as 1957 approached.[70]

Ruling By Consensus

Wagner's performance in the 1956 Senate contest made it clear that he would win reelection as mayor. He had compiled a distinguished record from 1954 through 1957 and had earned the right to serve again. Under his direction New York City built new schools, added more teachers, and reduced class sizes. His administration increased relief assistance for the poor and reduced caseloads for welfare workers; it built health centers in poor neighborhoods, inoculated the city's children against polio, and expanded programs for the mentally ill. The city opened three new hospitals and expanded a fourth to add 2,685 beds for New York's sick. The mayor put a record number of police on the streets and reduced major crimes by sixteen percent, increased the ranks of fire-fighters, and adopted new strategies to keep the streets clean. Playground facilities expanded, and special measures addressed the problems of juvenile crime. The mayor's office created the largest municipal middle-income housing program in the nation, and revamped the civil service regulations governing city employees. All of these measures occurred within a general context of improved management and efficiency of municipal employees.[71]

The public sensed the upward motion of the city. One couple wrote the mayor after he announced he would seek reelection: "We have lived here a life-time and with all the complexities and vexations . . . more people and problems than some countries have, New York City has [sic] and is improving. May God guide you in your campaign," they wrote. The letter included a P.S. "Thanks for ignoring Mr. Ibn Saud. . . . it is unfair to praise people so full of mean prejudices . . ." The Arab king had come to New York early in 1957 to attend the United Nations General Assembly, and Wagner deliberately snubbed him with the kind of sensitivity to the ethnic concerns of city voters that made him personally popular beyond the attraction of his competence. The Democrats considered no one else, and reform clubs and regulars organized for Wagner's reelection.[72]

The Liberals also backed the mayor. "Four years ago we did not support Robert Wagner for Mayor," David Dubinsky told a gathering of party members. "In the four years that have passed, Mayor Wagner has given us good reason to question our original judgement. He has . . . given evidence of his desire to conduct a liberal, humane and clean government in New York City." Alex Rose too believed that Wagner had earned the party's confidence, even though he cautioned that the struggle with Tammany for control of the city continued. "A large vote for the Wagner ticket on the Liberal line will insure a greater degree of independence from machine influence for the Wagner administration and will further the realization of many progressive and social objectives," Rose declared.[73]

Rose's comment attempted to respond to the quandary the Liberal party faced when the Democrats ran a strong progressive figure, especially in a municipal election. If the Liberals backed the candidate, they lost their separate identity, and to a degree tainted themselves with dirty Democratic baggage from the past that many Liberal party loyalists found offensive. But if the Liberals did not support Democrats who were honest and who held liberal views, they weakened the philosophical standing of their party and damaged the Democratic-Liberal alliance so important for success in statewide campaigns against the Republicans.

By the mid-1950s, in spite of some notable successes, the Liberals had begun to debate the possibility of folding themselves into the Democratic party because the long-term prospects for their independent organization seemed dim. The generation of Jewish workers that had provided the nucleus of the party was fading. The garment industry had begun to decline and the membership of Rose's Hatters' union, and more importantly Dubinsky's ILGWU, was shrinking. While a respectable share of the party's votes came from such union members, much more importantly, the labor organizations had always provided the hard core supporters who did the work that kept the party together and provided an alternative ballot line on election day. More and more, both unions were composed of black and Puerto Rican workers, rather than Jewish immigrants. The latter were retiring, or dying. The new workers, although philosophically in tune with the Liberal agenda, did not share the cultural solidarity of the Jewish labor movement that had created Socialists in the early part of the century, ALP adherents later, and finally Liberals. The new needle trade workers of mid-century made their political home in the Democratic party. The Jewish sons and daughters of the generation that created the Liberal party were not a source of new members either. Continual efforts to create a Coalition of Young Liberals, a vehicle within the party to attract youthful supporters, failed. The politically active among the younger generation of Jews had become Democrats, many of them members of the party's rising reform wing.[74]

Among some Liberals, there was the sense that with the Democrats nominating men like Wagner and Harriman, Tammany had finally reformed for good. In the future the machine would present only honest, well qualified, liberal candidates for important posts, they reasoned. The Liberal party, the thinking went, had therefore done its work, and consequently it had become safe to dissolve the organization and make common cause with the Democrats. At different times important members of the leadership, including former party chairman Adolph A. Berle, and at one point even Alex Rose, seemed to accept this logic. David Dubinsky never did. He retained a visceral distrust of New York's Democratic party until the day he died. Whenever others felt that perhaps the time had come to merge, he protested. Only the existence of the Liberal party, Dubinsky felt, with the threat it could pose to the Democrats if they did not nominate acceptable candidates, would keep the machine from degenerating back into a party of corruption and reaction. The Liberals should maintain their separate organization, he insisted, and join with the Democrats against Republicans whenever it made sense to do so.[75]

Joining with the Democrats behind Wagner in 1957 was easy. The mayor's record made him an attractive candidate for the Liberals, and his victory seemed guaranteed. To maintain some semblance of independence the Liberals ran separate nominees for City Council that year. The ploy did not satisfy the party's purists, who were embarrassed to be allied with Tammany, while the New York Post, which typically editorialized in favor of the Liberals, accused them of "surrender." But at least the Liberals had the good sense to surrender into victory.[76]

The Republicans, facing a hopeless task, dumped their nomination on Robert K. Christenberry, the first loser who agreed to accept it. A respectable Tennessee born businessman of some stature, with an adequate but uncompelling record in public affairs, the man was no politician. Shortly after he arrived in New York, Christenberry publicly denounced the police for not chasing undesirables away from the area surrounding the Hotel Astor, of which he was General Manager. Within twenty-four hours New York's finest responded by raiding an illegal crap shooting game taking place in the Hotel Astor itself. Reporters had been tipped to guarantee that the establishment got a full dose of negative publicity, and the gentleman from Tennessee learned something about talking tough with the cops who ruled New York's streets.[77]

The mismatch between Christenberry and Wagner started out large and grew. A confidential survey of city voters that the mayor's campaign staff commissioned from Louis Harris and Associates in August showed Wagner headed for a 350,000 vote victory. A follow-up study in October had him leading by even more. It also concluded that so few New Yorkers had an opinion about the unknown man running on the Republican ticket that the election had turned into a Wagner referendum.[78]

The Harris polls broke the totals down into component ethnic parts and analyzed what each of the city's major groups liked or disliked about the mayor. Italians, divided about evenly between the mayor and his opponent, were noticeably more apathetic about the election than others. Although Wagner was Catholic, he was not one of them, and some of his social policies sat uneasily with people concerned about rising taxes. The Irish too worried about taxes, but approved of the mayor's efforts to provide middle-income housing. Moreover, Wagner had been raised Catholic at the behest of his Irish mother, and according to the survey, her people "trusted" him in a way the Italians did not. The Harris study discovered that six Irish voters in ten planned to cast ballots for the incumbent as of October. The city's German voters normally tended to vote Republican, but they liked the son of the German immigrant running City Hall who had a strong respect for law and order. In August, this small group favored Christenberry slightly, but by October a bare majority had shifted to Wagner. The mayor's slum clearance program and good civil rights record made him popular with blacks. During the campaign New York's City Council considered legislation forbidding landlords to discriminate against minorities when renting apartments. The mayor announced he would sign the measure into law as soon as the Council passed it. Almost seven of ten blacks supported the man who made that commitment.

Although the mayor enjoyed majority support from most of the city's ethnic groups, the report concluded unequivocally that his most secure base of support was with Jews: "Wagner stands very strong, indeed with this group. It shows the least sign of defecting. . . . There is a tendency among the Jews to feel Christenberry is a 'reactionary.' Wagner's strength is positive and firm here. He is thought to be a New Deal liberal, strong on housing, and given growing credit for making good appointments in his Administration. The only weak point among Jewish voters is a skepticism about the Mayor's ties with Tammany Hall."

The report continued with the observation that: "Emphasis on the long-standing liberalism of the Mayor among Jewish voters will firm up this group. Also, it is important for Wagner to make a strong statement, repeated often, about his own personal dedication to honest and clean government. The only worry here is that corruption charges could dent the Jewish vote."

In early October, three Jews out of four indicated they would vote for Wagner, more than any other group. The polls also emphasized that "by and large, the people of New York City know and like Bob Wagner. . . . [They] consider [him] a warm and friendly man. He is thought to be a man of deep principle and absolute integrity. There is widespread feeling that he understands and champions the underdog and is conscientious about his duties as Mayor."[79]

While the polls told the story of Wagner's success with the average New Yorker, the mayor had also taken steps to ensure himself the support of the city's elite. Just after his election in 1953 he assigned Nathan Straus, a respected member of the city's German Jewish community, the task of creating the Mayor's Advisory Council. The goal, as its chairman understood it, was "to forge a new kind of instrument of city government. . . [to] lead to effective participation in municipal administration of New York's leading citizens." Straus hoped to spearhead the effort to "draw into city government the best brains in every field of New York life, as a continuing source of guidance and counsel for the new administration."

The mayor's objective was less ambitious and less noble: "If you get people into a room with you and talk to them, they will find it harder to be against you," he told a political aide. Wagner sought to co-opt the segment of New York society that had so often organized rebellion against the city's Democratic mayors. So successful was the effort, when matched with Wagner's record, that the Citizens Union, the bane of Tammany politicians past, wrote Wagner a glowing reelection endorsement in 1957.[80]

The coalition Wagner built stretched the length and breadth of the most diverse city in America; it reached from New York's gutters to its society ballrooms. The mayor beat his opponent by nearly one million votes, running stronger, apparently, with all segments of the metropolis than even his own polls predicted.[81]

Rumblings of Reform

During that same election, reform clubs mounted efforts to win Democratic leadership posts in twenty of Manhattan's thirty-three districts. The primary contests took place six weeks before the 1957 general election, and the neighborhood races had a different dynamic than the mayoralty campaign. Although DeSapio's candidates benefited from the boss's close association with the popular and powerful mayor, the reformers too had endorsed Wagner. To distinguish themselves from their opponents, the reformers accused the regulars of trying to keep power concentrated in the hands of a few instead of encouraging broader public participation, and of using their influence to undermine the independence of elected officials. Political manipulation of the judicial selection process was singled out as particularly offensive; judgeships were for sale, the reformers claimed accurately.

The campaign had some effect. The Lexington Club reelected Jack Baltzell without opposition. Just south of their domain Edward Costikyan, who became the second reformer to penetrate the Executive Committee of the Manhattan Democratic party when he defeated the regular district leader in 1955, won again. On the Upper West Side William Fitts Ryan and Shirley Kaye of the Riverside Club soundly defeated Tammany's choices. Even in DeSapio's home district the Village Independent Democrats mounted a surprisingly strong effort, though they could not displace the boss.[82]

By this time the reform clubbers were amateurs only in that few made their living at politics the way many regulars did. In other respects, they had much in common with Tammany. They assigned precinct captains to collect the signatures they needed to qualify their candidates for the ballot and to befriend neighborhood voters. Just as the regular machine had long helped local residents surmount the difficulties of urban living, so the reformers set up housing clinics to advise renters how to assert their rights. They provided free legal advice to those who could not afford to pay, and established polio inoculation clinics for those who had not found their way to government financed programs.[83]

The successful efforts of the Riverside reformers in 1957 depended in part on the Lexington Club's poll watchers, who had learned the tricks of the trade the hard way during the previous eight years and who traveled cross town on election day to help their fellow reformers. A defector from the regulars who was well connected with some of the West Side's wealthier Democrats raised an election fund that exceeded seven thousand dollars, a considerable sum for a campaign for an unpaid party position in the mid-1950s. The reformers presented a balanced ticket—tall, handsome, liberal, Irish Catholic Bill Ryan for male district leader, and a young Jewish woman, Shirley Kaye, for co-leader. (While both won, the latter out-polled Ryan in the heavily Jewish district).[84]

The reformers campaigned on the streets, put up posters, mailed literature, and sent sound trucks around their neighborhoods. In a tactic that would have made Richard Croker proud, on a hot summer night the Riverside Club parked a vehicle armed with huge loudspeakers outside the regular headquarters where Carmine DeSapio was trying to address the local party workers. In order to hear the county leader over the noisy entreaties to vote for Ryan and Kaye, the regulars had to shut the club door and endure the steamy summer discomfort of their unventilated quarters.[85]

But a few defeats in district leader campaigns are hardly enough to undo a political boss. DeSapio still held the loyalty of a comfortable majority of the New York County Democratic Party Executive Committee. He had the gratitude of a newly triumphant mayor, and the confidence of the governor, who would stand for reelection the next year. The boss, who had inherited a party under siege in 1949, by the end of 1957 had forged substantial peace among his party's feuding factions. The chinks in his armor were modest in comparison to his ability to keep Tammany's candidates in office. DeSapio had found a winning formula, or so it seemed.

SIX

Boss Blow-Out

1958–1960

Return of the Boss

Averell Harriman's renomination as Democratic candidate for governor of New York in 1958 was certain. There was no thought of unseating his lieutenant, George DeLuca, or the sitting Democratic controller, Arthur Levitt, so the Democrats had to consider nominations for only two statewide positions. Irving Ives, the incumbent Republican United States Senator, was retiring, and Louis Lefkowitz, the Republican attorney general appointed by the State Legislature following Jacob Javits's Senate victory in 1956, would stand for election for the first time. Custom gave an incumbent governor the principal voice in determining which candidates would run with him on his ticket, so Democrats waited for Governor Harriman to speak.[1]

Harriman was Protestant, and Jacob Javits a Jew, so the politics of the moment called for an Irish Catholic candidate for the other seat in the Senate. The demand was all the more compelling because in 1956 an alarming number of Catholics had abandoned the Democrats to vote for Eisenhower. More than a few of the old-time district leaders complained that the party was paying so much attention to the liberal Jewish wing that it was alienating its traditional supporters and needed to mend its fences. Wagner, who sought his party's nomination for Senate in 1952, and who had received it and run well in the face of a Republican landslide in 1956, was an obvious choice for the spot. Although the mayor had promised the electorate he would serve out a second term when he ran for reelection as mayor in 1957, he might have reconsidered had Harriman not insulted him. A series of petty scandals surfaced in the New York City Building Department early in 1958 and the governor, protective of his own reputation and presidential ambitions, told his political advisers that he would not have Wagner on his ticket for fear of being associated with graft. Harriman's high handedness left the mayor more than a little peeved when he got wind of the comment.

Once Harriman had vetoed the potential nominee around whom an easy consensus could have been built, he faced the task of developing support for an alternative. He proposed Thomas E. Murray, a one time member of the Atomic Energy Commission under President Truman. But Harriman, perfectly comfortable with powerful men in Moscow, London, and Washington, showed little skill in managing the men who ran political affairs in Manhattan, Albany, and Erie County. The governor never noticed that his choice did not sit well with important party officials in New York City and around New York State, including Carmine DeSapio. The bosses wanted to win, and they found Murray unenergetic and uninspiring.

The reform wing of the Democrats and the Liberal party arrived at a consensus of their own in favor of Thomas K. Finletter, former Secretary of the Air Force under President Truman and a high level speech writer for Adlai Stevenson. DeSapio disliked the former Stevenson aide who sympathized with the reform clubbers in their battles with the boss for control of Tammany. And Finletter was sure to back another Stevenson presidential bid in 1960, something DeSapio thought counterproductive. In short, neither Finletter nor Murray suited DeSapio, and with Harriman doing little to promote his candidate, the boss sensed an opening. He moved to fill it by garnering his forces behind Manhattan District Attorney Frank Hogan.

The Irish Catholic DA met the ethnic requirement for the nomination, and although he had never held a public policy-making post, by reputation he could be relied on to support liberal positions. Honest, well known, and well respected, Hogan, DeSapio reasoned, would be acceptable to the reform wing of the Democratic party and to the Liberals as well. The choice especially suited DeSapio because by boosting Hogan to the Senate, the Manhattan boss would then have the chance to put a new protege in the district attorney's spot. DeSapio rapidly organized his counterparts from the other boroughs of New York City, and to round out his position, cut a deal with Peter Crotty, party boss from Buffalo. Crotty had ambitions for the Senate spot himself, but realized he could not gather the votes. The upstate leader settled for DeSapio's commitment to back him for attorney general in return for his pledge to instruct his troops to vote for Hogan.

DeSapio held comfortable majorities for his candidates by the time the Democratic Convention opened in Buffalo at the end of August. In long meetings with DeSapio, Wagner, and state party chairman Michael Prendergast, who played second fiddle to the Manhattan boss, Harriman tried to force support for Murray. DeSapio, knowing he had the votes, refused to budge, while the mayor sat silently, seemingly uninterested. Finally, ignoring his earlier admonitions, the governor asked Wagner to accept the nomination for Senate in order to maintain party unity. The mayor, who had been urged by his family not to undertake the campaign, felt no obligation to rescue the man who had insulted him a few months before. Wagner refused to run, but made it clear that he would support Harriman's choice. He then left the feuding governor and political boss to arrive at their own decision.

Late on the evening of the convention's second day, long after it was scheduled to adjourn, came the announcement that the party's leaders could not agree on a candidate for the Senate seat. Hogan, Murray, and Finletter were all nominated, and on the first ballot the Manhattan district attorney won with 772 votes. Murray received 304 votes, and Finletter 66. Wagner had backed Murray as a courtesy to the governor's office, but to avoid antagonizing the party's liberals announced that Finletter also would have been acceptable to him. Harriman, although he had chosen Murray himself, also let party activists believe he did not oppose Finletter. The delegates named Crotty the party's candidate for attorney general without much controversy.

The next day, and in the weeks to come, newspaper stories about the Democrats had a single theme: "Mr. DeSapio, who has never held elective public office, had more influence in the Democratic party than the Governor of the state and the Mayor of its largest city, combined." In spite of nine years of concerted efforts to create an image of himself as an open minded political leader, DeSapio, in a single event, recaptured the label of autocratic boss. Wagner had been offended by De-Sapio's actions, and let the boss know it before leaving Buffalo, but he kept the conflict in perspective. The mayor had not paid much attention to the nominations that year, had backed a candidate late and without much enthusiasm, and unfortunately had not prevailed. To the long-time veteran, that was politics. Harriman resented not being allowed to pick his own running mates, but he never did understand domestic politics, and had brought the embarrassment on himself.[2]

The liberal wing of the Democratic party, however, steamed. Their darling, Thomas K. Finletter, never had a serious chance, yet they acted as if he had and took the loss personally. Two weeks after the convention, Pulitzer Prize–winning historian Arthur Schlesinger, a prominent liberal intellectual and New York City Democrat, wrote, "Tom Finletter's defeat in Buffalo was the New York County organization's revenge on the Lexington Democratic Club." He described the battle in apocalyptic terms that reformers echoed less eloquently in clubhouses around New York: "The essence of the know-nothing revolt, in short, is to wipe out the transformation wrought in the Democratic Party by Franklin Roosevelt and the New Deal and recreate something like the Democratic Party of the twenties . . . a party without ideas, program, energy or zeal." Then he got to the heart of the matter: "We will be told that [Hogan] will vote right on specific bills. But liberalism is more than voting the way the party leadership says; it implies intellectual curiosity, moral passion and a creative approach to public policy." Simply put, Frank Hogan would vote into law the policies liberal Democrats wanted, but somehow, the Irish Catholic prosecutor was not one of them. The liberals, long content to determine the policies of the Democrats while leaving the party administration to the professionals, now wanted to control the party outright. The formula that had worked since the days of Charles Francis Murphy was no longer acceptable.[3]

Shortly after the Democratic convention split that party wide open, the Liberals met. They had never endorsed a Republican in a statewide contest, but in the past they had run independent candidates when the Democratic choice displeased them. The practice effectively ensured a Republican victory even when that was not its express intent. Letters mailed to Liberal party Executive Director Ben Davidson ran about three to one in favor of championing Finletter for Senate, but the potential candidate did not want to burn his bridges with the Democratic party he hoped someday would nominate him. Finletter declined to run on the Liberal ticket alone. The membership "would have stampeded for an independent candidate" even then according to Adolf Berle, but Dubinsky, Rose, and others arranged to have the question put over for a week to allow for sober consideration.[4]

The Liberal party leadership sized up Congressman Kenneth Keating, the Republican nominee for Senate, and found him unacceptably conservative. They did not want to take any action that would help his chances, so they decided to endorse Hogan. At the same time, to demonstrate their displeasure with the "bossed" nature of the Democratic selections, they urged nomination of an independent candidate for attorney general. He would run against Peter Crotty, the Buffalo boss who held the Democratic line, and against the likable, liberal, Jewish, Republican incumbent, Louis Lefkowitz. In a circular distributed to Liberal party members, the party leaders wrote that they had adopted a policy "to elect to the U.S. Senate a candidate with liberal views of unquestioned integrity and ability as against an ultra-conservative Republican, whose voting record is bad on labor, housing, social security, taxation, public power, and on many key international issues." They had rejected Crotty because, "he does not measure up to our standard and because of his role as the Buffalo machine leader together with those from New York City who over-rode Governor Harriman's wishes and those of other great liberal Democratic leaders as Herbert H. Lehman on the question of candidates."[5]

The circular left much unsaid. The Liberal party leadership had a long-standing grudge against Crotty. For years they had tried unsuccessfully to establish themselves in the city that the Irish Catholic boss ran. They had appealed to Crotty to allow some of his candidates to run with the Liberal party endorsement, and had asked him to share some patronage with their meager ranks. The professional in Crotty never saw much reason for deference to the Liberals, who could muster only a few dozen active members in Erie County and typically delivered just a few thousand votes for local candidates.[6]

The party rank and file found the claim that Crotty did not meet Liberal standards easy to believe, for "reasons more visceral than logical," Daniel Patrick Moynihan, in 1958 a Harriman aide, would write later. Moynihan viewed the Buffalo Democrat as "a man of intellect, a diligent student of Catholic social theory, a formidable labor lawyer, and a passionate believer in racial equality." The distrust came because "organized liberals cannot help being suspicious of the liberalism of Irish Catholic county leaders who are at ease on city councils and who get along with police chiefs." The Liberals dumped Crotty because they wanted to steer clear of charges that they followed the lead of Democratic bosses, and they found it particularly convenient to make him the example. They nominated a fine young lawyer named Edward Goodell, who had no chance of victory, but whose candidacy guaranteed Louis Lefkowitz four more years in office.[7]

Meanwhile, the Republicans delighted in their opponents' disarray. They had nominated Nelson Rockefeller as their candidate for governor, and when his mouth was not filled with the ethnic food of one group or another as he campaigned around the state with ferocious energy, he carried on at great length about the bossed character of the Democrats, their lack of independence, the back room nature of their decisions, and the corruption that it all implied. Harriman appeared the dupe of Tammany Hall, while Rockefeller came across as strong enough to be his own man. *The New York Post*, normally supportive of Liberal party choices, endorsed Harriman late, but also said that it regarded Rockefeller, "as a man of liberal impulse and personal attractiveness." The Liberal party's Adolf Berle wrote a confidential seventeen-page economic policy memorandum for Rockefeller at the candidate's request, even though the Liberals had endorsed Harriman. In a radio interview he announced his intention to vote for Harriman," but, noted that "these are two first-rate men. . . . I am good friends with them both . . . New York is lucky to have them both."[8]

Among other inroads, Rockefeller seemed to be making headway among Jewish voters. Late in the campaign, in an effort to stabilize his standing with Jews, Harriman tried to tie Rockefeller to foreign policy decisions made by President Eisenhower and Secretary of State Dulles that were perceived as anti-Israeli. Dorothy Schiff, Publisher of the *Post* and a sometime lover of Rockefeller's, reacted to Harriman's comments by taking the extraordinary measure of printing the following letter on the front page of her newspaper:[9]

TO POST READERS:

Gov. Harriman's recent snide insinuation that Nelson Rockefeller is pro-Arab and anti-Israel should not be condoned by any fair-minded person. Rockefeller, far from being anti-Israel, has been a liberal contributor to the United Jewish Appeal for 12 years. It is deplorable but true that in political campaigns lower echelons on both sides indulge in vile demagoguery. But when the head of the ticket repeats such libels, he should be punished by the voters. If you agree with me, do not vote for Averell Harriman tomorrow.

Dorothy Schiff
Publisher

Rockefeller took the state by 550,000 votes. Newspaper analysts attributed the victory in great part to his success with liberal voters, primarily Jews, who thought Rockefeller a more independent millionaire than the boss controlled Harriman, and just as liberal and just as sensitive to Jewish issues. The assessment that Jewish voters caused Rockefeller's victory overstated the case, but Rockefeller did take more than twenty-seven percent of the Jewish vote on the Republican ticket in 1958, compared to Thomas Dewey's sixteen percent, while running with the advantages of incumbency, eight years earlier. The difference was significant. The rest of the Republican ticket also won, except William Lundy, candidate for controller, who lost to Arthur Levitt, the Democratic incumbent. Levitt, liberal, Jewish, uninvolved in the Buffalo fracas, managed to hold onto his office by a slim margin.[10]

The Democrats had placed Thomas Finletter in charge of the Citizens Committee for Harriman and Hogan in an effort to create party unity following the divisive convention. The disappointed candidate had the chance to prove himself worthy of future support by swallowing hard and helping the party to victory. But long time Democratic campaign staffers found that the information they sent to the Finletter team never got used. Speeches drafted by men skilled at finding the themes that touched New York's voters somehow got lost. Finletter's people, in the eyes of the regulars, sabotaged the 1958 election. The bitterness between reformers and regulars was growing.[11]

Harriman's loss was the first of an incumbent governor in New York State since 1922, and the Democratic debacle in New York contrasted sharply with the party's success in elections across the country in 1958. Liberal Democrats blamed the devastating defeat on Carmine DeSapio's impolitic display of power in Buffalo. The man who received the credit for key victories in 1953 and 1954 now got the blame for failure. That same year, DeSapio entered into a feud with black Democrats in Manhattan.

Politics Comes to Harlem

Harlem Congressman Adam Clayton Powell, Jr. was the most prominent black political figure in the nation in the 1950s. Born in New York in 1908, he was the grandson of a slave and the son of the pastor of the Abyssinian Baptist Church which, with its 10,000 black worshippers, was one of the largest congregations in the world. When Powell inherited his father's pulpit in 1937, he became an automatic presence in

New York City. Tall, athletic, and handsome, he cut a dramatic figure when he stood in front of his parishioners. He spoke with forceful, sophisticated eloquence. Educated first in Harlem's alleys, and then at Colgate College, he combined the words of a learned man with the cadence and rhythm of a black gospel preacher.[12]

Not long after he assumed his father's mantle, with the nation still suffering the harsh unemployment of the depression, Powell helped lead a boycott against white store owners on Harlem's 125th Street who refused to hire blacks. Ultimately, the "Don't Buy Where You Can't Work" campaign broke down the discriminatory hiring practices that prevailed in the very center of the country's largest black community. In 1941, Powell, nominally a Democrat, ran for City Council on the ALP and City Fusion tickets that had Fiorello LaGuardia at their head, and won easily. Congressional redistricting in 1943 combined black neighborhoods that had been split deliberately into three different parts to prevent election of a black. Powell, the obvious candidate for the newly created district, received the Democratic, Republican, and ALP nominations, and Harlem elected New York's first black congressman without opposition in 1944.

By then Powell had already adopted an inimitable style. Irreverently, irrepressibly, eloquently and continually, he reminded whites that they mistreated the people of his race. For that, the blacks in Harlem loved him. In Washington, a southern town in many ways in 1944, Powell insisted on all of the privileges due to a member of Congress. He would enter through no back doors, accept no second class treatment, and above all, not sit quietly and wait for the white leadership to decide what he could and could not do.

An outsider in the system, Powell doubted he would ever be treated fairly by the men who controlled the House of Representatives. Until he became chairman of the Committee on Education and Labor and sensed a real chance to accomplish important things, Powell did not even try to achieve legislative successes. He compiled a miserable attendance record, and according to even his most sympathetic colleagues was never to be found when the painstaking details of legislation needed to be worked out. But as a member of the Education committee he attached a clause to bill after bill intended to provide federal funding for school construction forbidding the money to be used for segregated institutions. The Powell Amendment, as it became known, time and again forced the Democratic party to confront the dilemma of race. The southern wing refused to pass any legislation that contained Powell's language, so no funds for schools flowed from federal coffers to northern cities, whose legislators desperately wanted them. The southerners hated him for nearly everything he did, and above all the way he did it, the northerners for preventing them from conducting business as usual until they confronted the plight of the black man.

The more that powerful whites disliked Powell, the more popular he became in Harlem. He drove fast cars, owned fancy homes and married a succession of beautiful women, including actress Isabel Washington, followed later by jazz pianist Hazel Scott. There were others along the way. He traveled to islands in the sun when it got cold, and took European tours when the climate was comfortable. He did, more often than not, what he damn well pleased. To an impoverished, oppressed and bitter people, it was a source of joy near delight that one of their own could dance in the white man's world with impunity, break all the rules that their race had been taught brutally to follow, and get away with it. The worse Powell's offenses, the happier he made his constituents. Between 1944 and 1958 Powell won reelection by margins of between two and four to one.

Just about the time of his first inauguration into Congress, Powell announced, "I will never be a machine man. I will represent the Negro people first. I will represent after that all of the other American people." Yet, for the purposes of congressional seniority, he was a Democrat. When he was present for party votes he generally sided with the leadership, except on matters of race. He was never part of the traditional Democratic organization in New York City, but never really opposed to it either, and one supposes that Carmine DeSapio understood that Powell was simply part of the political landscape. "Adam is unbeatable," a Harlem politician once observed. "My Lord, he has 10,000 parishioners—and every one is a campaign worker before election time. Who can build a better machine?" About one tenth of the congressional district's registered Democrats belonged to the Abyssinian Baptist Church. "I speak to 4,000 people every Sunday—that's more than a Tammany district leader sees in a year," Powell once said. [13]

And yet, there were limits to the degree of antagonism that other politicians would bear quietly, even from an invulnerable office holder. In 1956 the Democratic party, after a bitter fight over its national platform, adopted a lukewarm civil rights plank in an effort to appease its southern members. The compromise angered many blacks. Powell, who harbored a grudge against Adlai Stevenson for once having slighted him, decided to endorse Eisenhower. The event had no measurable effect on the black vote, but it did insult the New York County Democratic organization where such a display of independence ran counter to everything that the machine believed about party loyalty. And Powell held office in the borough that Carmine DeSapio ruled. The boss felt that for the good of the party, and to maintain his standing with his troops, he could not let the matter go unpunished. So, in 1958, when Powell's next election approached, and with the Harlem congressman under indictment for tax evasion, DeSapio called together the district leaders whose domains included pieces of Powell's congressional district. He informed them that the incumbent would not be the choice of the party. If Powell wanted to stay in office he would have to run against the machine candidate in a primary, except that the machine did not yet have a candidate.[14]

Perhaps to DeSapio it did not much matter who opposed Powell. He knew he could not unseat the man, and was simply making a statement that disloyalty to the Democratic organization would not be rewarded with the party's nomination. But by dumping Powell before naming someone to contest the seat, DeSapio became the target of Powell's brilliant invective. Suddenly, "Carmine, the Mississippi boss" was out to get Adam. "I ran away from the plantation in 1956 and now Carmine's trying to brand me," Powell said, reminding listeners that as a boy he had run his hands over the brand in his grandfather's back, put there by a slavemaster who had caught the man trying to flee. In the New York political vernacular, DeSapio normally came from "downtown," in Greenwich Village, Powell from "uptown," in Harlem. During the 1958 contest, DeSapio was from "down South,"—a reference to the part of Manhattan where the Tammany chief lived in terms that evoked an emotional response from black audiences. Powell's campaign issued pamphlets with the bold title: "The Truth About the Dixiecrat-DeSapio's Conspiracy to Remove Powell from Congress." Harlem's voters, who had often had an uneasy relationship with Tammany Hall, rallied to the cause of the man who embodied their dreams.

Two days after DeSapio's announcement Powell and Tammany's token black borough president, Hulan Jack, appeared together at an NAACP rally in Harlem. "Send that uncle Tom back downtown!," the crowd yelled when Jack, who supported his party's decision to dump Powell, tried to speak. The scene risked getting ugly until Powell rose and soothed his defenders. Hulan Jack, supposedly the senior black official in New York City, was shaken. A few days later, Powell, playing to a crowd rather than calming it, warned DeSapio and Jack to "stay off the streets of Harlem or we'll make it mighty uncomfortable." When they got around to naming his opponent, he declared, "we'll be waiting on the streets of Harlem." The respectable elements of New York, including the NAACP, immediately condemned the thinly veiled vow of violence. But the reaction among blacks to the civil rights organization's position was so intense that within twenty-four hours Executive Secretary Roy Wilkins retreated. "We have not denounced representative Powell," he declared apologetically.

Not surprisingly, no one wanted to run against Powell. Four candidates turned down the backing of the Democratic organization. Hulan Jack took his cue from the crowd that had threatened him and decided to wait for the end of the campaign in the safety of the borough president's office. Thurgood Marshall, the black lawyer who in 1954 tried the *Brown v. Board of Education* case before the Supreme Court and who ultimately become a justice of the court himself, said he and Powell were on the same side. Harlem Assemblywoman Bessie Buchanan declined. Her husband was a former partner of Powell's in a journalistic endeavor, and he objected to his wife's opposing an old friend. James H. Robinson, a prominent Harlem minister, refused, announcing that "the Democratic leadership, both of Harlem and of the city, seems neither to have fully understood nor accurately gauged the basic political attitudes, unspoken but deep resentments and desires of the people of Harlem."

Finally, Councilman Earl Brown, a fifty-five year old Harvard graduate, a seemingly respectable man who did his share of fighting with Hulan Jack and other Harlem Tammanyites, agreed to run for the good of the Democratic party. He insisted that Jack stay out of the campaign, and that the Democrats pay for every penny of the losing proposition, which they did. Brown waged a dignified, if doomed effort. He himself realized he was the "forgotten man" of the contest.

In years past, when Tammany confronted an adversary it could not defeat at the polls, it sometimes succeeded in the courts. New York's election law was (and is) a technical minefield laid quite deliberately by incumbents to explode the ambitions of the uninitiated. Powell, temperamentally unsuited for the kind of work involved in qualifying for the ballot, could have fallen victim to Tammany's election petition auditors and lost his place on the ballot before Harlem's voters ever had a chance to react, except for J. Raymond Jones.

If Adam Clayton Powell was the political general who inspired his troops to battle by the thousands, then J. Raymond Jones was the tactician who channeled the quasi-religious fervor to where it would do the most good. If the one was the star of Harlem's political show, the other was its director. Powell, from the start of his career, spoke over the heads of the local party leaders and established his position by virtue of eloquent leadership of Harlem's largest church. Jones had come up through Tammany's ranks. He had learned his politics house by house, electoral district by electoral district, in the trenches of Harlem's political warfare.

Born in the Virgin Islands in 1899, the son of a teacher, Jones finished grade school before World War I began. At the age of sixteen he shipped out to sea. He arrived in New York in 1918, worked as a redcap porter for the railways at Pennsylvania Station, then as a truant officer. For a time he ran his own bicycle shop, and later ran the ice concession for the first black cooperative residence in New York, the Dunbar Apartments. During the 1920s Jones lived in the predominantly white Twenty-Second assembly district on the northern border of Harlem, and he recognized that continued black migration into New York made politics a growth industry for a shrewd member of the race.[15]

He mastered the nominating petition process, worked diligently, and as the neighborhood became more and more black, Jones became an increasingly important lieutenant of Irish district leader John Kelly. His labors first bore fruit in 1936 when he was appointed Deputy U.S. Marshall. Afterwards, he held a series of government jobs. He assumed a district leader's post in 1941 when the local incumbent resigned, and with many of Manhattan's blacks gerrymandered into white districts, Jones was one of the few spokesman for his race inside Tammany. He played a prominent role during O'Dwyer's 1945 mayoralty campaign, and struck up a strong relationship with the Irishman. The political friendship between the two men landed Jones an appointment as Deputy Housing Commissioner in 1947, the highest city government job then held by a black. During O'Dwyer's complicated maneuverings with Tammany he was heard to remark remorsefully that if Jones were white, he would put him in charge of the Hall. O'Dwyer considered the Harlem leader the most astute politician in the city, but knew the party organization would revolt rather than obey a black man.

Jones entered into a sort of hibernation in 1953. He kept a city job, but resigned as district leader citing poor health. Rumors circulated that he had bumped heads with DeSapio, but over what is unknown. So Jones sat on the sidelines for five years, until, in 1958, DeSapio announced Powell could not have the Democratic party's support for reelection. Certain that Harlem would return Powell to Congress by a margin of ten to one, Jones, never a particularly close friend of Powell's, but never an enemy either, resigned his post with the city to manage the congressman's campaign. With a pro like Jones handling the mechanical side of the election contest, Tammany had little chance of knocking its opponent off the ballot. In an extraordinarily large turnout for a primary, Powell took more than three-quarters of the vote. On election day, Powell beat Brown by ten to one, just as Jones had predicted.

It had been a tough 1958 for Carmine DeSapio, and as the next year approached, Powell, at Jones's direction, set out to conquer Harlem's district leadership spots and organize them into a single unit of black politicians that would wield clout within Tammany. Another of New York's ethnic groups was coming of political age. Meanwhile, Herbert Lehman, the man who symbolized all that was good in politics to New York's liberal Jewish voters, had come to the conclusion that he must destroy Carmine DeSapio.

The Wrath of Herbert Lehman

Herbert Lehman became great by being good. He did not have the unique vision that charts a new course for a nation, nor did he own the oratorical powers that make hearts beat faster and chests swell. Rather, he possessed an unshakeable moral conviction, a rock solid confidence that he knew the difference between right and wrong. It was an attitude that could easily have led to arrogance, but by personal constitution Herbert Lehman was a humble man. He was a servant of the people, not their master. [16]

As governor, he brought the New Deal to the Empire State with energy and efficiency linking him directly to President Roosevelt and Mayor LaGuardia. The three men became a holy trinity of elected officials in the minds of New Yorkers. By the time Lehman entered the Senate in 1949, with Roosevelt and LaGuardia gone, he had become a symbol of liberalism in his own state, and around the nation as well. Never quite comfortable with the compromises needed for legislative success, Lehman left no lasting legacy on the nation's law books, but for seven years he served as the liberal conscience of the Senate. When Joseph McCarthy indicted men and women with innuendo Herbert Lehman rose on the Senate floor and asked to see the proof. When McCarthy accused people who criticized the dirty tactics of his staff attorneys, Roy Cohn and David Schine, of anti-Semitic motives, it was Lehman, the nation's preeminent Jewish statesman, who responded: "... I—a Jew, sensitive to any religious bias—have been strongly critical of the behaviour of these young men. . . . I am very certain that most members of my religious faith, not as Jews, but as Americans, are anything but proud of [them]."[17]

Lehman's religious beliefs were an integral part of his political and social philosophy. "In a very real sense, the aims and ideals of the Jewish religion are identical with the purposes of democracy," he wrote late in his life. "The sense of duty and right, the passion for freedom and justice, and the faithful obedience of the Law and the Word of God are basic tenets of the Jewish heritage and are also the heart and soul of America," Lehman believed. He defined his liberalism in intensely moral terms: "In essence, it means to do justice in every situation, to use every effort and legitimate means to insure equality to all people. It takes for granted the inherent rights of every human being to enjoy equal opportunity in every field, decent living and working conditions, adequate provision for the moral and spiritual development of his children, and free association with our fellow men as equals under the law and in the sight of God." He was proud that his appointment by President Roosevelt to lead the United Nation's Relief and Rehabilitation Administration was inspired, in part, because FDR, "wanted Hitler and the Nazis to know that he was appointing a Jew to bring relief and rehabilitation to the people and areas they had ravaged. My appointment was to be a symbol to the world."[18]

Lehman's eightieth birthday, in March 1958, was an event for New York liberals. It inspired a gala dinner in his honor, and a Sunday magazine article in *The New York Times* entitled, "Lehman at 80: Young Elder Statesman." In it, having exhausted all superlatives in the text, the author resorted to the bible to capture the meaning of Lehman's life: "Those who have had in any measure the joy of knowing him . . . will be tempted on his eightieth birthday to take up the Book of Wisdom and read there once again the just man: 'He shall show forth the discipline he hath learnt and shall glory in the law of the covenant of the Lord. Many shall praise his wisdom and it shall not be forgotten. And the memory of him shall not depart from the earth.' " In New York's liberal Jewish community, Herbert Lehman was "practically God," in the words of one young political activist. Following the 1958 Buffalo nominating convention, Lehman aimed his wrath at Carmine DeSapio.[19]

Lehman was lecturing and vacationing in Europe when the New York State nominating convention took place. Before leaving the United States, acting through Julius C. C. Edelstein, his chief assistant, Lehman secured a commitment from DeSapio to respect the wishes of the Democratic party's senior elected officials when it came time to nominate someone for the Senate. Lehman made it clear that he supported Finletter, but understood that Harriman was backing Murray, and respected the governor's right to run on a ticket with a candidate he preferred. In the days leading up to the convention Edelstein stayed in close contact with Lehman, who, in an effort to reaffirm his position, made several unsuccessful attempts to speak with DeSapio by transatlantic telephone. The Tammany leader avoided the calls. Lehman read about the convention in the newspapers, and shortly afterward received a long memorandum from Edelstein detailing the complicated backroom negotiations that preceded the final outcome. The episode infuriated Lehman.[20]

Up until 1958 Lehman's relationship with DeSapio had been cordial and proper, at times friendly. After the events of the nominating convention, it never would be again. In the first place Lehman felt that DeSapio misled him. The boss had agreed to honor the wishes of the party's elected representatives, but then launched a secret movement behind a candidate of his own choosing. Second, Lehman had profound respect for the governor's office that he had occupied for a decade. He was outraged that DeSapio publicly humiliated Harriman. Third, he felt that crude displays of power from top party officials discouraged young idealists from participating in politics. In November, when the Democrats lost the election because of Rockefeller's successful use of the charge that the Democrats were a "bossed" party, Lehman decided that DeSapio, and his style of rule, had to go. Meanwhile, Edelstein was devising a plan with the help of a top Harriman aide named George Backer.[21]

The Committee for Democratic Voters

The Democratic reform clubs that had emerged around Manhattan, and which to a much lesser extent were bubbling up elsewhere in the city, were independent groups that did not often act in concert in 1958. After all, the disciplined control that the regular organization exercised over party affairs was one of the main sources of frustration for the insurgents. It was only natural that they did not create a central authority of their own. The Lexington Democrats, as the most senior and experienced of the new clubs, and one of the wealthiest, helped some of the others to organize. But apart from that, there was little effective coordination. Edelstein and Backer reasoned that a citywide umbrella group, headed by senior officials of the Democratic party, could bring coherence to the diffuse and spastic movement to overhaul the machine.[22]

Efforts to get Governor Harriman and Mayor Wagner to join the cause failed. They did not like what DeSapio had done in Buffalo, but they were not impressed with the reformers and saw little advantage in splitting the party. Lehman plowed ahead nevertheless. He convinced Eleanor Roosevelt to add her prestige to the effort, and Thomas Finletter as well. Mrs. Roosevelt approved of a more open party, but brought to the task of removing DeSapio the special bitterness of a mother whose son had been wronged. By her own admission she never forgave the Tammany boss for his role in denying the gubernatorial nomination to FDR, Jr. in 1954. Finletter too, no doubt, desired a Democratic party more accepting of his ideas and of the wing of the party he represented, but as much as anything else he sought to reestablish his own political base. If he could not achieve his ambitions by working with the regular organization, then an alternate source of power made a lot of sense to him.[23]

On January 22, 1959, the three prominent Democrats declared that they were establishing the New York Committee for Democratic Voters. The objectives of the CDV were to promote the organization of all Democrats, to advance the principles of democracy within all the reaches of the Democratic party organization of New York, and to make the organization a vehicle to advance the party's political programs, rather than to serve the "urge for personal power of political professionals." They announced their opposition to the "unrepresentative character" of the party in New York City, and reiterated the belief that it was the stain of "boss rule" that had led the Democrats to defeat in the 1958 election, although they carefully avoided naming anyone as responsible.[24]

Immediately after the announcement, however, answering a reporter's question, Lehman said: "I think that Mr. DeSapio and some of his political associates gave Rockefeller and the Republican party a made-to-order issue of bossism by what happened at Buffalo and at other times. Obviously we are not going to support Mr. DeSapio. We will oppose Mr. DeSapio and hope voters of the state will take steps to remove him." Predictably, the next day's headlines read, "Democratic Liberals Open Drive to Remove DeSapio."[25]

The reform clubbers were angry with Lehman's remarks. Some felt that personalizing the campaign weakened the moral strength of their stand. Others did not want to alienate the Tammany leader because they hoped to use their emerging power to negotiate with him. Lehman was unconcerned. Although without question the least personally motivated of the CDV leaders, three decades of political battles had taught him that a human symbol helped to focus public attention on a cause. He discussed his strategy with Alex Rose, and the two agreed that Carmine DeSapio, with his "dark glasses and saturnine" appearance, was the target they needed for success.[26]

Besides, Lehman had no intention of compromising with DeSapio. He had decided that the boss system was damaging the party, and that he was going to destroy it. Period. Nothing could deter him from his objective. He tried hard not to allow his arguments to degenerate into the kinds of vicious personal accusations so much the currency of political campaigns, and admitted freely, "that there have been, and could still be worse bosses than [DeSapio]." But he remained unrelenting in his opposition to the man because "he is the present leader and symbol of the system of boss rule . . . [which is] a politically corrupting influence . . . whose habit of mind is to view the people as objects of manipulation rather than sovereign and wise."[27]

DeSapio sought to avoid a personal feud. "I will not rebut in kind," he said, the day that the Committee for Democratic Voters announced its intentions. "I respect Senator Lehman too much." He recalled the measures he had taken to encourage voter participation, to open the party and to make it more responsive to policy issues, and declared that he would continue to promote such practices in the future. The next day a *New York Times* editorial agreed with Lehman's stance in principle, but noted that, "Carmine DeSapio is a shining example of political enlightenment . . . compared with some other Tammany bosses of the recent past. The Committee, in its search for a successor, may find it easier to do worse than to do better." Far more than any leader before him, DeSapio had conducted the affairs of the party the way that the Committee demanded.[28]

Armed with that knowledge, and intent on preventing the party from splitting wide open, DeSapio arranged a meeting with Lehman. He made it clear that he was "very anxious to do everything to placate the Committee," short, one supposes, of stepping down himself. Lehman, speaking for the CDV, told the boss, "that we would not deviate from what we were trying to do." DeSapio was still not ready to launch a war, and he hoped to talk some more, but it was becoming increasingly apparent that the party was fracturing.[29]

Mayor Wagner was becoming concerned. He did not want to break with Carmine DeSapio, whose arrogance at Buffalo, and at other times, seemed less important to the mayor than his capable leadership of the party. And DeSapio, of course, was still a potent ally. But Wagner had no desire to fight with Herbert Lehman either, a life-long acquaintance whom he respected and admired, who had helped him in every political campaign he had ever run, and who wielded powerful influence over public opinion.[30]

In February 1959 the mayor reaffirmed his support for the Tammany leader, declaring, "I have always found him . . . to be a good man. He never attempted to interfere with the running of the city." But by April, as the annual Tammany fund-raising dinner approached, Wagner's "delicate sense of self-preservation" had already begun to tingle. The mayor's staff forwarded to him the draft of a speech to deliver before the party faithful that was filled with laudatory comments about the boss. "Do I have to say all these nice things about Carmine?" he asked Warren Moscow, his executive assistant who drafted the speech.

"Well, you don't have to go to the dinner at all," he was advised, "but if you do, you are a guest in his house, and then you have to say them."

Wagner wanted it both ways. He sent Deputy Mayor Paul O'Keefe to deliver the message, claiming, on the evening of the affair, that he could not leave Board of Estimate budget hearings. And the mayor watched the battle lines sharpen.[31]

The press portrayed the contest as one between old-line Democrats, led by DeSapio—and the liberal wing, led by Lehman, Eleanor Roosevelt, and Thomas Finletter. But that battle had long since been won by the liberal wing. DeSapio, by choosing well-qualified, liberal candidates, had helped to fight it. The notion that DeSapio and his followers were corrupt, while the other faction was virtuous, often lurked beneath the surface of the conflict. Yet, there had been no serious scandals involving Democratic party officials in Manhattan during DeSapio's decade as county leader. The closest the boss ever came to being tainted publicly with a charge of corruption occurred the day a cab driver found eleven thousand dollars in the back seat of his vehicle and reported to the police that the last passenger he had dropped off before discovering the loot was the well known Carmine DeSapio. The boss denied the money was his, to the cabbie's ultimate delight. A story circulated that the money had been the price paid for a promotion from Civil Court Judge to Supreme Court Judge, but no charges were ever levied, much less proven.[32]

Tammany district leaders saw nothing ideological or moral in the struggle at all: "The reformers in this city are a sham," one said, expressing a common sentiment. "[They] are young Jewish people who are trying to make a place for themselves in the sun, who are trying to break into politics." The reformers denied this, and took offense at having had their efforts defined in ethnic terms. Yet, the reform clubs were heavily Jewish in membership, and nearly all of the CDV's officers were Jewish. Before long Irving Engle, a former president of the American Jewish Committee, became its chairman. Ultimately the CDV created three new leadership posts expressly for the purpose of "includ[ing] in the roster of officers some non-Jewish individuals," as a matter of window dressing.[33]

The struggle was not over the philosophical orientation of the policies of the Democratic party in New York City, but over who would hold the reins of power. Herbert Lehman believed sincerely that as long as the ruling system endured, one that rewarded obedience and discipline rather than creativity and intelligence, some of the best citizens of the city would stay away from the party, even if its policy goals were commendable. He understood that to revolutionize the internal structure of the regular organization, it had to be utterly torn down and then rebuilt. What the Irish and Italian Catholics holding power understood was that, if Lehman succeeded, they would be replaced by the reform clubbers, most of whom were young Jews.

From the beginning Edelstein, Lehman's chief representative to the umbrella organization, discovered that mixed among the Democratic idealists that he hoped to shape into the spearhead of a newly energized party were more than a few "peanut stuff" politicians, possessed of the same "clubhouse mentality" that the reformers claimed to find so offensive. The efforts of these men, some of the most prominent of the reform club movement, were "neither geared nor focussed on the overall task before us, which is enormous, but rather on personality politics, on maneuver designed to capture power, for a purpose which I sense is quite different from that to which we are publicly committed." In a moment of despair he wrote to his chief: "If in the course of the original discussions, I had seen the faces which are now surrounding me, I would have suggested a good drink instead."[34]

Edelstein continued his sober work because Lehman insisted, but the loyal aide warned that he was, "possessed with fears and suspicions concerning . . . the motivations of the majority of those who have now been involved in the direction of the [Committee]. . . . the manner in which they have operated to date do not give me any confidence in either [sic] their judgment, perspective or overall purposes. . . . The DeSapio people charge, with some justification, that the effort being made is [to move the power to select candidates] from the Biltmore [the hotel where the Democrats traditionally set up campaign headquarters] to Park Avenue [location of the CDV offices]."[35]

Lehman understood the flaws in the group, but he refused to abandon what he considered a just cause, and he needed soldiers to help him fight his battle. He continued to lend his prestige to the movement, and served as chief financial supporter and fund raiser. Through Edelstein he monitored and tried to direct the CDV's evolving structure, but reserved the right to speak and act independently while he concentrated his energies on mounting a campaign to replace DeSapio sponsored district leaders in the September 1959 Democratic party primaries. It was the initial step in Lehman's drive to unhorse the boss himself.[36]

However pure his intentions, New York's preeminent Jewish statesman had become the leader of a push for power by a group of young Jewish political activists. Lehman's presence allowed the reformers to claim that they owned the liberal label, and that they were driven by disinterested virtue. These two characteristics, coupled with Jewish domination of the leadership of the CDV, made the organization culturally appealing to Jews. The Committee, through its prestigious leaders, was able to attract media attention to its cause, and succeeded in inspiring many hundreds of young Jewish volunteers to join the various reform clubs in Manhattan and, to a lesser degree, around the city. Many of these men and women came to fight the good fight, but the ones who made it to the top of the movement, with rare exception, were keenly interested in holding power. Some had actually tried to work within the Democratic political machine but had found it too frustrating, too tedious, and too foreign to suit them. More than philosophy or morality, what separated the regulars and the reformers was a cultural chasm—all of the differences that went into making the center of gravity of the one group working-class, middle-aged, and Catholic, and the other well educated, professional, young, and Jewish.

Substantial numbers of Jews participated in the regular party organization of course; they accepted its rules and benefited accordingly. They were usually distinguishable from their non-Jewish party coworkers only by their greater propensity to support liberal candidates, and in their special sensitivities to such Jewish issues as concern about anti-Semitism and the status of Israel. In some districts, Jews even constituted the largest part of the regular organization's membership, and there were ample numbers of Jewish district leaders and party officials by 1959. But there still had never been a Jewish county leader in the Bronx or Brooklyn, the city's two most Jewish boroughs, nor in the more Catholic boroughs of Queens or Staten Island. In Manhattan, only Hugo Rogers's brief and unimportant tenure saw a Jewish figure atop Tammany Hall. Catholics in general, and the Irish in particular—four of the five county leaders were of Irish descent, and all were Catholic in 1959—continued to play a disproportionately large role in the regular Democratic organization, and to conduct its affairs in a way that the young Jewish professionals of the reform movement found difficult to accept.[37]

DeSapio Wounded

In 1959, Manhattan had thirty-three party districts, each with a male and a female leader. The reform clubs launched battles in twelve districts, and in Harlem J. Raymond Jones, supported by Adam Clayton Powell's popularity, organized black political troops in four. Independent anti-DeSapio candidates emerged in four others. Reformers contested the regular organization in just a few districts in the Bronx, Brooklyn, and Queens as well. Typically, the party leadership elections that occur in New York City during the year before a presidential campaign attract little popular attention. But with the eighty-one-year old Herbert Lehman leading the reform crusade on hot summer streets during the day, and in sweaty political clubs at night, and with Eleanor Roosevelt doing the same, and Thomas Finletter as well, the election had a drama normally lacking.

The press followed the celebrities around Manhattan reporting to the public the speeches that portrayed the local contests as choices between the "bosses and the people." The CDV distributed money to the local candidates, most of it raised by Lehman himself, and provided technical staff and media coverage to boost their candidates' chances.[38]

Reform clubs took seven of the thirty-three districts in Manhattan, and did unexpectedly well in the other five where they ran. The modest success they achieved in 1959, more than they had ever won before, established the reform movement as a serious alternative to the regular Democratic organization. Lehman's strategy of using the insurgent clubs as a weapon to assault DeSapio's control of the party was beginning to wound the boss. The Harlem Leadership Team that Jones formed won three districts that year. While the blacks were not aligned with the reformers, neither did they take instructions from the boss. They were a new and independent power within Tammany Hall.[39]

DeSapio still commanded the loyalty of a majority of the district leaders in 1959, but his control of the party had weakened. And in his

Top: Fiorello H. LaGuardia was one of New York City's most successful builders of ethnic coalitions. Courtesy of LaGuardia and Wagner Archives
Bottom: LaGuardia, far right, is pictured with two more of New York's most skillful politicians, Alfred E. Smith, far left, and Herbert H. Lehman, next to Smith. Francis Cardinal Spellman is at center and Monsignor Michael J. Lavelle at his left. Courtesy of LaGuardia and Wagner Archives

Right: William O'Dwyer, an Irish Catholic immigrant, headed the Democratic party's first balanced ticket in 1945. Courtesy of Collections of the Municipal Archives of the City of New York

Above: The campaign banners show the 1945 Democratic ticket: O'Dwyer for mayor; Lazarus Joseph, a Jewish candidate for comptroller; Vincent Impellitteri, an Italian for City Council president. Courtesy of Collections of the Municipal Archives of the City of New York

Above: In 1949 a public feud between Eleanor Roosevelt (center) and Cardinal Spellman over public funding for parochial schools threatened Mayor O'Dwyer's ethnic coalition when Catholics and Jews took different sides in the controversy. Courtesy of Collections of the Municipal Archives of the City of New York

Left: Vincent R. Impellitteri (right) became acting mayor when William O'Dwyer resigned in 1950. Although he won a whirlwind special election to serve out O'Dwyer's term, Impellitteri never built a stable political base and lost his bid for reelection in 1953. Comedian Eddie Cantor is at left. Courtesy of Collections of the Municipal Archives of the City of New York

Top: Mayor Robert F. Wagner built one of the broadest based ethnic coalitions in New York City's history. He is shown here kissing Cardinal Spellman's ring at the St. Patrick's day parade. Courtesy of LaGuardia and Wagner Archives
Bottom: Wagner is pictured here on the reviewing stand at a later St. Patrick's day parade. Senator Jacob Javits is to his right, City Council president Paul Screvane to his left, and TWU chief Mike Quill. Courtesy of Collections of the Municipal Archives of the City of New York

Above: Wagner marching in the Columbus Day parade. Abe Stark is to his left.
Courtesy of LaGuardia and Wagner Archives

Right: Wagner speaking at the
54th Anniversary Dinner of the
Rabbi Jacob Joseph School. Jewish comedian Al Hirschfield is
seated behind Wagner at the near
end. Comptroller Lawrence
Gerosa is at the far end. The men
in the center are unidentified.
Courtesy of LaGuardia and
Wagner Archives

Right: Wagner greeting Doña Feliz
Rincon, Mayor of San Juan, Puerto
Rico. Courtesy of LaGuardia and
Wagner Archives

Above: Wagner greeting Dr. Martin Luther King, Jr. and Coretta Scott King at
a City Hall ceremony honoring Dr. King for winning the Nobel Peace Prize.
Courtesy of LaGuardia and Wagner Archives

Top: Carmine DeSapio (center) conferring with former President Harry Truman in Mayor Wagner's presence. At the peak of his power DeSapio wielded influence in the Democratic party's national affairs. Courtesy of Collections of the Municipal Archives of the City of New York

Bottom: DeSapio (left) made a crucial mistake when in 1958 he angered Herbert H. Lehman (second from right). Ultimately Mayor Wagner sided with Lehman in the battle between the two politicians. Abe Stark is at far right. Courtesy of LaGuardia and Wagner Archives

Right: In the 1961 Democratic primary Wagner ran for reelection to a third term as the reform candidate against the regular Democratic party organization. His campaign portrayed DeSapio as a villain who controlled Arthur Levitt, the candidate challenging Wagner. Courtesy of LaGuardia and Wagner Archives

Left: In an extraordinary repudiation of the regular Democratic organization Wagner won the 1961 primary with a majority of votes from almost every major ethnic group. The election night picture of Wagner kissing his wife, Susan, appeared on the cover of the *New York Post* the day following the primary. Running mates Paul Screvane and Abraham Beame are on Wagner's left. Courtesy of LaGuardia and Wagner Archives

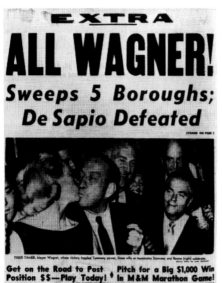

Greenwich Village home base, running against a Village Independent Democrat (VID) sponsored candidate, DeSapio won reelection as district leader by only 600 votes out of 9,000 cast. The rules of the Democratic party of New York County demanded that the boss be an elected district leader, so DeSapio's weak showing revealed a potentially fatal vulnerability. The South Village, where DeSapio had grown up, remained heavily Italian, and he ran as strong as ever there. Other areas of Greenwich Village, however, had become fashionable digs for young Jewish and Protestant professionals and intellectuals. In those parts of the community, where the VID gathered its forces, DeSapio ran weakly. And those areas were growing.[40]

Emboldened by their success, the reformers positioned themselves to play a role in the New York State delegation to the 1960 Democratic National Convention in Los Angeles. Many reform clubbers, hoping to launch yet another effort to nominate Adlai Stevenson, had an intensely negative reaction to John F. Kennedy. To them, the young Senator from Massachusetts—for all his Harvard education and Boston Brahmin manners—still smacked of an Irish Catholic pol. They distrusted his father, his family, his money, and him. So obvious were these sentiments from the earliest days of the movement that at one point Herbert Lehman had been forced to issue a statement that the CDV was not a "stop Kennedy" plan.[41]

The Kennedys had no intention of becoming embroiled in the local feud. They sent the State Democratic Party Chairman from Connecticut, John Bailey, across the border to gather support for Kennedy in upstate New York. In the city they relied on Charles Buckley, a friend of the candidate's father from the days when the Kennedys had lived in Riverdale, and on Brooklyn Congressman Eugene Keogh, another friend of Joseph Kennedy. By the time the delegates were chosen formally, support for the Irish Catholic politician from Boston had been substantially predetermined.[42]

Yet, for the New Yorkers, choosing a candidate for President was only part of the importance of their state delegation to the national convention. Determining who would speak for the party held just as much sway. DeSapio realized by the time the convention approached that there would be no truce with Lehman. Aided by New York State Chairman Michael Prendergast, the Tammany chief refused to grant a seat on the state's delegation to the former governor and senator who, except during wartime in 1944, had represented the state at every national convention since 1928. Outrage among Democrats issued forth fast and furious. Lehman called the decision "just another reflection of the short-sightedness and arrogance of the bosses." His cool demeanor made him appear above even so egregious a slight as this. Privately, for the first time, he began to harbor personal bitterness toward DeSapio.[43]

The effort of the two bosses to punish the Jewish statesman backfired badly. It was "evident to the dimmest clubhouse denizen that here were the makings of party disaster," one observer would later write of the episode. Mayor Wagner, trying to keep the Democrats intact, denounced the move immediately. Publicly he offered to give Lehman his own seat, saying, "there can be differences in the party, [but] a man of this stature certainly should be on this delegation." Privately, he put the screws to DeSapio and Prendergast. Within a week the state chairman resigned as a national delegate and Lehman took his place. Shortly afterward the two bosses would make a second blunder.[44]

Kennedy won the Democratic nomination on the first ballot. Party loyalty and political sense dictated a truce between the feuding factions in New York to help deliver the White House to their party's candidate. Robert Kennedy traveled to the city to make the point clear. Speaking to a group of reformers that included Lehman, Finletter, and others, he declared: "Gentlemen, I don't give a damn if the state and county organizations survive, and I don't give a damn if *you* survive. I want to elect John F. Kennedy."[45]

Within the city, the object of the Kennedy campaign "was largely to reach liberal Jews," according to Daniel Patrick Moynihan, so the Kennedy clan was properly respectful of the liberal leaders and their influence. A live local television spot was scheduled, during which prominent New York Democrats were invited to speak in succession on behalf of the candidate . After they were done, John F. Kennedy himself would speak. Prendergast, the loyal DeSapio man, tried to bump Lehman from the schedule. John Kennedy intervened personally with a telephone call to the state chairman and insisted that Lehman be on the program. The harried candidate, who did not arrive at the television station until just moments before he was to speak, was unaware that in spite of the commitment he thought he had received, Prendergast had indeed prevented Lehman from speaking.[46]

When Kennedy stepped out of the studio he found a fuming Herbert Lehman standing in his path. The aging but rugged Jewish politician looked the Irishman coldly in the eye and growled, "I've been double-crossed."

Kennedy was shocked. "You mean you didn't speak?" he asked. Lehman nodded. "You weren't double-crossed," replied the man who had been schooled in the 'don't get mad get even' ways of Boston politics, and who would soon be president. "I was, and I'll get the dirty son-of-a-bitch bastard if it's the last thing I do."[47]

Tammany received yet another blow that campaign season. On the Upper West Side Congressman Ludwig Teller, a Jewish law professor and liberal Democrat who had served his constituency well, ran for reelection. He was supported by the regular organization, and the Liberal party too. Lehman and his followers, however, refused to back anyone, of any quality, if they had DeSapio's endorsement. They ran William Fitts Ryan of the Riverside Democrats against Teller in the Democratic primary. They had a single issue—"bossism." Ryan's campaign workers swarmed the streets of their neighborhood looking for Teller posters on which to place stickers that said "Candidate of Carmine DeSapio." Ryan's fliers placed pictures of Lehman more prominently than photos of the candidate himself. The effect was to turn a campaign between a competent, liberal, incumbent Jewish Congressman, and an Irish Catholic newcomer, into a contest between an Italian Catholic political boss and a Jewish elder statesman. Ryan, riding on Lehman's, won.[48]

Mayor Wagner quietly watched events unfold, but stayed out of the fray himself. Shortly after the elections in 1960 he called a meeting of his top aides at Gracie Mansion. The next year was a mayoralty year, and Wagner would have to decide if he wanted to seek a third term. He asked for his advisers' comments. He sat silently and listened while they spoke, as was his habit. They analyzed the political landscape, discussed the issues that would be important, assessed the mayor's strengths and weaknesses, and speculated about his potential opponents, all with understanding and insight. The mayor, who had been born into politics, bred and raised in its practice, finally asked the only question on his mind: "After what happened to Lou Teller, what I want to know is how anyone can win if he has DeSapio's support?" No one had an answer.[49]

SEVEN

The Destruction of Tammany Hall

1961

During Robert Wagner's second administration the excitement of launching new programs gave way to the tedium of managing existing ones. The mayor had stamina, and displayed an extraordinary ability to sit through long bureaucratic sessions on the dullest of matters without losing concentration. One aide claimed that the secret to his effectiveness was his "cast iron bottom." Another, more reverent, observer thought him something of an "iron man." It helped, too, that in many instances the mayor knew the city's departments better than his commissioners, competent in their own rights, but almost inevitably less experienced than their boss. Yet, there was little in the daily routine to capture public attention and to remind the city that the man at the top was watching over them.[1]

New York, a city of perpetual motion, had a mayor who was a master of deliberate caution. Wagner liked to touch base with every center of power and carefully build a consensus before implementing new ideas. One of his favorite sayings, often quoted by his critics in ridicule, was: "When in doubt, don't." He believed that many problems left alone solved themselves, and that a lot of damage could be avoided, many political enemies could remain unmade, by doing nothing. Once, while still a young man, he was driving home to New York City after a weekend on Long Island with his father. He became exasperated with a slow moving automobile in front of him, and reached for the horn. Before he could hit it his father interrupted: "Don't honk Bobby, the man is a voter." Wagner always carried that lesson with him. As mayor, he rarely used the lights and siren in his official car. The notion of chasing after firetrucks, bashing slot machines with sledge hammers, or reading comics to the kids over radio, as LaGuardia had done, never occurred to Wagner. He preferred to travel around town quietly, performing his back breaking job in a subdued style.[2]

Among New York's elite were those who felt that the crushing problems of the country's largest city required continuous action. In October 1959 the liberal intellectual journal *The Nation* ran a special issue entitled "The Shame of New York." It consisted of sensationalist stories written by journalists Fred Cook and Gene Gleason claiming that New York City had more rats than people, that muggings and gangs, rapes in the schools and murders in the street, were the order of the day. They reported instances of corruption in the Building and Real Estate departments, reminded readers of scandals surrounding federal Title I Slum Clearance programs that had first surfaced in 1957, and profiled conflict of interest charges against two city councilmen whom the mayor had supported. The reporters implied that Tammany had selected Wagner in 1953 for his positive image, but that he was not competent. They asserted quite boldly that he had accomplished nothing as mayor. He was the hand picked stooge of Carmine DeSapio, they insisted, and they claimed that he made boss determined appointments on a political basis. They accused him of being part of a small group of "power barons" who spoke and listened only to each other in their quest for private profit. The city, they wrote, "has lost its very soul. . . . [Its] crushing problems demand swift, vigorous and decisive action. These positive traits that New York so desperately needs are the very ones most lacking in its mayor," they concluded.[3]

The Break

Confidential polling data compiled by Louis Harris at the mayor's request in May 1959 confirmed that Wagner's popularity had slipped substantially since his reelection. There "seems to be no call for the panic button," the study advised. The mayor still had a large reservoir of support with the average New Yorker. Still, Harris warned that the growing number of voters who had a negative view of the chief executive should be taken seriously. "If the situation remains that way for long, the political outcome will eventually turn for the worse." The poll also showed that the greatest threat to Wagner's public appeal as a likable and decent man, one of his most powerful assets, was the perception that he was "not strong enough in dealing with the political influences." The interview responses that led to that conclusion had "the thread of 'Tammany' running through them," Harris deduced from his study.[4]

Early in 1960 Wagner hoped, as he had in 1956, that his party would choose him as its candidate for Vice President. When the Democrats put John F. Kennedy, a northeastern Irish Catholic on the top of their ticket, Wagner's hope for the second spot faded. He then began to think about his reelection as mayor, and of his relationship to DeSapio. The events of 1960 that culminated in Ludwig Teller's primary defeat made it clear that popular perception of Tammany Hall and its boss had deteriorated badly over the preceding two years, and that affiliation with DeSapio had become a political liability.[5]

About the time the risk of maintaining his association with DeSapio was becoming clear to Wagner, a jury convicted Manhattan borough president Hulan Jack of accepting several thousand dollars worth of free work on his private apartment from a contractor who did business with the city. Jack resigned from office. Formally, it was up to the six members of the City Council from Manhattan to pick an interim replacement, but tradition provided for the Democratic county leader to make the selection. DeSapio sought out the mayor to discuss the post and to reach an agreement on a nominee. Wagner decided it was time to assert his independence from the Tammany chief. He refused to take DeSapio's telephone calls as part of a deliberate plan to force the boss to announce his choice alone. As soon as DeSapio did, the mayor nominated someone else. The boss's selection, Lloyd Dickens, and the mayor's man, Edward Dudley, were both able politicians. To Wagner, however, the important point was to split with DeSapio loudly to show the city that the mayor, not the party leader, was in charge.

DeSapio, however, was a skillful professional. Before he made his choice public he secured commitments from four of Manhattan's six city councilmen to vote for Dickens. In his first showdown with Tammany Hall, Wagner ran the risk of an embarrassing loss that would make him appear a political weakling. It was then that the mayor's

commissioner of investigation, Louis Kaplan, called two of the councilmen siding with the Tammany leader into his office for confidential
consultations. With one he discussed a particular case of fraud and some
bad checks, with the other some peculiar happenings surrounding certain city contracts. When the council cast its votes for an interim
borough president for Manhattan, Wagner's man won, four votes to
two. DeSapio accused the mayor of using his powers of investigation
for political purposes. The mayor, the commissioner, and the councilmen denied it, but Wagner's close assistant, Warren Moscow, did not
doubt that the mayor "called Louie and told him to throw his weight
around."[6]

On February 3, 1961 Wagner ended the partnership that had made
him mayor and DeSapio the most powerful political boss in the state.
"The time has come for the leader of the New York County Democratic
organization to step aside in the interest of the Democratic party," he
announced. He called for a more open party system, more active political clubs that would serve as community service centers, and more
attention to policy issues that affected the city. These were precisely the
changes the reform clubs demanded. But he tempered his comments:
"In restating these principles it is not necessary to affiliate myself with
any particular group within the party." Wagner wanted DeSapio out,
but the organization to stay.[7]

The point of no return had now been passed. "I am sorry that Mayor
Wagner has permitted himself to be euchered into his present position.
I am sorry both for his sake and for that of the party," DeSapio
responded. "In . . . allying himself with a small group of willful people," the boss continued, referring to the reform clubs and the CDV,
"who seek to rule or ruin the Democratic party—he has forsaken his
friends, his supporters and his own conscience." The boss ended with a
comment that sounded statesmanlike, but was in fact a threat: "Neither
the Mayor nor I determine the party leadership, or the party's candidates. The people will make that decision for themselves—as only they
can in the primary elections." The boss would not go quietly. He would
run a candidate against the mayor.[8]

Within days of the split DeSapio took the extraordinary measure of
presenting his case to the people of New York City in a half-hour
television spot purchased during prime viewing time. He outlined yet
again the positive steps he had taken to open the party to all who sought
to participate, and quoted from a speech Wagner made in 1959 praising
him for these initiatives. Responding to criticisms Lehman had leveled
at him regarding his influence over the judicial selection process, De-

Sapio asked how the current procedures "differ from those which prevailed when your brother, Irving Lehman, was nominated for the Supreme Court [of New York State] at the age of 32—yes 32! How do they differ from the circumstances under which he later was nominated for the State Court of Appeals?" DeSapio then read out loud a letter Senator Lehman wrote to him in 1956 complimenting him on his conduct as party leader. Finally, the Tammany chief accused the mayor of trying to turn him into a scapegoat for the city's unsolved problems as part of a reelection campaign hatched in cahoots with the Liberal party and the reform Democrats. The battle lines were being drawn.[9]

Ethnic Arithmetic, 1961

In March 1961 Wagner commissioned another confidential poll from Louis Harris. The results showed that the mayor's support among the greatly expanded ranks of black and Puerto Rican voters was strong. During the decade preceding 1960 the number of blacks living in New York City swelled from fewer than 750,000 to more than one million; the Puerto Rican population grew from fewer than 250,000 to more than 600,000. During the same period more than 750,000 whites moved from the city to the suburbs. By 1960 blacks and Puerto Ricans together accounted for more than one New Yorker in five. Harris's poll showed that the two groups were "almost invulnerable to Republican attack," and in the event of a primary, Wagner, not the machine, owned the image that attracted the minorities to the Democratic party. Only the proportion of the two groups that would actually turn out and vote on primary day was in doubt.

"The Catholic vote is not in good shape," the report continued. In particular, the study revealed that the Irish "now seem ready to leave the Democratic party in droves in this year's municipal election." They, and other Catholic groups, "should not be written off," the study counseled, "but they are at this writing far less likely to respond" to campaign efforts than others. "Inherent in these results," the study went on, "are the deeper roots of the internecine battle that now is seething in the ranks in the Democratic Party in this city," between the conservative Catholic wing and the liberal Jewish wing.

With Jewish voters, the mayor's position remained strong, but not invincible. Against a non-Jewish Republican like Congressman John Lindsay, the data revealed Wagner would win the votes of almost seven of every ten Jews. Against a well known Jewish Republican, like Attorney General Louis Lefkowitz, he would hold only some fifty-six per-cent. The study did not say what would happen if the mayor faced a Jew in a Democratic primary. Jews, Harris concluded, along with blacks and Puerto Ricans, should be "prime targets" for Wagner's campaign effort. The mayor, working principally with Louis Harris and Alex Rose, had already begun to develop a strategy for solidifying support with each of the city's ethnic groups.

The continued support of Rose's Liberal party was critical to the mayor's position among Jewish voters. The Liberals had backed Wagner in every campaign he ran with the important exception of his first race for mayor in 1953. Wagner acknowledged the lapse by dispensing sparse patronage to the party during his first administration, but after the Liberals supported him in his 1956 Senate race and his 1957 bid for reelection as mayor, the formal relationship improved. More important, Wagner and Rose had known each other since the two were young men. They were philosophically and temperamentally compatible, and Wag-ner had great respect for Rose's political judgment. As the mayor distanced himself from DeSapio he turned increasingly to Rose for advice.

In the months leading up to his break with DeSapio, the mayor sought Rose's counsel. The Liberal tactician advised Wagner that the public mood was such that he could win reelection without the ma-chine's backing. He also assured Wagner that even if his feud with DeSapio prevented him from winning the Democratic nomination, the Liberal party would still support him. That pledge was critical. It en-sured the mayor a spot on the ballot in November no matter what, and Liberal credibility was riding high at the time. The party had played an unusually important role in organizing John Kennedy's 1960 presiden-tial campaign in New York State because of the split between regular and reform Democrats, delivering 400,000 votes on their own line, more than Kennedy's margin of victory. In a somewhat fatuous but some-what believable way, the Liberals claimed credit for Kennedy's election. Without them, he would not have won New York, and if the state's forty-five electoral votes had gone to Nixon, so too would have the White House. The results proved that despite their softening core, the Liberals could still determine the outcome of a close election in New York.[10]

The pledge of support from the Liberals was one critical component of the mayor's plan to hold onto Jewish support. Reconciling his rela-tionship with the reformers was the other. On January 5, 1961, as the mayor neared a decision on his break with DeSapio, he arranged to meet with Lehman and some of the leaders of the CDV to test reform club waters. On the surface they were cold. Many of the reform clubbers viewed the mayor as a Tammany creation, and looked forward to launching a candidate to oppose him. Lehman, on the other hand, understood that governing New York City was no simple task. Wagner, in his view, was doing a commendable job despite some justifiable criticisms. Lehman also knew that victories in a few district leadership posts, and some primaries in Manhattan, hardly qualified the reform clubs to launch a serious citywide campaign for mayor.

Lehman therefore made it clear that he personally was inclined to support Wagner if the mayor actively helped to depose the boss. Lehman's backing was influential in its own right. Shortly after the meeting Harris's study would confirm for the mayor that "Democratic voters express a decisive preference," for Lehman over DeSapio when asked to choose sides in the battle between the two. Lehman's endorsement would also make it impossible for the reform clubs not to back Wagner. Winning this support would solidify the mayor's position among a significant segment of Jewish voters.[11]

Wagner's position among blacks and Puerto Ricans was strong. The mayor had appointed more blacks and Puerto Ricans to senior city government posts than any mayor before him, and he had supported local legislation to prohibit racial discrimination in housing. He favored integrated schools and in public speeches loaned the prestige of his office to the nationwide struggle for civil rights. His administration actively instituted policies designed to help the disadvantaged, and his political aides had consciously wooed the support of black and Puerto Rican politicians for many years, with great effect. Ensuring a high turnout among minority voters was the most important objective with the two groups. For this, Wagner turned to J. Raymond Jones, after 1959 virtual boss of Harlem. The two men had been friends since serving together in the Housing Department under William O'Dwyer, and as mayor, Wagner relied on Jones to distribute patronage in Harlem. When Wagner asked Jones to undertake the organizing effort in minority neighborhoods Jones accepted instantly and declared publicly that he would back the mayor "come hell or highwater."[12]

The mayor's position among Irish and Italian Catholics was more complicated. Wagner knew he needed to fight with DeSapio. Harris's poll had confirmed what the mayor's instincts told him earlier: "It is not too strong to say that [Carmine DeSapio's] backing will go a long way toward insuring the defeat of any city-wide candidate," Harris concluded from his polling data. He went on to advise Wagner to "keep alive his break with DeSapio, at every opportunity. . ." But the mayor hoped to limit the damage that such a battle was bound to cause to his standing among Catholics.[13]

Harry Van Arsdale, head of the powerful CIO Central Trades and Labor Council, and a long-time friend and ally of the mayor, assessed the circumstances and decided to form a new political organization to support Wagner—the Brotherhood party. He would use the trade unions he headed that were so heavily populated by Irish and Italian craftsmen as its center of gravity, and the party would serve, in a sense, as a Catholic counterpart to the Liberal party. If the mayor did not get the Democratic nomination Catholic voters, many of whom resented the Liberal party's influence because they felt the organization belonged to the Jews, would have a party line on which to cast a ballot for Wagner in religious and philosophical comfort.[14]

The mayor also hoped to maintain his relations with the Irish Catholic Democratic bosses outside of Manhattan, especially Charles Buckley in the Bronx and Joseph Sharkey in Brooklyn. Although these men practiced the same machine style politics as their Manhattan counterpart, they had not achieved the same notoriety with the general public. Wagner hoped he could force DeSapio to take the fall alone on the "bossism" charge. Managing this strategy was tricky. The mayor's split with the Tammany leader had to be portrayed as an attack on the system DeSapio represented and not just the man, which implicitly threatened Buckley and Sharkey. The county leaders would have to decide if it made sense for them to enter into an alliance, through the mayor, with the groups that were committed to taking power away from them. The mayor's effort to maintain his links to the county leaders beyond Manhattan was further complicated by the issue of charter reform.

Structural Changes

From his earliest days in office, Wagner had called for creation of a commission to revise the City Charter, the fundamental law detailing the powers of each municipal office in New York City. The structure, first implemented in 1901 and modified by reforms LaGuardia won in 1937, had some serious flaws. Among other things, the charter gave each borough president substantial control over significant municipal functions, including street and sewer repairs. The system meant that the mayor's authority over municipal workers was not equal to his charge to make the city work as a whole. It also meant that the Democratic party organization in each of the five boroughs had a source of patronage independent of the mayor. The borough president of Queens, for instance, had direct control of about two thousand jobs.[15]

The need for a new City Charter had been a major theme of Wagner's second inaugural address in 1958. The mayor tried to gather support from Democratic party officials for his initiative, but the politicians had little interest in a plan that would reduce their power. Wagner was not then willing to battle with his party's leaders. Republicans detected the friction between the mayor and his fellow Democrats, and in an effort to intensify the discord they pressed the issue throughout 1959. After a series of political maneuvers, a joint committee appointed by the governor and the mayor reported on the need for changes in the charter on January 16, 1961, just about the time Wagner was preparing to break with DeSapio. Good government was suddenly good politics. A push to revise the charter against the wishes of the political leaders would add to the mayor's image as an unbossed advocate for responsive government. Wagner asked for and received authority from the governor to create a formal Charter Revision Committee to draft major reforms and to submit them to the city's voters in a ballot referendum in November.[16]

Wagner's demand for changes in the charter damaged his relationship with Buckley, Sharkey, and the other county leaders because the proposed revisions threatened the boss's ability to control municipal employees, a vital element in maintaining machine discipline. In another way, more subtle and yet more profound, the mayor had already effected lasting change on the political leaders' power over city workers.

An incumbent mayor should hold powerful sway with municipal employees. He is, after all, their boss. Yet, before LaGuardia, the city's chief executive hardly controlled the workers nominally at his command. The most embarrassing evidence of this came in 1932 when a reporter asked the newly elected Tammany mayor, John O'Brien, whom he planned to name as commissioner of police. "I don't know," the hapless politician replied, "I haven't got the word yet." O'Brien did not choose the city's senior officials, or any others. The Democratic district leaders did, acting through their county bosses. Municipal workers, supposedly responsible to the mayor, displayed more loyalty to the local politicians who got them their jobs than to the city's titular head.[17]

LaGuardia forcefully implemented civil service rules in an effort to improve the mayor's ability to control city workers, but he enjoyed only partial success. The bosses found ways of encouraging friendly bureaucrats to ignore rules, or to reinterpret them, or managed to place just the right person in charge of reviewing applications, or to have just the right doctor perform mandatory physical examinations that eliminated some, while qualifying others, according to the health of their party loyalty. Although civil service regulations did reduce the district leader's power to place party workers in government jobs, even in their weakened state Democratic officials had more influence than anyone else over the city's staff. The battered machine emerged from the LaGuardia era poised to reassert itself. William O'Dwyer engaged Tammany and the other leaders in a personal war of attrition that prevented a wholesale revival of boss control over patronage, but under Impellitteri boss sponsored party hacks moved into important offices in large numbers. The struggle to control the loyalty of city workers continued.[18]

Measures that Wagner took during his first two terms had a profound impact on that loyalty. Just a few months after assuming office in 1954, the mayor issued an "Interim Order on the Conduct of Relations Between the City of New York and its Employees." The order guaranteed municipal workers the right to organize into unions without fear of reprisals. Groups of city employees had been forming associations and societies for decades, but Wagner's decision gave them a formal role for the first time. Three-and-a-half years later, in March 1958, Wagner implemented a staff recommendation to initiate collective bargaining with city employees. The plan authorized categories of workers to choose unions to act as exclusive representatives in negotiations with the city. But the city's Department of Labor, which the mayor controlled, had to certify which unions qualified to serve as the exclusive bargaining agents under the plan. This, in turn, determined who would command the loyalty of the workers, and who would wield the rapidly expanding resources municipal labor organizations were developing.[19]

Union certification, in short, was a rich form of patronage, and Wagner was the boss. "There was a conscious policy of Wagner's to get a lot of unions involved rather than trying to create one strong union," the mayor's Commissioner of Labor Relations told an interviewer. "Of course, what this did was to fragment generally the strength of the union power within the city, while at the same time keeping the various unions happy by giving them all a little piece of the action." The mayor did not intervene personally in every certification decision, but for the important ones, he "would just pick up the phone and call the people over at the Department of Labor and tell them who to certify and who not to certify." And the labor leaders knew it.[20]

The mayor's primary objective in recognizing municipal labor unions was to create an effective system of labor representation to promote smooth relations between the city and its employees, but he made sure to implement the program in a way that allowed him to remain master in his own house. The huge pool of city government workers, once viciously loyal to the Democratic machine, a loyalty softened by two decades of civil service reforms but never replaced, now had new objects of affection. Municipal unions began to determine how much city workers got paid, and what benefits they received. Labor representatives intervened on behalf of employees having troubles with their superiors, just as district leaders once had. Through the informal privileges that lead power in one sphere to follow from power in another, union officials began to have more than a passing say in who got city jobs, and who did not, just like political bosses.

The labor unions organized along functional lines, while the Democratic party remained geographically determined according to election district with obvious advantages for political work. But the new loyalties of city workers that competed with the old offered Robert Wagner a source of help in his incipient battle to hold on to City Hall. The incumbent mayor spoke with his long standing friends in labor, men with whom he worked and negotiated, with whom he shared casual talk and a few drinks—men whose power had been increased by the mayor's decision to certify their unions rather than some other—and asked for their help. Many thousands of city government employees who traditionally would have been expected to work for the regular Democratic organization would back the mayor in 1961. Robert Wagner's labor policies had quietly weakened the powers of the political machine in an enduring way. Even so, in the spring of 1961, the mayor hoped to salvage his relationship with the regular Democratic organizations in the boroughs outside Manhattan. Although weakened they remained powerful sources of experienced political workers. And the mayor feared that if they were not with him, they would be mobilized against him.[21]

Choosing Sides

When the mayor escalated his feud with DeSapio early in 1961, he cut off the Tammany leader's access to city patronage. Governor Rockefeller provided state jobs through his own party bosses with some deference to the Liberals, whose support he was trying to nurture. He offered DeSapio nothing. The Kennedy administration did not forget that Michael Prendergast, a DeSapio man, had broken his commitment to the President to let Herbert Lehman speak on television on Kennedy's behalf during the 1960 campaign. As a result, the Tammany chief had no access to federal appointments. The badly isolated Manhattan boss thought he would get some patronage relief when the State Legislature proposed thirty-seven new judgeships for the city, many of them in Manhattan and the Bronx. Wagner, realizing that the creation of the posts would help the Tammany leader, blocked the plan.[22]

At the same time that Wagner stopped offering jobs to DeSapio, he increased his generosity toward Buckley and Sharkey, although the mayor's relationship with the Brooklyn leader was strained. The mayor had decided that he did not want Brooklyn's Abe Stark as City Council president anymore. The amiable and popular Stark had no experience in city government and little in politics when he had ridden Wagner's coattails to office in 1953. The man had not distinguished himself since, and a lackluster successor, the mayor felt, would work against any plans that he might hatch to run for another office before the end of his term. During Wagner's 1956 Senate race Jacob Javits often reminded voters that sending Wagner to Washington would promote Stark to the city's top job. Although Stark had not come up through the Brooklyn machine, he was well liked in the borough, and dumping him could embarrass Sharkey.[23]

Buckley, with access to federal patronage, and a strong and well known relationship with the Kennedys, was on firmer independent ground in the Bronx than his counterpart in Brooklyn. Normally he got along well with the mayor, but he had grown nervous over Wagner's dispute with DeSapio. The Manhattan leader told the others that the fanatic elements of the reform movement had railroaded Wagner into his anti-boss position and that they would not be content with just the Tammany chief's scalp. If the reform clubbers succeeded in ousting him, DeSapio claimed, they would turn immediately to the other boroughs, and the mayor would not oppose them. To convince the other bosses that what he said was true, DeSapio reportedly played a tape recording of a public affairs television program during which a reform club member outlined this plan.[24]

To ensure this did not happen, Buckley wanted the mayor to announce his candidacy alone and to let the regular organization agree on the remainder of the ticket afterward. This would have made the interdependent relationship between the mayor and the machine clear. Wagner could not afford to abide by such a plan if he wanted to win reform support and maintain an independent image. After weeks of negotiating, on June 18, Wagner's office released a trial balloon. They leaked the news to reporters that the mayor was considering Deputy Mayor Paul Screvane, the former Commissioner of Sanitation and a well respected career bureaucrat, to run on his ticket as City Council president. He also proposed Budget Director Abraham Beame for comptroller to replace Larry Gerosa. The incumbent had fallen out of favor with the mayor and with the Bronx regular organization too. Screvane was an Italian from Queens, which by 1961 had become the second most populous borough. Wagner chose Beame, a Jew and a veteran Brooklyn regular, to balance the ticket. He also hoped the selection would defuse the reaction from the Kings County machine to his decision to drop Stark. And both men had strong credentials as municipal administrators, so the ticket could be presented to good government groups without apologies. Alex Rose had emphasized this last point in meetings with the mayor prior to Wagner's selections.[25]

The plan did not work. Stark rallied supporters to a City Hall demonstration forcing the mayor to backtrack half way and propose that Stark take the comptroller's spot. It was still a citywide post, but Stark would no longer be next in line for the mayoralty, solving Wagner's problem with the man. Stark's ethnic pride got in the way. He "bluntly told the mayor that he was next in line of succession to the City Hall throne and could become the first Jewish Mayor in the City's history," a newspaper report asserted. He would not step aside and lose that chance.[26]

On June 23, 1961 the mayor held a long meeting at Gracie Mansion with Buckley and Sharkey in an effort to reach a compromise. By 4:00 P.M. none had been found, and the mayor had scheduled a 5:00 P.M. press conference to announce his decision to run. In his car, on the way to City Hall, he decided to go ahead on schedule. In a long statement that reviewed his administration's many successes and that emphasized his personal experience and the competence of his staff, Wagner declared himself a candidate and said he expected to be reelected. He announced that his choices for running mates were Screvane for City Council president and Stark for comptroller. Wagner hoped that once forced into deciding between running with the mayor, or running against him, Stark would join the ticket. Most important, however, Wagner's announcement made it clear that he, not the bosses, had chosen his running mates. Even so, he hoped that all of the county leaders save DeSapio would ultimately support him and spare him the difficulty of a primary.[27]

Abe Stark rejected the mayor's gambit, and the Brooklyn machine stood firmly opposed to the mayor. A few days after his announcement, at an all day meeting at his Long Island home near Islip, the mayor made a last concerted pitch to Buckley. Wagner offered to allow the Bronx boss to select the candidate for comptroller in return for his support. Because Stark had not accepted the post, Wagner could offer it to someone else without fear of being called boss dominated. Buckley refused to break with the other county leaders and he made no secret of his contempt for the mayor's decision to allow his desire to keep the support of the Liberal party and the reform Democrats to determine his relationship with the regular Democratic leaders. Ultimately Abe Beame joined the mayor's ticket as the candidate for comptroller, and with the team he had originally proposed in place, Wagner prepared to take on the Democratic party organization in all five boroughs in the primary. No candidate had ever done that successfully before.[28]

By then the Liberal party had endorsed Wagner. Alex Rose and David Dubinsky pushed the mayor's name through their party's nominating convention amidst a small but loud protest from the supporters of Stuart Scheftel, an ambitious Liberal who had no realistic chance of winning a mayoralty race but who wanted to run. The Scheftel faction accused the two long-time party leaders of "bossism." They intimidated party members by sitting on the dais during the nominating process and taking a vote by show of hands instead of in a secret ballot, the insurgents complained. The protest was not unreasonable, but Dubinsky ridiculed the comment. "I was advised that my sitting on the platform intimidates the delegates. . . . Vote your conscience. I'll sit on the platform and close my eyes," he said. In fact, he also turned his back, leading one participant to ask what the point was. "Everyone knows Dubinsky has eyes in the back of his head," the man said.[29]

The outcome of the Liberal party convention was never in doubt. More unclear was the mayor's standing with the other pillar of his support among Jewish voters, the reform clubs. Even though Wagner had been taking steps for months to demonstrate his political independence from DeSapio, many reform clubs still hesitated to back him. Herbert Lehman, however, responded. In May, the Jewish statesman stopped just short of a formal endorsement saying in a television interview that if the mayor continued to fight to "improve the climate of the Democratic Party and to change the leadership . . . I wouldn't close the door to the possibility of the reform movement supporting him."[30]

In response to criticisms that Wagner was a latecomer to the anti-boss crusade, Lehman responded: "Whatever his attitude may have been previously, he is alive to the great problems of the City of New

York, and I believe that he has made up his mind and is determined to carry on the reforms which are necessary to bring about improved government." When Wagner announced formally his intention to run, Lehman said, "it is a refreshing turn in the political history of our city to have the public leader of the Democrats of the city, rather than the bosses, provide the leadership." The mayor's slate, Lehman continued, "commends itself to me," and he planned to support it.[31]

For months Lehman's assistant, Julius Edelstein, had been working diligently within the CDV to develop support for Wagner. After the mayor launched his campaign publicly, Lehman expressed his view to the Committee's leadership personally. Although by then he was eighty-three years old, Lehman spent the hot summer nights touring the reform clubs, punctuating his position in support of the mayor with his presence. Eleanor Roosevelt, no youngster herself, followed his lead. One by one the clubs fell into line. Even the most radical club, the Village Independent Democrats, who had announced in January 1961 that they would not back Wagner, finally relented. Rumors circulated that Lehman threatened to withhold up to $30,000 in campaign funds from the Greenwich Village radicals if they did not make common cause. Those who knew Lehman found it inconceivable that he would ever speak so crassly. They also knew that he could make himself very clear without resorting to crude terms. Herbert Lehman delivered the reform clubs. Without him, many would not have joined the mayor.[32]

Jewish Insiders, Italian Outsiders

The Democratic bosses aligned against the mayor agreed readily on one aspect of their strategy—they needed to run a Jewish candidate. Jewish voters cast between thirty-five and forty-five percent of the ballots in a Democratic primary—more than any other group by far. Wagner held Lehman's support, had pulled the reformers into his camp, and was personally popular with Jewish voters. The backing of the Liberal party gave the mayor added credibility among Jews, even among many registered Democrats. If the regulars did nothing to counter the mayor's strong position he would win Jewish votes in a landslide. Against a Jewish opponent, however, especially a liberal and respectable one, the mayor might be vulnerable. Moreover, the regulars' own strength was with the Catholics, especially the Irish, on whose loyalty they thought they could depend. "We expected to win the Irish votes, they were ours," remembered Pat Cunningham, in 1961 a low-level Democratic party worker in the Bronx.[33]

The most attractive Jew to be had was New York State Controller Arthur Levitt. He alone among the Democrats who ran in 1958 withstood Rockefeller's surprise victory. He had hung on by only a hair, but that was still several hundred thousand votes better than anyone else on the ticket. An accountant by profession, a respected and competent president of the school board for a brief time, Levitt was a gentleman drawn to public service, not a politician who thrived on power. The prospect of taking on the incumbent mayor in an internecine struggle for party control did not interest him. Just weeks earlier he had announced that he expected Wagner to be the party's choice, and that the mayor would be reelected. But the Brooklyn Democratic organization had launched Levitt's career, and Levitt felt indebted. The regulars needed him badly and they pressured him relentlessly until he gave in. On June 30, 1961 he announced that he would seek the Democratic nomination by running against Wagner in a primary. It was the first time since creation of the greater metropolis in 1897 that the regular Democratic party organization supported a Jewish candidate for mayor of New York City.[34]

As soon as the regulars convinced Levitt to head their slate, they had a problem. Sharkey had backed Stark in his dispute with Wagner, and had agreed to support him for City Council president. But the top two slots on the ticket could not both go to Jews, both from the same borough at that. Stark had to settle for the nomination for borough president of Brooklyn, and instead of standing in line to become the first Jewish mayor as he had hoped, he became instead the first candidate in the city's history to be dropped from two Democratic tickets in a single election. Buckley's organization chose the nominee for comptroller, a Bronx Italian named Joseph DiFede. An Irish Catholic from Queens, Thomas Mackell, became the candidate for City Council president. Conspicuous by its absence was a candidate from Manhattan. The regulars could not afford DeSapio's scent on their ticket, even though they continued to make common cause with their beleaguered counterpart.[35]

By the time Levitt entered the campaign the Republicans smelled a political opportunity. The sharp split among the Democrats gave GOP leaders hope that they could take control of City Hall. Governor Rockefeller was especially eager to launch the battle. In the first place, a Republican victory in the city would greatly strengthen his prospects for reelection in 1962. In the second place, he had every intention of running for president in 1964, and if he could mount a successful assault on the Democratic bastion of New York City it would raise his standing in his party nationally. Rockefeller looked first to Jacob Javits to carry the GOP flag. He was a proven vote getter from New York City, and Jewish. Javits toyed with the idea for a while, then announced he would stay in the Senate. The governor then turned to the next most popular Jewish Republican, New York State Attorney General Louis Lefkowitz.[36]

Lefkowitz was a GOP loyalist who grew up in the Lower East Side district where Sam Koenig had run Republican party affairs for half a century. In 1928, three years after earning his law degree from Fordham, Lefkowitz won a state assembly seat against a Democratic incumbent in a year of Republican landslide. He served just one term before losing the seat, then held a series of appointed city and state jobs, and became his party's legal counsel for a time. In 1956, when Javits resigned as attorney general to enter the Senate, the party's leaders tapped Lefkowitz for the spot—an appointment that left ethnic and regional political feathers unruffled. Competent, an able campaigner, liked by everyone, Louie Lefkowitz had no enemies. The strategy was clear—add Jewish votes to Republican party loyalists and build from there.[37]

During the first half of 1961, while Wagner battled with DeSapio but refused to announce his candidacy, Rockefeller tried desperately to win Liberal party backing for Lefkowitz. He met with Alex Rose to negotiate a deal, but the Liberal tactician played coy. Only if Wagner chose not to run would the Liberals consider joining the Republicans in a fusion campaign. After Wagner threw his hat into the ring, the Republicans were on their own. Still, with the opposition so badly fractured, they had hope.[38]

But there were splits where the Republicans normally got their support too. A cranky and flamboyant Republican named Vito Battista had organized the United Taxpayers party in 1957 and ran for mayor. Irrelevant then when Wagner's victory was assured, the conservative Italian was something of an irritant when he ran again in 1961. He accused Rockefeller and Javits of selling out to liberals leaving real Republicans with no place to go. New York, Battista complained, "was the most Sovietized city in the Western Hemisphere, outside of Havana." Lefkowitz, in his mind, was "a liberal—way over to the left." Battista had only the barest backing of his own, but his message, that the Republicans had learned to cater to New York's liberal voters moving the city's center of political gravity leftward, was largely true. Like the Democrats, the Republicans had discovered it was impossible to win in New York City without taking a large piece of the Jewish vote, and that Jews would not cast ballots for staunch conservatives. Yet, the Republicans wanted to keep conservative voters in their camp. They hoped that they would stay out of tradition and inertia. A lot of noise about how liberal the Republicans had become did not suit the GOP leadership. Late in the campaign Rockefeller and Lefkowitz met with Battista and offered him a patronage post if he would drop out of the race. The renegade refused the deal. Whether he was too sincere to be bought or displeased with the level of the offer is hard to say, but in response Battista announced that the governor and Lefkowitz made "DeSapio look like a saint."[39]

More important than Battista's campaign was Larry Gerosa's. The successful Bronx businessman had been chosen by that borough's Democratic party organization to run with Wagner in 1953 for city comptroller. Though he made something of a nuisance of himself during the first term, things were going so well no one wanted to make a change in 1957. After the reelection landslide Gerosa continued to criticize the mayor, even on minor issues. Wagner did not like the comptroller's posture, and felt that he was disloyal to the administration that brought him to power. The mayor's staff, however, insisted that Wagner could gain nothing by lowering himself to the level of petty daily squabbling that Gerosa seemed to enjoy.

Finally, one day in 1958, when the mayor was home with the flu and in a particularly irritable mood, he heard Gerosa launch another cheap criticism during a radio interview. The attacks had been accumulating for over five years by then. Wagner called his office and said to Deputy Mayor Paul O'Keefe, "I'm sick of this guy. Get something out on that bird that will finally shut him up." His staff decided that if they were going to respond it had to be definitive and issued a statement that began: "Larry Gerosa had no experience in city government when he was first elected comptroller, and he knows even less now." By the time 1961 arrived it had been clear for years that Wagner would not run with Gerosa on the ticket again. Bumped from the spot he held, the city's most prominent Italian elected official decided to enter the race for mayor as an independent, and created the Citizens party. Early polls showed that his candidacy would hurt a Democrat, but that it would hurt a Republican even more because a large number of Italians who typically favored the GOP would desert it for a fellow Italian.[40]

The Pivotal Jewish Vote, an Irish Last Hurrah

As the complicated political panorama took form, the campaigns armed their workers with pens and petitions and sent them into the field to collect sufficient signatures from registered party members to place their candidates on the ballot. When the filing date arrived on August 9, the Democratic machine showed that it still had the most potent political organization in the city, by far. It cranked out more than 280,000 signatures for Levitt, while the mayor's forces gathered only 55,000. Even Louis Lefkowitz, searching for Republican signatures in a Democratic stronghold, gathered more than the mayor by half. Levitt's staff, in a moment of euphoria, estimated that about a half-million Democrats would vote in the September 7 primary, and that their candidate would win the right to the Democratic ballot line by a margin of three votes to two.[41]

The mayor's team had known all along that it could not match the block by block politicking of the regular organization, but the enormity of the difference in the signature count hammered the point home. Even more alarming was an August update in Louis Harris's polling information. It revealed that the regulars were well prepared to bring their disciplined troops to the polls, and that if the general public did not respond to Wagner's appeal for support, the mayor would lose. The size and composition of the turnout on primary day would be critical.[42]

According to Harris, very few Italian Democrats could be counted on to vote for the mayor who was locked in a battle with the Italian leader of Tammany Hall. Blacks and Puerto Ricans, on the other hand, continued to support the mayor. "Among those Jews with the closest organization ties, the Mayor is running behind today," the survey revealed. However, many Jewish Democrats who were not affiliated with the machine would exercise their political independence and cast ballots for Wagner, if they voted. Harris emphasized, therefore, that the Jewish vote was "pivotal," adding that "this is one group where an all-out effort should be made" to increase voter participation. The way to appeal to Jewish voters was abundantly clear. "Jews will respond best of all to the bossism issue, and will vote almost unanimously against DeSapio, if the issue is cast this way." Harris went on to note that "the most popular Jew in New York is Herbert Lehman," and he recommended that Lehman and Eleanor Roosevelt, "campaign vigorously the last three weeks of the election, especially in Jewish neighborhoods and before Jewish groups."[43]

The study also discovered something less obvious. The Irish, who had seemed ready to reject the mayor several months earlier, were now apparently prepared to support him. "To a degree," the Harris report indicated, "they are against the bosses because they are opposed to machine politicians (in contrast to the Irish of two generations ago)." But much more important, "they are particularly opposed to DeSapio having emerged as the leading organization figure in recent years." The discomfort was less with the system than with the man, or more specifically his ancestry. Harris's interviews provided evidence of this by establishing that "without doubt, the key figure among the Irish is James A. Farley," the one-time King of the Irish political bosses who had helped launch FDR to the White House. In the strange bedfellow-ship that politics sometimes makes, Farley, the man who had once led his party's conservative wing and whose commitment to party "regular-ity" had been legion, had joined forces with Wagner and Lehman in an effort to stage a comeback. He appealed to the people who shared his heritage in a way the Italian running the affairs of the Democratic party could not. Farley "should campaign widely among [the Irish], making speeches and appearances. If possible, Farley handbills should be distrib-uted in Irish and other Catholic neighborhoods," the Harris report counseled.[44]

Farley evoked nostalgia among the Irish, a longing for the days when they ruled New York. The group objected less to the practices of the machine than to the bitter reality that they were being displaced. The city's top Democratic official was Italian, and the organization was backing a Jew for the party's nomination for mayor. Irish support for the machine became increasingly fragile as the group's standing in the party faded, and Wagner, the son of an Irish Catholic mother who sat in the most powerful office in the city, was one of the group's last links to formal political power in New York. They were not keen on losing it. Harris's figures revealed that Wagner could take a slight majority even among regular Democratic organization loyalists who were Irish. As the turnout rose, the mayor's performance with the group would improve.

The Wagner campaign moved on two levels to increase voter partici-pation. The first consisted of traditional campaign tactics. It was led by the reform clubbers, Jones and his team of black district leaders, and city workers loyal to the mayor. They talked with neighbors, handed out fliers, and plastered posters onto lamp posts. Letters went out urging every identifiable Wagner supporter to bring five friends to the voting booths on primary day. The second part of the strategy placed far greater reliance than ever before on mass media exposure, which required a simple image that could be captured in headlines and broadcast across airwaves.[45]

DeSapio's image was "easily the most negative in New York City" according to the Harris study. Forced to choose between the boss and the mayor, eight New Yorkers in ten would back Wagner. Moreover, the study determined that Levitt was virtually "unknown to over 7 out of every 10 Democratic voters." Pin "Levitt at every turn, [as] the faceless candidate who is being manipulated by predatory bosses, especially DeSapio, for their own selfish and corrupt ends," Harris advised. "It is important that the Mayor not give Levitt a chance to break out of the smoke-screen of boss dominated oblivion that he now is enveloped in." The strategy, in other words, was to run against DeSapio, the "sinister" Italian political boss, rather than Levitt, the respectable, Jewish public servant.[46]

Throughout the campaign "bossism" was the only issue that Wagner and his supporters recognized. Every time that Levitt tried to speak about the serious problems facing the city, the mayor blamed the conditions on boss rule. Rid the city of DeSapio, the mayor implied time and again, and New York will operate properly. For example:

> The boss system under Boss Carmine DeSapio has grown to proportions that, if left unchecked, will make a mockery of political democracy in our city . . . . He is planning now, and in fact has already begun, to dominate all nominations for legislative, judicial and administrative offices in our city. . . . The first line of defense of the predatory boss is to have his own men sitting on the bench. . . . He is planning to dictate the stands and votes of our legislators both in the City Council and the State Legislature . . . . Under Boss DeSapio, boss control has begun to create an appalling climate under which many with legitimate problems with the city were able to be mistakenly convinced that they first had to "clear it with Carmine."

and on and on.[47]

When Wagner's Commissioner of Investigation Louis Kaplan discovered that the Republican county leader of Queens, Frank Kenna, siphoned money from a middle income housing project under development in that borough, Wagner announced that the event, "illustrate[s] how the bosses, led by the likes of DeSapio and Kenna, can corrupt and subvert decent housing for our people. . . . I am frank to say that we cannot get decent middle income housing in this city unless the boss system—both democratic and republican [sic]—is smashed." DeSapio had nothing to do with the project. When Rockefeller forced Kenna to resign Wagner declared, "one down, nine to go," referring to the county leaders of the two parties in all five boroughs.[48]

Lehman, in his talks at reform clubs and on television, had been blaming all the ills of the city on Carmine DeSapio for months. At a meeting in Chelsea, on Manhattan's West Side, he recited this litany:

> In this neighborhood can be found compressed most of the heavy problems which confront New York City as a whole. . . the housing redevelopment and tenant relocation problems . . . the racial tensions . . . the juvenile gangs and violence . . . the crime . . . and the primary problem of personal safety in the streets, in the parks and squares, in your homes . . . the rackets preying on small merchants and small businessmen . . . the traffic problems . . . the air pollution by soot and poisonous dust . . . all these and many other problems are crowding in upon you in this district as they are upon the rest of the city, mounting up, piling up, and threatening to suffocate this neighborhood, this district, and this entire city.

And then the punch line:

> I consider the concentration of these problems a direct outgrowth if not an actual result of boss rule of the . . . Democratic party.[49]

The logic confused Carmine DeSapio. Of Wagner he said, "We are faced with the spectacle of a candidate who seeks reelection on a platform of cleaning up the mess which he himself has created." The boss recounted the mayor's career in a way that emphasized that Wagner was seeking, "a third term on the basis of his self-proclaimed independence from the political party of which he has been the favored beneficiary all his life." When Wagner accused DeSapio of leading a "battalion of corruption," the boss responded, "if there is indeed a 'battalion of corruption' it has been in control of City Hall for the past several years—and Robert Wagner has been its commanding officer." But the mayor's campaign was working. In the process of looking "through Mr. Levitt as if [he] were invisible," and blaming DeSapio for the city's ills, Wagner, still sitting in the mayor's office and in command of its political resources, succeeded in turning the Tammany leader into an unpopular incumbent in the public mind. Publicly, the mayor did not respond to the charge that he was running against himself. Privately, he reportedly chuckled, "I could find no better opponent."[50]

Time and again Levitt tried to find an issue that would seize the public's imagination and change the campaign from a discussion of the evils of boss rule to an assessment of the city's condition under the Wagner administration. He challenged the mayor to a debate declaring that he would respond to the "synthetic issue of bossism," but that he also wanted to discuss "our schools, our slums, our subways, safety in our streets and parks and the awful fact that parts of our city have been allowed to deteriorate into veritable jungles." Wagner refused, and neither he nor Lehman would allow DeSapio to recede from the public mind or forget that Levitt was the boss's candidate.[51]

Unable to find a means of running a campaign on the high road, Levitt surrendered to political pressures to travel the low one. In Harlem, he made a public promise to Adam Clayton Powell to give generous patronage to blacks if elected. When Wagner toured the same neighborhood he announced that "the only Negro in Levitt's office is his chauffeur," which the controller confessed was true. The mayor's staff distributed literature that detailed Wagner's impressive civil rights record, and listed the names of blacks he had appointed to high posts. The campaign also handed out fliers written in Spanish with the names of the mayor's Puerto Rican appointments. The contrast between the mayor's sensitivity to minorities and the controller's sorry record struck home. When Wagner walked along 125th Street blacks chased after him to tell him that they planned to vote for him.[52]

For a brief period, a corruption scandal revealing thievery of school construction funds surfaced, and Levitt gained some ground. But Wagner reacted decisively by calling for the resignation of the entire Board of Education. Governor Rockefeller, trying to make political hay of the affair, offered a heavy handed proposal for the state to take control of the city's educational system. The city's newspapers unanimously condemned interference from Albany, and Wagner suddenly became the defender of home rule against an upstate power play. Moreover, the mayor portrayed the scandal as the obvious consequences of boss rule. Once again, DeSapio got blamed.[53]

By mid-August Levitt's campaign, with no where else to go, was reduced to a deliberate effort to attract Jewish voters through straight ethnic appeals. He toured Williamsburg in Brooklyn where he conversed with Hasidic rabbis in Yiddish, and he visited Jewish delicatessens in the Washington Heights section of Manhattan. At one he ate lukshen kugel, a Jewish baked dish, but when he washed it down with a beer, "a combination not in the Jewish tradition," a journalist noted, he ruined whatever effect he hoped to have. His comment, that he was "a sincere devotee of the knish," might have been cute from a non-Jewish campaigner, but Jews were surprised that a member of their faith felt he had to say it. *The Jewish Daily Forward,* the only Yiddish newspaper in the city, with socialist roots that made it strongly sympathetic to the Liberal party, objected to the transparent effort to win Jewish votes. "Jews must be especially aware of the fact that the Tammany gang has purposely selected a Jew to serve as a front for them," the editor wrote. "It is quite clear that Tammany is not certain of the 'Jewish' vote. We hope that Jews will teach these agents of corruption and reaction a lesson; that principles play a more vital role than conniving tricks with Jewish menus."[54]

The mayor had a healthy store of support with Jewish voters. When Levitt walked the beach at Coney Island he got friendly handshakes, but he also heard chants of, "We want Wagner." When he accused the mayor of having allowed the city to neglect a site dedicated to the heroes of the Warsaw ghetto uprising in Riverside Park on Manhattan's Upper West Side, the Hebrew comment from the audience, "*yashe-koach*" (more power to you), generated an immediate response from another onlooker: "Where's the marionette operator, Carmine De-Sapio?" Wagner had David Dubinsky and Alex Rose to organize his appearances in the garment district, and when he descended to the Jewish stronghold of the Lower East Side, he took Herbert Lehman with him. While walking the neighborhood with the elder statesman the mayor spoke never of himself, only of Lehman and the crusade against the evils of bossism. "To those of middle age and beyond," wrote a journalist, "Mr. Lehman was the greater attraction. . . . one elderly citizen after another pressed forward to greet the former Governor. One bent and kissed his hand." In the battle to win Jewish votes, Herbert Lehman was an unmatchable weapon.[55]

Anti-Semitism: The Last Refuge of a Losing Candidate

As the campaign entered its final week, Levitt's backers felt his candidacy fading. In a last ditch effort to swing voters back to the regular organization's hope for retaining power a henchman of Bronx boss Charles Buckley prepared pamphlets that implied Wagner was a communist puppet controlled by Lehman, Dubinsky, Rose, and Eleanor Roosevelt. The regulars sent them to "special Irish mailing lists." Another piece portraying Wagner as an anti-Italian bigot went to Italian voters. But the piece that made headlines was this:

> Irish American Democrats
> Vote for Wagner
> on Primary Day
> Thurs. Sept. 7th
> or Else You Will Have
> A Levitt or a Lefkowitz as Mayor

Queens district leader Matthew Troy brought the piece to Levitt's headquarters, and the Jewish candidate immediately accused the mayor of allowing his forces to inject anti-Semitism into the campaign. Levitt said that reports had been confirmed that six hundred Sanitation Department employees canvassing Irish and Italian neighborhoods in Queens were using the argument that, "a victory for Levitt will leave a Jew to run against a Jew. . . . The Sanitation Department is intended to clean up dirt—not to spread it," he declared. Then he called on Herbert Lehman "to denounce and repudiate these racist tactics of . . . anti-Semites" in the Wagner organization. He also denounced the mayor's Brooklyn campaign manager for reportedly telling fellow Jews that Levitt did not warrant their support because he was "not Jewish enough." The next day Levitt asked Attorney General Louis Lefkowitz, who of course was also running for mayor against Wagner, to investigate the bigoted electioneering practices.[56]

Herbert Lehman steamed at the accusation of anti-Semitism leveled against Wagner, and by association, against him. The Jewish statesman's office told a reporter who called that Lehman was so "outraged by the charge that he did not trust himself to make immediate comment." The next day he had recovered sufficiently to call the episode, "a transparent, despicable, foul blow . . . the most malicious tactic of any campaign I recall." Wagner, although angered himself, barely missed a beat. He attributed the false charge to boss DeSapio's "bag of Tammany tricks," and said that more efforts to portray him as a bigot were in the works. The comment was based on information Wagner had received from members of the Bronx organization who remained quietly loyal to the substantially Irish Catholic mayor who had always treated them fairly. "The people will not be fooled," Wagner declared. "They will reject these foul tactics. . . . The forces of decency will prevail, and will smash the DeSapio forces this Thursday in the Primary."[57]

Ultimately the Attorney General's Office confirmed that the charges against the Wagner campaign were false, and that the regulars, not the mayor, had distributed bigoted literature. The anti-Semitic piece was a fraud, but Levitt probably did not know it. So much of his campaign was conducted by the party leaders without his knowledge or consent that at one point he almost quit in protest. Later, he would recall the entire campaign bitterly: "They made me run, they made me do it," friends recalled him as saying.[58]

On September 7, primary day, Charles Buckley was up before six in the morning. He dressed quickly and drove around the Bronx to check on each of his district leaders personally. He made sure that every polling station was covered. Loyal workers were handing out literature in support of Levitt and the regular party candidates for local offices. All of the machinery was in place to ensure that the Bronx organization's disciples made it to the voting booths to cast their ballots. Satisfied, Buckley returned home about eight o'clock to have some breakfast. His Irish born maid served him cereal, and the long-time political veteran engaged in small talk with the woman.

"Did you vote while I was out?," Buckley asked.

"Aye," came the noncommital response.

"Who'd you vote for?," Buckley continued.

"Wagner," the woman replied as she turned quickly and walked back to the kitchen without looking her boss in the eye. That was when Buckley knew that the organization would lose.[59]

Wagner slaughtered Levitt in all five boroughs. About 740,000 Democrats turned out, and Wagner won by 160,000 votes. He ran well with party members of every persuasion. Running on the mayor's slate, reform club candidates won seven City Council races, and every district they contested for party leadership posts. Littered among the electoral casualties lay Carmine DeSapio.

After the 1959 primary contest showed the Tammany boss vulnerable in his home base, the CDV convinced James Lanigan to move into Greenwich Village and prepare to face DeSapio in the 1961 district leader race. A Harvard trained lawyer and former aide to Averell Harriman, Lanigan had the kind of education and liberal credentials the reformers liked. He had campaigned for Stevenson and was also a favorite of Eleanor Roosevelt, who had discovered him in his youth working for her husband's Civilian Conservation Corps. But he was not just another "egghead." Since he was fourteen years old, when his father ran for Congress in his native Nebraska, Lanigan had worked on political campaigns, and at the age of forty-three, he was an experienced politician himself.[60]

As he was running against DeSapio, Lanigan's candidacy attracted substantial media attention, and the CDV funneled extraordinary resources into his effort. The campaign cost more than $40,000 according to some estimates, unheard of for a district leader contest. The Village Independent Democrats, "pathologically anti-DeSapio," took to the streets with fanatic fervor to topple him. Bossism, of course, was the principal issue. Only when the "small oligarchy at the top of the [Democratic party] pyramid" was replaced would there be a chance for good government in New York, Lanigan wrote.[61]

DeSapio countered by accusing Lanigan and the VID of being outsiders in Greenwich Village. He appealed to the neighborhood people to protect themselves against the intruders, but his argument found resonance only among his fellow Italians. The boss went down, 6,165 votes to 4,245. In defeat, DeSapio maintained "the grace that will never leave him in life," wrote journalist Murray Kempton, present as the returns flowed into the boss's headquarters. DeSapio apologized to all those who had worked for him for having let them down. To lift the mood of gloom from the room where he spoke, he declared himself "a lively corpse, down but not out." It was a brave performance, but it was the end of the road for the last of New York's big-time bosses. He would stage a vigorous, yet unsuccessful comeback campaign in 1963 against an ambitious young VID member, Edward I. Koch, and lose a final grasp for power in 1965 before fading entirely from the political scene.[62]

The day after the primary the reformers insisted that they were responsible for Wagner's success, and demanded he support one of their members to replace DeSapio as Manhattan county leader. "I did a lot more for them than they did for me," Wagner responded, and the voting pattern proved his point. The mayor had pulled together a broad coalition. It consisted of blacks, Puerto Ricans, Irish, and significant numbers of other Catholics, for whom the reform clubs held little attraction, in addition to polling well in the Jewish districts where reform clubs organized. With the general election still to come Wagner decided to duck the potentially divisive issue of a new boss and he appointed a respected attorney, Simon Rifkind, as interim leader. The mayor had no authority to take the step, but no one had the power to stop him.[63]

Wagner's stunning primary victory made it clear that Lefkowitz had no chance of defeating him in the general election, and the campaign that followed was almost friendly. The opponents met at the offices of the American Jewish Committee on October 5 and signed an agreement to ban appeals to bigotry from their election efforts. In a televised debate, both candidates proved themselves able, and changed no one's mind. Just before election day, Lefkowitz tried to boost his vote by accusing Wagner of implying that anyone who grew up on the Lower East Side was not good enough to be mayor. The effort to turn Wagner into an anti-Semite was more subtle than Levitt's had been, but neither that, nor Lefkowitz's earlier tactic of campaigning in resort hotels in the Catskill Mountains, a Jewish vacation mecca ninety miles from New York City, won him noticeable support. Comptroller Lawrence Gerosa, running on his Citizen's party ticket, accused Wagner of having split the Democratic party and billed himself as the only real Democrat in the race. He built a strong following among his fellow Italians, but could find little support among others.[64]

When the results came in Wagner won 400,000 ballots more than Lefkowitz. He took a clear majority—fifty-one percent—always a feat in a three way race. The outcome surprised no one, but political professionals found the election returns intriguing. Lefkowitz took thirty-four percent of the vote on the Republican line, more than any other mayoral candidate, even LaGuardia, had ever polled on that party's ticket alone. If the 211,000 votes Wagner had won on the Liberal party line had gone to Louis Lefkowitz, the Republican would have won by a nose. The Liberals had seemed prepared to back Lefkowitz against almost any Democrat other than the mayor. The Liberals further proved their potency that year by backing Joseph Periconi, the Republican candidate for borough president of the Bronx. In a razor close election they delivered his margin of victory. It was the first time ever that the Bronx borough president was not a Democrat. Gerosa won more than 320,000 votes, mostly from Italians who might otherwise have voted Republican. The 55,000 votes Wagner won on the Brotherhood party line would not necessarily have gone to the GOP, but they underlined the cleavages in the Democratic party that could work to Republican advantage. Louis Lefkowitz's honorary campaign manager, John Lindsay, thought the results were very interesting indeed.[65]

The End of An Era

The 1961 Democratic primary contest for mayor in New York City was the culmination of the conflict between the party's conservative wing, dominated by Irish Catholics, and the liberal wing, dominated by Jews. Since early in the century, Democratic victory in New York City elections had depended on an unwritten alliance between Irish Catholic politicians and Jewish voters. The one group controlled the Democratic machine and enjoyed the power, prestige, and privileges that went with it. The other insisted that the city's politicians pay due deference to their demands for liberal social policies, respond to their particular concerns about discrimination and anti-Semitism, and apply some sense of moral standards to the practice of city government. Since the 1940s Italian voters had been a weak third force within the party, generally following the Irish pattern of seeking positions of party control, but without the same degree of success. In the 1950s Carmine DeSapio was the notable exception to the rule.

By the time of the Buffalo nominating convention in 1958, the liberals had clearly established themselves as the dominant ideological force in the New York State Democratic party. More and more Irish and Italian voters were abandoning the Democrats for the Republicans, with whom they felt more comfortable philosophically. As a consequence, the predominantly Irish and Italian Democratic party leadership rested on an increasingly narrow base of Catholic supporters. In many heavily Jewish areas Irish district leaders held office only because replacing the existing leaders with members of their own faith was relatively unimportant to Jewish voters and party workers. A number of Jews had of course risen to positions of organization leadership over time, but they had done so patiently, and in disproportionately small numbers considering the weight of their vote within the Democratic party. Hugo Rogers's brief and unmemorable tenure as Tammany chief was the only time a Jew had ever been a county leader in New York City.

Jewish willingness to accept Catholic party leadership began to change with the development of the reform movement. This younger generation of professional, well educated, American born, Jewish, political activists were determined to participate in the management of Democratic party affairs. While the group was not anti-Catholic in any overt way, the cultural gap between themselves and the existing party office-holders was simply too great to bridge. When Herbert Lehman declared that DeSapio had to go, he was declaring an end to the arrangement that had left control of the Democratic party in Catholic hands and policy orientation in Jewish minds. It is worth repeating that there is no evidence of a conscious push on the part of Lehman to displace people who did not share his faith. Rather, the machine system of political organizing disturbed him, increasingly as time passed. As Lehman aged, he felt less and less need to compromise with machine bosses. With no further ambitions to hold office, it was especially easy for him to break with the party leadership.

There is little doubt that it was Herbert Lehman, armed with his own unassailable prestige and the emerging force of the reform movement, that pushed Robert Wagner to break with the machine. And in early 1961 when the mayor contemplated the political consequences of splitting with the Tammany chief, Alex Rose was his most important counselor. The Liberal party leader's assessment that Wagner could win reelection without DeSapio's support was critical to the mayor's decision to reject the boss because Wagner had great confidence in Rose's political judgment. Rose's pledge to deliver the Liberal party line to Wagner ensured the mayor a spot on the ballot in November no matter what, and enhanced his standing with liberal Democrats in his own party primary. New York's liberal Jewish political forces were behind the mayor's decision to run against the regular Democratic organization.[66]

That Wagner ultimately won Catholic votes too should not obscure the nature of the party conflict. To the contrary, the mayor's success with the Irish was due in part to the regular organization's selection of a Jewish candidate to oppose him. The machine knew it had to do something to try to appeal to Jewish voters under the circumstances, and misjudged the effect that placing a non-Irish candidate on the top of the Democratic ticket would have on their traditional party loyalists. If one accepts Wagner as Irish Catholic, and most of the Irish did, Levitt's candidacy was only the second time since 1909 that the organization's leaders had selected a non-Irish politician to run for mayor. The other was the 1950 candidacy of Ferdinand Pecora. Both instances brought defeat. Wagner actually maintained the traditional pattern that had brought Democratic victories to New York—an Irish Catholic candidate with appeal to Jewish voters—even as the formula became obsolete. And as was so often the case in the past, the 1961 New York mayoralty campaign had been reduced ultimately to an effort to win Jewish votes, an unsuccessful one on the part of the regular Democratic organization and on the part of the Republicans who sported Louis Lefkowitz as a candidate.

The rise in the number of blacks and Puerto Ricans living in New York, and the decline in the city's white, especially Catholic, population helped to swing the balance within the Democratic party away from the conservative wing. Democratic party liberals placed strong emphasis on advancing the cause of civil rights, and using the tools of government to guarantee economic opportunity, so the city's racial minorities were philosophically comfortable with the candidates promoted by liberal Democrats. Blacks and Puerto Ricans voted overwhelmingly for Wagner, for instance. But it would go too far to say that there was a meaningful alliance within the Democratic party between its liberal wing and New York's minorities. J. Raymond Jones organized black politicians from Harlem into an independent unit, generally siding with liberals on matters of race and economic policy, but with the more conservative district leaders on matters of party control, provided he received his due. The Democratic organization in Manhattan had thus fractured into three pieces: a regular faction that was heavily Catholic, a reform faction that was heavily Jewish, and a black faction. Ironically, DeSapio's conflict with Powell in 1958 accelerated political organizing among blacks, to the boss's detriment. The task of brokering these groups, and getting them to cooperate, would prove virtually impossible after 1961.

The other regular Democratic organizations around the city also emerged from the 1961 conflict badly weakened. Although the reform and minority factions in the Bronx and Brooklyn were not so strong as in Manhattan, they existed and created similar, if less intense conflicts in those boroughs. Moreover, the charter reform referendum that Wagner had placed on the ballot passed. The new rules would eliminate the administrative functions of the borough presidents beginning in 1963, which would reduce the independent patronage power of all of the county organizations in New York City by about ninety percent. And the municipal unions Wagner had done so much to create were beginning to exercise greater power over city workers as well, further weakening the machine. Before his primary victory, Wagner had been careful not to fire many of the city's Democratic patronage appointees. He did not want to subject himself to accusations that he was using his office for political purposes, and he did not want to give wavering Democrats reason to oppose him. After winning the party contest he let go over four hundred senior municipal employees, and hired back only those he felt he could rely on. "We don't want people around who tried to kick my brains out," the mayor explained. He planned to finish the job of transforming the Democratic party in New York City, but it would turn out that breaking the party up was easier than putting it back together.[67]

The 1961 Democratic primary and general election broke new financial ground for a mayoral contest. When Wagner announced his candidacy in 1953 his campaign committee had five hundred dollars in the bank—no more. Piecing together the actual amount spent on his primary and general election campaign that year is very difficult, but $250,000 is a plausible estimate. Running as the incumbent, without a primary in 1957, he spent about $350,000. That year, he had the entire Democratic party organization campaigning on his side. In 1961, when he broke with the machine and had to reach the voting public through the use of mass media to a much greater degree than ever before, the cost of his campaign escalated to beyond one million dollars. For the first time in his political career the mayor resorted to formal fund-raising functions with groups of Real Estate developers who did business in the city. At one luncheon, a municipal employee serving as a co-chairman of the mayor's finance committee asked each of the business-men present to stand and announce publicly how much money they would pledge to the mayor's campaign. The tactic caused an outcry and led to the man's resignation. When the Democratic party was strong, its support was the scarce resource in the electoral politics of the city. Running without a machine in the age of mass media required money on a grand scale, creating a new dimension to the quest for the mayor-alty.[68]

EIGHT

The Ambitions of John V. Lindsay

1961–1965

Mayor Wagner's third administration took on a harsh political tone even before it started. The day before Thanksgiving, 1961, Brooklyn boss Joseph Sharkey called together a high powered team of loyal Democrats from his borough and asked them to make peace for him with the mayor. The contingent invited itself to Gracie Mansion where Wagner greeted them cordially, unaware of the exact purpose of their visit. When they sat down to talk one began:

"Bob, we know you've been through a hell of a fight, but Joe Sharkey has done a lot of good for all of us throughout the years, and he's been good for the party. It's Thanksgiving after all, a good time for forgiveness, and . . ."

The mayor cut the speaker short.

"Now wait just a minute. What did Joe Sharkey try to do to me in the primary?" No one answered.

"He tried to f_____ me!" the normally mild mannered mayor exclaimed pointing his index finger at his own chest. The guests were stunned. They had never heard such language from the mayor.

"Now f_____ him," Wagner finished, thrusting the accusatory finger toward the men in the room. The meeting ended, and several months later Wagner displaced Joseph Sharkey as Brooklyn Democratic leader.[1]

The Party Falls Apart

For a brief time a triumvirate replaced Sharkey. Assemblyman Stanley Steingut, a long-time veteran of Brooklyn politics, whose father Irwin had once been speaker of the New York State Assembly, coveted the spot. He met with Wagner and thought he had secured a commitment of support from the mayor, but when the time came to make the choice, Wagner backed Steingut's rival, Assemblyman Aaron Jacoby. The latter was a long-time favorite of Alex Rose, the mayor's most influential political adviser by this time. More than a few of Brooklyn's Democrats resented the Liberal party leader's interference in their affairs, and within a few months Steingut managed to garner just enough votes to win the county leader's position himself. In the process, he initiated a struggle with the mayor that lasted the duration of Wagner's third term and kept the Brooklyn organization badly split and embittered. There was a certain irony to Steingut's victory. He was the first Jewish politician in the city's history to rise to the top of a Democratic county organization on his own ability, and he was as much a machine politician as the Irish pol he replaced. Yet it was only after Herbert Lehman, the Jewish reform clubs, and the Liberal party toppled the Irish regime that Steingut was able to assume the county leader's post.[2]

In the Bronx, boosted by the support he received from the Kennedys, Charlie Buckley fought to hold onto his control of that borough's Democratic organization. A strong reform movement developed in his home district, and to win reelection to his congressional seat in 1962 the boss had to beat back the effort of a young Jewish attorney named David Levy. In a fierce primary in 1964 a young Protestant lawyer named Jonathan Bingham, once an assistant to Governor Averell Harriman and the husband of Herbert Lehman's grand-niece, pushed Buckley from the federal office that had been his since 1934. The boss kept his post as county leader, but he was badly weakened, and the Bronx party badly fractured.[3]

The bitter cultural collision between the Jewish reformers and the Catholic regulars in Manhattan offered little hope for the return of a strong party organization there. Reform clubs controlled thirty of Manhattan's sixty-six Democratic party districts after the 1961 primary. The system for electing the county leader grouped the party districts according to assembly district, and gave each district leader a fraction of a vote equal to the proportion of the assembly district represented. As a result, the reformers held 6 5/6 votes, the regulars 5 1/6 votes, and J. Raymond Jones held power over the balance, four votes.

To replace DeSapio the reformers backed John Harrington, one of their own from the Lexington Democratic Club, but they did not have a majority. Their own shrill rhetoric and the intense hostility of the 1961 primary battle made it impossible for them to reach an accommodation with the regulars. The prospect for an alliance with the blacks was also dim. "I have a suggestion for all these bright young idealists," J. Raymond Jones said of the reform clubbers with more than a little disdain, "they can join the Peace Corps." He wanted jobs for his people and power for himself, and that meant working with the mayor.

Wagner did not want to return power to the regulars and create an image of a Democratic party regressing to "bossism," but he had no intention of handing power over to the reform clubs. His relationship with them had always been uneasy, and the inconsistencies between their rhetoric and their actions was so apparent that the mayor did not trust them. For example, the reformers complained that the patronage-infested machine was corrupting the governmental process by making appointments on a political rather than a professional basis. But when reform club darling Bill Ryan was district leader he sent lists of job seekers to the mayor's patronage dispenser just like the regulars did. A respected officer of the Lexington Democrats asked Julius Edelstein to intervene with the mayor and secure patronage posts for some club members because it was the surest way of strengthening his power. Another reform clubber arranged an appointment with the mayor to petition for the county leadership post for a colleague who had been nominated by a reform club caucus. When the man arrived, he asked the mayor to name him to the spot instead. The reform clubs accused the machine of unethical electoral practices, but Herbert Lehman found himself asking the CDV to intercede with reform club candidates who claimed falsely that he had endorsed them. A good government group wrote to one prominent reform candidate, who would serve for years in the State Senate, to ask him to correct errors in his campaign literature that were dishonest attempts to discredit his opponent, and on and on.[4]

The tightly controlled, well disciplined nature of the regular organization had kept them from breaking into politics on the terms they sought, so reform clubbers glorified the idea of an open, "unbossed," Democratic party. They took this idea to such an extreme, however, that they were "not radicals but anarchists," according to Julius Edelstein. If the reform club leaders did not believe in discipline and found virtue in noncooperation, how reliable could they be as allies? And if they practiced all the tricks of the political trade while assailing the regulars for doing the same, who could trust them? Certainly Wagner did not. Over a period of several months the mayor convinced the regulars and J. Raymond Jones to support Edward Costikyan. Costikyan, an Armenian, neutral in Tammany's ethnic wars, was first elected a district leader as a reformer in 1955. He had stayed away from the fanatics in the movement, and had earned a reputation for keeping his word that was somewhat rare among reform club leaders. In March 1962, with all of the reformers except himself and his female coleader voting against him, Costikyan became the Democratic county leader. With no independent base of support, however, he found himself in a perpetual struggle. After two years he resigned from the daily frustration of trying to keep the party together to spend more time at his law practice.[5]

The mayor chose J. Raymond Jones to replace Costikyan and for eight nights straight met from early in the evening until past mid-night with reform club district leaders to convince them to endorse the decision. He pointed out the obvious political advantage of currying favor with blacks, whose political presence in the city was continuing to rise, and the symbolic importance of selecting as county leader a member of a group that had been kept at the margins of power for so long. The mayor reviewed Jones's durable career, praised the general high quality of his patronage recommendations, and emphasized the man's reasonableness and shrewd political judgement. It took hours of effort, but finally the mayor outlasted the reluctant reformers who agreed to his choice. Wagner then picked up the phone and called Duke Viggiano, a Lower East Side district leader who had assumed the role of coordinating the regulars.

"Duke, I want you and your fellows to consider Ray Jones for the county leadership post, and let me give you some reasons why."

"Just a minute Mr. Mayor," the loyal regular interrupted. "If Ray Jones is your man that's all we need to know. I'll line up the vote."[6]

The conversation ended, and Wagner marveled at the difference between dealing with the regulars and the reformers. J. Raymond Jones became the first black Democratic party county leader anywhere in the country. But he was only modestly more successful than Costikyan in keeping peace, and the feuding among Democrats in Manhattan, and around the city, continued.

The reform clubs never did fashion themselves into a coherent force. The one issue that had united them, DeSapio's rule, had disappeared. Within days after Wagner's reelection, Herbert Lehman ended his association with the CDV. He would continue to work for the causes he believed in, he announced, but implied that he could no longer participate in the committee's affairs as actively as he had because his years were catching up with him. Anyone who had seen him campaign along Coney Island's boardwalk in the hot summer sun, or climb up scaffolding ladders in the Bronx to appear beside the mayor at outdoor rallies, could only wonder at Lehman's sudden realization that he was old.

The elder statesman of the reform movement left the CDV because it had become something other than what he had intended. In May, 1961, Edelstein had warned him that, "our creature has grown, if not into a Frankenstein's Monster, at least into an entity with glaring defects and deficiencies." Its mood, he wrote, was "basically negative, iconoclastic, violent and intolerant." Edelstein was taken aback that within the reform movement, "there should have grown up, so quickly, the same proprietary attitude by the clubs—the same clubhouse mystique—that exists in the boss ridden machines. The reform clubhouse boys have developed the same sense of exclusive jurisdiction that the Tammany clubhouse boys have always had." Days after the 1961 primary Edelstein warned that the reform club activists would try to use Lehman for their own private gain. "These are not pretty people all of them. Some of them are decent enough, [but] . . . many are overambitious; some are wicked." Lehman cut his ties to the CDV because he did not think the reform clubs that the committee held together represented the goals of the movement he had led, and he had no interest in being used for personal gain by petty politicians, whether working-class and Catholic or well educated and Jewish.[7]

The divisions within the Democratic party had their effect. In 1962 polls showed that Governor Rockefeller's popularity was sagging and that there was real opportunity for a Democratic victory in the state. A "Herbert Lehman type candidate"—an upper crust Jew perceived to be above politics—had the best chance to defeat the incumbent according to a confidential public opinion survey. The Democrats set out to find someone who fit the description. Wagner conferred with a number of people, and ultimately took President Kennedy's suggestion to tap Robert Morgenthau, Jr., the son of Franklin Roosevelt's New Deal era

Treasurer, whom Kennedy had named United States Attorney for New York's Southern District. To balance the ticket the Democrats chose an Irish Catholic, James Donovan, to run for Senate against Jacob Javits. Donovan, a successful corporate lawyer, had been a World War II navy commander and a member of the Office of Special Services (OSS), the wartime intelligence operation. He was an active participant in a number of international causes, and had won some celebrity for his success in helping to negotiate the release of Gary Powers, the U.S. pilot shot down over the Soviet Union in 1959 in the U-2 affair. Arthur Levitt stood for reelection as controller, and the Democrats nominated Edward Dudley to challenge Louis Lefkowitz as attorney general. Dudley was the first black man ever chosen by the Democrats to run for statewide office.[8]

Morgenthau, a highly competent and decent man, turned out to be a miserable campaigner. "Whoever chose him never heard him give a speech," Warren Moscow reasoned. He lost ground wherever he appeared, and the regulars resented a strategy that allowed the party to choose an inept candidate as long as he fit a liberal Jewish image. Even on that basis Morgenthau had been a poor choice; he was too far removed from the day to day life of the city's Jews to generate much ethnic appeal. Sometime after his failed election bid he bumped into black civil rights activist Bayard Rustin standing on a street corner eating a knish, a popular Jewish food. "What's that you're eating?," Morgenthau asked. Rustin was shocked. "I'm eating the reason you're not governor," answered the black man in touch with the city's ethnic pulse. The liberal wing of the party resented the Senate candidacy of James Donovan with the same bitterness that the conservatives objected to Morgenthau. Donovan's rhetoric became so right-wing by the end of the campaign that liberal Democrats and the Liberal party all but disavowed him.[9]

The disjointed Democratic campaign allowed Javits to win by a million votes, and Louis Lefkowitz beat Dudley by seven hundred thousand ballots. As in 1958 Arthur Levitt was the sole Democrat returned to office. Rockefeller beat Morgenthau by more than five hundred thousand votes. Normally that would have been an impressive margin, but it was well behind the successes of the other prominent members of his ticket, and scarcely half what his campaign staff glibly predicted in the days leading up to the election. The performance was considered weak, a setback to Rockefeller's presidential ambitions. There were two principal reasons for the result. The first was that Rockefeller took a much lower share of the Jewish vote than the two Jewish men who shared the ticket with him. The second was that the newly formed Conservative party, established specifically to weaken the influence of Rockefeller and other liberal Republicans within the GOP, turned out to be more successful than even its own organizers had dreamed possible.[10]

The Conservative Backlash

At the 1960 Republican national convention, Nelson Rockefeller made heavy handed demands for liberal concessions in the party platform. His posture infuriated a large number of party loyalists. Many New York Republicans found Rockefeller's liberal attitude—and Javits's as well—out of touch with the national organization's beliefs. Late in 1961 two young Wall Street attorneys, Kieran O'Doherty and J. Daniel Mahoney, along with a half-dozen friends who felt Rockefeller had all but sabotaged their efforts on behalf of Nixon in New York State the year before, launched an ambitious drive to create a permanent Conservative party. Borrowing a technique from Wall Street's financial firms they mailed a "Conservative Party Prospectus" to about 50,000 likely supporters they identified around the state. The strategy behind the enormous undertaking could not have been more clear. In the opening letter of the plan the organizers wrote:

> The Rockefeller-Javits leadership, confident that conservative New York Republicans are a captive vote, is leading the Party in an unabating march to the left.
>
> The Rockefeller-Javits elements must be made to realize that so long as they abandon Republican principles in pursuit of liberal backing, they will be denied the support of the conservative Republicans who constitute the backbone of the party. . . .
>
> The Conservative Party's endorsement will become essential to Republican victories in New York statewide elections, just as the Liberal Party's endorsement is considered essential by the Democrats.

"Our intention is to gain for conservative Republicans the same recognition in party policy-making that the Liberal party has gained for liberals within the Democratic party," O'Doherty explained publicly. A blunt journalist described the Conservative objective as an effort to "make Rockefeller and Javits stop licking the liberals' boots." The movement aimed its sights at dissatisfied Republicans, but organizers also understood that liberals "are purging old-line Democrats from the Democratic party," and offered shelter to those who no longer felt at home in a Democratic party so heavily laced with liberalism.[11]

The process at work was evident. The Liberal party had organized a large segment of the liberal Jewish population into a coherent force that could at times determine the outcome of close elections. First the Democrats, and then the Republicans, learned this and had adopted the practice of offering liberal candidates to the public because it was the way to win. The Conservatives were the almost inevitable reaction, an effort by those whose voices were increasingly ignored to reassert themselves. The leadership of the new party was overwhelmingly Irish Catholic. Its membership too, in its early years especially, consisted mainly of Irish Catholics, with some German Catholics and Lutherans, and some Italians. As Irish Democrats confronted the loss of control over the Democratic party that they once had ruled, many searched for a new political home among the Conservatives.[12]

The small team of lawyers that launched the effort to create the Conservative party worked with the zeal of converts to attract volunteers and to gather enough petitions from each of New York's sixty-two counties to place their candidates for statewide office on the ballot in 1962. They succeeded, and running a virtually unknown upstate businessman named David Jaquith for governor they polled more than 140,000 votes. New York State law rewards any party that wins 50,000 votes in a statewide election with an automatic place on the ballot until the next gubernatorial contest. As a result, a Conservative party candidate would be on the ballot in the 1965 New York City mayoralty contest.

The Ambitions of John V. Lindsay

Early in 1965 *Herald Tribune* journalist Joseph Carter reported that "political experts and analysts," believed that to win City Hall away from the Democrats, the Republicans needed to do three things: get the Liberal party endorsement, come up with a candidate who could carry the Jewish vote, and build a party organization that could carry Queens.[13]

The first two objectives were old news, and closely related. New York City had seven registered Democrats for every two Republicans. Liberal party support bolstered the base of loyal voters a Republican candidate could count on, and attracted those liberal Democrats dissatisfied with their party's nominee. Typically, these were Jews voting against the tactics and politics of the city's regular Democratic organization. New York's politicians understood in 1965 that "the Jewish vote is now the swing vote in the city." It had been for some time, and its influence seemed on the rise. Catholics were moving out of the city and into the suburbs at a faster pace than Jews, so that the Jewish proportion of the New York City electorate increased, from about twenty-five percent in the 1940s to more than thirty percent by the early 1960s.[14]

The political significance of Queens grew with its population. Since the 1920s large numbers of German, Irish, and Italian Catholics had been moving to Queens from elsewhere in the city as they climbed up the economic ladder, out of apartments and into homes. The commitment of many of these New Yorkers to the Democratic party weakened as their property values and income levels rose. By 1940 Queens voters typically delivered a heavy Republican majority, splitting their votes more evenly when the Democrats offered an especially attractive candidate. By 1952 Queens boasted more voters than any borough except Brooklyn.[15]

Starting in the late 1940s large apartment complexes went up in Jackson Heights and Kew Gardens, in Flushing and Forest Hills, and elsewhere in Queens. The new buildings attracted large numbers of younger middle-class Jews looking for dwellings and neighborhoods more pleasant than those in Manhattan and Brooklyn, but cheaper and nearer than those in the surburbs. In 1940 some 120,000 Jews lived in Queens, constituting less than ten percent of the population; by 1961 nearly 420,000 Jews lived there, about a quarter of the borough's total population. Whether these new residents would vote Democratic or Republican—whether they would vote like Jews traditionally had, or could be convinced to vote like their middle-class, homeowning, neighbors—remained an open question in the early 1960s. In overwhelmingly Democratic New York, Queens was an island of Republican opportunity. As elsewhere in the city, Jews were the swing voters.[16]

Given the conditions for a successful campaign for mayor, Jacob Javits was the most attractive Republican possibility. He was Jewish, had been supported by the Liberals in the past, and was an experienced and effective campaigner. By 1965, however, he had settled into the Senate and had begun accumulating the seniority so important to influence in that body. He saw no reason to give up a job he enjoyed for the headache of trying to govern the metropolis. Like many other Republicans, he wanted his party to nominate Congressman John Lindsay.[17]

John Vliet Lindsay was, at first blush, an unlikely man to win a New York mayoralty campaign. White Anglo-Saxon Protestants had no standing in the ethnic equations politicians used to calculate the chances for electoral success in the city, and Lindsay was very WASP. Six feet three inches tall, fair haired, blue eyed and "heroically handsome,"

Lindsay's physical bearing seemed a reflection of what the city's Protestant elite considered a proper upbringing—the Buckley School in New York City for elementary education, St. Paul's prep in New Hampshire for high school, Yale University for college, and later, Yale Law School. The best he could do for immigrant roots was a grandfather from the Isle of Wight, off the coast of southern England. His father laid claim to some Irish blood, but from so many decades past that it had been diluted beyond detection. His mother's Dutch ancestors had been in America for generations, and the Lindsay children were raised Episcopalian, the faith of New York's wealthy.[18]

As a teenager, Lindsay met Fiorello LaGuardia during a class trip to City Hall. The impressionable youngster concluded that the Republicans were the party of virtue in New York because LaGuardia "was with the good guys, fighting the bad guys—Tammany Hall." When World War II broke out Lindsay volunteered for the navy. By the time peace came he was a full lieutenant wearing five battle stars. He was also a chastened man. A college roommate had been killed, as had several of his closest friends, and a quarter of his graduating class from St. Paul's. It was then that Lindsay made a moral decision to enter public life. "I felt something had to be done to make sure it wouldn't happen again, and politics finally seemed to me to be the way to get most fully involved instead of sitting in a business or profession," he reasoned.[19]

Lindsay completed law school, and in 1952, at the age of thirty, became president of the New York Young Republican Club. He described the group as "an independent lot . . . filled with energy and ambition [and] a thorough and deep seated disgust with the way political affairs were conducted in New York City." Lindsay spearheaded the club's drive to elect Eisenhower, and in return became a special legislative assistant to the newly appointed attorney general, Herbert Brownell, an old family friend. In 1958 he returned to New York and launched his own political career. In a well managed primary effort and election campaign he won a seat in Congress representing Manhattan's Upper East Side. He rapidly established a reputation as a liberal legislator who exercised independent judgement. He won reelection comfortably in 1960, and in a landslide in 1962. In 1964, when the right wing of his party insisted on a harshly conservative national platform, Lindsay disavowed it and refused to endorse Barry Goldwater, the Republican presidential candidate. Lindsay's district returned him to Congress with more than seventy percent of the vote, even though a strong majority voted for Democrat Lyndon Johnson for President. Although running on the Republican ticket, Lindsay never once referred to the party during his campaign. He adopted the slogan: "John V. Lindsay— The District's Pride, The Nation's Hope." Clearly he had national ambitions, and the press had already begun to think of him as a potential presidential contender.[20]

The seventeenth congressional district that Lindsay represented was known as the "silk stocking" district, a metaphor for the great wealth and upper class bearing of so many of its residents. It offered a young politician an unusual degree of visibility because it contained the headquarters of the country's three national television networks, and *Time* magazine and *Newsweek*, and a horde of publishing companies and advertising firms. It was home to the executive offices of more Fortune Five Hundred corporations than any other district in the nation, and to New York's rich, along Fifth Avenue and Sutton Place, and to its powerful, like Nelson Rockefeller, and former Governors Dewey and Harriman, and Herbert Lehman and Eleanor Roosevelt, and on and on. Still, no congressman had been elected President since William McKinley in 1896. Lindsay recognized that even if the unique nature of his district gave him a boost, his political journey had more chance of ending in the White House if he could find a launching pad with wider geographic spread, more power and national importance.

By early 1965 Lindsay's desire to move on was keen. His unorthodox Republicanism had left him so isolated in the House that he had rendered himself "pretty nearly ineffective," as a congressman, he admitted. But the obvious paths for advancement were blocked. Between 1958 and 1964 New York had a Republican Governor, Nelson Rockefeller, and two Republican Senators, Jacob Javits and Kenneth Keating. Keating's loss to Robert Kennedy in 1964 offered scant encouragement—the seat would not come around for six long years, and who ever looked forward to running against a Kennedy? Only the mayoralty seemed to offer a way up, and maybe out.[21]

The Mayor of New York instantly becomes a national figure. Yet, paradoxically, the office has always been a dead end job. It seems to use up its occupants, exhausting them politically and otherwise; it taints them in the minds of anyone outside the five boroughs. Lindsay thought the national attitude toward New York's top official could change. For years gerrymandered voting districts gave disproportionate strength to non-urban areas across the country. Legislators representing regions with declining populations successfully resisted the loss of political power that should have followed. A 1964 Supreme Court decision ruled that the districting practices in six states, including New York, violated the one man, one vote protections of the Constitution. As states across the country took steps to see to it that their laws conformed to the ruling, it appeared that national political power would shift markedly toward urban centers. President Johnson declared 1965 the "Year of the City" in a special address to Congress, and then elevated metropolitan problems to cabinet status by creating the Department of Housing and Urban Development. As the nation's priorities became increasingly urban, Lindsay reasoned, a politician identified across the country as "Mr. City" would be well placed to seek national office. What better way to win the title than as Mayor of New York? [22]

After the 1961 mayoralty contest Lindsay concluded that he would have run a better campaign than Lefkowitz. He realized then that running for mayor in 1965 might be the next step in his career, but he did not dwell on it. When Republicans began thinking about choosing a mayoral candidate late in 1964, Javits and Lindsay discussed the city's political circumstances. The two politicians publicly identified three conditions that they felt were essential if their party were to have any chance of mounting a successful fusion effort: a treasury of one and a half million dollars; a free hand for a candidate to wage the race without interference from Albany or New York City's GOP leaders; and selection of a candidate by March 1, 1965, without a primary, to allow sufficient time to build a campaign organization. The message was meant for Rockefeller as party leader, and Lindsay indicated that if the conditions were met, he would run. [23]

Rockefeller was prepared to commit the party's coffers, and his own, to a mayoralty race, and he understood the need for a campaign in Democratic New York City to be free from apparent control by Republican bosses. The March 1 deadline created a problem. Rockefeller had an ambitious agenda on the floor of the New York State Legislature in early 1965, and it was being held hostage in a complicated political war between Mayor Wagner and Stanley Steingut. Until that was resolved, Rockefeller did not want to poison relations with Wagner by launching a mayoral candidate against him. When the March 1 deadline came and went without a nod from the governor, Lindsay announced he would not run. [24]

Yet, Javits and Lindsay were the only potential Republican candidates who had a chance of making a credible race for the city's top post. Javits had little cause to change his mind, so prominent Republicans began telephoning Lindsay and sending him letters urging him to make the race for the good of the party and for the good of the city. Someone leaked poll results to the press that indicated Lindsay would do well against the mayor. By early May, John Lindsay was losing sleep over the matter. He discussed the possibility of changing his mind with his campaign manager, Robert Price.[25]

Price, thirty-two years old, had grown up in the Bronx the son of an orthodox Jewish grocer. He had an oblong face and a balding head, a pointed nose and dark rimmed glasses that sat atop a husky six foot frame. In physical appearance he was half nerd, half middle linebacker, with a temperament as unpredictable as his confusing image suggested. He had an abrupt, often arrogant manner, but that was inconsequential to Lindsay. Price began working with Lindsay during his first campaign for congress, and had proven himself a political wizard who could read the public, manipulate the media, and run a campaign from his head, even one that was New York sized. "There was never a better contribution to anything than Bob Price to John Lindsay," one close Lindsay acquaintance told an early biographer of the congressman. "Bob Price *is* practically John Lindsay."[26]

After a weekend of listening to the prospective candidate's agonizing, Price "could tell he was ready to go." Without checking with Lindsay he called *The New York Times* and "leaked" the news that the man was running. The enthusiastic response that followed encouraged the Hamlet-like politician. Two days later, after financial arrangements had been confirmed and the GOP nomination had been promised by party leaders, Lindsay led an eleven car caravan of supporters and journalists on a tour of the five boroughs, stopping in each to declare his crusade:[27]

> I enter this fight because conscience and duty compel me and because I believe that with proper leadership our city can once again be restored as the Empire City of the world.
>
> Cities are for people and for living, and yet under its present tired management New York City has become a place that is no longer for people or for living. In these long years of one-party rule, we have witnessed the decline and fall of New York City. . . .
>
> There is no leadership, and in such a vacuum of leadership there is no standard, no tone, no quality of excellence. . . .
>
> I for one cannot stand by while the decline and fall of New York continues headlong. . . .
>
> To all of the people of our city I pledge my total effort. I will carry my message to every person, and I express the hope that every person who feels as I do will join with me to bring to our city the greatness that it so richly deserves.[28]

Lindsay was not asking for a chance to govern the city—he proposed to rescue it.

A Graceful Exit

The man in City Hall whom Lindsay blamed for New York's dire circumstances shrugged. "Can you beat him?," reporters asked Wagner of his impending race with Lindsay. "Sure I can beat him," replied the political pro who had won three mayoralty campaigns and two citywide primaries. He gave Lindsay short shrift. "I'm not going . . . to waste my time in the next few weeks talking politics. I've got too much to do attending to the problems of the city," he said. The battle lines seemed to be falling into place.

For many Democrats, the unsuccessful campaign to unseat Governor Rockefeller in 1962 had called into question the quality of Wagner's leadership of the party, but there was no one to contest him. Herbert Lehman died in 1963, and after that Wagner stood alone in stature among New York State Democrats. When Robert Kennedy descended on New York to run for Senate in 1964, Wagner withheld his endorsement until it was clear that the mayor would continue to act as the state's top Democratic official whatever the outcome of Kennedy's race. The mayor found brokering the endless petty feuds over party control tiresome, but in the balkanized environment that obtained after 1961, no one else could do it for him, and he had no intention of surrendering the power that it gave him as long as he had to function as mayor.[29]

While ethnic fissures made the city's politics increasingly complex, running the city's government became no simpler. Problems of noise and pollution, traffic congestion and public sanitation, water supply and fire control for eight million people remained as intractable as ever. The flow into the city of poor blacks and Puerto Ricans continued, as did the outflow of white middle-class citizens to the suburbs. Increased levels of violent crime and insufficient resources to combat it, the seemingly endless need for low-income housing, the strain of providing education for more and more children who lived in deprived environments, all combined to give the impression that the quality of life in New York, and the ability of the government to improve it, was declining.

The march for civil rights for blacks surged forward throughout the country in the early 1960s, and no pace of change, it seemed, could satisfy a people so miserably oppressed for so long. Tensions rose everywhere. In New York, protesters accused the mayor of acquiescence in the face of discrimination, and militants launched sit-down strikes in City Hall and in city agency offices. One hot day in July 1964, a white police officer shot a black youth in Manhattan and six days of rioting erupted in Harlem and Bedford-Stuyvesant. The picture of police battalions locked in combat with the people of New York's ghettos flashed across television screens confusing and frightening the city. Intellectuals had already begun to ask, "Is New York City Ungovernable?," and in her popular book, *The Death and Life of Great American Cities*, Jane Jacobs wrote that the country's urban centers were headed for disaster as a consequence of inadequate and unsound planning. Early in 1965 the *Herald Tribune* ran a series entitled "City in Crisis," detailing the problems accumulating daily in New York, for which no solutions were apparent. Faced with an atmosphere of decline, many New Yorkers felt a need for new leadership. Still, when in February 1965 Wagner made an off-the-cuff remark that he planned to run for an unprecedented fourth term, the Democrats prepared to line up behind him.[30]

Then, on May 28, 1965 a story leaked that Wagner might not seek reelection. It looked like the standard political ploy to create momentum for a draft. Lindsay bet Price one hundred dollars that Wagner would run. Two weeks later the mayor called a press conference, and journalists lined up to report what they expected to be his announcement that he would stick around because the city needed him. City Council President Paul Screvane was on a golf course at the time. When the mayor's staff reached him to ask him to return to City Hall for the event, Screvane decided there was little excitement in hearing that the mayor would continue in office for four more years. He stayed to finish his game.[31]

Wagner stunned the city's politicians and touched its people with his announcement that he would not run again. The reasons were principally personal.

In March of 1964 Wagner's wife of twenty-two years had died of lung cancer. "In 1961," the mayor told the city softly, "I promised Susan that if I were re-elected, it would be my last term as mayor." She had insisted that their sons needed "the guidance of a full-time father." As he explained his pledge to his late wife, with Robert, Jr., twenty-one, and Duncan, eighteen, standing off to one side, the mayor looked down and wiped tears from his eyes. Many others present did the same. Only a handful of Wagner's closest friends and political advisers had known of his decision, but many had detected a decline in the mayor's spirit after his wife's death. He seemed to find the unrelenting burdens of his office heavier without his companion, and his responsibilities had left him no time to grieve. Even as he left his wife's bedroom the afternoon that she died someone fell in behind him with papers that had to be signed before a deadline passed. With both his boys away at school Wagner tried to escape the loneliness of Gracie Mansion by moving into a hotel, but it had not helped.[32]

"One of my major and continuing considerations was simply the fact that much of the pleasure and satisfaction I have always derived from even the day-to-day work schedule had been drained from me," Wagner confessed. "While I continued to respond to each day's major challenges—and the challenges are many—I caught myself feeling that four more years would be four more years of the same thing. I feared I might go stale, and I felt this would be unfair to the city."

"If there is anything I relish," he told New York, "it is a good political fight. I have never walked away from one. This one especially intrigued me," he said of Lindsay's challenge. "I began to feel the old excitement of political combat. I knew I could take this candidate's measure." He had briefly reconsidered his promise, but determined that his two sons, "one on the very thresholds of manhood, [the other] approaching that state . . . have a claim upon me." Under no circumstances would he run. He was a father before he was a politician.[33]

Liberals and Conservatives

Of a sudden the race for mayor was wide open. While the Democrats tried to regain their balance, Price made a beeline for the Liberal party. The Lindsay campaign rapidly issued a strong statement in support of continued rent controls in New York City, and another in favor of proportional representation for City Council elections. The first declaration eliminated a usual source of friction between the Liberals and the Republicans. The second put Lindsay on record as backing a proposal long desired by the minority party because it would help them to win office. The pair of announcements was a deliberate signal to the Liberal party that Lindsay could do business with them.[34]

As long as Wagner had been a potential candidate, Alex Rose made it clear to the Republicans that the Liberals would consider no one else. By and large, the party's members liked and respected Wagner, and during the mayor's third administration Rose's influence had grown considerably. He was the only politician among a small group of advisers that the mayor organized for monthly meetings at the Lotus Club on East 66th Street. At those sessions, over lunch, Wagner took the city's economic and political pulse, relying heavily on the Liberal party chief for the latter. He solicited Rose's advice when making decisions about Democratic party leadership posts, City Council committee chairmanships, and before setting governmental goals. A deputy mayor's post, several commissionerships, some judgeships, and scores of lesser jobs had been awarded to men Rose had recommended. "Alex was very smooth," Wagner remembered, "he would say Bob, I have a fellow, well qualified, who is willing to make the sacrifice for public service." Wagner, of course, knew that "they wanted the jobs." The relatively small number of registered Liberal party loyalists, and the high number of patronage positions Rose commanded under Wagner, meant that he could deliver more jobs per party supporter than any person in New York. The mayor himself once implied that the Liberals held up to five hundred important positions.[35]

"Credit Rose with recognizing Santa Claus when he sees him," one journalist wrote of the Liberal leader's strong support for Wagner. Rose's access to patronage during Wagner's third term was higher by far than it had been after 1953 when the Liberals had not supported Wagner, or even after 1957 when the party simply joined the Democrats in what was the mayor's sure reelection. Governor Harriman had shown the Liberals only modest generosity between 1954 and 1958, even though the party had delivered his margin of victory. The additional resources Wagner offered the Liberals after 1961 were very important. As the garment industry unions that supplied the bulk of the Liberal party's workers continued to shrink, so too did the number of dedicated party loyalists. Its members continued to age, die, and retire, and keeping the organization together was difficult. The tedious political work increasingly "was being done by people with jobs," Donald Harrington, who would become the party's titular chairman in 1966, remembered. As a generation of Jewish immigrants slowly passed from the scene, the glue that kept the Liberal party together was shifting away from the ethnic bonds so important to its origins, and toward the standard political resource of patronage.[36]

Once Wagner dropped out of the race, Liberal support was up for grabs. The party's leaders had no particular relationship with the obvious Democratic contenders, and Rose concurred with the assessment that compared to Wagner, the others were "pygmies," as one Democrat would put it before the campaign ended. Dubinsky, Rose, and other leaders feared that without Wagner a Democratic administration could rapidly degenerate into a clubhouse regime that would pay little attention to the pressing needs of the city. Lindsay, on the other hand, was a bonafide liberal. His views were certainly acceptable to the party, and there was strategic advantage in supporting him too. The Democrats would run a primary all summer long before choosing their candidate in September. If the Liberals waited, their endorsement would have minimal effect. If they chose wrong in June, they would be stuck with a third party candidate. The day after Wagner's announcement, newspapers reported that the Liberals "are shopping not only the Democratic market, but the Republican one as well."[37]

On June 19 Lindsay met with an eight-person Liberal party screening committee chaired by Rose. "I have been a liberal Republican in Congress. Everybody knows that I have been independent in my decisions," Lindsay told the committee. "I want a non-partisan city administration and not a Republican administration. I want a fusion ticket with a qualified Democrat and a qualified Liberal alongside myself," he said. He pledged that "personally . . . I will get as far away from the Republican party as possible," during the campaign. Rose asked if Lindsay would create a "cabinet" of distinguished citizens to advise him. Lindsay agreed that he would, and the unspoken understanding seemed to be that Rose would be part of it. Rumors swirled that for the first time in twenty years the Liberals would back a Republican for mayor.[38]

While Lindsay's candidacy gathered momentum, the leadership of the Conservative party fumed. After he had refused to endorse Barry Goldwater for President in 1964, even after the Arizona Senator won the GOP nomination, Lindsay ranked behind only Rockefeller and Javits on the Conservative party's list of villains. Kieran O'Doherty was so angered by Lindsay's posture that he had mounted a congressional campaign against him in 1964 in a symbolic act of retribution. After the Republicans chose Lindsay as their mayoral candidate in 1965, the Conservatives felt that they had to respond. They recruited William F. Buckley, Jr., the acerbically brilliant thirty-nine-year-old editor of the conservative journal *National Review* to carry their banner.

On June 24, Buckley, a Republican, announced he would run on the Conservative ticket, "because the Republican designation is not, in New York, available nowadays to anyone in the mainstream of Republican opinion." The proof that this was so, Buckley claimed, lay in the behavior of "Mr. John Lindsay, who, having got hold of the Republican Party, now disdains the association; and spends his days . . . stressing his acceptability to the leftwardmost party in New York, the Liberal Party."[39]

The obvious purpose of Buckley's candidacy was to draw support away from Lindsay and force the Republican party in New York to respond to the philosophical imperatives of its conservative wing. His candor in stating his intention made for amusing reporting. Immediately following his announcement he answered questions from the press:

> Question: Do you want to be Mayor, sir?
> Buckley: I have never considered it.
> Question: Do you think you have a chance of winning?
> Buckley: No.

Later in the campaign Buckley entertained the public with a self-administered interview:

> Question: Why didn't you run in a Republican primary?
> Buckley: Why didn't Martin Luther King run for Governor of Alabama?
> Question: What would you do if you won?
> Buckley: Demand a recount.[40]

Democratic Chaos

Meanwhile, an air of anarchy swirled around the potential Democratic candidates as they prepared to confront each other in a primary. Early in the year Upper West Side reform Congressman William Fitts Ryan had threatened to challenge Wagner for his party's nomination. When his effort to generate enthusiasm for his candidacy fizzled, he dropped out. After Wagner exited, Ryan re-entered. Reformer Paul O'Dwyer, the brother of ex-Mayor William O'Dwyer and a councilman-at-large from Manhattan since 1963, also announced he was running. He had little support and less organization. City Council President Screvane decided that under the circumstances he needed to go "up or out," and declared he would run too. Queens District Attorney Frank O'Connor, a handsome prosecutor as Irish in heritage as his name implied, joined the fray. He had bid for his party's nomination for governor in 1962, but the politics of the moment had called for a Jewish candidate then. He did not want to be mayor, but thought that by entering the race he would keep his name in prominent display and improve his chances to win backing for the governor's spot in 1966.[41]

By the end of June a fifth candidate, Comptroller Abraham Beame, declared that he too would seek the Democratic nomination for mayor. Months earlier he had gone to see Wagner to ask the mayor about his reelection plans. When Wagner played coy, Beame got worried. The two politicians had been exchanging verbal salvos for some time in a low key but significant feud over the direction of the city's deteriorating financial position. Beame remembered that his predecessor, Larry Gerosa, had argued with Wagner and lost his job. Moreover, Beame carefully maintained his political base in his home borough of Brooklyn, which meant keeping close ties to Stanley Steingut, Wagner's consistent foe. With no reason to believe Wagner would not seek reelection, Beame feared that the mayor's reticence might mask a plan to choose a new comptroller for his ticket. He therefore took steps to organize an independent citywide primary campaign for comptroller, just in case. When Wagner decided to retire, Beame reassessed his target. After two weeks of conferences with his supporters, he decided to risk losing the job he had for a chance to win the one he wanted, and he joined the battle for City Hall.[42]

Never before in the city's history had there been such a contest for the Democratic line on the ballot in a mayoralty campaign. In the past, even when party discipline broke, two clearly defined opposing factions lined up against each other. The free-for-all unleashed in 1965 signaled the advent of a new, post-Tammany era. "Nobody knows who father is," lamented one regular, nostalgic for the days when a handful of political elders gave their loyal Democratic children instructions. The county leaders still mattered—they could still garner troops and organize a campaign—but their ability to control events had been shattered by the ethnic cleavages that culminated in the 1961 drive that removed Carmine DeSapio as de facto citywide boss and destroyed the political system that he had come to represent. No longer could anyone find enough common ground among the ethnic groups that made up the Democratic party to create a consensus; no one had a formula that satisfied the competing tribes sufficiently to bind them to a single Democrat.[43]

Lindsay's Kosher Label

All of the Democratic hopefuls except Beame, who had entered the contest late, tried to win the Liberal endorsement. Rose and Dubinsky, however, decided to direct the party's support toward Lindsay. "We need a government not beholden to any political party," Rose told the Liberal delegates the night they assembled to make the decision final. "We need at the head of that government a man of integrity and ability and imagination. . . . Let us help elect Congressman John Lindsay as the next mayor of New York," he enjoined the crowd. Dubinsky also took to the podium to speak strongly in favor of Lindsay, and with the two long-time leaders of the party firmly committed, the outcome of the convention was a forgone conclusion. A small band of renegades protested the effort to "put the Kosher label on this Lindsay . . . You can't fuse fire and water. The Liberal Party and the Republican Party are fire and water," they complained, while tempers flared in Yiddish and English. But the delegates awarded Lindsay an overwhelming endorsement.[44]

The Liberals then brought forth Timothy Costello, a college professor of Irish Catholic descent and the party's titular head, to run as City Council president on Lindsay's ticket. Finding a Jewish Democrat to round out the team for ethnic balance and maximum fusion appeal was left to Price. After several unsuccessful contacts, somewhat desperate to complete the slate, the campaign manager convinced Milton Mollen, Chairman of the Housing and Redevelopment Board under Wagner, to run for comptroller. The choice drew some criticism. Mollen oversaw an area of the Wagner administration that the Lindsay campaign had criticized harshly, and Lindsay himself had read a long attack on Mollen's policies into the congressional record just a few months before. But Mollen was the best Jewish Democrat available. "We've already got the good government people, now we'll get the bad government people too," Price commented privately with a mischievous smile. What he understood was that Lindsay would have to win or lose the mayoralty on his own.[45]

Price had already set in motion a ferocious drive to create a citywide campaign machine independent of the local Republican party. He planned to open Lindsay election store fronts in every one of New York City's seventy-six assembly districts and staff them with volunteers. He was trying to re-create the kind of network that the regular Democratic organization traditionally commanded. The campaign strategy also called for Lindsay to be everywhere. He needed to meet the people of the city in their own neighborhoods and on the most familiar terms possible, Price theorized, to dispel the notion that Lindsay the WASP was strictly "silk stocking" material. The tall, fair haired, charismatic campaigner shook hands, walked the streets in shirtsleeves, and spoke to small crowds in front of grocery stores and delicatessens. Stripped to his boxer bathing trunks, his broad shoulders and muscular chest bared before admiring women, he campaigned at pools around New York. One man emerged from a locker room and announced to the press that he just shook hands with Lindsay under the shower, "where all men are equal." If Lindsay was searching for familiarity, he certainly found it.[46]

He looked for it most in Jewish neighborhoods. Price's analysis of New York City voting patterns led him to conclude that for Lindsay to succeed he had to win the support of Irish Catholics and Jews who traditionally voted Democratic. In the 1964 presidential campaign a majority of the city's Irish had voted Republican, and Price hoped that the trend would continue. The Jews, however, had remained loyal Democrats and therefore needed the most attention. Rose concurred with the assessment, and with the strategy of sending the candidate into as many Jewish neighborhoods as possible to show that he was sensitive to the matters Jews cared about. The candidate kept three *yarmulkes,* the traditional Jewish skullcap, in his car and donned them at the slightest opportunity. His speeches and literature highlighted his strong civil rights record for two reasons: civil rights was a traditional Jewish concern, and he hoped to poll much better among the city's minorities than the paltry few percent Republican Barry Goldwater won with his conservative rhetoric in 1964.[47]

Lindsay traveled to the resort hotels of the Catskill mountains, irreverently known to New Yorkers as the "Jewish Alps." The candidate ate kosher food in the dining rooms; he ordered gefulte fish for breakfast at Grossinger's; he called a heckler *meshugunah.* All of these gestures were designed to make the city's Jews comfortable with the candidate who did not share their faith, nor their allegiance to the Democratic party, but who did share their liberal politics. Price hoped Jews would think of him as a "Franklin Roosevelt type of candidate," a man from the upper class, but one who understood the needs of ordinary people.[48]

The campaign generated powerful momentum by mid-summer with up to five Lindsay store fronts opening daily. They proved so effective that Price decided to open more even after achieving his goal of one in every assembly district. Ultimately some 10,000 volunteers responded to Lindsay's plea to help him save New York City from a headlong decline. A near life size poster of the challenger appeared in subway stations throughout the city. It showed the tall, young, dynamic candidate walking the city's streets in shirtsleeves, Kennedyesque in appearance, striding with confidence. The caption quoted *New York Post* columnist Murray Kempton: "He's fresh when everyone else is tired." Whether talking about crime, or housing, transportation or schooling, Lindsay always sounded the theme of moral regeneration, of saving the city's soul. And the Democrats had yet to choose a candidate.[49]

A Jewish Democrat

Screvane started out the favorite to win his party's primary. He was the obvious heir to Wagner, and he hoped to hold onto the mayor's coalition. He attracted Orin Lehman to his ticket to run for comptroller, and Daniel Patrick Moynihan for City Council president. Lehman, the deputy budget director in Wagner's third administration and a nephew of Herbert Lehman, added an image of managerial competence and a touch of the late Senator's luster to Screvane's campaign. Moynihan, Under Secretary of Labor in the administrations of Presidents Kennedy and Johnson, and a native New Yorker who had once worked on Governor Harriman's staff, was a liberal intellectual of Irish Catholic descent. The ticket had ethnic balance, but little else; the three men were bureaucrats, not politicians. Screvane spent much of his campaign trying to disassociate himself from criticisms of the Wagner administration, but he had little political identity apart from his relationship with the mayor. The contradiction left him trapped. His impatient personality seemed to irritate the public, and his effort was further complicated by the campaigns of William Fitts Ryan and Paul O'Dwyer. Both those men, who ran with balanced tickets of their own, had some claim to the allegiance of the reform clubs weakening Screvane's standing with that wing of the party.[50]

Screvane could be his own worst enemy. He inexplicably cold shouldered Harry Van Arsdale when the labor leader approached him to offer support. With an unacceptable response from his preferred candidate, and little admiration for the others, Van Arsdale decided not to mobilize the Central Trades & Labor Council or to use his influence with the city's municipal unions during the Democratic primary. As a candidate, Screvane allowed an important endorsement to slip away, and as a party, the Democrats allowed one of their most effective organizational tools to sit unused.[51]

While Screvane lost ground, Beame gained some. The comptroller strengthened his bid considerably by striking a deal with Frank O'Connor. The Queens D.A. agreed to drop out of the mayor's contest and join Beame's ticket as candidate for City Council president in return for Beame's commitment to back O'Connor for governor in 1966. A Bronx judge, Mario Procaccino, became Beame's choice for comptroller. Procaccino denied any ties to county leader Charlie Buckley, but the Bronx boss soon joined Beame's camp, where Brooklyn county leader Stanley Steingut was already hard at work. By July 20, when Beame named

Edward Costikyan, the former leader of Tammany Hall, as his campaign manager, the long-time Brooklyn regular had the strongest organization of any of the Democrats in the primary. He was also the only Jewish candidate fighting for the mayoralty.[52]

On primary day Abraham Beame became the first Jew in history to win the Democratic nomination for mayor of New York. In the four way race he captured a respectable forty-five percent of the vote, easily beating Screvane's thirty-six percent while overpowering weak performances by the two Irish candidates. "Jewish Vote Cited in Beame Victory," read the headline in *The New York Times* the next day. "Mr. Beame's strength among the Jewish voters, which you could see him winning during the campaign, was a major factor in his victory," announced pollster John F. Kraft, a former associate of Louis Harris working for the Beame campaign. Screvane's pollster, Oliver Quayle, also a former member of Harris's team, announced that his figures showed that "the Jewish vote went massively to Beame," and "this accounted more definitely than anything else for Mr. Beame's victory." The analysts estimated that Jews had cast nearly forty-five percent of the ballots in the Democratic primary. In the general election it would be only two-thirds as large a proportion of the total, but still the largest voting group.[53]

Price had prepared a post-primary strategy to run against Screvane, whom he had been convinced would win in spite of a weak campaign effort. Beame's victory made the contest tougher. One journalist reported that the Lindsay "forces said Mr. Beame was the most formidable of the potential antagonists because Mr. Beame, a Jew, could make a strong appeal to the Jewish voters." Yet, the primary results also showed that there was opportunity. William Fitts Ryan, although he ran a distant third overall, showed great strength among younger, upper income Jewish voters—the reform club Jews. Price was certain Lindsay could win those votes, and even garner votes in Jewish working class neighborhoods by persisting in his aggressive moral campaign and by emphasizing his liberal positions. Beame also ran noticeably less well among blacks than Wagner had in the primary four years earlier. With his local government experience in finance, the comptroller had no particular standing on civil rights matters. This contrasted sharply with Lindsay's record, which included sponsorship of the 1964 Civil Rights Act and the 1965 Voting Rights Act.[54]

Price detected a third area of opportunity. He understood the fierce competition between the Irish and the Jews for control of the Democratic party, and reasoned that Irish Democrats would resist voting for a ticket headed by Beame. As a WASP, Lindsay at least was neutral in the ethnic struggle for power. As a second line of defense, those Irish who would not adopt Lindsay might be convinced to vote for Buckley. The Irish presence at Conservative rallies was readily apparent, and not only was Buckley Irish Catholic, but so were his two running mates, Rosemary Gunning and Hugh Markey. Lindsay's staff started to think that Buckley's campaign might help their candidate more than it would hurt him. It appeared likely that more Conservative votes would come from Democratic defectors than Republican ones, and by constantly attacking Lindsay's liberalism Buckley gave his nemesis the liberal image that the Democrats usually enjoyed, and that helped them to win Jewish votes in New York City.[55]

Despite Beame's surprise victory, Lindsay's team lost no time in pressing ahead with a campaign that blamed the Democrats for the city's ills. Up until the primary Price's objective had been to establish Lindsay's moral and liberal identity in the public mind and to build a physical presence in every area of the city through the use of the campaign store fronts. The citywide network continued to operate in high gear, but the day after the Democratic primary Lindsay's public relations team supplemented Price's political fundamentalism with a media blitz designed to convince the city's voters that it was time for a change. The shift in emphasis was so strong that Lindsay's advance man, Sid Davidoff, thought of the effort as "two entirely different campaigns." The second phase was led by a young public relations consultant named David Garth, and it featured television and radio clips of ten or twenty seconds each that delivered a simple compelling message over and over. One example went like this: "With dirty streets, polluted air and broken down schools, things could be worse," a voice said while still photographs of a city in decline appeared on the television screen, "Lindsay could lose. Change things November 2," it concluded.[56]

Beame's campaign team seemed as surprised as everyone else that their candidate had won, and confusion prevailed immediately following the unexpected victory. But as the Democratic standard bearer Beame had an automatic advantage. A late September poll showed that if undecided voters cast their ballots the same way as those who had already made up their minds planned to vote, Beame would win about fifty percent of the total to Lindsay's thirty-nine percent, with Buckley amassing less than ten percent. The key to maintaining Beame's standing, the survey revealed, was holding onto his image as a traditional

Democrat. So Beame accused Lindsay of issuing position papers that imitated his own long held Democratic views, and he reminded New Yorkers that his challenger had voted for Eisenhower and Nixon, not Stevenson and Kennedy. Beame also pointed out that, as a Democrat, he would have easier access to officials in Washington to ensure generous federal funding for city programs.[57]

Lindsay responded by linking Beame not to his party's liberal traditions, but to its disreputable political past. "The Beame candidacy will bring into City Hall the most dismal elements of our political structure," the crusader warned, invoking the name of Charlie Buckley as the boss who would rule a Democratic mayor. He accused Beame of repudiating the cause of reform by supporting Stanley Steingut for county leader in Brooklyn, and announced that his opponent was, "part and parcel of a cynical conspiracy that is poised to take over our city government for predatory purposes." Price ridiculed Beame's claims that Lindsay was stealing the comptroller's liberal policy programs. "The best kept secret in New York City for the past twenty years is any new idea that Mr. Beame has had," Price declared in a press release.[58]

In late September more than half of the city's Jews indicated that they would back the man who shared their faith in his quest to be mayor, while fewer than three of ten expected to vote for Lindsay. Considering that Beame did not have the Liberal party endorsement, it was not a bad position. An additional fifteen percent of the city's Jewish voters had not yet made up their minds, and almost none contemplated casting a ballot for Conservative William Buckley. Then, on October 18, Beame campaigned in Harlem with Adam Clayton Powell. Standing at the pulpit of the Abyssinian Baptist Church, the eloquent champion of black pride exhorted a crowd of listeners to vote for the Democratic candidate. "It's time we proved we can elect a Jew in New York as mayor. If I don't get . . . these Jews, these Catholics into office, how can I ever expect to be President of the United States?" Powell asked.

Beame sat silently. "I know I should have jumped up and said I didn't want votes on that kind of basis," he said later, "but it happened so fast. I didn't know what to do." It took a little time for the impact to set in, but soon the Beame camp realized that Jewish voters resented Powell's appeal to his supporters to vote for a candidate on the basis of religion, and that Beame's silent response had disappointed them. Jewish voters began abandoning Beame in large numbers.[59]

"To stem the exodus of Jewish voters, once thought so securely in the fold, a kind of vote-for-a-Jew campaign sprang up," one analysis of

Beame's election strategy explained. A letter signed by a rabbi went out to Jewish neighborhoods in Manhattan, the Bronx, and Queens urging Jews to vote for Beame because he would bring "distinction to our people." Another, a touch more subtle, highlighted Beame's affiliation with more than forty Jewish charities and social organizations. One party strategist suggested that they try a "sentimental argument . . . the idea that this is indeed a 'miracle' that Abe Beame should be so close to becoming Mayor of the City of New York and that, as the song in *Fiddler on the Roof* goes, . . . the city can 'Make a Miracle.' The net effect, "was simply to make more people furious, lose more votes," the analysis concluded. "What kind of a schnook is he?" one member of Beame's faith asked.[60]

Jews disillusioned with Beame had only Lindsay to turn to. Buckley made statements that sounded like blatant appeals to Catholics to vote for him on the basis of his religion, and the policies he proposed jarred the city's most liberal ethnic group. When the Conservative candidate proposed that welfare recipients be removed from New York and sent to rehabilitation camps so that they could learn how to live properly, Javits, speaking for Lindsay in Jewish neighborhoods, summarized the plan as a call for "welfare concentration camps." Buckley lashed out in response: "That phrase conjures up Nazi visions of horror specifically aimed at the Jewish people," he declared. The Lindsay campaign, he continued, is "trying to do to Jewish voters what the Ku Klux Klan . . . [does] to white people in the South—keep them scared." Probably, but the tactic was effective. Buckley also denounced the Lindsay campaign for sending under-cover volunteers to infiltrate Democratic clubs in Irish districts and encourage voters to vote for Buckley, the Irish candidate, rather than for Beame, the Jew.[61]

In late October the three candidates met in a series of televised debates. Beame seemed ordinary, Buckley nasty. The television cameras were kind to Lindsay, whose good looks and cool style played well. He came across as the leader, the man best suited to run the city. The Americans for Democratic Action endorsed him, and a few reform Democrats drifted into his camp. Congressman Ryan never came out for Beame, leaving his supporters free to vote their consciences. The day before the election Edward I. Koch, the Democratic district leader from Greenwich Village and since his defeat of Carmine DeSapio during the boss's 1963 comeback effort one of the "saints" of reform, endorsed Lindsay. It made the front page of the *Daily News* on election day.[62]

Top Democrats, including Robert Kennedy and Vice President Humphrey, campaigned for Beame, but throughout the contest President

Lyndon Johnson remained strangely silent. Rumors circulated that he hesitated to speak on Beame's behalf because he did not want to offend his good friend David Dubinsky whose Liberal party had supported him in 1964. The 1965 mayoral campaign was almost over by the time Johnson's press secretary, Bill Moyers, announced that the President approved of the Democrat running for New York's top job. The anointment was tepid, and distant, and late. Johnson never spoke the words publicly himself, leaving Beame's legitimacy with his party's national leader in doubt. The coyness hurt Beame badly with black New Yorkers, who had great affection for the Texan who had masterminded the passage of the most far reaching civil rights legislation since the Civil War. During the last days of the battle Price detected Beame's weakness with the group and had Lindsay campaign especially hard in black ghettos, right up until three in the morning as election day dawned.[63]

An Unlikely Coalition

On election night, the Lindsay team gathered in its campaign headquarters in the Roosevelt Hotel. Early on it became clear that a record number of New Yorkers had gone to the polls and that they had elected Frank O'Connor and Mario Procaccino to the Board of Estimate. At first Lindsay trailed, and at 10:45 P.M. *The New York Times* called Price to say that it planned to project Beame the winner by 60,000 votes. "I think you'll be making a mistake," he replied coolly. Price had been collecting numbers from a sample of one hundred key districts that he had identified around the city. Shortly before midnight, when the returns came in from a neighborhood in the Riverdale section of the Bronx that consisted of a mix of Irish Catholic and Jewish voters, he turned to Lindsay and told him, "I think we're in." Lindsay was.[64]

The mayor-elect threw away a concession speech he had drafted, and at 2:30 A.M. descended to the ballroom to thank his supporters. "We had faith we could win this election. And we did. We had faith we can govern this city. And we will," he told the euphoric crowd. "I plan to give New York the most hard-working, the most dedicated and, I hope, the most exciting administration this city has ever seen. We will work together to make our great city once again the Empire City of the world," he concluded, and left amidst cheering and yelling.[65]

When the votes had all been counted, Lindsay was the victor over Beame by 102,407 ballots. He had taken forty-three percent of the total, Beame thirty-nine, and Buckley thirteen. Beame had edged Lindsay out in heavily Democratic Brooklyn and the Bronx, but Lindsay's pluralities in his home borough of Manhattan, and in Queens, gave him the margin of victory. He had won in Staten Island as well.[66]

The ethnic composition of Lindsay's vote was unusual. A variety of groups had given him their support, but each for different reasons. It would make maintaining a coalition challenging.

New York City contained a modest number of white Protestant voters, but more than six of every ten cast their votes for the moralizing challenger. Italian Republicans remained loyal to their party. Lindsay won forty-one percent of Italian votes in 1965, about the same as the forty percent that Barry Goldwater had garnered in 1964. Irish Catholic New Yorkers had cast fifty-five percent of their votes for Goldwater in 1964, and German voters nearly sixty-five percent. For Lindsay the figures dropped to forty percent and fifty percent respectively. The declines were significant, but the bulk of the difference went to Buckley, not Beame. Lindsay held on to all but the most staunchly conservative Republicans. These voters appeared to back Lindsay's call for a more efficient and effective government.

About four blacks in ten chose the Republican candidate with the impressive record on civil rights and the charismatic personality, while the year before only about one in twenty had voted for the Republican presidential candidate running against Lyndon Johnson. A quarter of the city's Puerto Ricans cast ballots for Lindsay, whereas only six per cent had done so for Goldwater. These voters responded to Lindsay's dedication to equality for people of all races, and an implicit commitment to expand government benefits for the poor.

Forty-three percent of the city's Jewish voters cast their ballots for Lindsay in November, fourteen percent higher than the level of support he held from the group in late September. If Beame had maintained the kind of backing among his coreligionists that had enabled him to win the Democratic primary, he would have been elected mayor. But Lindsay's campaign for moral regeneration, his success in seizing the liberal image, and his vigorous campaigning in Jewish neighborhoods won him Jewish votes. As always, many Jews cast their ballots on the Liberal line. The party polled 280,000 votes, providing Lindsay with his margin of victory. Once again, Alex Rose had picked a winner, and the Liberal party line helped determine the outcome of a New York City election.[67]

William Buckley's campaign cut into Beame's support among Catholics, and the defeated Democrat had ample reason to attribute his loss to the Conservative party candidate. But the two groups that shifted away from Beame and toward Lindsay most strongly were blacks and

Jews. Increasingly, the politics of the city were being told in terms of these two groups.

Another trend was apparent in city politics. In 1961 Wagner had spent over $1 million to win reelection, three times the cost of his 1957 campaign. Beame's unsuccessful effort in 1965 cost more than $1.5 million, while the Lindsay team spent more than $2.5 million. A significant portion of Lindsay's funds, perhaps $500,000, maybe more, went to pay for radio and television advertising. But more than two thirds of the expenses—at least $1.8 million—went to pay for printing literature and to cover the expenses of creating the Lindsay campaign citywide storefront network. By far the greater part of the money was therefore spent building a political organization to do the work that a well functioning political machine normally performed, only without the obligations inherent in relying on the city's traditional party structure. More than increased use of the media, the weak state of party affairs in New York City was driving up the cost of local elections, and money now competed with political party support as the key ingredient to building the kind of coalition necessary for electoral success in New York City.[68]

NINE

The Politics of Polarization

1966–1969

Lindsay's victory catapulted him onto the national stage just as he had hoped. A non-Democratic mayor of New York was news, a fresh Republican presidential contender was news, and Lindsay was a natural media star. "John Lindsay was the best mayor New York ever had before he took office," Wagner press secretary Debs Myers commented about the coast to coast barrage of favorable publicity Lindsay received in the weeks following his election. The nation's eyes were on the man its premier metropolis had chosen to do great things, but Lindsay began to have trouble even before he entered City Hall.[1]

The Irish Boss and the Protestant Reformer Redux

For years Mike Quill, chief of the Transit Workers Union, had been treating New Yorkers to the spectacle of negotiations between his labor organization and the city. Quill was a tough, tyrannical, irrepressibly iconoclastic Irish immigrant who spoke with a brogue and claimed proudly that his limp was the result of a wound suffered while fighting the British in the early years of the century. He feared nothing so much as the possibility that someone might accuse him of being respectable. "I'll begin to worry the day the papers say something nice about me," he once said. If that was his standard, he lived his life more worry free than most. By the time Lindsay came to office Quill, then sixty and almost a full generation older than the forty-three-year-old mayor, called himself, "an elder statesman of public monsters." He delighted in the role and regularly threatened to shut the city down by calling a transit strike if some demand or other that he concocted were not met.[2]

Despite Quill's intimidating bombast, during Robert Wagner's dozen years in office a negotiating pattern emerged between the union leader and the mayor that astute New Yorkers perceived as a kind of charade. The collective bargaining contract between the city and the TWU would expire every two years on December 31. In the weeks leading up to the dramatic deadline, the mayor's labor negotiators would offer a minimal wage increase. Quill would then yell and scream and accuse his adversaries—though never Wagner personally—of cruelty, brutality, idiocy, and anything else that came to mind. Next, Quill would convene a meeting of his members, and in a thunderous speech secure their permission to call a strike if necessary. Then, as the deadline approached, usually on New Year's Eve itself, Quill would negotiate directly with the mayor and reach an agreement much more favorable to Quill's union than the one originally offered. Publicly, the transit leader claimed victory. Wagner, however, always took care to see that the accords were in line with what the city treasury could afford.[3]

Quill combined attention to the bread-and-butter issues that concerned TWU workers with the rhetorical style of an Irish nationalist. When Quill joined the union in 1926, and in the decades that followed while he rose to power, Irish workers dominated the membership. By the mid-1960s, however, the union had changed. Large numbers of blacks, and some Puerto Ricans, entered what had once been almost exclusively an Irish domain. The labor chief's ability to control the workers with emerald oratory weakened, and by the time Lindsay prepared to assume office, some observers thought Quill would have to call at least a token strike to assuage union militants.[4]

Such circumstances did not augur well for negotiations, nor did the personal chemistry between the mayor-elect and the union chief. "John Lindsay looked at Quill and he saw the past. And Mike Quill looked at Lindsay and he saw the Church of England," wrote newspaper columnist Jimmy Breslin as the two men squared off in the weeks before the TWU contract expired with the year 1965. Quill said of Lindsay: "He is a Republican, no matter if he tries to pass himself as a fusion guy and friend of labor. He's strictly Silk Stocking and Yale. This nut even goes in for exercise. We don't like him." Lindsay announced that during his administration the "power brokers" would not run City Hall by entering through the back door to cut private deals. When asked who the power brokers were, he replied: "They know who they are." Quill certainly did.[5]

Each man had an audience. Quill needed to show his members that he was tough and demanding, that he could win concessions from City Hall. It was the aging Irishman's last stand, his last chance to insist that the city's respectable people take him seriously and deal with him on his own terms. Lindsay, on the other hand, was determined to show New York that while he was mayor, negotiations in the public interest would be conducted above board—responsibly, professionally, respectably. It was a cultural collision that had more to do with symbolic power than dollars, as each man sought to make a statement about who should rule New York.

Lindsay, not officially mayor until January 1, 1966, decided to remain aloof. He refused to be drawn into negotiations until the very last days of December. When he finally did meet with Quill, instead of bargaining he lectured the union leader on civic responsibility. It was more than Quill could endure. "Coward! Pipsqueak! Ass!" the union leader shrieked at the man who would be the city's chief executive in a matter of hours. "We'll take no more *bubkes* from a *schmuck* like you!," he finished, treating the advisers present to the colorful combination of Yiddish curses spoken in an Irish brogue. Quill stopped the city's transit system just past mid-night, New Year's Eve, minutes after Lindsay became mayor.[6]

"One day on the job and John Lindsay has ended crime in the subways," Sammy Davis, Jr. quipped at the mayor's inaugural ball. Gallows humor prevailed, and one New Yorker who descended into an abandoned subway station, still bleary eyed from the festivities of the evening before, supposedly gasped: "My god, Wagner left and took all the trains with him." At a news conference the next day a reporter asked Quill if there had been any new developments. "We explored [Lindsay's] mind yesterday and we found nothing," he replied. So the tenor of conversation continued for two weeks, while New Yorkers struggled to get around the city in the snow and ice of post-Holiday New York. The event was crippling.[7]

Ultimately, the two sides worked out an accord twice the size of any ever granted by Wagner, but Lindsay took credit for not succumbing to an effort to blackmail the city, and the public approved. Still, the intense hostility that erupted between an Irish union leader, even one as infamous as Quill, and the upper-class Protestant mayor did nothing to create harmony between the new administration and the group that had run the city's politics for so long, and that still held a disproportionate amount of power in the city's bureaucracy and in its municipal unions. The event was an indication that Lindsay's moralizing style risked alienating large segments of the city.[8]

Ethnicity and Bureaucracy

The transit strike also made it clear that as time passed, the municipal unions that Robert Wagner had helped to create were becoming more and more powerful. New York had not suffered a single significant strike by municipal workers during Wagner's first half-dozen years in office. In the six years that followed his 1958 executive order authorizing exclusive bargaining rights, there had been six. One, a two-week walkout by welfare workers, was a major event. After 1965 the change in leadership at City Hall relieved many of the union chiefs from the sense of loyalty and obligation that they felt to Robert F. Wagner personally, and to the party he represented as well. The Democrats had long been the advocates of national legislation that helped labor, and locally, Wagner had implemented the system that so greatly expanded the power of municipal unions. With Wagner gone, and his party out of office, labor leaders felt little responsibility to anyone other than their members. This was a palpable shift in the distribution of power in New York. Under Wagner, most of the city's union leaders perceived a strong relationship between the fortunes of the man in City Hall and the welfare of the city's employees. As a result, job actions that generated public hostility had to be avoided. With Lindsay's assumption of office, this control, already weakening, was lost.

The transit strike failed to temper the new mayor's desire to attack the city bureaucracy head on. Confrontation marked Lindsay's initial months in office. The new staff at City Hall—principally young Jewish attorneys who became known collectively as the kiddie corps—launched a plan to reorganize the city's departments into ten superagencies, each headed by an administrator answerable to the mayor. The Democratic City Council examined the reorganization proposals item by item, changing them to make sure that they did not greatly enhance the mayor's authority before approving them. When Lindsay announced that he would transform the store fronts that had been established during his election campaign into "Little City Halls" to bring government closer to the people, the City Council and Board of Estimate flatly refused to fund them. As far as the council members and borough presidents were concerned, the idea was a plan to create Lindsay political clubs to compete with the local Democratic organization. Ultimately, Lindsay managed to open just a half dozen offices around the city.[9]

Within weeks of Lindsay's inauguration his administration initiated an assault on the Police Department by leapfrogging police deputy inspector Sanford Garelik over another senior official to make him Chief Inspector, the highest career rank in the department. Later, Lloyd Sealy was promoted to Assistant Chief Inspector. The first man was Jewish, the second black. One journalist reported that the actions were a deliberate effort to move the men "into jobs previously considered the private property of the Irish hierarchy that traditionally controlled the Police Department." Garelik himself remembered reading a memo circulated to the department's top brass in 1964 regarding security arrangements for the Pope, who was planning a visit to New York: "There must have been sixteen or seventeen names on the memo, all the senior people, and every single one was Irish." But the initial confrontation with the Police Department was mild in comparison to what was to come. On May 2, 1966, Lindsay announced that he had signed an executive order to create a civilian controlled review board to examine citizen complaints against police officers.[10]

After the 1964 race riots, a number of civil rights leaders and public officials proposed that a panel of civilians be empowered to review charges of police abuse. The existing system provided for senior level police officials to examine such cases, and although the mayor retained ultimate power over their disposition, in perception and practice oversight of police actions was largely an internal affair of the department itself. During the 1965 mayoralty campaign the issue arose, and Lindsay pledged that he would create a Civilian Review Board. His May 2 announcement fulfilled his promise, but infuriated the police. They perceived the decision as an implicit indictment of their integrity. They feared a witch hunt, and resented the outside control. Police Benevolent Association president John Cassese announced that the city's police officers did not accept the mayor's decision, and launched a campaign to place a referendum on the ballot that would allow the citizens of New York to decide if they wanted a Civilian Review Board or not.[11]

Most referendums placed on the ballot in New York City generate little interest, but this one struck a nerve. The liberal community rallied a well organized, well financed, campaign to keep the Board. A wide range of citizens groups joined with the PBA in opposition. The liberal faction tried to twist the issue into a litmus test of fairness; if you were against the Board, they implied, you were racist. The Board's opponents adopted scare tactics. Around the city they put up posters of a young white woman emerging alone from a subway station where she faced a dark and menacing street: "The Civilian Review Board must be stopped! Her life . . . your life . . . may depend on it," the caption read.

The emotional campaign resulted in a resounding rejection of what had become known as "Lindsay's Review Board." Two of every three New Yorkers voted to abolish it, leaving the mayor's prestige badly damaged and liberals shocked. For more than a decade the civil rights movement had achieved one success after another. Activists believed that an inexorable march toward a harmonious society was underway. For an issue that they had defined as a matter of civil rights to lose in New York City, the citadel of liberalism, seemed unimaginable. A careful study launched immediately after the referendum showed that most of the citizens who voted to dissolve the board perceived it as a special concession that was being offered to blacks that no other group enjoyed. Most New Yorkers did not believe that the cop on the beat was racist, so they did not think that the board was necessary to protect the civil rights of minorities. Many citizens also feared that the review board would reduce the ability of the police to maintain law and order.

Analysis of the voting results revealed that blacks and Puerto Ricans overwhelmingly favored the Civilian Review Board, and that Catholics of every European descent opposed it vigorously. There was a slight softening of Catholic opposition among wealthier, better educated members of the faith, but nearly ninety percent of all Irish and Italian Catholics, and more than eighty percent of non-Hispanic Catholics of other heritages, rejected the board. The pattern among Jewish New Yorkers was more complicated. Working-class Jews at the lower end of the economic and educational spectrum, many of whom lived in neighborhoods that bordered black ghettos, voted against the Board in large numbers. The notion of law and order was very real to these people. Upper-income Jews, well educated professionals in particular, who lived in the city's safest neighborhoods, voted fairly strongly in favor of the plan. The daily threat of crime and violence was more distant to them. The outcome reaffirmed that, as a group, Jews were far more liberal than the city's Catholic voters. It also revealed limits to Jewish liberalism. Strong support for civil rights did not overpower a desire to live in safety.

In so far as the vote was a referendum on the Lindsay administration, which is how many New Yorkers perceived it, the balloting showed that, after a year in office, the mayor had developed powerful support among minorities, that his position among Jews was weakening, and that he risked losing his standing with Catholic voters altogether.[12]

The Overpowering Politics of Race

The level of tension in New York stayed exceptionally high during the next two years. Nationwide, it was a time of student protests against the Vietnam War, of strident black militancy, and white middle-class backlash against both movements. In city after city, riots erupted in black communities. In New York, the generous distribution of federal anti-poverty funds to potential protesters, the exceptionally skillful use of police intelligence and riot control techniques under Chief Inspector Garelik's command, and the almost magical effect Lindsay's personal presence had on young blacks as he walked the streets of the city's ghettos night after summer night, kept minority slums from exploding. Lindsay's success in defusing potential racial violence came to national attention in 1968 when President Lyndon Johnson appointed him Vice Chairman of the Kerner Commission, convened by the President to determine the causes of the violent protests sweeping the country.[13]

In spite of the obvious advantage to the entire city of the mayor's remarkable ability to keep peace, white resentment toward Lindsay built. "I can't stomach that Lindsay," a cabbie told a journalist. "If you're colored, you're all right with him. If you're white, you got to obey the law." When Lindsay showed up one night in Little Italy a teenager expressed shock. "That's Lindsay? You're kidding. There ain't no niggers here." The perception grew that the mayor represented only part of the city.[14]

The consequences of what many whites perceived as favoritism spilled over into the mayor's ability to manage New York. In 1968, the city offered the heavily Italian Sanitation Workers union an attractive contract package. When union president John DeLury presented it to his members, "he was hooted off the platform, pelted with eggs, and required police assistance to get out of the crowd," Lindsay's deputy budget director recalled. The workers were not so much dissatisfied with the contract proposal as they were "angry at the city . . . angry at the apparent preference shown the minorities; they felt like second-class citizens ('garbagemen') and wanted to strike almost for catharsis."

They did, and the city suffered the stench and ignominy of a two week halt of garbage collection. Ultimately, Lindsay handled the conflict well, and forced a reasonable settlement in spite of damaging interference from Governor Rockefeller. Still, people wondered if it had all been necessary.[15]

Then, in the fall of 1968, New York City suffered the longest and most bitter school strike in its history. In 1967 Lindsay's budget office made the important discovery that the economic formula New York State used to allocate educational aid to localities would generate more money for New York City if it divided its school system into five administrative parts, one for each borough. Decentralization was already being proposed by some as a way of improving management of the schools. The new information gave the idea a push. About the same time, the notion of "community control," allowing local residents to have greater power over the institutions that governed them, began to catch on as a practice that might help improve life in the ghetto. Schools received special attention because some academics thought that sending black youths to institutions with predominantly white teaching and administrative staffs reinforced feelings of inferiority in minority communities.[16]

Several pilot projects tested decentralization in practice, including one in the Ocean Hill-Brownsville section of Brooklyn, an impoverished black ghetto. The rules governing the newly chosen board, and its powers, were ill defined. The experiment was not particularly successful, but a report prepared under the direction of Ford Foundation president McGeorge Bundy recommended that the city pursue a decentralization strategy anyway. In May 1968, Lindsay asked the State Legislature to pass a law that would effectively decentralize the school system, and go a long way toward granting community control.

The terms of the proposed law were not adequate in the mind of Rhody McCoy, the administrator of the experimental Ocean Hill-Brownsville board. McCoy, who was black, was an eighteen year school veteran and bitterly angry at the shabby treatment he felt he had received from a white, specifically Jewish, bureaucracy. On May 9, 1968, in what appears to have been a deliberate effort to create a confrontation in order to establish his authority, McCoy, fired thirteen teachers and six administrators. All but one were white, almost all were Jewish. McCoy claimed to have charges to levy against the educators, but he did not. The Board of Education refused to accept the action, and a battle began. It ended with the school year in June, but festered throughout the summer. In September, on the day school was scheduled to reopen, Albert Shanker, the president of the United Federation of Teachers, called a citywide strike. What had started out as an experiment in improved education had turned into a battle between a self-declared black spokesmen and his supporters, and a largely Jewish union.

The bitterness that the strike created between blacks and Jews is difficult to exaggerate. During the course of the struggle black community control advocates baited picketing strikers with taunts of "Jew pig." Some handed out anti-Semitic literature. The UFT publicized the slurs widely in a campaign to discredit their adversaries, exacerbating tensions in the process. Among the teachers Rhody McCoy brought into the Ocean Hill-Brownsville schools was a black militant named Leslie Cambell. Shortly after the strike ended, he appeared on a black radio station and dedicated a poem entitled "Anti-Semitism" to Albert Shanker. Cambell called the work "beautiful" and "true." Its opening stanza went like this:

> Hey Jew boy, with that yarmulke on your head
> You pale-faced Jew boy—I wish you were dead;
> I can see you Jew boy—no you can't hide,
> I got a scoop on you, yeh, you gonna die.

The conflict was finally settled in mid-November on terms that reaffirmed the authority of the labor contracts negotiated by the Board of Education with the UFT, and that did not allow local community boards to dismiss teachers. New York's children left the streets and ball fields to return to the classroom. But the city was badly polarized. Lindsay's efforts to defuse the crisis made it appear once again that he had sided with the city's blacks, this time against Jews. The effect of the strike on Lindsay's popularity among whites was devastating. As 1969 arrived, a mayoralty election year, New Yorkers perceived Lindsay as a leader who represented only one segment of the population, its racial minorities. White New Yorkers of every background felt abandoned.[17]

Running Against the Odds

On February 10, 1969, fifteen inches of snow fell on New York City. It caught the weather forecasters off-guard, and the mayor too. The city, especially in neighborhoods with private houses and small streets, like those in Queens where the storm hit hardest, came to a standstill before

Department of Sanitation plows finally managed to make the roads passable. For many people, the event symbolized Lindsay's inability to govern the city. It was as if the gods themselves had turned against the mayor.[18]

Early in 1969 Lindsay had polls taken that confirmed what he already knew—his standing with New Yorkers was weak, and his chances for reelection, poor. Racial minorities supported him strongly, but no others. Irish contempt for the mayor was fierce. The group viewed his assault on the status quo as a direct threat. Most other Catholics also hated Lindsay. They felt that "he had done too much for the blacks and nothing for anyone else," and they had no intention of voting to return him to office. The Italians displayed some slight remorse about their resentment toward Lindsay's policies, but still offered him only modest opportunity for political gain.

Only among Jews was there any softness in the white middle-class hostility toward the mayor. Deep in their hearts, many Jewish New Yorkers were very sympathetic to minority demands and thought that the government ought to play an active role in helping blacks to overcome the effects of discrimination and its debilitating legacy. Like other whites, the group felt that Lindsay ignored the legitimate demands of hard working middle-class people for fair and proper treatment from their government. They also thought that he had responded to sincere concern about the effects of his policies with high handed arrogance that assumed all his detractors were racist. But there was no fundamental conflict between Lindsay's intentions and the political philosophy of most of the city's Jews. With the right campaign, the mayor might be able to win enough of them back so that, when added to his strong support among minorities, he would have a chance to win.[19]

Robert Price, who had run Lindsay's 1965 mayoralty campaign virtually as a one man show, left the administration after serving a year as deputy mayor. Lindsay needed a new political manager, one willing to take on what appeared a near hopeless effort. He asked Richard Aurelio, a one time news editor of *Newsday*, and long time Washington staff assistant to Senator Jacob Javits, to do the job. Aurelio, who had run the Senator's successful reelection bid the year before, had just left Javits's staff in search of a new challenge when Lindsay approached him. After several days of contemplation, the experienced professional accepted the job because he thought that Lindsay had become such a symbol of the movement to provide equal opportunity for racial minorities that his defeat in New York would be a blow to the cause of improved race relations across the country. Once Aurelio signed on, the candidate and his campaign manager met with Alex Rose to discuss strategy.[20]

For a brief period in 1966, the Liberals had been embroiled in an episode that put Rose at odds with the Lindsay administration. Robert Price, still Lindsay's chief political operative then, cut a deal with J. Raymond Jones to give joint Democratic and Republican backing for the Manhattan surrogate to New York State Supreme Court Justice Arthur Klein, a product of the Democratic machine. The two leaders would then back a Republican for a Supreme Court judgeship as the *quid pro quo*. Rose had not been consulted on the deal, and he liked neither the arrangement, nor the fact that he was being ignored by an administration he had helped elect. He convinced Robert Kennedy to oppose Klein, and the Senator tapped another Supreme Court Justice, Samuel Silverman, to run for the Democratic nomination. Kennedy inspired reform Democrats to his side, and Silverman ended up winning the primary and the election. Not only did the victory remind the city's political figures that the Liberals were not to be trifled with, but it also won the party a rich source of patronage as well.[21]

In 1966, New Yorkers also chose a governor. Rockefeller ran for reelection, and the Democrats made good on their 1965 promise to deliver their party's nomination to Frank O'Connor. Polls taken in May 1966, showed the Democrat a strong favorite over the incumbent, but Alex Rose resented the deal that made O'Connor the Democratic candidate. The Liberals refused to support him, and Rose talked Franklin Roosevelt, Jr. into running for governor on the Liberal line alone. The decision ensured O'Connor's defeat. Some charged a plot by Rose to keep Rockefeller, always solicitous of the Liberal leader's favor, in office. During an interview O'Connor made no secret of his frustration with Rose's decision. "I think there is a strange suspicion among many leaders of the Liberal Party and many Reformers concerning an Irishman. . . . No matter what your record . . . it's hard to convince them you're really liberal," O'Connor told a journalist. Rose blasted the implied accusation of ethnic discrimination, and in a sense, the charge was unfounded. Rose harbored no petty bigotry. But if being Irish Catholic was not just a question of kinship, but of cultural values and political style as well, there was something to the complaint. O'Connor's traditional brand of politics was unacceptable to the largely Jewish membership of the Liberal party.[22]

The decision to play spoiler once again established the Liberals as a dangerous political force to ignore, but it also caused a serious split among party supporters. In March 1966, David Dubinsky had retired as head of the ILGWU, and Louis Stulberg, the union's long-time secretary, replaced him. Stulberg objected to FDR, Jr.'s candidacy, and harbored personal resentment toward Rose and his domination of the Liberal party. The new president of the union that provided so much of the party's financial support, and whose members remained the nucleus of its loyal workers, refused to accept Rose's decision and backed the Democrat.

The United Federation of Teachers was another traditional source of support that had soured on the Liberals by 1969. The principal leaders of the Liberal party backed Lindsay's effort at reconciliation during the school strike. Donald Harrington, the party's titular chairman, Rose, and a handful of others, believed that the mayor's policy ultimately would increase the chances for an integrated school system and racial harmony. Albert Shanker and many members of the union he headed belonged to the Liberal party, and the UFT had long been among the party's most important financial contributors. They felt betrayed. Shanker resigned and ended his union's relationship with the party over the issue. Quite a number of Liberal party rank and file resigned as well. They were offended by a stand that seemed to align the organization with anti-Semites.[23]

Lindsay appreciated Rose's unswerving support on the school board issue, and the Liberals had backed his Civilian Review Board proposal as well. The mayor had great regard for Rose's political wisdom, met with him frequently, and made good on promises to provide the Liberal party with high-level patronage posts, even though Rose never seemed satisfied with the number of jobs his party received. "John," he once told the mayor, "there was a Russian peasant who had two horses. One was pretty and the peasant gave him everything, even though he never pulled very hard. The other was strong, but ugly, so he got very little. One day, John, the ugly horse who did all the work—he died. And the other one could not pull." Rose did not need to mention that the horses' names were Republican and Liberal.[24]

Other times Rose was even more indirect. Sid Davidoff dispensed the Lindsay administration's patronage for a time, and he remembered that occasionally the Liberals would make a request he simply could not fulfill. "They would have some young rising star who was pushing coat racks in the garment center," Davidoff recalled, "and they would ask me to make him a deputy commissioner of finance or something. I would say no, and a few days later I would get a call from John [Lindsay] telling me he had seen Alex, who asked why Sid Davidoff was always giving him the cold shoulder. I wouldn't have spoken to Rose, wouldn't know what it was all about, and then I would realize—it was the guy with the coat racks."[25] The mutual dependency between Lindsay and Rose was as great as the mutual respect.

Rose had as keen a sense as anyone of the public mood in New York. He knew Lindsay faced resistance that bordered on the pathological in many of the city's white middle-class neighborhoods, and he knew that many members of the Liberal party harbored bitterness toward the mayor as a result of his stand during the school strike. Yet, Rose felt that the Liberal party had an obligation to stand with Lindsay. He believed that the mayor had tried to do what he thought was best for the city, and that he had achieved some notable successes. He also felt that the mayor's efforts to open more opportunities to blacks and Puerto Ricans were critical to improve the climate of life for everyone in the city. He feared that if a surge of white backlash defeated Lindsay in New York City, the bastion of the nation's liberal thinking, it would send a chilling message to politicians across the country and initiate a long period of reaction. "New York had to become a political Stalingrad," he said of Lindsay's reelection campaign, "like the city where the forces of Hitlerism were turned back. . . . the backlash had to be turned back. We felt it better to lose than to run away from it."[26]

Rose had read the polls that Lindsay had taken, knew that the battle would be long, hard, and uncertain, and that the key to the outcome would be the city's Jewish voters. He quietly arranged for Lindsay, Aurelio, and himself to meet with pollster Louis Harris in the latter's home in Riverdale, far from public view, to plan strategy. Harris by then ran a national polling agency that concentrated on market studies for corporations. He still took political polls, but did them primarily for news services. He did not want to associate himself publicly with a particular candidate. But he and Rose were close friends, and he shared Rose's concern about the dangers of white backlash and its potential consequences for the city and nation. So he agreed to help develop a campaign strategy, and he outlined for the three men what years of gathering survey information in New York had taught him about the city's Jews and their voting patterns.

Harris divided the group conceptually into a number of categories based on economic, educational and professional achievement. At one end of the spectrum were the upper-income, well-educated Jews of Manhattan, Riverdale, and a few other neighborhoods. At the other, the intensely protective and isolated hasidim of Brooklyn, poorer than most of the city's Jews and intensely concerned with maintaining their traditions. In between were several degrees of working-class and professional Jews, some more religious, some less, some better off, some worse.

The plan that emerged from Harris's explanation required the mayor to spend little time among wealthier Jews. The campaign needed only to "prick the conscience" of this segment of the population, and their liberal convictions would bring them back to Lindsay as a matter of course. The hasidim were a small, well organized sect whose security concerns and specific needs could be addressed successfully by the resources available to an incumbent mayor. The candidate would need to spend the bulk of his time in neighborhoods of Jewish workers and accountants, of school teachers and shop owners, in Brooklyn, Queens, and the Bronx. And John Lindsay would have to humble himself. He would have to admit that he had made mistakes, show that he understood that it was not immoral for New Yorkers to criticize their mayor and that not all of the anger directed at him was motivated by racism. It was the only way Lindsay would be able to regain the confidence, and the votes, of the city's Jews.[27]

John Lindsay "had a tough time learning to eat crow," Dick Aurelio remembered. The mayor remained adamant that the causes he backed were just, and his commitment to them remained firm. But his advisers wore him down until he finally accepted the idea that for the good of the city even just policies needed to be implemented in ways that were sensitive to the demands and perceptions of the average New Yorker. By the end of January 1969, Lindsay began meeting with Jewish groups in his capacity as mayor. He talked about his administration, its successes and failures, and tried to make Jewish voters believe that if they gave him another chance, he would accept their vote of confidence with humility.[28]

Law and Order

GOP stalwarts wanted no more of Lindsay, humbled or otherwise. Staten Island Republican State Senator John Marchi was so offended by Lindsay's handling of the school board controversy that he decided to challenge the mayor in the Republican primary. Marchi felt Lindsay had capitulated to the demands of extremists who used illegal tactics, and wanted to make it clear that, "everybody has an obligation to obey the law." New York was fertile ground for that idea. An opinion poll taken in March, 1969, revealed that, "preoccupation with race and its auxiliary issues—the school crisis, crime, police problems—was an obsession among voters." The perception had developed that Lindsay's concern for blacks and Puerto Ricans—what many middle-class white New Yorkers saw as favoritism toward the groups—encouraged the criminal elements among them to act with impunity. It became increasingly apparent that attitudes toward race relations, expressed in terms of "law and order," would overpower other concerns during the 1969 mayoralty campaign.[29]

Lindsay's team knew that their candidate had no chance to win a contest confined to the GOP. The strength of that party came from the groups that had lost all confidence in the mayor. About four out of ten New York City Republicans were Italians, like John Marchi, and another ten percent were Irish. A Jewish Republican was a rarity, a black Republican an oddity. About a quarter of the party's registered voters were Protestants, like Lindsay. Only these offered the incumbent some base of support within the GOP, and there were simply not enough for victory. Aurelio and Rose proposed that they run a "once over lightly" primary campaign while conserving their resources for a general election bid running on the Liberal ticket. But Lindsay's chief money backers, men like financier John Hay Whitney, publisher of the New York *Herald Tribune* and scion of two of America's most distinguished and wealthiest families, and Gustave Levy of the Wall Street investment bank Goldman Sachs, and a few others, had spent years trying to develop the liberal wing of the Republican party. They did not want to abandon their dream and promised to raise the money Lindsay would need to run a campaign and primary both, so the race was on. No one thought Lindsay could win the Republican nomination, but a respectable showing might keep the wing he represented intact, and provide some momentum for November as well.[30]

For running mates, Rose urged Lindsay to pick well qualified city employees to strengthen his appeal to good government voters. For comptroller, the campaign team tapped city finance administrator Fiorvante G. Perrotta. The choice had the added benefit of offering some recognition to the Republican party's Italians. For City Council president Rose suggested Sanford Garelik. The Police Department's chief inspector was the ideal choice to prove Lindsay's concern for law and order, and he was Jewish. He was also a registered Democrat, which would allow Lindsay to claim he was mounting a fusion campaign. But Garelik declined. "They must have asked me to run fourteen times," he remembered, but he told Lindsay and assorted emissaries that he was a policeman, not a politician.

Aurelio looked for an alternative, but found none who could match Garelik's unique appeal. Vince Albano, the Republican county leader from Manhattan, was loyal to Lindsay and friendly with Garelik. He arranged for himself and Aurelio to meet with Garelik in a suite at the Roosevelt Hotel one evening for a last effort to convince the man to run. "If we don't get him tonight, we won't get him," the county leader told the campaign manager as they entered the building. The two men tried unsuccessfully for several hours to break down the resistance of the reluctant candidate. Finally, having exhausted all other ideas, Aurelio began to impugn Garelik's manhood.

"Are you going to be a cop all your life Sandy? Here's a chance to really do something for the city, to have the power to change things, and you don't have the guts to do it?" the political operator sneered. Aurelio could tell it had an effect, so he continued.

"What kind of a man are you?," he asked the cop who had been the youngest captain in the history of the police force, who as a rookie had won the department's battle star his fifth day on the job. Albano leaned over to Aurelio and whispered half in jest, half not: "Christ Dick, remember he's got a gun."

"What kind of a man are you Sandy?," Aurelio persisted, "What are you afraid of? . . . Where are your balls, Sandy, huh? . . . Don't you care about this city? . . . Where are your balls?"[31]

Before the night was over Garelik had agreed to run for City Council president, and Lindsay had a Jewish law-and-order candidate to bolster his ticket. After some maneuvering, John Marchi ended up with an Irish Catholic assemblyman named Robert Kelley as his City Council president running mate, and Vito Battista, hero of the city's anti-tax forces, for comptroller. The Marchi slate also got the Conservative party endorsement.

While the Republicans prepared for a clear battle between their conservative and liberal wings, the Democrats began a confusing struggle that showed how badly split and weakened their party had become.

After his candidate lost the surrogate's race in 1966, J. Raymond Jones could no longer hold on to what remained of the Democratic organization in Manhattan. Frank Rossetti replaced him and inherited the fractured structure that had led to Jones's decline. In the Bronx, in 1967, Charles Buckley died. He was replaced by Henry McDonough, who became ill himself, and died early in May 1969. The Democratic primary was half over by the time Patrick Cunningham received the organization's vote of confidence and became county leader. Brooklyn too had a new boss, Meade Esposito, more experienced than the others, but still building his base of power. Robert Kennedy's tragic assassination in 1968 robbed New York State of its senior elected Democrat. The party that dominated the registration rolls in New York City had no leadership, and was headed for a primary free-for-all worse than the one it suffered in 1965. At one point a dozen Democrats seemed prepared to run for the spot. Ultimately five candidates vied for their party's nomination for mayor.

Bronx Congressman James H. Scheuer was the first to announce. A moderate liberal from the party's reform wing, educated at Swarthmore, Harvard Business School, and Columbia Law School, Scheuer had enjoyed a successful career building government-sponsored middle-income housing before entering politics. His campaign strategy combined concern for safety in the streets with a direct ethnic appeal to his fellow Jews: "the little old Jewish lady who's lived all her life on Jerome Ave. should be able to walk out of her apartment without fear after sundown Friday to go to her synagogue," was a typical line from his speeches. His campaign aides readily conceded that "much of his strategy is being pegged at the Jewish vote." After all, up to forty-five percent of the ballots in the Democratic primary were expected to come from Jews, according to estimates based on polling data.[32]

Herman Badillo, the Puerto Rican politician elected Borough President of the Bronx in 1965, understood the ethnic arithmetic of a Democratic primary as well. He had become the first member of his group to win a seat on the Board of Estimate when he edged out Republican Joseph Periconi, and he knew the coalition that had voted him into office consisted of minorities voting for one of their own, and Jews supporting his liberal politics. When Badillo announced he was in the race for mayor in 1969, he chose two Jewish running mates, Elinor Guggenheimer of Manhattan for City Council president, and State Senator Harrison Goldin for comptroller, both from the party's reform wing. It did not hurt that Badillo's wife, Irma, was Jewish. He called himself the only liberal in his party's primary.[33]

In spite of Badillo's assertion, he was not liberal enough for author Norman Mailer. After listening to the city's preeminent Puerto Rican politician give a speech one night, Mailer concluded that he had to run himself if he wanted to inject a truly liberal agenda into the campaign. He talked the irreverent columnist Jimmy Breslin into joining him as candidate for City Council president. The two writers explained how they would replace the existing government of the city with a completely decentralized structure, make New York City the fifty-first state, and "kiss off the boredom of the Democratic machine." They passed out buttons that said "Vote the Rascals In," and adopted "No Bullshit" as a campaign slogan. For many their campaign was a joke, but they persisted straight through the primary election.[34]

At the opposite end of the spectrum was Comptroller Mario Procaccino, the Italian born son of a shoe maker whose family emigrated to New York when he was still a child. He got his start in politics when Mayor LaGuardia appointed him to a position as an assistant corporation counsel in 1944. When O'Dwyer came to office, the Democrats made it clear to Procaccino that if he hoped to advance his career he would need to join the Democratic club in the Bronx neighborhood where he then lived. Procaccino did, and over time, the party rewarded him with several appointments before finally tapping him to add ethnic balance to Abraham Beame's 1965 mayoralty race as the Italian candidate for comptroller. Procaccino's mayoralty campaign was designed to appeal directly to the white middle-class voters so angry at the state of affairs under Lindsay. "We can have the best schools, the best hospitals, the best housing, the best museums, the best of everything, but it will be to no avail if we can't make the city safe," he told New York. He accused Lindsay of handcuffing the police and demoralizing the department, and declared that as mayor, he would clean the "punks, pushers and perverts," from the streets. Everyone must obey the law, he insisted.[35]

Then Robert Wagner entered the campaign. Out of city government for four years, he was bored. He found little happiness in a new marriage that ended in annulment, and a stint as Ambassador to Spain served simply as a diversion. Restless, with his party in obvious need of leadership, encouraged by his sons and many supporters to run, the old pro tossed his hat into the ring. "I had a vacation," he explained to the city during the campaign. "I suppose its good for a mayor to have a vacation. I think the present mayor should get a vacation." Wagner was the instant front runner, and he went to talk with Alex Rose to see if his old friend would help him to re-create the kind of coalition that had brought Wagner victory in 1961.[36]

The Lindsay campaign got very nervous. "The Liberal party is the ball game," admitted one aide who knew that there was great support for Wagner among the Liberals. But Rose refused to switch his allegiance. He thought Wagner's comeback as mayor did not make sense, and he continued to feel that it was important to reelect Lindsay to make it clear that the conservative backlash could not drive committed liberals from office. Rose refused to allow his party to hold a primary, which Wagner might well have won, and working with other members of the leadership who felt as he did forced the party he controlled to accept Lindsay. The ILGWU split with the Liberals formally over the issue, and backed Wagner.[37]

The Democratic contest rapidly reduced to a three way race. Procaccino was the right wing candidate, even though he often disliked the image. Badillo was the farthest left of center, and Wagner the candidate of reconciliation, somewhere between the other two. Scheuer simply failed to reach the public with his message and hovered in obscurity, while Mailer was a protest candidate without serious standing. On primary day, to everyone's surprise, the fractured party elected Mario Procaccino its candidate for mayor.

Procaccino took less than a third of the Democratic ballots cast. That was still more than anyone else in the scattered field. He won almost seventy percent of the sizable Italian vote giving him the strongest base of any of the contenders, and he polled over a quarter of the Jewish votes, mostly in lower-income working class neighborhoods. Wagner and Badillo between them took nearly fifty-seven percent of the Democratic vote—it was Wagner's old coalition, but split between two candidates. The former mayor polled almost forty percent of the Jewish ballots, and sizable portions from other groups. Badillo took nearly ninety percent of the Puerto Rican vote, more than half the black vote, and more than twenty percent of the Jewish vote. Jews concerned about rising crime in New York, but who maintained their liberal convictions, voted for Wagner. The former mayor made it clear that he would give high priority to making the city's streets safer, but he also had a progressive reputation on social policies that Procaccino could not match. Badillo's Jewish support was strongest in upper-income neighborhoods, far from the street crime growing ever more common in the city.[38]

For City Council president, the Democrats voted for the incumbent, Francis X. Smith, appointed when Frank O'Connor stepped down to run for governor. For comptroller they chose Abe Beame. The veteran politician launched an independent campaign to regain his old job when Procaccino announced he would seek the mayoralty. The Democratic primary, as it happened, elected a balanced ticket—Procaccino, a Bronx Italian; Beame, a Brooklyn Jew; and Smith a Queens Irishman. But something was wrong. The traditional purpose of the balanced ticket was to offer a symbolic gesture to the ethnic voting blocs that supported the Democratic party, thereby keeping the organization unified. By that standard, in 1969, the Democrats needed a minority candidate on their ticket, and they did not have one. A ticket headed by an Italian was not the strongest that the Democrats could offer because among the city's major ethnic groups Italians were the least Democratic in registration. Procaccino, who had won less than a third of the primary vote, was clearly not the first choice of a strong majority of the city's Democrats, and to many his conservative outlook was simply unacceptable.[39]

While Procaccino won a weak victory in the Democratic contest, Lindsay lost the Republican primary with a strong showing. Marchi beat him by only 6,000 ballots out of more than 218,000 cast, and both of Lindsay's running mates beat Marchi's men. On the one hand, there was no escaping the conclusion that Lindsay's defeat was personal. On the other, he had run much better than expected. In spite of his loss, Jacob Javits, Louis Lefkowitz, and other liberal Republicans announced that they would back the mayor, who was still in the race on the Liberal party line. "We may be the rescue operation for John Lindsay," Rose said coyly. That was of course the plan from the start. And the mayor's campaign staff created the Independent Citizens party to give Lindsay a second line on the ballot for those who would refuse to vote on the Liberal ticket.[40]

The Lindsay team, which had expected to face Robert Wagner, viewed Procaccino's surprising win as a blessing. Aurelio threw out campaign ads he had already prepared that consisted of montages of negative headlines from Wagner's third term. Lindsay announced immediately that both Marchi and Procaccino wanted to ride to victory on "fear, reaction and the backlash." The mayor was the only liberal candidate still in the race, and the Lindsay camp knew that many Democrats, particularly the liberal Jews who made up the reform wing, would find it impossible to vote for their party's nominee.[41]

The Perennial Quest for the Jewish Vote

Over the next two weeks Lindsay spoke personally with almost every reform Democrat of standing in the city to ask for support. A well-respected former Democratic district leader from the party's reform wing, Ronnie Eldridge, found the prospect of Procaccino controlling her party for four years unnerving. She launched an effort to recruit prestigious Democrats to Lindsay's cause, and a handful rapidly announced that they would back the mayor. Lindsay's campaign staff arranged press conferences for each of the defectors and spaced them a few days apart so that it would appear as if a flood of Democratic backing were flowing to their candidate. Aurelio organized a Fusion Advisory Council to bring the Democrats into the campaign structure. Some were offered top staff positions, others were asked to recommend people for city jobs. As the summer wore on local politicians took the pulse of their districts. Many who represented upper-income Jewish areas, like Assemblyman Benjamin Altman in Riverdale, and Assemblyman Leonard Stavisky in Queens, determined that their followers would vote for Lindsay. They decided to back the mayor. Black politicians like J. Raymond Jones, Charles Rangel, and Shirley Chisolm did the same.[42]

Procaccino seemed to understand the risk of being labeled a conservative in a city as liberal as New York, even at a time when anger and the sentiments of white backlash were riding high. He did not want his "law and order" campaign to brand him as racist. "If you think my record is that of a bigot, you're out of your mind—your cotton picking mind," he told the press, and he tried to portray himself as an independent moderate. "There's Alex Rose's man, John Lindsay on the left. There's Kieran O'Doherty's man, John Marchi on the right. And in the middle there am I—a moderate progressive Democrat. That's what I am and that's what I'll stay," he said.[43]

But Procaccino was a political incompetent, and his campaign staff was no better. His manager, a Bronx Democratic district leader named Victor Campione, made no attempt to achieve a reconciliation with the liberal Democrats flirting with Lindsay. "We come from the school which believes that when you win the primary the party comes to you," he said. The reformers never did, and even the regulars lost enthusiasm. In the Bronx, Pat Cunningham thought that Procaccino was simply an accident and found working with his people difficult. In an effort to bring the party together Meade Esposito arranged for Procaccino to meet with Louis Stulberg of the ILGWU, and with Robert Wagner, whom the Brooklyn boss had backed in the primary. Wagner asked the candidate for a "White Paper," explaining his positions on a number of issues. "Why don't you cut the shit," Procaccino told the former mayor, according to Esposito. "You're the number one Democrat in this town and I expect your support." The meeting ended abruptly. In the middle of the campaign, Esposito, wanting no part of Procaccino, left the city for a three-week vacation.[44]

In campaign stops throughout the Bronx, Brooklyn, and Queens, Procaccino accused the city's glamorous WASP mayor of running a "Manhattan Arrangement," that favored the city's influential midtown elite at the expense of the middle class. He called the mayor's supporters "limousine liberals," implying that they were out of touch with the problems faced by the average New Yorker. He suggested that Lindsay's wealthy backers found it easy to promote special privileges for the city's minorities because their jobs were not at risk, and because their neighborhoods were effectively out of bounds to poor New Yorkers. His campaign fit the polarized times.[45]

Lindsay, meanwhile, campaigned principally in the city's Jewish neighborhoods. In Crown Heights he reminded residents of the success of operation Hasidic Rabbi, a police undercover ploy that disguised patrolmen as religious Jews who then collared unsuspecting muggers. At Temple Isaiah in Forest Hills, he confronted the crowd directly: "I've been accused of caring too much for minorities. I plead guilty. I have cared about minorities in New York—all of them," he told the gathering of Jews, a people whose legacy has been to live always in the minority. In a visit to the same site just a few months earlier he had been booed and jeered. "Last winter, I wouldn't have given three cents for his chances," one man in the audience commented, but things were changing. While the mayor himself toured Jewish neighborhoods, his office launched a publicly funded voter registration drive in minority ghettos. Everyone knew who the newly inscribed citizens would vote for in the mayoralty contest. Procaccino attacked the effort as "discriminatory," because it focused on just a few areas. Marchi called it "a total waste of taxpayers money." The accusations sounded racist and cheap. After all, what kind of a leader was opposed to helping the poor to exercise their democratic rights?[46]

In 1965 Price had been forced to build a citywide campaign network to organize support for Lindsay. In 1969 the incumbent mayor had a ready made campaign team of loyal assistants and employees who owed their jobs to the man in City Hall. Moreover, the municipal unions, whose members were so angry at Lindsay, found the administration unusually cooperative in negotiations that took place during the spring and summer of 1969. Generous wage settlements were reached, long standing disputes resolved, many accommodations made. When asked if a deal had been struck Lindsay aide Sid Davidoff replied simply that, "budgets are always political documents." The union leaders were powerless to convince their members to vote for Lindsay, but their political committees worked closely with the mayor's staff putting up posters, arranging for crowds to appear when the mayor spoke, staffing telephone banks, and the like.[47]

With logistical operations easily managed by the mayor's existing staff and city workers, the campaign team was free to focus its attention on media advertising to an extraordinary degree. Public relations consultant David Garth worked together with the advertising company of Young & Rubicam to create Lindsay's commercials. In the most important television spot of the contest, Lindsay, shirt open at the collar, stared into the camera with a firm and earnest gaze: "I guessed wrong on the weather before the city's biggest snowfall last winter, and that was a mistake. But I put 6,000 more cops on the streets—and that was no mistake. The school strike went on too long—and we all made some mistakes. But I brought 225,000 new jobs to this town—and that was no mistake." The mea culpa was critical. It allowed voters who approved of Lindsay's liberal convictions to believe that the mayor had learned from the conflicts of his first term, and that he would not make the same administrative blunders and errors of judgement again if they returned him to office. The sense of humility so important to winning back the support of Jewish voters was there, coupled with a reminder that Lindsay had accomplished some difficult things as well. By the end of the summer the mayor's campaign adopted the slogan, "It's the Second Toughest Job in America!" No wonder, voters were urged to think, Lindsay had made mistakes. They were also expected to wonder if the Democrat running against the incumbent was up to the task.[48]

By mid-September, when summer holidays ended and the mayoralty campaign began to pick up speed, both sides admitted what had been true from the start of the contest: "The Jewish vote will determine whether John V. Lindsay, Liberal and Independent party candidate, or Mario A. Procaccino, the Democratic candidate, will be the city's next Mayor," a *New York Times* reporter wrote after interviewing members of the two campaign teams. One Procaccino strategist assessed the political reality of New York City this way: "Is an Italian going to vote for Lindsay? How much of the Negro vote can we possibly get? . . . What we're really talking about this year is the Jewish vote. Most of the other vote is locked in." Procaccino's staff felt confident that their candidate would win the support of the key voting bloc. Most Jews, they reasoned, are "worried about the same things their Irish and Italian neighbors are—crime, garbage, you name it."[49]

Something else was important to Jews as well. During September and October Aurelio sent volunteers, mostly Manhattan lawyers, to walk the streets of Jewish neighborhoods in Queens, Brooklyn, and the Bronx and gauge the impact of the campaign. The young attorneys talked with people sitting on park benches or standing on street corners and asked them what they thought about the mayoralty race. The clearest message of the interviews was that New York City's Jews wanted the war in Vietnam ended. It had nothing to do with municipal government, but everything to do with what was on the minds of the voters who would determine who controlled City Hall. Lindsay had long opposed United States involvement in Southeast Asia, and declared repeatedly in campaign speeches: "We have to take money out of the drain of death and put it into the work of life." In synagogues around the city the line "won thunderous applause." His stand, one political analyst wrote, "not universally appreciated by any means . . . did win favor with the group whose support he needs most desperately, the Jews."[50]

Then, in the last days of September, Israeli Prime Minister Golda Meir traveled to New York to attend the United Nations General Assembly. Her visit coincided with the Jewish holiday of Succoth. An orthodox rabbi suggested to Sid Davidoff that the city build a succah— a tent-like abode traditionally erected during the holiday to serve as a symbolic reminder of the Jewish flight from Egypt—as a gesture to the prime minister and the people she represented. Davidoff convinced Lindsay that the plan had merit. The succah went up outside the Brooklyn Museum, where the city hosted an extravagant dinner for the visiting chief of state attended by more than 1,400 of the city's most influential Jews. "If there was an important Jew in the city who wasn't there, it was because they were dead or dying," Davidoff insisted.[51]

Before the reception Lindsay and Aurelio met privately with Meir. They explained to her that more was at risk in the New York City mayoralty election than the career of John Lindsay. It was a fight for liberal and humane government, they told her, for racial harmony and equality. In a "very self-interested" way, they convinced the woman who led the spiritual homeland of world Jewry that the "soul of New York's Jews was involved" in Lindsay's contest for reelection. The chief of a foreign state could not properly favor a candidate for the mayor of a city in another country. The best Aurelio thought Lindsay could hope for from Meir were some quiet words of support to some of the more important Jewish leaders present. But the prime minister was so moved by the explanation of the stakes involved that when she rose to speak before the largest gathering of prominent Jews ever assembled for a single event in New York City, she practically endorsed Lindsay.[52]

Then the Mets won the World Series. The mayor was at Shea Stadium when the final game ended, and Sid Davidoff grabbed him by the arm and thrust him into the locker room on an impulse. There, Mets pitcher Tom Seaver raised his pitching arm and doused His Honor all over with champagne. The next morning the picture appeared on the front page of the city's newspapers. Twenty years later Aurelio still smiled at the event. "We spent the whole campaign trying to cut Lindsay down to size, to humble him," he would reflect. "We never could have planned anything that effective." The tall, elegant, WASP mayor, in a Queens locker room, just one of the guys, and yet a champion.[53]

By October Lindsay's campaign was winning over large numbers of Jewish voters. Procaccino decided that he had to respond by confronting his adversary and he agreed to debate Lindsay and John Marchi on television. Marchi appeared thoughtful, articulate, and distinguished looking. Lindsay, as always, came across as a matinee idol. Bared before viewers, Procaccino seemed harsh and mediocre, disorganized and emotional, outclassed by his rivals. He was on the defensive; he looked tense and excitable, a little too eager to play the cop, too much like the harsh man Lindsay accused him of being. He failed to portray himself as a reasonable representative of the middle class, and what came through strongest was the impression that the mayoralty was over his head.[54]

As the campaign came to a close, one confident Lindsay aide told a journalist, "talking about voting for a law-and-order candidate is one thing, doing it is another. The Jewish voter has always been the most liberal voter in America. On election day, they just won't be able to pull the Procaccino lever." Although the speaker underestimated the effect of racial tensions on New York's Jewish population in 1969, the statement remained true enough to elect John Lindsay mayor. He took just under forty-two percent of the total vote. Procaccino won thirty-five percent, John Marchi twenty-three percent.[55]

Jewish voters split their support evenly between Lindsay and Procaccino. Each of the two candidates won about forty-four percent of the group's ballots, while Marchi got only the crumbs. The wealthier the Jewish neighborhood, the more likely it was to vote for Lindsay. Middle-class and less well off Jews tended to back Procaccino. Simply put, the Jews at greatest risk of paying the consequences for policies designed to benefit racial minorities backed the harsh sounding Democrat preaching law and order. They voted for self-defense. The ones who backed Lindsay were farther removed from blacks and Puerto Ricans physically and occupationally, and more able to afford the financial burden of programs designed to help minorities. Under those conditions, the traditional liberal attitude of Jewish voters persevered. Yet, for the first time in a New York City mayoralty election, a majority of Jews cast ballots for candidates who were clearly not liberal. The political outlook of New York City's Jews was changing.[56]

The rest of the voting pattern was predictable. The two Italians took more than eighty-five percent of their countrymen's votes, and nearly as high a proportion of the Irish ballots as well. Between them, they ran strongly everywhere that white Catholics outnumbered other voters. Lindsay of course won overwhelmingly with the city's minorities; more than eight of every ten votes cast by blacks, and more than six of ten cast by Puerto Ricans.

Campaign financing records for the 1969 contest are very incomplete, but it is clear that Lindsay's effort cost well over two million dollars, perhaps three million. Although he did not have the formal backing of the city's Republican party, Lindsay did have the support of the GOP's wealthiest contributors, which meant that Marchi did not. The Republican-Conservative challenger had a tough time paying for a serious citywide effort. Nor could Procaccino match Lindsay's warchest. The law-and-order candidate was out of step with the philosophical views of his party's traditional financial supporters, many of whom ultimately favored Lindsay. Because the mayor had the resources of the incumbency to develop the kind of neighborhood campaign that political parties typically organized, the bulk of his election treasury went for television and radio advertising making the discrepancy in resources greater still.

Yet, Lindsay's huge treasury, and his extensive and sophisticated use of the media, explain little about his victory. Neither of these advantages, nor the power of his incumbency, nor the efforts of the more skillful and more experienced campaign staff he commanded, enabled him to build support beyond the city's minorities and the wealthier segments of its Jewish community. The coalition that returned him to office consisted principally of the same voters who had favored the Civilian Review Board in 1966, suggesting that what his campaign had accomplished was to repair some of the damage the 1968 school strike had done among Jewish voters, and no more. No amount of money and no amount of television time, would have won him support with New York's Catholics, and there is little reason to believe that more funding would have made him more successful with working-class Jews. Had Lindsay faced only one of his foes in 1969, he would almost certainly have lost in spite of his many advantages, even without a fairer distribution of campaign finances. Even in a three way contest, a Democrat more in touch with his party's traditions than Procaccino would almost certainly have beaten Lindsay. More than anything else, Lindsay owed his victory to Mario Procaccino's utter unsuitability as a candidate to liberal Jewish voters and to the city's racial minorities.

The importance of Jewish voters became apparent in another way in 1969. Four years earlier, the coincidence of Beame's loss in his bid to become mayor, and the loss of Lindsay's Jewish running mate, Milton

Mollen, in his bid to become comptroller, left the Jews without a citywide representative on the Board of Estimate for the first time in memory. Abe Stark, Brooklyn borough president since 1961, was the only member of his faith who held a seat on the city's most important governing body after 1965. In 1969, the voters returned him to office, and they returned Abe Beame to the comptroller's post he once held. To the surprise of the city's political analysts, Sandy Garelik defeated incumbent City Council President Francis X. Smith. In the Bronx, a Jewish reform Democrat named Robert Abrams won the borough president spot that Herman Badillo vacated when he ran for mayor. A Jewish politician named Sidney Leviss was elected borough president of Queens. In Manhattan, tradition left the borough presidency in the hands of a black man, Percy Sutton, and on Staten Island Robert Connor, the lone politician of Irish descent among those who ruled New York, was the top elected official. For the first time in the history of New York City, a majority of the politicians serving on the Board of Estimate, five of eight, were Jewish.

And New York had yet to elect a Jewish mayor.

TEN

The Jewish Assumption

1970–1977

Lindsay Leaves Town

Soon after winning reelection as mayor on a campaign of humility, John V. Lindsay began running for President. He had been unable to win the Republican nomination for his race in New York City in 1969, and his aides had little trouble convincing him that it was hopeless to seek the nomination for President against the Republican incumbent, Richard Nixon. So in 1971, Lindsay switched his political affiliation and prepared to compete in Democratic presidential primaries around the country the following year. He knew that the chance for success was small, but he planned to use the nationwide publicity of such a campaign to establish himself as the country's preeminent spokesman for urban issues, and to prepare the way for a future race.[1]

To be heard and to maintain his political credibility, Lindsay had to run acceptably well. He did not. Alex Rose and Louis Harris warned him that Democratic voters would resent his quest for their party's nomination for President when he had only just changed his political allegiance. They also cautioned that the people of the city would resent him for setting off on a series of primary runs around the United States while compelling problems required his attention at home. But Lindsay listened to others who were seduced by the allure of the White House, and he listened to his own unbridled ambition. There was a spark of light when he ran well in the Arizona delegate poll, but he finished a weak fifth out of seven candidates in Florida. The state was home to many transplanted New Yorkers, retired Jews in particular, so he had expected to run better. During that contest, a Manhattan man who disapproved of Lindsay's handling of his job as mayor arranged for an airplane to fly over crowded Florida beaches trailing a banner that carried the message: "Lindsay spells *tsouris*." The Yiddish word for trouble was meant as a warning to Jewish voters, and Lindsay ran poorly among the group that he had hoped would bolster his position. His campaign effectively ended with that performance, but he had made an unbreakable commitment to political supporters in Wisconsin that he would run in that state's primary. With little money and less enthusiasm, he ran badly there too, compounding his embarrassment.[2]

New York City did not hold still while its mayor chased the presidency. Racial tensions continued to threaten violence and New Yorkers remained obsessed with the level of crime in the city. Riots in 1970 in the Tombs, the city's municipal jailhouse, punctuated the precariousness of the government's ability to control the city's criminals. An initiative to develop scatter site housing—medium-sized government sponsored apartment complexes for low-income tenants that were located in middle-income neighborhoods—met fierce resistance in white communities. Lindsay appointed a local attorney named Mario Cuomo to negotiate a compromise over a housing plan in Forest Hills, Queens. The capable attorney's skillful work did little to improve the mayor's popularity among the citizens who wanted no housing projects at all near their homes.[3]

Municipal unions continued to make demands that strained the city's coffers and the patience of the public. Police and Firemen threatened to strike and engaged in illegal work slowdowns. In 1971, the city agreed to a generous pension package with District Council 37. At Governor Rockefeller's urging the State Legislature refused to approve the plan, and in retaliation the union's chief, Victor Gotbaum, declared what he promised would be the "biggest, fattest, sloppiest strike we have ever seen." Laborers fulfilled the pledge by opening twenty-seven drawbridges throughout the city, making circulation all but impossible, and by opening sewer lines so that raw waste floated onto metropolitan beaches. The public reaction was fierce. The Legislature refused to succumb to the blackmail, the strike ended, and the city worked out a modest compromise with DC 37 some months later. Public perception of municipal unions, already souring, turned rancid as a result of the episode. Lindsay's image suffered too. He seemed simply unable to govern New York City.[4]

Serious financial trouble loomed as well. Lindsay had inherited a significant deficit from Wagner in 1965, but during his first term as mayor he had made tough fiscal decisions. His administration implemented a city income tax and imposed higher real estate and business taxes so that he could present the city with a succession of balanced, or nearly balanced, budgets. That changed during the second term. The welfare rolls increased from a half million clients when Lindsay entered office, to twice that size by 1970. Continued middle-class flight to the suburbs reduced the tax base that generated the revenues that helped to pay for the poor. It took a little time for the cost of labor agreements to have their full impact on the city treasury, but by the final years of Lindsay's second term they had arrived. "We are going to hell in a pension cart," one city budget expert sighed. New York implemented open enrollment in the City University system promising a college education to anyone who finished high school. The number of publicly sponsored students grew rapidly, as did the need for staff and the cost of the system. Generous day care and health care programs, far more comprehensive than other cities offered, added to the budgetary burdens.[5]

By 1973, a mayoralty election year, Lindsay had become a man without a party. He had left the Republican camp only to receive a cold welcome from the city's top Democrats. Alex Rose, who continued to exercise one-man control over the Liberal party's nominations, told Lindsay, "some of your best friends, including myself, feel you'd be better off not to run again." Rose knew that the mayor's presidential campaign had badly damaged his political standing, but the disillusionment went deeper. As long as Lindsay had remained Republican, wealthy backers of that party, members of New York's social and business elite, had lent their financial support to Lindsay's ambitions with few strings. After he switched political affiliations Lindsay lost access to that money. His national campaign in 1972 was financed to a considerable degree by firms doing business with New York City. "John was really never that good with city government," recalled pollster Louis Harris, a confidant of Alex Rose, and a Lindsay supporter until the 1972 race. "The one thing [John Lindsay] had was a certain fundamental integrity on the issues. When he lost that, he had nothing. When I learned he had taken money from city contractors, I told him he had sold his soul for a pittance." According to Harris, Rose felt the same way.[6]

Just how much the Liberal party could do for a candidate by 1973 was unclear. To be sure, it still had a ballot line, and could therefore still influence political events in New York, but its core of support had been decimated. So much of the generation of Jewish immigrants who had founded the organization had retired or died by then that few were left to carry out the party's work. Many of those who remained had been so alienated by the stand that the Liberals had taken during the school strike that they no longer supported the organization. The dissension that had divided the country over United States policy in Vietnam pushed its way into the Liberal party's executive committee. Titular chairman Donald Harrington insisted on an antiwar stance while Louis Stulberg refused to accept a policy he thought unpatriotic. The strained relationship between the party and the ILGWU finally ended definitively with Stulberg withdrawing his union's support.

The genius of Alex Rose, the patronage network he had built during the previous dozen years, and the determination of a handful of committed men—Dubinsky, Executive Director Ben Davidson, a few others—kept the organization alive, but it was gasping. Ironically, in 1969, the party had received its largest vote ever, just as it reached its weakest state since its creation. The ballots in the race that pitted Lindsay against two conservatives, Procaccino and Marchi, had come from people with no place else to go, not from loyal supporters. Such circumstances could of course occur again, but neither the times, nor John Lindsay, were prepared for such a campaign.

By the end of his second term in office, Lindsay was tired. He had concluded that the people holding power in Albany and Washington had more control over the future of New York City than its own mayor. In March, 1973, he announced that he would not seek a third term as mayor amidst rumors that he would run for governor in 1974, or for the Senate in 1976.[7]

The Evolution of Racial Politics

The imposing array of problems that faced the next mayor should have limited the number of people seeking the job, but the power of the office is a political aphrodisiac. Long before Lindsay dropped out, politicians began maneuvering to replace him. The coalition that had elected Lindsay in 1969 consisted of blacks and Hispanics, and liberal Jews. It did not deliver a majority—in neither of his election victories did Lindsay win the confidence of even half the city's voters—but there were liberal politicians who thought they could develop a stronger coalition by adding ethnic appeal as a Jew or a minority to Lindsay's base. Without the taint of the controversies so closely associated with the retiring mayor, the votes of moderates might be won as well.

Lindsay's 1969 victory also showed that a majority of New Yorkers were prepared to vote against a candidate perceived as too liberal, particularly with respect to crime. Maintaining law and order was the single most important issue to New Yorkers in 1973. Catholic voters had long been sensitive to the topic, and many Irish and Italian voters believed that government programs offering preferences to racial minorities exacerbated lawlessness. By the end of the 1960s, so did many Jews.[8]

In the wake of the 1968 school strike the Ford Foundation commissioned a detailed and extensive citywide survey on the state of black-Jewish relations in New York City. The data revealed that in spite of evidence of continued Jewish suspicion of Catholics, and "the sense among Jews that right-wingers and members of the WASP establishment are anti-Semitic, . . . as of mid-1969, it could be said that the blacks had supplanted these more traditional enemies."

The report continued: "One of the most striking findings of this study has been the change in attitudes as a result of black-Jewish conflict and confrontation among a substantial section of the Jewish community, in the past in the forefront of liberalism and tolerance in New York. This change makes possible an alliance between this section of the Jewish community and much of the rest of the white community, particularly the large Catholic group."[9]

It would go too far to say that Jews, as a group, had abandoned liberalism wholesale. It is more precise to say that fears of black militancy led many Jews, especially those who lived near black neighborhoods, to establish a clear sense of priorities. First the government must enforce the law and keep people safe. Then it can try to improve the world. In 1969, Mario Procaccino's political ineptitude, and almost hysterical style, had prevented him from benefitting fully from the transformed political outlook of a large number of Jewish New Yorkers. But the makings of a new political coalition was apparent. It would consist of a core of middle-class Jews whose liberalism had been tempered by the racial conflicts of the 1960s, and the city's Irish and Italian Catholic voters. Racial animosity would hold it together.

Congressman Mario Biaggi was one candidate who thought the new political climate would help him to win the mayor's office. Biaggi, the Manhattan-born son of Italian immigrants, grew up in the poverty of East Harlem. He joined the police department in 1942, and began a career as a cop that is a confusing collage of apparent blunders, and worse, that he managed to turn to his advantage. From his earliest days on the force Biaggi viewed the police department as a resource to use to launch a political career. He started out building a base within the Patrolmen's Benevolent Association, but that organization represents only patrol officers, so when Biaggi made sergeant he had to drop out. He then turned his attention to the Columbia Society, a fraternity of Italian civil servants, ultimately becoming its president. In 1961, he offered Robert Wagner the society's backing in the Democratic primary if the mayor would agree to make Biaggi a deputy police commissioner after the election. The mayor's staff sought to clear the proposal with Police Commissioner Murphy, but they learned that the city's top cop "wouldn't have that SOB around under any circumstances," so they let the offer die. The Columbia Society then backed Levitt in the primary, and after he lost, Lefkowitz in the general election.[10]

With his political career momentarily stalled, Biaggi, although not a college graduate, received special permission to attend New York University law school at night on a scholarship. On his third try he passed the bar, and then used contacts built up through the Columbia Society to attract business for himself and some law partners while remaining politically active. In 1968, with law and order becoming the most pressing concern of New Yorkers, Biaggi ran for Congress in the heavily Italian twenty-fourth congressional district of the northeast Bronx. He billed himself as the most highly decorated man in the history of the New York City Police Department. The claim was not true, but it won him election, and reelection in 1970 and 1972. In 1973, he decided to run for mayor.[11]

While Biaggi prepared to campaign in the Democratic primary, he also maneuvered to win the endorsements of the Republican and Conservative parties. It was a strategy to pull together an unorthodox fusion coalition behind his candidacy of all the political organizations in the city that were to the right of center, and add them to the support of Democrats in search of law-and-order.[12]

The prospect of Biaggi as mayor frightened some New Yorkers, including Alex Rose and Nelson Rockefeller. Neither man thought

Biaggi was up to the job of running the city. They disagreed with his politics, found his rhetoric polarizing, and they distrusted him. Together, they set out to stop him from getting the Republican endorsement. Their plan called for Rose to deliver the Liberal line to a competent candidate, and for the governor then to use the prospect of fusion with the Liberals, a combination that had brought victory before, as a means of convincing the Republican leaders to go along. The key was to find an acceptable nominee. Rose suggested his old friend Robert Wagner, and Rockefeller agreed.

The disarray among New York's political parties was evident. A Republican governor and the leader of the Liberal party were trying to convince a life-long Democrat to serve as their candidate for mayor, to prevent another Democrat from winning the Republican nomination. Wagner was only casually interested, but did not rule out a race, so Rose went ahead and delivered the Liberal endorsement. "Bob Wagner is the only man who can beat Biaggi and win a victory for New York," announced the Liberal Party Policy Committee, just a week after the Conservatives endorsed the Italian congressman from the Bronx. Despite his use of harsh tactics, Rockefeller could not deliver the Republicans to Wagner. Faced with the prospect of a Republican primary, of all things, the former mayor withdrew. The Liberals were momentarily without a candidate, but the ploy had accomplished what Rose and Rockefeller wanted. The stiff resistance to Biaggi led the Republican leaders to endorse John Marchi as their party's candidate for mayor.[13]

The Democratic Contenders

To avoid entering another mayoralty contest as badly divided as they had been in 1969, the Democrats had the State Legislature pass a primary run-off provision. It required a second election between the two top primary candidates if none won at least forty percent of the vote in the first round. Winning the Democratic nomination would therefore be harder in 1973 than it had been before, but the additional hurdle did not reduce the number of candidates who sought the spot. There was a group of liberal reformers among the contenders. They included Edward Koch, the Greenwich Village district leader who had been elected to the City Council in 1966, and to John Lindsay's old congressional seat in 1968; Robert Postel, a Manhattan councilman; Jerome Kretchmer, an Upper West Side assemblyman whom Lindsay had named Environmental Protection Administrator in 1970 in return for Kretchmer's backing during the 1969 campaign; and Albert Blumenthal, another West Side assemblyman and deputy minority leader of the New York State Assembly. None had much standing beyond his home district, all appealed primarily to liberal Jewish voters, and by March all were having trouble raising the funds necessary to mount a campaign that would allow them to distinguish themselves in the mind of the electorate. All of these candidates sought the endorsement of the New Democratic Coalition as a means of breaking out of the pack.[14]

The New Democratic Coalition (NDC) was an umbrella group Paul O'Dwyer pulled together in the late 1960s to organize politically active Democrats opposed to the Vietnam War. It consisted largely of the city's reform Democratic clubs, a looser version of the Committee for Democratic Voters that Herbert Lehman created in 1959. The NDC was the closest thing to an institutional voice that the liberal reform wing of the Democratic party had. On the evening of March 3, 1973 several hundred delegates from reform clubs around New York City met in a high school auditorium on Manhattan's West Side to try to reach a consensus on candidates for citywide office.[15]

With little contention, they agreed on O'Dwyer for City Council president and Harrison J. Goldin, a reform State Senator from the Bronx, as candidate for comptroller. Herman Badillo, who won election to a South Bronx congressional seat the year after losing his bid for the Democratic nomination for mayor in 1969, was running for mayor again. He thought he had the inside track for the NDC endorsement. He had worked closely with the reformers, was philosophically one of them, and no other reformer came near to matching Badillo's standing with Puerto Ricans and blacks. His candidacy offered a chance to marry minority supporters to liberal Jewish voters with more strength than the other contenders. The combination seemed so attractive that Badillo simply assumed he would win. He appeared so certain of himself that many delegates found his bearing arrogant. They felt that he acted as if their endorsement belonged to him by "divine right," one journalist reported.[16]

While Badillo assumed victory, Al Blumenthal was working for it among the delegates. He had some advantages. Like the CDV before it, the nucleus of the New Democratic Coalition was in Manhattan, on the West Side in particular, Blumenthal's political home. Also like the CDV, its members were mostly well-educated liberal Jews. On a personal level they had more in common with Blumenthal than with the Puerto Rican from the Bronx. On the night of the endorsement meeting, Blumenthal's supporters enforced membership rules with a rigidity that had been lacking in the organization's affairs up until then. They succeeded in eliminating a number of Puerto Rican delegates who had come to back Badillo. When the votes were counted, Blumenthal had won.[17]

The West Side assemblyman instantly became the Democratic party's liberal standard bearer, and some weeks later the Liberal party added its support. An enraged Herman Badillo accused the NDC of racism. "We can't have a coalition that says a fellow can't be Mayor because he's Puerto Rican," he announced. He implied that Blumenthal's support was limited to upper-middle-class Jews, too narrow a base for victory in a citywide election. Badillo vowed to run in the primary in spite of his setback, and predicted that many black and Puerto Rican members of the NDC would leave the organization to back him. Jerry Kretchmer and Robert Postel dropped out of the race after they lost the endorsement. Congressman Koch, citing an inability to raise funds, ended his candidacy a short while later. The stage was set for Badillo and Blumenthal to compete for liberal and minority votes.[18]

Meanwhile, Comptroller Abraham D. Beame was quietly planning to win the Democratic nomination for mayor. Since 1969 Beame and City Council President Garelik had been the only Democrats with citywide standing. Garelik, in spite of his formal party affiliation, had been elected on the Republican and Liberal lines, whereas Beame's victory came on the Democratic line. The comptroller's staff dwarfs the City Council president's, so his ability to reward loyal party members with patronage posts is much greater. Perhaps most importantly, however, the former chief inspector of the police department never really adapted to the compromises the political arena requires. Beame had been immersed in the city's politics for nearly four decades, and he thrived on it. He had become, de facto, New York City's Democratic party leader.[19]

In January 1973 Beame commissioned Peter D. Hart Research Associates, a polling firm specializing in gathering data on Democratic party voters, to conduct a survey and determine what New Yorkers thought of him. The results revealed that more New Yorkers thought Beame did his job well than thought the same of Mayor Lindsay or of Council president Garelik, who also entertained thoughts of a mayoralty race. More than anyone else in New York, Democrats named Beame as the public figure who knew the most about running city government. More than any other potential candidate, registered Democrats considered him the most respected and trusted member of their party. It was therefore unsurprising that he was the first choice for mayor of more

New York City Democrats than any other politician. By an even wider margin, more named him than anyone else as their second choice, a matter of some significance in a primary election with a chance for a run-off.[20]

Beame's greatest support by far was with Jewish voters, but he was well known throughout the city and his reputation for fiscal conservatism gave him standing among Italians and other middle-class whites. He had no particular strength among minorities, but had committed no offenses either. By the end of February Beame had assurances of support from Meade Esposito's Brooklyn Democratic organization, and from Bronx boss Pat Cunningham as well. Both men viewed Beame as the candidate with the best chance to win, in no small measure because of his Jewish heritage. They also knew he was a politician who would remember his supporters when he did.[21]

Since J. Raymond Jones's retirement in 1966, Manhattan Borough President Percy Sutton had become the political voice of Harlem's people. He did not wield the power Jones once had, but he controlled the most effective political organization left in New York's oldest black community. Adam Clayton Powell had allowed a series of petty but debilitating law suits, personal problems, and political troubles to destroy him. In 1970 he finally lost his grip on New York's blacks, and Assemblyman Charles Rangel, with Sutton's backing, won Powell's congressional seat. Sutton detected a "mood of Jewishness" to the city's politics in 1973, and he wanted to be on the winning team. He also wanted to be mayor someday. Beame was then sixty-seven, and claimed he would serve only one term. In return for Sutton's support in 1973, he promised to back the black politician for mayor in 1977. Sutton convinced Rangel, and Harlem State Senator Basil Paterson, another ally, to join with him behind Beame. With more organized support than any other candidate, and a well known and respected reputation in city government, newspaper reports noted that, "Beame starts out the race as the front runner, even his opponents concede."[22]

Winning and Losing Jewish Votes

Yet, Mario Biaggi, with his pledge to end the "climate of fear [that] permeates this town," gathered more publicity. His campaign got a big boost when the Queens Democratic party endorsed him, and county leader Matthew Troy became his manager. The new campaign chief counseled Biaggi to expand his appeal by speaking more often of his work on behalf of prisoners in Northern Ireland, and of his efforts on behalf of Soviet Jews. In front of Jewish audiences, while always insisting he would be tough on crime, Biaggi began describing himself as a moderate liberal. He pointed out that he received high voting ratings from the Americans for Democratic Action, a liberal watchdog group. Biaggi was adding an appeal to the Jewish social conscience to his message that he would protect Jewish voters from violence. The campaign was working. Biaggi's standing was improving, even among middle-class Jews where Abe Beame's support was strongest.[23]

Al Blumenthal, too, hoped to cut into Beame's large Jewish constituency. The assemblyman's own backing was most solid with members of his faith, but it was concentrated in Manhattan's upper-income neighborhoods. He had no chance of winning without expanding his appeal, and the logical place for him to try was with the Jewish populations in Brooklyn, Queens, and the Bronx. Jews were expected to account for more than forty percent of the Democratic primary vote in 1973, and Blumenthal's effort to attract the group was blatant. "At synagogues and fraternal meetings, Mr. Blumenthal is apt to say that he wants to become 'the first Jewish Mayor of New York' " one journalist reported. "It is a frankly sectarian appeal that some of his coreligionists find troubling, particularly in what is already seen as a polarized city." Blumenthal understood that after the racial conflicts of the Lindsay years, the challenge for a liberal reformer like himself, even among Jews, was to prove he could be tough on crime. An orthodox Jewish supporter took out an advertisement for him in *The Jewish Press*, an English language weekly, that declared: "Blumenthal would prevent Flatbush from becoming another Brownsville." It was a thinly disguised appeal to racial fears, and Blumenthal apologized for it, but other ads of a similar nature appeared from time to time throughout his campaign.[24]

Herman Badillo's position among blacks and Puerto Ricans was strong, so he too campaigned principally in Jewish neighborhoods in an effort to broaden his base of support. He found the going tough. Jews who might have favored his politics found a philosophically similar candidate in Blumenthal, who had the added attraction of being Jewish. Badillo's ungracious if accurate remarks following the NDC endorsement of his rival alienated some of the most active reform Democrats who might otherwise have backed him. And in middle-class neighborhoods concerned about law and order, a Puerto Rican committed to helping the city's minorities was hardly a popular choice.[25]

Badillo was becoming cast as an isolated candidate of the minorities, Blumenthal a splinter candidate of die-hard liberals, primarily from the

West Side of Manhattan. Beame and Biaggi settled into competition for votes among the white middle-class, the one firmly rooted in the city's Jewish community, the other the champion of its Italian neighborhoods. Beame was ahead, Biaggi closing, when the *New York Times* ran a front page story revealing that a few years earlier, Biaggi had invoked the Fifth Amendment before a grand jury investigating allegations that he had abused his authority in a variety of ways. More important, Biaggi had lied to the public and to political leaders a number of times when he denied that he had refused to answer questions under oath.[26]

For several weeks a series of complicated legal and political maneuvers followed while Biaggi tried to convince the public that he wanted to release the grand jury transcripts. In fact, he worked to prevent further disclosure. The episode dominated the headlines, and as day after day went by without an unsealing of the records, the public became increasingly skeptical. Biaggi appeared on television to condemn his "trial by press." He talked of the pain the incident caused his family, and asked the public, his voice cracking with emotion, "how do you tell a fourteen year old kid [Biaggi's son] about dirty politics?" Then, with release of the documents imminent despite Biaggi's efforts to bury them, he finally confessed. The transcripts showed that the candidate had invoked the Fifth Amendment on sixteen occasions to avoid answering questions that he feared would land him in the penitentiary.[27]

Fallout from the event was rapid. CBS News polling data revealed that Biaggi lost fourteen percent of his support during the two weeks that the controversy surrounding his testimony dominated the campaign. The tough law-and-order advocate maintained some backing among Italian and Irish voters, but top Democrats concluded "that his inroads into middle-class Jewish areas, where the law and order issue is strong, would be reduced by his action before the grand jury." The polls also revealed that almost all of the voters who had abandoned Biaggi went to Beame. In Co-op City in the Bronx, home to many elderly Jewish Democrats, a journalist noted that residents felt Biaggi had betrayed them. Beame, whose campaign team distributed literature in the area with the headline: "I'm going to put the cop back on the block Mrs. Zimmerman," in what the journalist called "a direct appeal to the community's most significant voting bloc," was the only other candidate the residents of such communities trusted to protect them.[28]

The Biaggi scandal shared headlines with the Watergate revelations that were surfacing daily during the spring of 1973. The anger people felt toward government officials who lied to them compounded Biaggi's problem. The public mood worked to Beame's advantage. "He's an honest sincere person. He's getting on in age but he's like a good relief pitcher—he can still throw a strike when it counts," one New Yorker commented. As the tumult of the Lindsay administration came to an end, another noted, "Beame has the personality of a loaf of Wonderbread . . . but I guess I've had enough of charisma for a while." Others thought back with regret to the 1965 election: "If you ask me, it was because Beame was Jewish," that he lost, Esther Levine of Brooklyn told a reporter. In 1973, she hoped he would win.[29]

No issues distinguished the four politicians running for the Democratic nomination for mayor: All vowed to put more police on the streets; all said they would reduce the racial tensions that plagued the city; all portrayed themselves as fiscal conservatives. They promised to cut waste in government and to hold down real estate taxes to keep the middle class from fleeing. Each candidate said he would undo the super-agency management structure that Lindsay had created, and each pledged to trim the bureaucracy. Each did, however, portray a distinct image: Beame claimed he had the most experience; Badillo claimed he could reconcile the city's poor minorities and its middle-class; the public viewed Blumenthal as the true liberal. For many that meant he was not tough enough to govern, and try as he might Blumenthal could not alter the perception. His repeated sorties into Jewish communities always ran into the shadow of Abe Beame, somehow the more authentic representative of Brooklyn, Queens, and Bronx Jews. Biaggi, the law-and-order candidate, refused to step out of the race even though his campaign was mortally wounded. In a desperate effort to bolster his strength with Jewish middle-class voters he arranged for a young Jewish man he had helped to secure an exit visa from the Soviet Union to fly to New York from Israel for a press conference. The ploy was simply too blatant to have much effect.[30]

Ten days before the primary, the *New York Times* and the *New York Post* both endorsed Herman Badillo as the candidate with the best chance of bringing hope and help to the city's minorities without alienating the middle-class. Badillo's campaign, short on money until then, received a generous infusion of contributions as a result of the praise. He launched a television blitz designed to bring the news to the public. The last minute endorsements and publicity had an effect.[31]

On primary day Beame won, but the thirty-four percent of the vote he took was disappointing, and short of the forty percent he needed to avoid a run-off. Herman Badillo, with twenty-nine percent, finished much closer behind Beame than anyone had anticipated, and he earned the right to challenge the leader in a head to head race. Predictably,

Beame took a strong majority of the Jewish ballots, but Badillo too owed his surprising performance to Jewish voters. His success with Jews living in upper-income areas, when added to his solid support in minority communities, made him the runner-up. Blumenthal could hold only sixteen percent of the vote, primarily from upper-income Jewish and Protestant areas of Manhattan. Biaggi won twenty-one percent, concentrated overwhelmingly in Italian and, to a lesser degree, Irish areas.[32]

Race Run-off

Badillo's strong performance energized him. He envisioned himself as a candidate on the rise with the *Times* and *Post* endorsements having finally brought his message to New Yorkers. In his eyes, Beame sat stagnant and tired, more or less at the same point where polls had shown him weeks earlier. A close look at the primary results, however, revealed that in almost every district that Biaggi won, Beame ran second. Beame took his share of votes in the districts where Blumenthal ran well too. Badillo could hardly run better than he had among minorities—more than ninety percent of the Puerto Rican ballots and seventy percent of black votes—and there was little reason to expect him to make inroads with Italian and Irish voters who showed no inclination to cast ballots for a Puerto Rican candidate. Badillo could only win if he could convince Jewish voters that he would represent them better than his well-respected Jewish, opponent.[33]

He launched a vigorous effort. In a television ad Badillo's Jewish wife, Irma, appeared: "I'm a New York housewife. I guess you'd call me middle-class. I have the same concerns you do—safe neighborhoods, good schools, fair taxes," she said in an appeal hardly targeted at the special concerns of the city's blacks and Puerto Ricans. She campaigned tirelessly in Jewish areas where she used yiddish terms in her conversations, a strategy that one campaign worker described as, "Mrs. Badillo's Jewish rye bread. You don't have to be Puerto Rican to like Herman." An advertisement in *The Jewish Press*, an English-language weekly, informed its readers that, "large numbers of Jews joined with hundreds of thousands of other New Yorkers to vote for Badillo June 4," and it urged them to support him again. Meanwhile, Badillo himself campaigned vigorously in middle-class Jewish neighborhoods, particularly in Queens. Many of the reformers who had abandoned him earlier, now with no place else to go, joined his team for the run-off contest.[34]

Beame knew that Democrats who had cast their ballots for Biaggi were sure to prefer him over Badillo. His main concern was to make sure that these voters did not stay away from the polls altogether now that their first choice was no longer in the race. Even in the age of mass communications, the direct personal efforts of the loyal members of the regular Democratic organization remained the most effective means of getting a carefully targeted pool of Democratic voters to the polls, and Beame had their backing. On June 18, five congressmen, twelve state senators, twenty-nine assemblymen, and twenty-nine councilmen, all from the regular wing of the Democratic party, met on the steps of City Hall to join in a mass endorsement of Abe Beame and to promise a spirited drive to bring party members to the polls on his behalf.[35]

With the campaign reduced to a contest between one politician associated with the white middle-class, and another associated with the city's minorities, the more vulgar of the regulars relied on racial fears to increase turnout. In the Bronx, Councilman Stanley Simon and party functionary Stanley Friedman produced pamphlets that featured a picture of a burned out block with a caption above that read: "This is the Bronx Herman Badillo helped build." A caption below pleaded with voters: "Don't let him do this to New York." In *The Jewish Press*, the Beame campaign ran an ad that called upon New Yorkers to, "vote as if your life depends upon it, because it does." Beame's staff denied responsibility for some of the fiercest works, but they appeared in large quantities throughout the city's middle-class neighborhoods.[36]

During a television debate Badillo tried to make the tactic backfire by denouncing *The Jewish Press* ad as "an appeal to fears in the Jewish community. It's an ethnic appeal to the Jewish community and it's the kind of appeal that should be repudiated." Beame disarmed his opponent by denouncing the piece and claiming that it had been placed by local party members before his campaign had reviewed it. He then moved rapidly to the offensive accusing Badillo of telling Puerto Ricans to vote only for a Puerto Rican candidate. "Now if I said Jewish people should only support Jews, I would be ridden out of politics," he concluded. Beame also accused Badillo of using numbers runners in ghetto areas to help pull out the vote. And so the tenor of the campaign continued. Badillo finally lost his composure during the last television debate of the contest when he called his diminutive opponent a racist, and "a vicious little man."[37]

The First Jewish Mayor of New York

Beame won a commanding sixty-one percent of the ballots cast in a run-off that had a higher turnout than the original primary. With Biaggi's supporters crossing over to Beame, he won more than three quarters of the Italian votes cast, and nearly as high a proportion of the Irish ballots. Just under seven of every ten Jewish voters chose Beame as well. Nine of every ten Puerto Rican New Yorkers voted for Badillo, as did seven of ten blacks. He added a significant, but insufficient, number of upper-income Jewish voters to that base to finish with thirty-nine percent of the total. In short, Catholics and Jews came together in opposition to Puerto Ricans and blacks, with a small number of Jewish liberals willing to vote for a Puerto Rican who shared their philosophy.[38]

Badillo immediately threatened to mount an independent candidacy. Blumenthal was committed to running on the Liberal ticket in November, just as Biaggi had agreed to run on the Conservative line. John Marchi would head the Republican ticket. But the strength of Beame's victory made the other candidates inconsequential. He had won the nomination of the city's majority party in a landslide, and victory in November seemed assured. If there had been any doubt, it was dispelled when many of the city's reform Democrats, who had backed Blumenthal in the primary and endorsed Badillo in the run-off, one by one announced their support for the Democratic nominee for mayor. At a Democratic fund-raising dinner held for Beame before the election ended Manhattan County Leader Frank Rossetti told a reporter: "For the first time in many years the various factions of the party . . . are working together on behalf of the Democratic ticket."[39]

A dozen years earlier the reformers refused to work with politicians from the regular wing of the Democratic party under any circumstances because, they had claimed, all of the regulars were corrupt. A moralizing posture had been easy then when reform politicians were on the outs and had nothing to lose by refusing to accept the regulars' political rules. Their uncompromising stand made them the politicians of virtue in the public mind.

In the years between 1961 and 1973, however, many reformers had won office, as assemblymen, state senators, councilmen, congressmen, and district leaders. In 1969, almost all of the movement's prominent leaders had backed Lindsay for reelection. The entry of many members of the reform faction into responsible positions in city government was a logical conclusion of that campaign. As a result, by 1973, the reformers were no longer insurgents in search of power, but a part of New York's Democratic ruling class with a stake in keeping the party together. The two politicians who would share the Democratic ticket with Beame for citywide office were tangible evidence of how far the reformers had come. Paul O'Dwyer, who won the primary for City Council president, and Harrison Goldin, who was the candidate for comptroller, were both reform Democrats. Abraham Beame, unlike Mario Procaccino, was not ideologically threatening to reformers. Beame described himself as a fiscally responsible New Deal liberal, tempered and moderated by the tensions of the 1960s. The sixty-seven-year old Jewish man who had lived first on Manhattan's Lower East Side, and then grew up in Brooklyn, could have been the father of almost any of the reform politicians. [40]

The campaign limped through the summer and fall heading for Beame's inevitable victory. Unable to gather momentum for an independent race, Badillo ultimately met with his party's nominee and the two politicians declared a truce. What one newspaper headlined as, "The Campaign That Never Was," another journalist summarized as, "the most boring, tedious, wearisome, monotonous, spiritless, stale, musty, dreary, banal, flat, prosaic, insipid, pedestrian, blank, motheaten, tiresome and dull election in memory." Yet, he concluded, his vocabulary exercise finished, "it remains a work of genius." Beame had pulled toward him all of the pieces of the Democratic party. In November, in what was theoretically a four way race, he won a commanding fifty-seven percent of the vote. The Democratic party ruled again, and for the first time in history, New York City had a Jewish mayor. [41]

Jews perceived Beame's election as an ethnic triumph. "Abe Beame is the summary of the whole Jewish experience in this city, isn't he?," pontificated a hasidic Jew at a celebration shortly after the election. "In one generation you can be elected Mayor." That was not entirely true, for Beame's career spanned two generations, almost three. Beame's factory worker father had been first a Socialist, later a member of the American Labor party, and then a Liberal party member. This was the political experience of a broad segment of New York's Jewish immigrants. Abe Beame grew up in it, and was influenced by it. Yet, while technically an immigrant himself, having been born in London while his parents were en route to New York from Poland, Beame arrived on the Lower East Side at the tender of age of six months. His entire experience was American. [42]

About 1930, at the age of twenty-four, Abe Beame joined the Madison Democratic club in the Crown Heights section of Brooklyn without journeying through any of the other political organizations that immigrant Jews found ideologically appealing. He was a liberal, but regular Democrat. His loyalties were forged in the age of Al Smith and Franklin Roosevelt. He was willing to pay his dues and work his way up the party hierarchy, but remained faithful throughout his life to the New Deal social philosophy that guided his generation through the depression and beyond. The Jewish reform club politicians, who rose later, shared much of Beame's outlook, except that they had been unwilling to work slowly up through the party system to achieve power. Once the reformers held a share of power, which they did by 1973, they had little reason to begrudge a man like Abe Beame his position. He was not one of them, so they were unenthusiastic about his victory, but they accepted it without great fear.

The peace Beame brought to the Democrats won him the majority of the votes of all of the city's ethnic groups, except the Italians, who split between Biaggi and Marchi. The Irish backed Beame strongly in 1973, which contrasted sharply with his disappointing performance with the group in 1965. Part of the reason was that there was no Irish candidate in the race to attract conservative Irish voters as William Buckley had done eight years before. But there was more to it than that. Jewish displacement of the Irish as the dominant power within the Democratic party was just climaxing in 1965, the first year that a Jew had ever won the party's mayoral nomination. Irish resentment at the time was strong. Lindsay's 1965 campaign manager, Robert Price, targeted Irish Democrats for special attention because he felt they would resist voting for a Jewish candidate that year. The intervening period had given the Irish time to adapt to their lesser role in the city's political life. And the intensity of racial polarization had given the Irish and the Jewish middle class a common enemy—the minorities that both perceived as the bearers of crime and the destroyers of white middle-class neighborhoods. Simply put, racial solidarity helped overpower ethnic differences between the Irish and the Jews. The Italian vote for Beame over Badillo in the primary run-off made it clear that they too feared minority control more than Jewish control of the city, but because they had the option of voting for candidates of their own heritage in the general election, they did.[43]

The overwhelming support that the city's minorities gave Herman Badillo in both the primary and run-off made it clear that they would prefer to see one of their own in City Hall. When that option faded, they reverted to the party of Franklin Roosevelt, the Kennedys, and

Lyndon Johnson. Eight years earlier, Lindsay's impressive civil rights record and dynamic campaign, and the lukewarm support that the Democratic party's national spokesmen offered Beame, had allowed the Republican-Liberal to eat into the traditional Democratic constituency in minority neighborhoods. In 1969, Lindsay swept those voting districts against Mario Procaccino, a Democrat perceived as threatening to blacks and Puerto Ricans. In 1973, Beame did not seem hostile at all. Some expected Al Blumenthal to pull minority votes away from Beame by portraying himself as a more aggressive civil rights activist than the comptroller, but the Liberal candidate targeted Jewish middle-class areas throughout his campaign, and made little headway among blacks and Puerto Ricans.

Beame's campaign used radio and television advertising, but the plain looking candidate, barely five feet tall, was hardly a media star. His expenses were fairly balanced between mass communications and more traditional campaign expenditures. The standard stuff of elections—shaking hands, talking to small crowds, handing out literature, conversing with newspaper reporters, telephoning registered party members, bringing voters to the poll on primary day—were all part of the successful effort. The victory highlighted that the regular Democratic organization, the base of Beame's early effort, had not yet been exhausted as a source of political power in New York City. The party, citywide, had split into so many factions that it could no longer determine who would be the Democratic candidate. It was weaker by far than it once had been. But the regular Democratic party had pulled itself back together sufficiently that it was more effective than any other political organization in the city.[44]

Fiscal Doom

History would not be kind to the man who, shortly after his victory, told a reporter: "All I ever wanted in life was to be Mayor of the greatest city in the world." The day after his election Beame appointed a transition team to review the city's affairs and establish an agenda for mayoral action. One of their most important findings should not have surprised the outgoing comptroller. The city's budget deficit in the coming year, Beame's experts estimated, "should easily exceed $1 billion." Actually, it would top $1.5 billion.[45]

Throughout the second Lindsay administration the deficit grew, but with creative if uncautious budgetary manipulations, city bureaucrats continually pushed the problem forward into the next fiscal year. There was a limit, of course, to how long that could endure. "A sum of this magnitude cannot be raised painlessly by raising accruals, suspending payments to the rainy day fund, ending the fiscal year one week early, switching from cash to accrual on payables, etc.," the transition report warned, providing a summary of the tricks used over the years. Beame would have to find the funds to cover the massive deficit.[46]

It was impossible. New York City had spent itself into a hole from which it could not get out. Soon recession came and tax receipts fell. Financial institutions realized how perilous the city's circumstances were and stopped rolling over borrowings. Slowly, the mayor who had bragged during his campaign that people should vote for him because "he knows the buck," realized that the city he governed faced bankruptcy. The state helped engineer a rescue plan, but the cost was dear. The governor and his aides established financial control boards that all but robbed New York City of its sovereignty. The new institutions began to make decisions that once had been the province of the mayor. The fiscal crisis forced cutbacks in city services that exacerbated relations with municipal unions, and that caused the people of the city to suffer.[47]

The worst of it came late in 1975 when New York City, at desperate risk of not being able to pay city employees, sought emergency assistance from the federal government. President Gerald Ford refused Gotham's plea. The *Daily News* ran its now-famous banner headline "Ford to New York: Drop Dead." The huge reserves that had accumulated in the pension funds of the municipal unions were finally used to buy risky New York City debt, and disaster passed by for a moment. Nevertheless, a crisis atmosphere prevailed throughout 1976, and Beame got the blame. He was mayor, and he could not easily cast the guilt over his shoulder saying that his predecessors, not he, were responsible. Since 1948, when O'Dwyer named Beame deputy budget director, he had been near the center of the city's finances, save the period from 1966 to 1970 when he was out of office. He had been comptroller for eight of the twelve years before he became mayor.[48]

Beame had declared in 1973 that he would serve just one term. By 1977 he was determined to stay in office, in part it seems, to restore his reputation. Although he was the incumbent, with the power that implies, the strains of the fiscal crisis badly damaged his public standing. A *Daily News* survey showed that as the election year began, a majority of New Yorkers thought the mayor should not run for reelection. Clearly, Beame was vulnerable, and a number of politicians prepared to challenge him. Most prominent among them was Bella Abzug.[49]

Tribal Politics

In the late 1960s Bella Abzug was one of the advocates of the Women's Strike Force for Peace, an anti-Vietnam War group that organized protests in New York City. Sid Davidoff thought that her aggressive speaking style and irrepressible personality were very effective with the politically active women on Manhattan's West Side. He invited her to join John Lindsay's 1969 reelection campaign, which she did. The very next year, she ran for Congress on the Upper West Side of Manhattan, and won.[50]

Abzug was Jewish and radical, way to the left of the typical New York City liberal. She was even extreme for the left wing politics of the West Side neighborhood where she lived. She had a distinctive, forceful style, and never appeared in public without her trademark big floppy hat. The attention-getting head gear, and her heavyset, bear-like shape, were so distinctive that in one of her political campaigns she used buttons that had nothing on them save her silhouette. A redistricting in 1972, manipulated by the regulars to eliminate a reform congressional seat, forced her into a primary against William Fitts Ryan. Ryan beat her soundly, but died before the election leaving Abzug to inherit the office in a safe Democratic district. For four more years she used the platform her congressional seat gave her to pursue liberal causes and to establish her image in the public mind. In 1976 she ran for the Senate. The early favorite, she made mistakes, spoke too harshly, and scared off potential supporters. One journalist wrote that she did not understand that "being tough is not the same as being out of control." Yet, her tactics made her as well known as any politician in New York, and many thought that her ferocious style would play better in the city than it had upstate. By the time she announced her candidacy for mayor in May 1977, she had already won the support of the New Democratic Coalition, and she led Beame in the polls. That victory, however, had not come easily. It had taken four ballots for Abzug to win the sixty percent of the vote the NDC required for endorsement, because of the strong battle waged by another liberal Jewish reformer, Congressman Edward I. Koch.[51]

Koch was born in the Bronx in 1924, the son of Jewish immigrants who arrived in the United States about 1910. Like so many of their contemporaries, Koch's parents found work in the garment industry and built a simple but comfortable life, until the depression struck. Koch's father lost his job along with hundreds of thousands of other laborers, and the family moved to Newark to live with relatives. The bout with poverty lasted several years and made a strong impression on Koch. Eventually, his father recovered, opened a small business, and moved the family to its own apartment in Brooklyn in 1941.

Koch entered City College that year, but was drafted in 1943 and sent to Europe to fight against Hitler's army. He survived front line combat and returned home intent on going to law school, which he did evenings at New York University under a special provision for returning veterans who had not completed college. He graduated in 1948, passed the bar in 1949, and set up a small private practice in civil law in lower Manhattan.

In 1952 Koch got caught up in the enthusiasm for Adlai Stevenson's first presidential campaign. Through his NYU connections he worked actively with Stevenson's Greenwich Village supporters, even though Koch was still living with his parents in Brooklyn then. In 1956 he moved to the Village just in time to work on Stevenson's second bid for the presidency.

After Stevenson's 1956 defeat the activists Koch had worked with created the Village Independent Democrats to continue their struggle for a new brand of politics in Carmine DeSapio's home district. Koch opposed the decision as impractical, and joined DeSapio's club. But the young, liberal, Jewish lawyer had little in common with the Irish and Italian working-class Tammany loyalists that populated DeSapio's fiefdom. Within two years the pragmatic Koch returned to the VID, and the club supported him in a failed bid for the New York State Assembly in 1962. He then became the candidate chosen to stop DeSapio from returning to power as district leader in 1963. The race was razor close, and a judge ordered a second election after abuses during the first were uncovered, but Koch and the VID persevered.

In 1965 Koch made headlines when he, and his female VID counterpart, Carol Greitzer, were the only Democratic district leaders to publicly endorse John Lindsay on the eve of the mayoral election. In 1966, when Greenwich Village councilman Theodore Kupferman won Lindsay's vacated congressional seat, Koch ran for and won the council post Kupferman left behind. In 1968 Kupferman decided not to run for reelection to Congress, and Koch beat out Republican candidate Whitney North Seymour, Jr. for the spot.

Throughout, Koch was fanatic about criticizing wrongs he perceived in government practices and in advocating local constituent needs. On many issues he held bona fide liberal convictions—he was a strong and active supporter of the civil rights movement and took an early stand against the Vietnam War—but more than anything else what comes through his early political career is a pragmatism bordering on opportunism. Those who knew him best thought that his reputation as an ultraliberal exaggerated his personal views. One VID member close to Koch in his early years concluded that what "fueled his engines [was] not a vision of society but personal success in his chosen career." Koch's measure for success was clear: he wanted to be mayor. He told a close friend upon the birth of the man's son in 1966 that the child's bar mitzvah would take place in Gracie Mansion, because Koch planned on being the city's chief executive by the time the boy reached the age of thirteen.[52]

Since the day his campaign for mayor ended in 1973, he had been planning to run again. That year, he had dropped out shortly after losing the NDC backing because he could not raise enough money to wage a campaign. In 1977, he was determined not to let that happen a second time. By May, Koch had already gathered more than $300,000. He expected to raise and spend $1 million before the primary vote in September.[53]

The city's minorities did not know who Koch was, and they did not know what to make of Bella Abzug. The fiscal crisis had made it hard for Mayor Beame to offer any special programs to New York's poor, who often suffered the most from cutbacks in municipal services. Manhattan's black borough president, Percy Sutton, who in 1973 had backed Beame in return for a commitment that Beame would back him in 1977, launched his campaign for mayor without the support he expected to have. The deep voiced son of a Texas slave, Sutton could speak in rousing terms that inspired his people, and he had tried to maintain his standing with white liberals as a responsible leader as well. He hoped for the same coalition that gave Lindsay the mayoralty in 1969. But Herman Badillo once again announced he would run for mayor. With the leading spokesmen of the city's Puerto Rican community and its black community in the race, the minority vote was sure to split.[54]

In Albany, Governor Hugh Carey, elected in 1974, watched developments with concern. He had worked closely with Beame during the darkest days of the fiscal crisis, and he considered the man unfit to be mayor. The governor knew that there were more financial hurdles ahead, and he did not want to rely on Abe Beame to help overcome them. He was just as uncomfortable with the prospect of Bella Abzug running City Hall, Beame's strongest opponent according to early voter surveys. He liked Ed Koch, but did not think he could win, so Carey needed a candidate of his own. He turned to Mario Cuomo, then New

York Secretary of State, a patronage plum normally awarded to a loyal political ally of the governor. Cuomo was the attorney who had negotiated a compromise to the Forest Hills scatter site housing controversy in 1972, and who later helped end a rent strike that Co-op City tenants launched against their quasi-public landlord, the Riverbay Corporation, for failing to live up to contract requirements. At first Cuomo was reluctant to run because he did not really want the job, but Carey insisted, and pledged to provide him with campaign support. Cuomo finally relented and announced his candidacy amidst charges that he was the governor's stooge.[55]

Delivering the Liberal party endorsement to Cuomo was the first step in Carey's plan. The Liberals, along with Robert Wagner and Bronx boss Pat Cunningham, had helped elect Carey. For the Liberals it had been a critical victory because with Republicans in office in Washington, and an unsympathetic Abe Beame in City Hall, the party was virtually bereft of tangible support. Carey's victory turned out to be Alex Rose's last hurrah. The long-time leader of the Liberal party died in 1976. The leadership void Rose's passing created left Carey holding powerful influence over the party. He had an easy time heading off an early effort in 1977 to create a Liberal-Republican fusion campaign behind State Senator Roy Goodman and delivering the Liberal line to Cuomo. Then the governor had the Democratic primary moved to September from June so his preferred candidate would have more time to make himself known.[56]

A Protestant businessman named Joel Harnett, with no standing of any significance, also entered the Democratic primary, making a total of seven candidates for that party's nomination.

Without great ado, the Republican leadership selected Roy Goodman. The choice was in part because he "is Jewish in a Jewish town," Vince Albano, the Manhattan GOP leader reported, and because Goodman had a strong record of local service and a reputation for honesty. As heir to a family fortune that flowed from the sales of *Ex-Lax*, he had the means to run a campaign. The Conservatives chose a transplanted southern radio personality, Barry Farber, also Jewish, as their candidate for mayor. The entertainer opened his campaign with a pledge to "offer amnesty to every liberal who admits he was wrong," and challenged Goodman in the Republican primary. But neither Goodman nor Farber had any hope of winning the mayoralty. The serious battle would take place within the Democratic party.[57]

By summer, it became clear that the Democratic contest had become tribal. Sutton was the black candidate, Badillo the Puerto Rican. Cuomo was the Italian, or sometimes the Catholic candidate, sometimes the "white ethnic." Jewish voters were perceived as choosing between two members of the faith: Abe Beame, the choice of elderly, middle-class, Jewish, regular Democrats—and Bella Abzug, preferred by the younger, professional Jews who made up the reform wing. Koch was considered a weak prospect who would win only a smattering of Jewish votes. Harnett, for lack of a better name, was the businessman's candidate, but it meant nothing. He had no base of support.

Each candidate tried to expand beyond ethnic limitations. Sutton opened his campaign headquarters in a white middle-class neighborhood in Queens, a symbolic gesture designed to show that he would represent more than just Harlem if he ruled the city. Surveys taken half-way through the campaign revealed that he was making no headway among whites, so he redirected his energies to draw black voters to the polls. Badillo could not break out of the Puerto Rican barrios, save a little support in black communities outside of Manhattan. Cuomo spoke about creating a coalition: "I need a lot more than Catholic votes. I need a sizable portion of the Jewish vote, and I still think I can get black and Puerto Rican votes," he told a reporter. One of his political strategists assessed the campaign otherwise: "Cuomo talks to Cuomo about issues; but I look at reality. There are three Jews in this race, and there is only one Italian, right? . . . While issues may mean something in Manhattan, people who vote in the other four boroughs are more interested in the candidate's last name. And many are especially interested, thank God, in how many vowels are in that name."[58]

Many Italians continued to register in the Republican party, and even those who were Democrats were less likely to vote in primary elections than Jews, who went to the polling booths in large numbers. Cuomo instinctively understood that he needed more than just Catholic votes, but he allowed campaign strategists to concentrate his appearances in Catholic neighborhoods. A few of his advisers, principally Professor Richard Wade, one of the nation's preeminent scholars of urban history and an experienced political adviser to liberal Democratic candidates in New York, warned Cuomo that his "white ethnic" campaign was becoming "anti-Manhattan." In the process, it was alienating well-educated, liberal professionals—Jews and Protestants—whose votes Cuomo needed to win. Others in Cuomo's camp were defiant in rejecting such voters. One even drafted a document that "proved" the Italian could win without Jewish, black, or Puerto Rican support.[59]

Other political analysts counted differently and concluded that only a Jewish candidate could win the Democratic primary in 1977. "Abe or Bella," read the headline in one article. A *New York Times Sunday Magazine* story assessed the contest the same way: "Beame's Scenario: How to Beat Bella," was its title. It reported that the mayor's campaign staff was confident of victory. Their candidate had the backing of the city's regular Democratic organizations, and their campaign treasury was ample, filled with money donated by real-estate developers and labor unions. One important part of the incumbent's campaign strategy was to make him, rather than Abzug, the preferred candidate of Jews. To do this, the *Times* article reported, the campaign staff would make "quiet, subtle suggestions that the first Jewish Mayor in New York history might have been a victim of anti-Semitism. . . . One campaign official alludes to the *Daily News* headline at the time of the city's pleas to Washington for fiscal relief : 'Ford to City: Drop Dead.' 'Remember that headline' [the campaign official said], 'Drop Dead Jew.' " That was the message the Beame staff hoped would make its way into the minds of Jewish voters. But events took a course of their own that badly hurt the candidacy of Abe Beame.[60]

Curtains for Abe Beame, Spotlight on Ed Koch

On July 13 the lights went out in New York City. A massive power failure early in the evening left the metropolis in the dark for the entire night. In contrast to a similar incident that had happened some years before, when the city had remained calm, the ghettos erupted in a wild orgy of looting and wanton destruction that left commercial strips devastated and the city's psyche assaulted. It happened on Beame's watch. "What good is a mayor who allows anarchy to rule?" New Yorkers asked themselves. Then in August, the Securities Exchange Commission released a detailed assessment of the causes of the fiscal crisis that had brought New York to the brink of bankruptcy in 1975. Its conclusions about Beame's stewardship of the city's finances were damning. "The City employed budgetary, accounting and financing practices which it knew distorted its true financial condition," the report said. It implied that the mayor lied to the city.[61]

Bella Abzug should have won the allegiance of voters who soured on Beame, but she did not. On July 7, she insisted that firemen and police had the right to strike, just like any other workers. That was bad politics in a city preoccupied with law and order. Just a few days later the blackout riots brutally reminded New Yorkers what could happen when respect for public safety deteriorated. Besides, New Yorkers in 1977 were angry at municipal unions. The generous pension benefits paid to public employees were perceived as a major cause of the city's fiscal woes, and the continual threat of job actions involving government services for which there were no substitutes made citizens feel like hostages. Abzug alone among the candidates did not vow to take a tough line with city unions.[62]

Her positions reinforced the image many had of Bella Abzug as the kind of liberal that got New York into its financial mess in the first place. Her style, "the Bella Boogie" one reporter called it, while flamboyant to some, was grating to others. Cuomo described her politics as, "agree with me or I'll make you deaf." A Sutton worker said "her message is a growl." Abzug could scarcely deny the charges. When one woman told the candidate that she did not believe Manhattan liberals care about the people in the other boroughs, Abzug responded: "Then go vote for that *schmuck* we have." After a comment like that, the woman probably did. Abzug's fierce personality inspired an admiring reporter to call her, "the Muhammad Ali of feminist politicians." The same style drove another to draw a cartoon that showed the politician riding high above the New York skyline on a broom. The well known silhouette was outlined in the light of a haunting full moon, the ever present hat was pointed, and a banner that read "Bella Abzug for Mayor" trailed behind.[63]

With Beame battered by circumstances beyond his control, and Abzug's positions and personality creating "Bellaphobia" among city voters, the third Jewish candidate, Ed Koch, began to get a hearing. Up until the blackout he remained in the shadows of the two better known members of his faith. The morning after the blackout, even before the shattered glass had been cleared from ghetto streets, Koch announced that, had he been mayor when the rioting started, he would have insisted that the governor call out the national guard to enforce the law. It was the kind of language that attracted attention, and that many New Yorkers wanted to hear. It fit perfectly with Koch's campaign strategy.[64]

Most New Yorkers did not know Koch at all when the campaign began, and the ones who did associated him with the liberal wing of the Democratic party. "Ultraliberal," according to some. That image would never win him favor with middle-class voters in Queens, Brooklyn, and the Bronx. Koch knew that to win, he needed to reach New Yorkers who did not know him with a message that would convince them that he would deal harshly with those who broke the law. The national guard announcement helped. Koch discovered that support for the death penalty worked even better. As the campaign wore on, he used the issue relentlessly.[65]

In the summer of 1977 a psychopathic killer terrorized the city by shooting young women and then reporting his actions to the police under the name "Son of Sam." The press dubbed him, "The .44 Caliber Killer," because of the size weapon he used. For several weeks running, the city's tabloids headlined the desperate search for the murderer. The police caught the killer before long, but to the frightened city it seemed like an eternity. Koch seized the chance to push his toughness into the public mind. "Hi. I'm for capital punishment, are you?" he asked citizens on the streets in the middle-class neighborhoods outside of Manhattan. With that he got their attention. The mayor has no authority to institute the death penalty, but that did not matter. New Yorkers wanted to express their outrage at criminals, and Koch's "rhetorical executions" seemed to help.[66]

In his home district, where Koch was popular, his campaign literature announced: "Five Reasons Why Manhattan Needs Ed Koch as Mayor: 1) Safe and affordable housing; 2) preserving middle-class neighborhoods; 3) safe streets and neighborhoods; 4) a fair shake for your tax dollars; 5) safe schools that teach." These were printed on one side of a page, and an editorial endorsement on the other. In Queens, however, instead of the editorial, the flip side offered five additional reasons to vote for Ed Koch: "1) The blackout and the national guard; 2) policeman and firemen do not have the right to strike . . . ever; 3) the death penalty . . . for good reasons; 4) protect our senior citizens; 5) New York employees should live in New York City." Koch knew, however, that reaching hundreds of thousands of New Yorkers by campaign flier was a hopeless task. He needed a different tactic.[67]

In 1973 Koch had used a large portion of his campaign fund to pay a staff and to set up a traditional campaign structure complete with pamphlets, posters, field captains, and the like. In spite of that, in 1977, he was still a political unknown outside his congressional district. Typically, candidates relied on political organizations to stretch their reach, but Koch had no standing with the regular Democrats, and only pockets of support within the reform wing. Television commercials offered the only means of bringing his name to enough of the electorate to give him a chance to win. That in turn meant raising money. Koch worked at the task relentlessly. He received some large donations from a few wealthy friends, but most of his fund raising took place in an endless series of small meetings. They were held in the living rooms of his upper East Side congressional constituents, in any home in Queens where an invitation to talk with a few neighbors could be had, or in the meeting rooms of synagogues around the city, where he asked for modest donations, and got them.

To manage the media campaign Koch hired David Garth, who had worked for John Lindsay in 1965, and again in 1969. In 1974, Hugh Carey, then an unknown congressman, used Garth to handle the media strategy for his gubernatorial race. The success of that effort confirmed the reputation of the communications expert as a man shrewdly capable of interpreting public sentiment and creating an image to satisfy it. In 1977, that meant improving Koch's appeal in middle-class neighborhoods outside of Manhattan.[68]

Garth's first step was to recruit Bess Myerson to act as his candidate's escort. She was the nation's first Jewish Miss America, and Commissioner of Consumer Affairs under John Lindsay. Quite a lady about town, with ambitions of her own, she brought more than glamour to the campaign. Koch was a fifty-two year old Greenwich Village bachelor. That was sure to lead the residents of Queens, Brooklyn, the Bronx, and Staten Island to speculate that he was a homosexual. By appearing with Koch everywhere he went, Myerson defused the insinuation. Cynics referred to the relationship as the "immaculate deception."

Next, Garth wrote a slogan to distinguish Koch from Beame, the opponent who had the best standing among Jewish middle-class voters, and from Lindsay, the man many middle-class New Yorkers thought of, with remorse, when they contemplated a liberal politician from Manhattan. "After eight years of charisma and four years of the clubhouse, why not try competence?" Koch advertisements read. Garth encouraged Koch to emphasize his support of capital punishment so he would not appear so liberal, and to condemn strongly municipal unions to prove he was a fiscal conservative.[69]

The net effect of these efforts was to make Koch acceptable to the city's middle class, particularly to middle-class Jews. Many continued to hold onto the liberal ideas of a simpler time, even as they became concerned about law and order and had come to fear that efforts to help minorities had lost their sense of fairness. Koch sounded like one of them. And Garth took to the airwaves with an ample treasury to carry the image of Koch as a tough representative of the middle-class to every living room in New York. He got some help. Australian publisher Rupert Murdoch bought the *New York Post* in 1977. Under the long-time guidance of publisher Dorothy Schiff, the *Post* typically endorsed Liberal party candidates, or liberal Democrats. Murdoch was decidedly more conservative than his predecessor, and his newly acquired newspaper endorsed Koch. The *Daily News* also endorsed Koch. The *News* was the city's largest daily and the one most read by New York's Catholics. The editorial in favor of Koch said he was the man most likely to make the tough decisions that were needed to restore the city to fiscal health.[70]

Mario Cuomo, like Koch, relied heavily on television. He had the governor's support, but Carey was at odds with the regular Democrats in Brooklyn, and in the Bronx, Pat Cunningham, once the governor's able ally, was crippled by investigations into his conduct. In Queens, Cuomo's home base, Borough President Donald Manes had replaced Matthew Troy as Democratic leader. Manes was a faithful follower of Abe Beame, and neither the governor nor Cuomo had particular ties to Manhattan. Cuomo's commercials told New Yorkers that he "was as angry" as they were about crime in the streets and mismanagement of the city. It was directed, like Koch's commercials, to the middle-class residents in the outer boroughs.[71]

Unlike Koch, Cuomo did not believe in the death penalty, and said so. The press made much of this difference between the two candidates, one of the few that distinguished them. It left Cuomo frustrated. "Should New York lead the league in vengeance?" he asked one audience. "I could win the election just by coming out for capital punishment," he complained to one reporter, "and I could absolutely clinch it if I came out for capital punishment preceded by torture." Yet, a poll taken shortly before the primary vote showed that voters were lining up behind candidates whose image they liked, not whose views they agreed with. Cuomo, a Queens Italian, did not have to prove he was conservative on matters of law and order—it was assumed. The death penalty issue helped Koch because it allowed voters to believe that he was not a typical liberal; it did not hurt Cuomo whose credentials were not in question.[72]

By the time primary day approached, Percy Sutton and Herman Badillo had faded into their respective political ghettos, hopelessly outnumbered by the ethnic arithmetic of the city. Newspaper polls revealed that Beame and Abzug continued to lead, but that Koch and Cuomo were both within striking distance. No one doubted there would be a run-off; no one knew who would be in it. Koch and Cuomo crowded the airwaves with their ads in an effort to pull supporters to the voting booths. Beame unleashed the regular organization, Abzug established an elaborate telephone operation designed to reach thousands of likely supporters in liberal Jewish neighborhoods.[73]

Almost 900,000 registered Democrats went to the polls on September 9 to divide their votes among the candidates. Koch came in first with twenty percent, then Cuomo with nineteen, then Beame with eighteen, and then Abzug with seventeen. Blacks turned out in larger numbers than usual to vote for the first man of their race to launch a bid for mayor, and Sutton polled fourteen percent. Badillo took eleven percent, and Joel Harnett got just one percent of the vote. Koch would face Cuomo in a run-off on September 20. A tearful Abe Beame announced that he accepted, "tonight's vote without apology. I gave this city every ounce of my strength and my fullest devotion during its most trying years of crisis. I've not let this city down." With that ended a four decade career in city politics that brought a Jewish New Yorker to the pinnacle of power for the first time. A second waited in the wings.[74]

Jews versus Catholics

The election results broke down along fairly predictable lines. Koch, Beame, and Abzug all had their strength in Jewish neighborhoods. In three reform dominated assembly districts on the West Side of Manhattan, Abzug came in first. In two of the three Koch, himself a Jewish reform politician, came in second. Beame came in first in ten districts, six of them in his home borough of Brooklyn where the regular organization was strongest. In all ten districts that Beame won, Koch placed second, often just a few hundred votes behind the mayor. Koch's campaign to reach the middle-class had worked in Jewish neighborhoods. He himself came in first in ten assembly districts, three on Manhattan's East Side in his own congressional district, one in the Flatbush section of Brooklyn where he narrowly beat out Beame and Abzug, two in the Bronx also by slim margins, and four in the middle-class bastion of Queens. Jews made up the largest group of voters in all of the districts where Koch came in first, but the sections he won in the Bronx, like Riverdale-Kingsbridge, and in Queens, like Woodside-Forest Hills, also had significant numbers of Irish Catholics. Over half of Koch's total primary votes came from Jews, and just under a quarter from Catholics, the better part of them Irish as far as can be told. The tribal election campaign had left the Irish without an obvious chieftain, and many decided that Koch was the candidate who suited them best. A fair proportion of the city's white Protestants lived in Koch's congressional district so he won many of their votes, and a smattering of blacks, Puerto Ricans and others made up the rest.[75]

Beame lost citywide by just a few thousand ballots, but he won in Brooklyn, making it clear that the regular organization there could still turn out a vote. Koch wanted that support, and so the candidate who had begun his political career as a reformer denouncing party boss Carmine DeSapio, made the pilgrimage to meet with Meade Esposito in the home of the Brooklyn boss's mother. Koch had come prepared to strike a deal. All Esposito told him was: "Make a good mayor and be honest with me." The *quid pro quo* was understood. Then the two men ate meatballs together, and with that, the Brooklyn Democratic organization was on Koch's side. Esposito had little affection for Koch, but Cuomo was the candidate of Governor Carey, who was battling with the Brooklyn organization, and Koch looked like a winner.[76]

In Harlem, Percy Sutton fumed angrily. He resented white unwillingness to cast votes for a black candidate, and was frustrated that he had won only some fifty-five percent of black ballots. A substantial portion of the remainder went to Herman Badillo in black neighborhoods outside Manhattan. The rest scattered among the various candidates. Sutton threatened to start a black political party, but cooler heads assessed the situation and determined that of the two Democrats in the run-off, Koch was the better candidate, the one most likely to win in their districts. Congressman Charles Rangel, Basil Paterson, and others, endorsed the Jewish candidate in the run-off. Herman Badillo endorsed Koch as well. Bella Abzug's backers gravitated toward him as a natural alternative to their fallen champion.[77]

Cuomo's support had come from the city's Italians. A *New York Times*/CBS exit poll reported that two thirds of his ballots had come from Catholic voters, but his performance was strongest by far where the Italian population was greatest. Less than a fifth of Cuomo's votes came from Jews, and very few from New York's minorities. The survey also indicated that those who voted for Cuomo, and those who voted for Koch, "were almost identical in their concern for issues." Ethnicity, not policy positions, would decide the contest.[78]

In the days leading up to the run-off, journalists noted "a growing perception of the election as a Roman Catholic-Jewish confrontation." The realization bothered Cuomo. He did not want to polarize the city, and he also knew that without Jewish votes he could not win. He tried to confront the conflict head on: "You're a Jew. I'm a Catholic. It doesn't make any difference in this election," he told heavily Jewish audiences in Borough Park and elsewhere in Brooklyn. But of course, it did.[79]

More than three quarters of the city's Jewish Democrats voted for Koch in the run-off on September 20, almost nine out of ten Italian Democrats cast their votes for Cuomo. There were more Jews in the party than Italians, so Koch had the bigger base. Koch also ran about even with Cuomo in Irish districts. With Sutton and Badillo out of the running, the city's blacks and Puerto Ricans turned apathetic. As a result, turnout in the run-off was about one hundred thousand lower than in the primary. Koch ran perceptibly better than Cuomo among minorities, except in a few middle-class black areas in Brooklyn and Queens where Cuomo had the support of local political figures. There, the two candidates ran about even. Koch won in every borough except Staten Island, where the heavy Italian presence brought Cuomo a victory of small proportions. The final score made Koch his party's nominee with fifty-five percent of the vote.[80]

With the Democratic nomination, Koch's election seemed assured. Financial and political support came to him easily, and party officials and workers began to recognize him as the new power in New York City. Cuomo prepared to run on the Liberal line alone, while Governor Carey, who had at first agreed to back Cuomo through November even if it was only on a third party ticket, inched his way out of the commitment. Carey did not want to enter into a political conflict with Koch, who would almost certainly be elected mayor. The Republican candidate, Roy Goodman, and the Conservative's Barry Farber, limped toward the general election representing their respective parties, but they made little impression on the public.[81]

On November 9, 1977, half of the 1.4 million New Yorkers who went to the polls gave Edward I. Koch their votes. Cuomo took forty-two percent, and Goodman and Farber about four percent each. Koch again won about three quarters of the Jewish votes, and he ran substantially better among blacks and Puerto Ricans in the general election than he had in the primary run-off against Cuomo. When asked to choose between Democrats, minorities had given Koch just a slight edge. When choosing between the candidate of the Democratic party and the candidate of the Liberal party, a strong majority cast their ballots for the former. In spite of a significant loss of minority support, Cuomo ran just about the same in the general election as he had in the primary. Large numbers of Italian voters who were not registered Democrats, and who therefore could not cast ballots for Cuomo in the primary, went to the polls to support him in November, making up the loss among minority voters.

Koch's victory meant that a Jewish mayor continued to rule New York. Edward I. Koch's rise to power was a personal triumph, but it was also part of the historical evolution of Jewish political participation in New York City. A period of Jewish predominance had arrived.

ELEVEN

The Chutzpah of Edward I. Koch

1978–1988

Edward I. Koch began his mayoralty in search of a political consensus that would help him to grapple with the city's fiscal woes. Upon entering office he appointed seven deputy mayors. The group included men well respected by the city's senior bankers in an effort to inspire confidence in the new mayor's commitment to good government and his determination to restore budgetary soundness. The team also included Herman Badillo and Basil Paterson, tangible gestures to the city's minorities that all New Yorkers would be represented while Koch was mayor. The new chief executive made a gesture to the Irish too by appointing Bob McGuire police commissioner. When he did, a reporter asked, "Mr. Mayor, isn't this just a continuation of the old Irish Mafia syndrome?" referring to the practice of naming Irish police commissioners.

The mayor, feigning disbelief, turned to McGuire and quipped, "Bob, I thought you told me you were Jewish?"

"No, I didn't Mr. Mayor," the new commissioner deadpanned. "I just told you I look Jewish." It was a far cry from the days when the Irish ruled New York.[1]

Chutzpah

By the time Koch became mayor New York had already suffered the worst of the fiscal crisis. Some 65,000 municipal employees had lost their jobs. Free tuition at City College—a century-old tradition that had helped make New York unique—was gone. Subway fares, which rose just five times between 1904 and 1975, had risen three times since. Expenditures on middle-income housing projects had been delayed indefinitely and programs to help the poor were cut. Governor Carey, aided by Felix Rohatyn of Lazard Freres investment bank and a highly competent team of private citizens and state officials, had already fashioned a path out of the financial abyss. New agencies, the Municipal Assistance Corporation and the Financial Control Board, oversaw New York City finances with unusual regulatory powers designed to restore confidence in the city's fiscal management. The development of a credible program for recovery induced the federal government to guarantee New York City short-term debt for three years, subject to strict demands for progress toward solvency. The complex arrangements limited the power of the mayor to control city programs, but saved New York from the unacceptable consequences of default or bankruptcy.[2]

Despite real progress, the city had not restored investor confidence fully by the time Koch assumed office. To have enough time to make the transition back to fiscal soundness New York needed federal endorsements of its long-term bonds. During his first weeks as mayor Koch studied hard to understand the city's revenues and expenses and mastered the intricacies of the municipal budget. In the months that followed he negotiated agreements with labor unions that allowed him to present himself in Washington as a responsible steward of the city's check book. He testified before Congress with an air of confidence and met with his old friends in the House of Representatives to ask for their support. With the help of the governor, the city's congressional contingent, and others, he won the commitments the city needed.[3]

The new mayor's initial progress toward restoring the city's fiscal health was important, but the most striking thing about his first year was its inspired tone. Since 1975 New York had teetered on the brink of financial collapse and an unaccustomed darkness hovered over the city. At one point laid-off police officers and firefighters pressured

Top: Following Wagner's split with the regular Democratic organization, Liberal party leader Alex Rose, shown conferring with Wagner at Gracie Mansion, became one of the mayor's most influential advisers. Rose continued to wield substantial power during the Lindsay administration. Courtesy of LaGuardia and Wagner Archives

Bottom: John V. Lindsay, shown here campaigning in 1965, viewed the New York City mayoralty as a stepping stone to the White House. Robert Price, Lindsay's campaign manager, is standing on the far right. Seated next to Lindsay is Queens Assistant District Attorney Nathan Hentel. Courtesy of Collections of the Municipal Archives of the City of New York

Top: Lindsay developed enormous popularity among black New Yorkers. He is shown here at a graduation ceremony of the Clairol Leadership Program in 1968. Courtesy of Collections of the Municipal Archives of the City of New York

Bottom: Many white New Yorkers perceived Lindsay's programs as favoring minorities at the expense of public safety. This paved the way for the 1969 law-and-order campaign of Mario Proccacino, shown shaking Lindsay's hand. Courtesy of Collections of the Municipal Archives of the City of New York

Top: In a bid to improve Lindsay's law-and-order image, and to appeal to Jewish voters, Lindsay's campaign staff convinced the Jewish Chief Inspector of the police department, Sanford D. Garelik, to run on Lindsay's ticket as City Council president. Garelik is shown announcing his candidacy with Lindsay, along with his wife, Catherine, and his son, Neal. Courtesy of the Daily News

Bottom: With a carefully orchestrated plan Lindsay's 1969 reelection campaign staff boosted the mayor's standing with Jewish voters by convincing Israeli Prime Minister Golda Meir (at Lindsay's right) to indicate her support for the mayor. Courtesy of Collections of the Municipal Archives of the City of New York

Top: As New York City's first Jewish mayor Beame's political strength was greatest among Jews. He is pictured here at a ceremony honoring the Greater New York Conference on Soviet Jewry. Stanley Lowell is at the far left standing next to Brooklyn district attorney Eugene Gold. Manhattan borough president Percy Sutton is on the far right. Courtesy of Collections of the Municipal Archives of the City of New York

Middle: The fiscal crisis Abraham D. Beame inherited in 1974 crippled his ability to exercise the traditional powers of the mayor and to build a successful political base. Beame is pictured here on the grounds of Gracie Mansion conferring with former Mayor Lindsay. Mary Lindsay is at the far right talking with Mary Beame. Courtesy of Collections of the Municipal Archives of the City of New York

Bottom: Beame spent much of his single term in officenegotiating fiscal relief measures with state and federal officials. He is pictured here with members of New York City's congressional delegation. From left to right, Edward Koch, James Delaney, Hugh Carey, Beame, Bertram Podell and Mario Biaggi. Courtesy of Collections of the Municipal Archives of the City of New York

Top: Mayor Edward I. Koch enjoyed strong support among white New Yorkers but had problematic relations with black New Yorkers during most of his twelve years in office. He is shown here on the steps of City Hall being endorsed for Governor in 1982 by "All New Yorkers for Koch," a coalition of twenty ethnic groups. From left to right are Congressman Mario Biaggi, Erie New York Congressman Henry J. Nowak, Koch, former Mayor Robert F. Wagner, and Franklin D. Roosevelt, Jr. Courtesy of Collections of the Municipal Archives of the City of New York

Bottom: Koch seeking the endorsement of black community leaders for governor. Courtesy of Collections of the Municipal Archives of the City of New York

Top Left: Koch's popularity among Jewish voters remained strong throughout his three terms. He is shown here with Israeli Prime Minister Menachem Begin. Courtesy of Collections of the Municipal Archives of the City of New York

Top Right: Former Mayor Wagner (r) holds the bible as his son, Robert F. Wagner Jr., is sworn in as deputy mayor by Mayor Koch. The appointment perpetuated the Wagner family tradition of public service to New York City.

Bottom: Koch beat Mario Cuomo in the Democratic primary for mayor and the general election for mayor in 1977, but lost to Cuomo in the 1982 Democratic primary for Governor. Koch is shown here endorsing Cuomo for governor following the 1982 primary contest. Courtesy of Collections of the Municipal Archives of the City of New York

Top: On January 1, 1990 David Dinkins became the first black elected mayor of New York City. His wife, Joyce holds the bible while he is sworn in while Judge Fritz Alexander administers the oath of office. Mayor Koch and Governor Cuomo can be seen in the first row, and above them from left to right Councilmembers Archie Sprigner, June Eisland, and Arthur Katzman. Jazz singer Hazel Duke is at the far right. Courtesy of the Mayor's Photo Unit, Joan Vitale Strong, photographer

Bottom: In the summer of 1991 an accident involving the motorcade of Lubavitcher Rebbe Menechem Schneerson and a young black boy set off three days of riots in Crown Heights, Brooklyn. Mayor Dinkins traveled to the site of the riots in an effort to ease tensions. Courtesy of the Mayor's Photo Unit, Edward Reed, photographer

Right: City Council president Andrew Stein (center) has expressed mayoral ambitions. Courtesy of the Office of the City Council President

Left: Rudolph Giuliani lost his 1989 bid for mayor by a narrow margin against David Dinkins

Right: Bronx Borough president Fernando Ferrer, one of the city's most prominent Hispanic politicians, may seek citywide office in 1993. No Hispanic has yet held citywide office. Courtesy of the Office of the Bronx Borough President

politicians to rehire them by welcoming tourists arriving at airports, train stations, and bus terminals with pamphlets that described New York as "Fear City." At another moment labor leaders threatened Mayor Beame and the city with a general strike. Subway trains came less often, garbage collection slowed down, the police and fire departments responded to emergencies less rapidly, and on and on.[4]

Koch banished the doom. In his inaugural address he declared that New York had "been shaken by troubles that would have destroyed any other city. But we are not any other city. We are the City of New York, and New York in adversity towers above any other city in the world." The mayor made a show of eating in restaurants around town and he praised his favorites publicly. He extolled New York's night life, its culture, the excitement of its streets, the remarkable diversity of its people. He emphasized how much more New York did for its citizens than most other municipalities even as he insisted on fiscal austerity. He rode the subways and asked the passengers, "How'm I doing?" with an energy that sparked the riders. It gave them the sense that the mayor was one of them, that they had access to him—that the man at the top was in touch with their needs.[5]

Koch spoke to the public in terms so informal they bordered on the vulgar. Such candor from a politician refreshed people who had been lied to by Watergate's conspirators and who were rapidly tiring of the stilted and moralizing monologues emitting from Jimmy Carter's White House. The mayor dismissed his detractors as kooks, nuts, wackos, and crazies. When asked why he did not support one program or another his favorite reply was, "because I'm not a schmuck." It was not just words that made people respond to Koch. Every day, or so it seemed, the mayor proposed a new program or a different policy—often a visceral reaction to whatever he had come across the day before. "My own feeling is that I am an ordinary guy with special abilities," Koch wrote of himself. "But I want the things the average person wants. And so I do the things the average New Yorker would do if he or she were the mayor."[6]

Koch insisted publicly that while he ruled City Hall merit, not patronage, would determine appointments. He revamped the system for choosing municipal judges and pledged to fire any employees who stole from the city. He insisted loudly on a full day of productive work from anyone receiving a city paycheck. Koch's initiatives were basic and reactive. There was little sense of a grand vision, but common sense prevailed; and New Yorkers felt that the darkest days of the fiscal crisis had been left behind. They had a leader who in his early days in office "seized the city's soul, and asserted it, thumbs up, marching up Fifth Avenue," according to New York Senator Daniel Patrick Moynihan.[7]

By 1979 the mayor had won the confidence of the people, and their approval gave him confidence in himself. That year he reorganized his office and reduced the number of deputy mayors. Peter Solomon continued as deputy mayor for economic policy and Haskell Ward retained the post of deputy mayor for Human Services. Koch named Nat Levanthal deputy mayor for operations, and he appointed Robert F. Wagner, Jr., deputy mayor for policy, perpetuating the Wagner family tradition of public service to New York City. Badillo left in the restructuring. Paterson was already gone, appointed Secretary of State of New York by the governor. The all-inclusive, consensus-building meetings of the early administration, when at times sixty people showed up to decide important policies, came to an end. The mayor settled down to govern in his own style.[8]

At the start of his administration Koch decided that he would have to take on the public employee unions. In 1980 the transit workers struck and he got his chance. The TWU contract expiration date had been moved to March 31st to avoid another dead-of-winter walk-out like the one that had greeted John Lindsay on January 1, 1966, but the new deadline still arrived two months before the bulk of the city's labor contracts came up for renewal. As a result, the accord with the transportation union set the standard for the others. As a matter of fiscal concern the mayor wanted to keep the TWU settlement low, and because it was the union in many ways most able to cripple the city, confronting it would have great symbolic importance.

Faced with a transportation strike in 1966 the Lindsay administration counseled all New Yorkers not involved in vital services to stay home. In 1980 Koch told them all to go to work. He forbade municipal employees to stay away from their jobs and decreed business as usual to the greatest extent possible. Most mornings and evenings throughout the strike he stood on the Brooklyn Bridge and yelled encouragement to thousands of New Yorkers clad in business suits and sneakers walking to lower Manhattan. "Go out and make money!" the mayor yelled to men and women headed for Wall street.

"We love you," they yelled back. "Don't give in, you're doing fine," they shouted in implicit response to his trademark question, "How'm I doing?"

Koch did not like the contract ultimately agreed to by the governor and MTA negotiators, and he said so. But despite his disappointment with the agreement, his posture created a new climate for negotiating with municipal unions, and he made it clear that while he was mayor the labor unions would not dictate to the city.[9]

Race

When Koch named Basil Paterson deputy mayor for labor relations black political leaders thought they detected something new at City Hall. Mayors had named black deputies in the past, but the jobs were political payoffs that carried little responsibility. Paterson's appointment was different. A skilled conciliator, his job was as important as almost any in city government. The inspired choice held the promise of sound race relations for the administration. The hope did not last.[10]

Koch brought another exceptionally qualified black man into his government, Haskell Ward, whose initial task was to reorganize a series of poverty programs rife with ineptitude and corruption. In no small measure the programs ran that way by design. During the Lindsay Administration, when riots erupted in ghettos around the country, the mayor and his staff adopted a practice of buying peace in New York. They identified leaders in different black communities and channeled federal money to them through the Great Society programs Washington funded. The programs did of course direct resources into poor neighborhoods and create some jobs, but more important they gave the potential organizers of disruption a stake in the system. The city government did not monitor too closely how the money got used as long as no riots occurred. Under Beame, the system persevered with the mayor's patronage dispenser, Stanley Friedman, determining which politicians, community leaders, or churches, would hand out the jobs and money. It was machine politics as usual, updated to include the poverty programs of the 1960s.[11]

Koch resented the system. With a fiscal crisis still dominating city business in 1978 the inefficiencies offended him, and ample evidence of corruption compounded his anger. Blackmail was implicit in the formula the Lindsay team worked out—"We'll pay you not to riot," and the Beame Administration's approach smacked of injustice. The insiders got jobs, others got nothing. Koch wanted programs that were fair and effective. Ward moved competently to achieve that. In the process, programs that boosted the position of many local black politicians and community leaders lost their status because they did not meet the new standards. That alienated some from the mayor, but it was the least of his difficulty with blacks. The main problem was that Koch brought the same *chutzpah* to reorganizing the poverty programs that he brought to other areas of public policy. He did not explain calmly that efficient government required a new approach, but rather condemned "the poverticians" and the "poverty pimps" who used the taxpayers' money to advance themselves. To black leaders, this smacked of race baiting.

During his 1977 campaign candidate Koch had sounded the same theme. Once the run-off narrowed to a contest between him and Cuomo, he met with a group of Harlem political leaders that included Charles Rangel, Basil Paterson, and Assemblyman Herman "Denny" Farrell to seek their support. They gave it in return for two pledges—the would-be mayor agreed to appoint more senior black officials to city government than his three predecessors combined, and to stop using words like povertician that inflamed racial tensions. Koch abandoned the term during his campaign, but not long after winning office reverted to his earlier ways. For many New Yorkers it was just Koch being Koch, insensitive perhaps, but sincere. For black leaders there was something more to it. Charles Rangel concluded that, Koch "happens to be bright, he is witty, he is a politician, and he knows how to win—you put all this together and you get the sense that the son of a bitch is not just insensitive. He knows exactly what he is doing. He has consciously cultivated the back lash." [12]

The mayor's relations with black leaders were already tense when in 1979 journalist Ken Auletta wrote a profile on the mayor for *The New Yorker* and cited a comment that Koch had shared with a Columbia University oral history interviewer. The transcript was meant to be sealed until far into the future, but Koch authorized its release. In it he declared that in his experience, "blacks are anti-Semites." The blanket statement was a shocker, and Koch's effort to temper the comment by saying it referred primarily to black leaders helped but little. [13]

Then Koch decided to close Sydenham Hospital and Metropolitan Hospital in Harlem. The latter was simply used inefficiently and could not be justified on the basis of cost. Ultimately a special federal program instituted there rescued it. Sydenham, the smallest of the seventeen municipal hospitals the city ran at the time, had a long-standing reputation for sub-quality care. Old and dirty, it lacked adequate facilities and its low level of usage did not justify the investment to upgrade it. The city pledged to build four clinics to provide out-patient care and showed that the community was well served by other hospitals for emergency and in-patient care. It did not matter. Opposition to the proposal was fierce. The people of Harlem felt they were being singled out to suffer the consequences of fiscal retrenchment even though the neighborhood's residents suffered from more medical problems than most. And the community would lose several hundred jobs to boot. Union leaders, local activists, and political officials protested.

For a full year a pitched political battle raged. Opponents accused the mayor of racism, and Koch responded with equally harsh rhetoric. Haskell Ward, by then a deputy mayor and the president of the city's Health and Hospitals Corporation, resigned in the midst of the controversy leaving Koch without a senior level black among his top aides. Ultimately the hospital closed, but the cost to the mayor and to the city was great. A dozen years later it was the one thing Koch wished he had done differently in dealing with black leaders. After the Sydenham episode Koch's relationship with New York's principal black politicians would never be good again.[14]

Democrats and Republicans and Whites and Blacks

The Sydenham closing blemished what was measuring up as a highly successful first term in office for Koch as the 1981 mayoralty race approached. Koch's popularity was extraordinary and comparisons with Fiorello LaGuardia abounded; there was little chance for anyone to unseat him. A small group of liberal Democrats led by Arthur Schlesinger, Jr., labor mediator Theodore Kheel, and John Lindsay tried to develop some momentum against Koch because they thought his posture antagonized minorities and polarized the city's races. Herman Badillo briefly threatened to run, but he found little enthusiasm for his campaign and it ended before it really began. Finally, a liberal Brooklyn assemblyman named Frank Barbaro decided to challenge Koch in the Democratic primary because no one else would. He accused Koch of sending a subliminal message to the white middle class that the mayor "was going to put minorities in their place," and of giving the city away to real estate developers. But the accusations did not capture the public's imagination, and the Democratic primary rapidly turned into a general referendum on Koch's first term.[15]

So too did the Republican primary. Since late 1979 Koch had been plotting to add his name to the ballot on the Republican line as well as the Democratic one. His public rhetoric was in tune with the party's philosophy, and the fiscal crisis had made a virtue of city government austerity—a traditional strong point with GOP voters. In 1980, at odds with President Carter's policies toward Israel, Koch had invited Republican presidential candidate Ronald Reagan to visit him at City Hall to take pictures before the election. The mayor also invited Alfonse D'Amato, the Republican candidate for United States Senate, to City Hall and he had been careful throughout his first term not to antagonize the upstate Republican leader of the State Senate, Warren Anderson. In a series of meetings with the city's Republican party leaders he actively courted their support, appointed some of the people they recommended to office, and pledged more patronage in return for their help. As a result, the leaders agreed to allow Koch's name to appear on the ballot in the Republican primary in 1981. His only opponent was a little know Queens Assemblyman named John A. Esposito.[16]

On primary day the city's voters gave Koch overwhelming majorities. He won sixty percent of the Democratic vote to Barbaro's thirty-six percent, and more than sixty-six percent of the Republican vote. The only source of weakness was clear. In spite of his huge overall success, Koch lost black districts by a vote of greater than two to one in both the Democratic and Republican races. In the general election, with the two principal ballot lines carrying his name—the only time in history a New York City mayoral candidate had both major party nominations—Koch took three quarters of the vote. The opposition was so weak Koch won virtually every neighborhood in the city. But he conquered white districts by margins of ten and twelve to one; in black districts his margin was five to one. In his victory speech Koch cited racial unity as an important goal for his second term.[17]

The 1981 contest for borough president of Manhattan made it clear that the issue of race would not go away. Four years before, when Percy Sutton sought the mayoralty, a hard fought battle had ensued for the job he vacated. Political tradition had reserved the Manhattan borough presidency for a black since 1953 when Carmine DeSapio and Robert Wagner chose Hulan Jack to run for the post. The often unspoken but unchallenged logic was that a city with a population more than twenty percent black and about one third racial minorities should have some minority representation on its most important governing council. Manhattan had the highest concentration of blacks, so its borough presidency became the seat allocated for the purpose.

The destruction of Tammany Hall and the breakdown of an effective citywide political machine eliminated the organization that could impose such a rule on the city. The custom endured because more often than not the black politician in the job moved on to higher office in mid-term leaving a vacancy to be filled by the borough's City Council members, most of whom abided by traditional party rules. Sutton's decision to run for mayor in 1977 created a vacancy in a city election year. Harlem's politicians nominated one of their own, David Dinkins, to succeed Sutton, but a Jewish assemblyman, Andrew Stein, also sought the office, as did Robert F. Wagner, Jr. son of the former mayor and a councilman-at-large from Manhattan.

With Sutton running for mayor Harlem's attention focused on him rather than on the race for borough president. Andrew Stein had a well-financed campaign and had earned a reputation as a crusader by exposing maltreatment of the elderly in the city's nursing homes. Robert Wagner, Jr. also raised a substantial campaign fund, and had his father's name and considerable influence working to his advantage. Stein defeated Wagner by a small margin, and Dinkins ran a distant third. As a consequence, the Board of Estimate lacked a minority representative. Koch of course became mayor in 1977, and Jay Goldin won reelection as comptroller. In an outcome that surprised the city's political analysts Carol Bellamy, a Protestant woman who held a Manhattan State Senate seat, beat Paul O'Dwyer in the Democratic primary for City Council president and won election in November. Bellamy rode into office on the rising wave of feminism that Bella Abzug had not quite been able to make work for her. With O'Dwyer's departure the Irish lost their last remaining seat on the Board of Estimate. In Staten Island, an Italian named Anthony R. Gaeta was elected borough president. Each of the other boroughs had Jewish presidents in 1977—Robert Abrams in the Bronx, Donald Manes in Queens, and Howard Golden in Brooklyn. By 1981 Robert Abrams had won election as New York State Attorney General and the Bronx Democratic party replaced him with Stanley Simon, also Jewish. Thus, six of eight members of the Board of Estimate, holding eight of the board's eleven votes were Jewish men.[18]

In 1981 Dinkins again challenged Stein for Manhattan borough president. The other contests for city office generated little drama that year so the battle for the top post in Manhattan received a lot of attention, and during the campaign Dinkins raised the issue of minority representation on the Board of Estimate. Dinkins lost the Democratic primary by just a few percentage points, and Manhattan's voters returned Stein to office easily in the general election. But black turnout for Dinkins had been unusually high, and the edge to the battle had been sharp. Minority political leaders made it clear they felt something was wrong with a system that denied so significant a proportion of the population representation on the city's most important governing body—and that allowed six positions of eight to be held by Jewish politicians.[19]

More Chutzpah

Despite weakness among minorities, Koch's 1981 victory was stunning. He won a higher proportion of the vote than any mayor had ever won before and he became drunk with his own popularity. A few close friends encouraged him to take advantage of his extraordinary public standing to run for governor when Hugh Carey, faced with a sharp decline in his political fortunes, announced in January 1982 that he would not seek reelection. A short while later *New York Post* publisher Rupert Murdoch launched a crusade to draft the mayor to run for governor, and Koch responded by contemplating a statewide campaign.

Many of his closest political advisers counseled him not to do it. The city would resent it, they pointed out, if fresh upon winning reelection as mayor he tried to leave the city to become governor. Besides, the city's people would not believe that he really wanted the job. Koch loved being mayor and had announced repeatedly that he planned to serve three terms to see his programs to completion. On a trip to Jerusalem the mayor had pledged before the wailing wall that he would seek no other job. Koch, by then a fifty-seven year old bachelor, had convinced New Yorkers that their city was the only true love in his life. But he wanted to run. More than anything else, it seemed, Koch simply wanted to campaign. He enjoyed the thrill of political combat and the gratification of winning. Against the judgment of his most trusted counselors he announced his candidacy.[20]

Mario Cuomo too declared himself a candidate. The year after he lost the mayoralty to Koch, Cuomo ran for lieutenant governor on Hugh Carey's ticket and won the superfluous office. The demands upon him were not great, and he spent most of his time positioning himself to run for the state's top job. Even before Carey stepped down Cuomo's intentions were clear. Koch's announcement scared everyone else contemplating running out of the race. City Council president Carol Bellamy was considering a bid, but if Koch won—and almost everyone thought he would—she would become mayor. It seemed the better bet by far. New York State Assembly Speaker Stanley Fink had considered running, as had New York State Attorney General Robert Abrams. Both changed their minds after Koch declared himself a candidate. Cuomo, on the other hand, stood fearless. He thought Koch had peaked and would slide from his 1981 high. The mayor was too-New-York-City in demeanor for upstaters, and his flirtation with Republicans would hurt him in a primary against a solid Democrat with a clear message, Cuomo believed. Besides, he ached for the chance to repay Koch for the 1977 defeat in the mayoralty campaign.[21]

Unwittingly Koch set the tone of the campaign the day after he announced his candidacy. Several months before he had granted an interview to a *Playboy* magazine journalist. Advance copies of the story were distributed twenty-four hours after Koch's declaration. In it, among other things, the mayor said, "Have you ever lived in the suburbs? I haven't but I've talked to people who have, and it's sterile. It's nothing. It's wasting your life." He continued later on: "Anyone who suggests I run for governor is no friend of mine. It's a terrible position, and besides, it requires living in Albany, which is smalltown life at its worst. I wouldn't even consider it." The mayor's gaffes throughout the campaign—he sometimes did not know what county he was in to the malicious delight of local reporters—hurt his credibility. Cuomo, a state official by then for nearly eight years, was practically on home turf. His messages were simple, yet eloquent, and he portrayed himself as the underdog committed to taking on Ed Koch—a political goliath—because he believed he would do the better job, one more consistent with Democratic party principles. Running behind the whole campaign, Cuomo defeated Koch by a modest margin in the Democratic primary, and then beat Republican Lew Lehrman in a similar close contest in November.[22]

A Strong Undertow

Koch was gracious in defeat. He could afford to be. He remained mayor of New York and the city was riding a wave. Fueled by a rising national economy and changes in federal tax legislation, New York's financial sector experienced one of the greatest periods of dealmaking in its history. Wall Street bankers got richer than ever and the allure of money attracted thousands of young ambitious men and women to work in the city's investment houses. The growing number of New Yorkers earning handsome incomes wanted to live in comfortable housing. The mayor's real-estate programs offered incentives to builders who threw luxury apartments up toward the sky with breathtaking speed. Apartments once offered to renters converted to cooperative ownership as landlords discovered financial opportunities hidden in the buildings they owned and city dwellers saw a chance to accumulate equity in the walls that surrounded them. Poorer areas on the edges of more stable neighborhoods held a new attraction for builders. Gentrification—the economic upscaling of the population of a community—

became a common event around Manhattan, in Brooklyn Heights and Park Slope, and to a lesser extent in other areas of the city.

The general tone of New York in the early and mid-1980s was upbeat and optimistic. People got rich and spent their money. They went to discotheques and fancy restaurants; they rented limousines and threw parties. Shops prospered, and the city's tax base expanded. During his second term the mayor found the money to restore many basic services to the levels they were at before the fiscal crunch. Some efficiencies were achieved, but mostly the city hired more staff. That in turn fueled the economy more. The metropolis that had flirted with financial disaster suddenly had budget surpluses of five hundred million dollars.[23]

The mayor's hubris fit well with the times. He wrote a provocative and entertaining book about his political career entitled *Mayor*. It named names, pointed fingers, told the truth, told tall tales, rewrote history, changed details to suit the mayor's fancy—and it sold by the thousands. It became a best-seller and the mayor got rich. A Broadway musical of Koch's exploits appeared. One had been produced about Fiorello La-Guardia, so naturally Koch wanted one too. LaGuardia's had come years after his tenure in office and his death. Koch's appeared while he still reigned. The mayor seemed not to understand the difference. The play bombed.[24]

Glitz had its limits, and the rising tide of prosperity had a sharp undertow. The powerful economy helped New Yorkers across all economic spectrums—the number of families on welfare began to drop—but there were pockets of hard core poverty in New York with long-term problems that a short-term boost could not solve. With almost the same speed that huge luxury cooperatives rose so too did the number of homeless appearing on New York's streets. Soon the problem emerged across the nation, but in a densely populated metropolis like New York the impact on daily life was great. Dozens of seemingly broken men and women, often with vacant stares, pitiable visages, and alarming demeanors, began to haunt New York's streets. They congregated *en masse* in public spaces like Grand Central Terminal, Pennsylvania Railway Station, and the Port Authority Bus Terminal. They slept and lived on benches in comfortable neighborhoods as well as poor ones. The dozens turned into hundreds, then into thousands. Ultimately more than ten thousand homeless single men would sleep in city-run shelters on any given night. Social workers claimed that at least that many, perhaps more, rode the subways and roamed the streets.

The number of homeless single men had the greatest effect on the city's physical space, but the number of homeless families laid a greater claim to the city's heart. Typically a young and husbandless mother with more than a single child, the families generated pity in a way that men without homes did not. The obvious victims—young children, in no way responsible for their plight—painfully reminded New Yorkers of the unfair cruelty of poverty. Each and every night, twenty thousand family members, in addition to the ten thousand single men, needed room and board. New York City became ward to a population of more than thirty thousand, the size of a substantial city itself.[25]

Compassionate people urged the mayor to build sufficient public housing to provide the suffering city of homeless with permanent residences. The mayor rejected the simplistic proposal as a prescription for bankruptcy. If the government offered a free or cheap apartment to every person or family that asked, Koch reasoned logically, then the numbers of people asking would skyrocket. The city therefore provided dormitory style shelters, or placed families in hotels, or sought other short-term solutions. The numbers were overwhelming, the daily task of caring for the homeless daunting. The quality of some of the facilities, particularly the later ones, was humane and impressive. The quality of others, particularly the ones established when the numbers first began to balloon, were deplorable—beneath any standard of decency and dignity. The mayor's critics condemned his policy harshly. And they looked at the composition of the homeless population, overwhelmingly black and Puerto Rican, and accused the mayor of racism. If New York's homeless were white, they implied, Ed Koch would find them some place to live.

Racial tensions ran high for other reasons too. In 1983 Michigan Congressman John Conyers held hearings on New York City police department abuses against blacks and Puerto Ricans. The accusations were substantial, detailed, and embarrassing. Koch responded by naming a black Police Commissioner, Benjamin Ward, but the gesture had little effect and race relations remained sour.[26]

A pair of episodes occurred late in 1984 that made things worse. In one, a group of five black youths riding on a New York City subway asked a white passenger to give them five dollars. The man shot the teenagers and fled. After hiding out for several days while public debate raged, Bernhard Goetz gave himself up. Some praised the man for defending himself against the menacing toughs, others thought him guilty of attempted murder. The facts were not entirely clear, nor did they seem much to matter. New Yorkers formed opinions based on their ability to sympathize more easily with the shooter or the teens. Initially, a grand jury declined to indict Goetz. Then additional evidence revealed that after firing a first salvo, Goetz turned to one victim lying on the subway floor, said "You don't look so bad. Here's another," and fired again. A second jury indicted him for attempted murder. Koch joined in the public debate. First, he condemned vigilantism. Then he defended Goetz's right to protect himself from the threatening behavior of the youths and praised the grand jury that declined to indict Goetz. When the second grand jury returned an indictment, Koch fell silent.[27]

That same year in the Bronx a white police officer shot and killed Eleanor Bumpers, an elderly black woman with a history of mental illness. The police had been called to evict the woman from a city owned apartment. She refused to leave, became violent, and attacked the police at the scene. A grand jury indicted the officer who shot her, but a judge later dismissed the case. Blacks cried foul; Koch publicly praised the decision.[28]

Something else happened in 1984 that gave political weight to the mounting anger many minorities felt toward the mayor and his administration: Jesse Jackson ran for President. His inspirational rhetoric thrilled young black men and women who heard him preach that, "hands that once picked cotton could now pick a President." The Jackson campaign launched an energetic registration drive in black neighborhoods around New York City to counter the typical low turnout of the voters most likely to support their candidate. The registration roles in black neighborhoods soared. On primary day, against two opponents, Jackson won more than one third of the ballots cast in the five boroughs of New York City, including nearly ninety percent of the city's black votes.[29]

Jesse Jackson's bid inspired hope among blacks, but fear among many of the city's Jews. Jackson had once referred to New York as "Hymietown" in derogatory reference to the city's large Jewish population. His sympathy for the PLO alienated supporters of Israel. Louis Farrakhan, a Chicago-based Black Muslim with a notorious record of anti-Semitism, endorsed Jackson. The candidate disowned some of Farrakhan's more outrageous comments, but accepted his backing. Jews reacted to Jackson with suspicion and anger.

As the 1985 mayoralty campaign approached racial polarization remained high. No one doubted Ed Koch would run for a third term, something only Fiorello LaGuardia and Robert Wagner had done before successfully. The question was who would run against him, and would they have a chance to defeat the popular but controversial mayor.

The Coalition That Never Was

Shortly after the 1984 presidential primary in New York a group of minority politicians began thinking about how to displace Koch. Jackson's success had shown that a coalition of blacks, Puerto Ricans, and a small core of white liberals could produce a powerful citywide vote. Some felt Koch could be beat in 1985, others felt that at the very least the stage could be set for a more serious race in 1989. The key, though, was to unite Koch's disparate opponents. In an effort to pull the pieces together forty leading black and Puerto Rican political officials and community activists announced the creation of the Coalition for a Just New York and named Brooklyn assemblyman Al Vann their chairman.

Harlem Congressman Charles Rangel, David Dinkins, who then held the appointed post of City Clerk, and Assemblyman Herman "Denny" Farrell, who was Manhattan's Democratic County Leader, proposed Basil Paterson as the consensus candidate. Herman Badillo still hungered for the chance to run City Hall, and City Council president Carol Bellamy wanted the job as well. Comptroller Jay Goldin had mayoral ambitions, but his posture was more circumspect than others. Badillo declared himself a candidate but announced that he would run only with the support of the coalition and that he would back their selection. Carol Bellamy met with the group but kept her options open. Paterson declined to reveal his intentions for months as the press continued to view him as the favorite. Ultimately Paterson declined to run for reasons of health and Herman Badillo replaced him as the leading minority contender. Badillo lined up a majority of the coalition's votes, and it appeared he would run against his former boss with the support of the city's minorities lined up firmly behind him.

Harlem's black political leaders could not accept Badillo's candidacy. To do so would have ceded control of the coalition, and potentially City Hall, to a Puerto Rican. It was a matter of ethnic pride and of self-interest as well. They wanted Koch out, but they wanted themselves, not others, in. And on a personal basis they did not trust Badillo, whose independence made him highly unpredictable. To break the support Badillo had cultivated among the coalition's black politicians they had to offer a black candidate as an alternative. After a series of delaying maneuvers, on February 11, 1985, two days before the coalition met to choose its candidate, Denny Farrell finally agreed to run himself. He won the coalition's support amidst charges that his candidacy was just a ploy to stop Badillo. A dozen years earlier the Jewish reformers of the

New Democratic Coalition had rejected Badillo for one of their own. Blacks had now done the same. Badillo was outraged, but saw little point in running without support. Bellamy, on the other hand, had already announced that she was in the campaign to stay. With Bellamy running for mayor Manhattan Borough President Andrew Stein announced he would run for City Council president. That in turn allowed David Dinkins to mount a campaign for the top political post in Manhattan without serious opposition.[30]

Koch could only smile as he contemplated the ineptitude of his opposition. By the end of March the coalition had split into feuding factions while the mayor's popularity was as high as ever. Farrell had no money for a campaign, little support outside of Harlem, and it became apparent he did not plan to make a serious run. Bellamy's challenge was far more energetic, but doomed as well. The mayor declared a one hundred day moratorium on political announcements and avoided any dialogue with his opponents that would only give them more exposure than they could win on their own.

At the same time, Koch put his reelection machinery into motion. He had been impressed with the impact the Jackson campaign had on the ethnic composition of Democratic party voters. Blacks had constituted seventeen percent of the vote in the 1981 Democratic primary for mayor, but as a result of the Jackson campaign's registration drive and the city's changing demography, about thirty percent in the 1984 presidential primary. The Hispanic component reached thirteen percent in 1984, also higher than it had been. Jews, who once cast as much as forty-five percent of the total vote in a Democratic primary, had fallen to about half that level. White Catholics had declined as a proportion of the party's voters as well. Koch reasoned that he knew well enough who his supporters were; making sure they went to the polls to vote was the most important measure he could take to ensure his reelection.[31]

The mayor also knew that the best way to bring out a targeted vote was not with television commercials, but with street organizing of the kind the Jackson team had used. He split his enormous reelection treasury evenly between the media and a grass roots effort, and relied heavily on the power of the incumbency to boost his public standing. He was his usual charismatic self on the campaign trail and ended up winning sixty-four percent of the Democratic primary vote. Three quarters of the Jewish voters cast ballots for Koch, as did more than three quarters of the Italians, and more than eighty percent of the Irish. Koch also took seventy percent of the Hispanic vote, creating a clear break in the minority coalition his opponents had hoped would defeat him. Predictably the mayor ran worst among blacks, but even so took almost as many black votes as Denny Farrell—a far better performance than the mayor had managed four years before. The Manhattan assemblyman simply ran no campaign to speak of and paid the price. Bellamy's effort never caught on.[32]

In the general election the mayor demolished the inconsequential opposition of Diane McGrath running on the Republican ticket and City Council president Bellamy who held the Liberal line. Koch took more than three quarters of the total vote and actually beat his 1981 landslide by a slim margin. As in the primary he ran weakest among blacks, but better than expected. Political analysts wondered if Koch's conflicts with the city's black leaders were more severe than his problems with the black population at large. If so, perhaps in his third term, with an eye on his historical legacy, the mayor would manage to temper his provocative remarks and make peace with black New Yorkers. Just maybe, many hoped, the mayor would unite the entire city yet.[33]

Betrayal

Koch's 1985 reelection lacked drama, and few of the other city government campaigns of that year offered much excitement of their own. David Dinkins's persistence paid off. He won election as borough president of Manhattan and became New York's highest ranking black municipal official. Jay Goldin won reelection to the comptroller's office and Andrew Stein won his bid to become City Council president. Howard Golden, Donald Manes, and Anthony R. Gaeta all won reelection to their borough presidencies. In the Bronx, the borough most heavily populated by Hispanics, Stanley Simon retained his presidency by holding off a spirited race by Puerto Rican assemblyman Jose Serrano. When the election results all were counted, six of the Board of Estimate's members were still Jewish men, including all three citywide office holders. They held nine of eleven votes. The Democratic county leaders of the Bronx, Queens, and Brooklyn were Jewish while Manhattan's head was black and Staten Island's Italian. At the peak of Mayor Koch's power, Jewish politicians controlled the Board of Estimate and the Democratic party almost as completely as the Irish once had. Then, within weeks, bizarre events began to change that.

Not long after Mayor Koch's triumphant third inauguration a highway patrol unit discovered Queens borough president and Democratic party leader Donald Manes weaving his car dangerously across the

Grand Central Parkway. The powerful politician had slit his own wrist. At first Manes concocted a story about a mugging, but then confessed from his hospital bed that he had tried to end his own life. Within weeks the distraught politician plunged a knife into his own chest in the kitchen of his home and died as his horrified wife and daughter tried bravely but helplessly to revive him. The politician was corrupt, and he had become despondent over the unbearable burden of the discovery of his guilt by U.S. Attorney Rudolph Giuliani. Manes's fatal decision ended the investigation into his actions. For dozens of politicians and city government workers, it was just the beginning.

In the months that followed a remarkable series of revelations left the city numb. Donald Manes, Bronx Democratic County leader Stanley Friedman, Bronx Congressman Mario Biaggi, Bronx Borough President Stanley Simon, Brooklyn's recently retired boss Meade Esposito, and a host of less well known city government officials were indicted, tried, and convicted of bribery, extortion, thievery, influence peddling, and other crimes. The arrogance of the men stunned New Yorkers. In his law office Stanley Friedman proudly hung a sign that read, "Crime does not pay . . . as well as politics." Stanley Simon extorted money from his own chauffeur. The Democratic machine that had atrophied since 1961 as a political force was still powerful enough to enrich scores of petty local politicians.[34]

As the details unfolded before Giuliani's relentless pursuit, district attorneys and federal prosecutors around the city felt compelled to investigate officials in their jurisdictions to avoid accusations of protecting the powerful. A series of trials followed. The endless reports gave New Yorkers the impression that their government was corrupt to the core. *Village Voice* journalists Jack Newfield and Wayne Barrett wrote a book entitled *City for Sale*, in which they recounted the vulgar story of the scandals in excruciating detail. Their thesis was simple: It had all happened on Ed Koch's watch. He was friends with and a political supporter of Manes and Friedman and Esposito and many of the others exposed as betraying the people they were supposed to represent. The mayor bore the final responsibility for the political climate that allowed the Democratic leaders to steal with impunity, the crusading journalists wrote.[35]

Koch felt betrayed by his cronies, but the city felt betrayed by the mayor. No one doubted that Koch had never stolen from city coffers, but few found the mayor's defense that the villains were independent of him interesting. To be sure, the main culprits held elected public or party offices that they won on their own accounts. But the mayor had maintained close relationships with the county leaders and many of the others caught up in the scandals. He had been personal friends with Donald Manes and Stanley Friedman for nearly twenty years. Koch had praised them publicly, endorsed them and their candidates, and helped them to raise money for their campaigns. He had appointed their political workers to responsible government jobs, jobs that those men then used to pilfer the city.

"If a sparrow dies of a heart attack in Central Park, I'm responsible," Koch once told a journalist in a colorful explanation of how the average citizen viewed the office he held. While the mayor did not feel personally responsible for the actions of politicians he did not control, he well knew that New Yorkers held him accountable for virtually every public event that took place within the five boroughs of the city. The mayor's fall from grace was particularly hard because of the image he had brought with him when first elected. He had been the outsider, the radical reformer, the man who had battled and defeated Tammany's Carmine DeSapio when the boss staged his political comebacks in 1963 and 1965. As a candidate, Koch had vowed to throw out Beame's clubhouse politics. As mayor he had attacked the corruption of the poverty programs with a vengeance, and he had established himself as Mr. Clean. New Yorkers close to city politics knew that Koch worked willingly with the borough's Democratic organizations. But to the average citizen the intimacy of the ties, and the ultimate consequences, shocked and offended. Being close to the "bosses" remained bad politics in New York.[36]

The scandals damaged the mayor's public standing, and they weakened him personally too. Bess Myerson found herself on trial for trying to influence a judge in a divorce case that involved a lover of hers who owned a construction company that often did business with the city. Joe DeVincenzo, a long time aide and Koch's chief patronage distributor, shred documents that he thought might embarrass the mayor. The cover-up did more harm to the mayor than the evidence that the administration took job recommendations from the county leaders. It went on and on with the mayor's confidence in some of his closest colleagues and friends shattered. At times the beleaguered chief executive had no recourse but to sit by himself in Gracie Mansion and cry. In the summer of 1985 the mayor suffered a "tiny, trivial" stroke. Many thought the unrelenting pressures of his job compounded by the weight of the scandals were proving too much for the sixty-two year old man.[37]

Other things soured as well. A series of scandals surfaced in New York's financial industry that were as startling as the revelations crippling New York's politicians. Prosecutor Giuliani's office found case upon case of insider trading and organized cheating at the most successful houses on Wall Street. Ivan Boesky, a man with a reputation as a remarkably shrewd investor turned out to be a crook. He went to trial and jail, as did Michael Milken, the celebrated creator of the "junk bond" market. Enough Wall Street bankers at enough firms turned out to have engaged in illegal activities that New Yorkers began to wonder if all of the rich and powerful men in the city were corrupt.[38]

In October 1987 the stock market crashed. The relentless upward motion of share prices that had helped carry the profits of Wall Street to dizzying heights finally broke, and a profound reassessment of the strength and direction of the city's financial industry occurred. The future looked bleak in comparison to the easy money of the past. Fragile firms rapidly collapsed while stronger ones began to lay off staff. Bonuses and salaries dropped as precipitously as market indices. Cooperative apartments and condominiums bought when salaries were pushing relentlessly upwards suddenly became unaffordable. The luxury buildings under construction no longer had eager owners waiting on line to buy them. The need for office space declined, and the city had an enormous and overpriced glut. Building stopped, construction workers lost their jobs, and real estate developers sweated as they assessed their finances. New York's upbeat mood faded, and Koch's triumphant return of the city to fiscal health began to appear ephemeral.

Lynchings and Liars

In the winter of 1986 three black New Yorkers suffered car trouble in the Howard Beach section of Queens, a white middle-class neighborhood. They left their automobile to seek help. A group of local teenagers crossed paths with the three men. Without provocation the youths beat the black men with bats and fists, and chased one onto a parkway where he was killed by a passing motorist. Racial bigotry and the vicious fear it creates appeared to be the sole motivation for the conflict that led to the death of an innocent black man and the brutal beatings of two others. Mayor Koch, likening the event to a modern day lynching, vowed that it would be punished. Police arrested the attackers, but black militants Al Sharpton, C. Vernon Mason, and Alton H. Maddox, Jr. saw a chance to use the tragedy for their own purposes.

Professional provocateurs, Sharpton, Mason, and Maddox made their careers by fanning racial flames in an effort to create heat so intense it would melt the rules of a society they believed institutionally racist. The three militants got themselves appointed advisers to the victims' families and convinced the survivors not to cooperate with Queens district attorney John Santucci. Blacks could never expect a fair trial from the "system" they claimed, and they demanded that the governor appoint a special prosecutor to try the case. Their rhetoric was inflammatory and divisive, their legal tactics obstructionist. Ultimately, Governor Cuomo negotiated the appointment of Charles J. Hynes as special prosecutor. An Irish Catholic New Yorker whose background included a stint as a special prosecutor for the state, Hynes rapidly and competently brought the assailants to justice, winning convictions and substantial prison sentences.[39]

The hot racial embers of the Howard Beach trial had not quite cooled when in December of 1987 a young black teenager named Tawana Brawley declared that she had been abducted for four days and repeatedly raped by white men, including law enforcement officials, in Dutchess County, upstate New York. It had nothing to do with New York City, but the accusations generated publicity and Sharpton, Mason, and Maddox drove north. Once again they succeeded in having themselves appointed advisers to the family. Mason and Maddox publicly accused the Dutchess county assistant district attorney of raping Brawley, and likened Attorney General Robert Abrams to Adolph Hitler. Mason declared that Abrams had masturbated over photographs of Brawley. They went on and on with their wild, unsubstantiated accusations. They once again convinced the family not to cooperate until a special prosecutor was appointed. When officials subpoenaed Tawana Brawley's mother, Glenda, the three men brought her into New York City and offered her sanctuary in a Queens church, creating a media extravaganza. The militants continued to refuse to cooperate until certain demands were met.

It was all a hoax. Tawana Brawley was a troubled teenager whose stepfather frightened her. She had played hooky from school to visit her boyfriend in prison and feared she would be severely punished if her stepfather found out. She had stayed away from home to avoid confronting what she had done and her stepfather's wrath, and invented a story upon her return to hide the truth. The advisers had known it almost from the start but to them it did not matter. They played on and exacerbated the racial tensions of the city because it suited them temperamentally and philosophically, and because they made their living at it.[40]

Jews Would Have To Be Crazy . . .

By 1988 racial tensions in New York were as bad as they had ever been, and presidential politics brought the Democratic contenders to town. The field of significant candidates had narrowed to three by April when New York State Democrats went to the polls to vote for Michael Dukakis, Jesse Jackson, or Albert Gore. Dukakis was clearly the leader by then, but as in 1984 Jesse Jackson's campaign sparked the hopes of the country's racial minorities. In 1984 a number of New York's black leaders had backed Walter Mondale over Jackson, but by 1988 Jackson's candidacy had become a litmus test of racial loyalty among black politicians. All of New York's senior black political spokesmen, and most of the Puerto Ricans as well, strongly supported Jackson. Many of the city's largest labor unions, heavily populated by blacks and Hispanics, also endorsed Jackson and mobilized their members on his behalf.

The shadow of Jesse Jackson's links to anti-Semites followed the black man as he campaigned around the city that was home to more Jews than any other in the nation. At one point a journalist asked Koch about Jackson's support among Jewish voters. "Jews and other supporters of Israel would have to be crazy to vote for Jackson," the mayor responded in his typical blunt style. The comment enraged blacks and offended Jews. The former took it as more evidence of what they viewed as Ed Koch's racist politics. The latter objected to Koch giving them instructions as if they had to vote the way he said. Most New Yorkers found the comment egregiously antagonistic in a city already struggling to maintain racial harmony.[41]

Koch endorsed Tennessee Senator Albert Gore, and on primary day Gore won only eleven percent of the vote in New York City. Jackson won a stunning forty-five percent within the five boroughs, a razor slim plurality over the leading Democrat, Michael Dukakis, who ran much stronger upstate and won the primary. City politicians found the results telling. A black candidate, supported by a solid coalition of black and Hispanic politicians, with strong help from organized labor, won a citywide vote. More than nine blacks out of ten voted for Jackson; more than sixty percent of Hispanic voters cast ballots for him, and a small but crucial number of white liberals completed his coalition. If it could be duplicated in a race for mayor, Koch could be defeated.[42]

TWELVE

A City in Search of Harmony

1989

Not long after Jesse Jackson left town New York politicians began talking about David Dinkins. As the borough president of Manhattan he was New York's senior black elected official and he possessed three attributes that made him particularly attractive to a disparate group of politicians looking for a black candidate to back for mayor in 1989. As the product of a political clubhouse he could be counted on to reward his supporters. He had a low-key and courteous style that contrasted sharply with Koch's confrontational bluster in a city searching for harmony. And while he had an unblemished record of supporting minority causes, he did not practice the kind of protest politics that scared white voters away from minority candidates. To the contrary, throughout his career Dinkins had been a steady supporter of Israel, and had been one of the few black politicians to condemn anti-Semitic remarks emanating from the likes of Louis Farrakhan. Dinkins could appeal to Jewish liberals in a way few other black politicians in New York could, and therefore had the potential to hold together a coalition to defeat Koch.[1]

The Challengers

David Dinkins's career was a study in the slow, predictable rise a competent soldier of a political machine could achieve. He was born in Trenton, New Jersey in 1925, where his father owned a barber shop and would later develop a successful real-estate business. As a seventeen-year-old high school graduate Dinkins tried several times to enlist in the Marines, but the quota for "Negro" recruits was filled. Finally an opening occurred, but by the time he finished boot camp World War II had ended, and instead of going to war Dinkins went off to college at Howard University in Washington, D.C. He graduated with honors in mathematics in 1950, and after trying his hand at a few jobs, earned a degree from Brooklyn Law School in 1956 and became an attorney.

By then Dinkins had married Joyce Burrows, the daughter of a Harlem assemblyman, and like so many young lawyers he discovered that political activity helped his practice. He joined J. Raymond Jones's Carver Democratic Club and became a loyal worker, then a captain. In 1965 Jones tapped Dinkins to run for the New York State Assembly. He served one year before reapportionment eliminated his district, and in 1967 he became a Democratic district leader, a post he held for the next twenty years. In 1970 he became counsel to the Board of Elections, a part-time position that allowed him to continue to practice law, and in 1972 received a seat on that board, and was named president by the other members. Many assumed that Percy Sutton, Manhattan borough president at the time and a close friend and colleague of Dinkins, had arranged the appointments. Dinkins soon left the tedious job, but newly elected mayor Abraham Beame, indebted to Percy Sutton and the Harlem gang for their support in 1973, offered Dinkins a post as deputy mayor.

A routine investigation into the nominee's background revealed he had failed to file federal, state and city income taxes for four years. Dinkins's only explanation was, "I was busy taking care of other people's business," and never got around to it. The embarrassing revelation forced him to withdraw his name from consideration. Two years later, with Dinkins's back taxes paid, Beame appointed the Harlemite to the office of city clerk, a position responsible principally for processing marriage licenses. Dinkins held the job for the next decade, all the while continuing to pursue elected office. His two unsuccessful bids for Manhattan borough president kept him in the public eye in 1977 and 1981, and he finally won election to the post in 1985.[2]

As early as May 1988 political analysts saw Dinkins as the favorite to challenge and to defeat Koch. With typical caution the potential candidate kept his own counsel publicly, but his backers created a committee, raised money, and in October 1988 commissioned a poll. It showed that the groups most dissatisfied with Koch were the ones that Dinkins appealed to most strongly. In a head to head race with the mayor in a Democratic primary, a coalition composed of black voters, a substantial majority of Hispanics, and a small but crucial number of liberal whites out of sorts with the mayor could deliver the nomination to Dinkins.

Minorities across the city, intent on ousting Koch, quietly traveled to Dinkins's office in Manhattan to pledge their support. A second poll taken in January 1989 reconfirmed the October findings. By then Dinkins's support among black and Hispanic politicians was virtually complete. On February 15, 1989 Dinkins announced his candidacy. "I am running [for mayor] because our city has become sharply polarized. We need a mayor who can transcend differences so we can work together to solve our problems," he said. He referred to New York as a "gorgeous mosaic" of peoples, each one contributing something unique to the quality and character of the city, each one worthy of respect.[3]

Dinkins's announcement knocked out several potential candidates. Shirley Chisolm, a black woman and a former congressional representative from Brooklyn had contemplated running, but rapidly changed her mind. Upper West Side councilwoman Ruth Messinger was a favorite of many New York liberals. Her name had floated briefly as a possible anti-Koch candidate, but her appeal was too limited for a citywide race. She opted to run for Manhattan borough president instead. Charles J. Hynes had considered a mayoral campaign as well. An Irish Catholic who had served as a special prosecutor, he could easily represent the city's white middle-class so concerned with law and order. At the same time, he held moderately liberal views on social issues and his sure-footed handling of the Howard Beach case earned him unusual credibility with minorities. A brief stint as the city's Fire Commissioner added administrative experience to his credentials. Against Koch, Hynes was likely to win black votes overwhelmingly while cutting heavily into the mayor's Catholic support. Against Dinkins, Hynes's standing with minorities would melt. He decided to run for district attorney of Brooklyn instead. Some political analysts speculated that City Council president Andrew Stein might seek the mayoralty in 1989, but ultimately he decided to hang on to the safety of the office he held.[4]

Harrison J. Goldin decided he would run for mayor. For sixteen years the city's comptroller, he viewed himself as exceptionally well qualified to manage city government affairs, and in 1989 he saw a chance to replace Koch as the candidate of the white middle class. These voters still wanted someone who shared their priorities, Goldin reasoned, but one who spoke to the city's people in gentler tones than the three-term incumbent. He thought of himself as the right man for the times.[5]

New York businessman Richard Ravitch also decided to run for mayor. A native New York City Jew who grew up in East Harlem, Ravitch graduated from Columbia University and then Yale Law School. He made a fortune building housing in New York City, and participated in a variety of civic organizations where he often crossed paths with politicians and government officials. A committed Democrat who typically supported the party's candidates for national office, Ravitch had steered clear of local politics to avoid the appearance of conflict of interest with his construction firm. Then, in 1978, Governor Carey called on him to rescue the New York State Urban Development Corporation from failure. Ravitch accepted the challenge, succeeded at the task, and was then named by the governor to head the Metropolitan Transportation Authority. Once again Ravitch successfully oversaw the renewal of a struggling public agency. Mayor Koch was impressed enough with Ravitch that in 1986 he asked him to head a commission to update and revise the City Charter. Labor leaders who had worked with Ravitch, politicians who had relied on him to solve complicated problems, public minded peers who respected his ability, all urged him to run for mayor because they thought him an exceptional manager of public agencies. Many agreed that he would make the best mayor, but just as many doubted that he would be a viable candidate against a team of seasoned political professionals.[6]

The Republicans too had a Jewish businessman candidate, but one far less familiar with city government than Dick Ravitch. Ronald Lauder, scion of the Estée Lauder cosmetics fortune and a Republican party stalwart who served briefly under Ronald Reagan as ambassador to Austria, decided to run for mayor. He had no qualifications at all for the job. His candidacy was the outgrowth of a political battle between United States Senator Alfonse D'Amato and federal prosecutor Rudolph Giuliani.[7]

D'Amato was New York State's senior Republican official and he guarded his status jealously. A machine politician who built his career through loyal service to the powerful Nassau county GOP machine, D'Amato practiced his trade like the gruff local party hack he was rather than as a high minded U.S. Senator. Credible if unproven accusations of corruption cast shadows over his reputation. Giuliani was also a Republican. He had converted to the GOP in 1980 after youthful flirtations with the Democratic party, and while Giuliani had political ambitions of his own, he was a very different sort than D'Amato. Almost inevitably the two men ended up at odds.

Giuliani was born in Brooklyn to parents of Italian descent. His father was a hardworking plumber and tavern owner and his mother a believer in the strength of tradition. They instilled strong Catholic values in their only child. The first member of his family to get a higher education, Giuliani won an academic scholarship to Manhattan College. For a time the young man contemplated joining the priesthood, but at the age of twenty decided against a vocation that required celibacy. After college he went on to New York University Law School and then on to a legal career. He joined the office of United States Attorney Whitney North Seymour, became chief of the anti-corruption unit and established a reputation as an ambitious, hardworking and capable prosecutor. Giuliani spent a few years in a private law practice until in 1981 Attorney General William French Smith offered him a high ranking job in the Justice Department in Washington. Two years later, in 1983, Smith appointed Giuliani U.S. Attorney for New York, an office that gave him the power and autonomy to pursue the cases he chose.

The ambitious man rapidly built an impressive prosecutorial record. The political corruption trials, the Wall Street scandals, and hard hitting investigations into organized crime made the U.S. attorney a media star. A constant barrage of publicity attended the arrests, indictments and convictions of some of New York City's most powerful men. The public perceived Giuliani as a bold and relentless champion of justice who took on anyone who broke the law without fear or favor. Journalists and politicians noticed that the prosecutor sought out and enjoyed the attention he received. Some said he chose his high profile targets with the potential for publicity foremost in mind, and speculated that he planned to seek elective office and a broader forum for his crusading zeal.[8]

Initially, Giuliani and Senator D'Amato made common cause in New York. One night, in search of headlines, the two Republicans accompanied drug enforcement agents on an undercover bust. D'Amato wore the uniform of a United Parcel Service worker, Giuliani dressed like a Hell's Angels bike rider. They claimed unconvincingly that their quest for photo opportunities was meant to dramatize the ease with which drugs could be bought on city streets. One indignant FBI agent commented off the record that the next time the two wanted attention they should dress in Bozo the Clown outfits, but celebrity status and a law-and-order image suited both men.[9]

In 1988 D'Amato wanted Giuliani to challenge New York's veteran Democratic Senator, Daniel Patrick Moynihan. The Republicans, however, were not likely to defeat the twelve-year incumbent whose reputation as one of Washington's brainiest politicians on complex matters of national importance made him a formidable opponent. Still, as his party's leader, D'Amato wanted the Republicans to wage a respectable race and Giuliani was the strongest potential contender. With several important investigations at critical stages, and the prospects for victory slim, Giuliani declined to leave the U.S. attorney's office. The timing of Giuliani's decision left D'Amato without a serious candidate and feeling burned. More important, the discussions between D'Amato and Giuliani revealed a brewing conflict.

As the senior Senator belonging to the President's party, tradition gave D'Amato a strong say in the selection of a U.S. attorney in his state. Had Giuliani run for Moynihan's seat D'Amato would have played a role in choosing his successor. Rumors circulated that he planned to propose someone who would not pursue the cases against Wall Street's bankers because the firms involved raised large sums of money for D'Amato's political campaigns. Giuliani wanted to be certain that his successor would continue to pursue investigations underway. As 1989 arrived, and Giuliani contemplated a race for mayor, the conflict over his replacement became severe.[10]

Giuliani was popular, and in a climate of corruption and rising crime who better to run against a tainted mayor than a prosecutor? He was clearly the most attractive Republican candidate, and hoped to win the Liberal party endorsement as well. Neither Dinkins nor Koch had close ties to Liberal party leader Ray Harding, and neither Goldin nor Ravitch could match Giuliani's standing in the polls. Harding was a political pragmatist who consolidated his control as party boss after a bitter fight with the remnants of the philosophically motivated core of the organization. His practice was to deliver the party's backing to whichever candidate had the best chance to win and to give the Liberals the best political reward. Giuliani appeared to fit the criteria, and the federal prosecutor also thought he had a good chance to win the backing of the Conservative party. That would give him three lines on the ballot.

Giuliani's posture threatened D'Amato. If the prosecutor succeeded in naming his own replacement it would be a blow to the Senator's prestige, and if he won election as mayor he would have an independent base of support with far more patronage power than D'Amato. Giuliani would become New York's top Republican. To throw nails in his rival's path D'Amato convinced Ronald Lauder to run for the Republican nomination for mayor. The candidacy would ensure a GOP primary and a chance to damage the prosecutor's image. Why Lauder did it is hard to discern. He had no background in urban affairs, or elected office, and he was not even from New York City. To the amusement of political professionals, on January 4, 1989, he announced his candidacy for the New York City mayoralty standing on the steps of the state legislature in Albany. "At least the announcement wasn't made in Vienna," Ray Harding commented. Lauder clearly was no match for Rudolph Giuliani, but he had personal assets in excess of $300 million with which to wage a campaign designed to expose Giuliani's weaknesses.[11]

Within days after Lauder's announcement Giuliani declared that he was leaving his post as U.S. attorney. His interim replacement, Benito Romano, was an experienced and competent prosecutor who had worked for Giuliani and who intended to pursue vigorously the corruption cases in progress. When asked if he would run for mayor Giuliani replied, "I have not ruled out that option." He took a position with a private law firm, and soon began campaigning.[12]

Koch the Underdog

By January 1989 Ed Koch's private polls showed that only a hard core of about seventeen percent of the city wanted him to be mayor again. That was even lower than John Lindsay's rating twenty years before, and as low as Koch's had ever been. Public polls revealed that barely one New Yorker in three approved of the way he was handling his job, compared to nearly three quarters of the city's residents at the height of his popularity. Worse, more than half of the city now disapproved of Koch compared to barely one New Yorker in five in January of 1985 when his last reelection campaign had begun. Several close friends thought he should not seek reelection at all and instead exit gracefully from City Hall.[13]

Koch never really considered not running. "I was too proud to put my tail between my legs and get driven from office," he would later say. "And I knew that things were going to get very bad, and I didn't want whoever took over to be able to say that I made a mess and left.

[By going] to the mat to hold onto power myself, they could never say that by the time they got it it wasn't worth anything." For Koch, this last point was especially important if the city elected a black mayor. He was determined not to be the scapegoat of minority politicians.

A formal announcement would not come for months, but Koch made it clear he would run and he adopted a strategy. With the city headed for a new round of fiscal crises, the mayor reasoned, New Yorkers would want the most capable man available in City Hall. With a dozen years experience, having rescued the city from crisis once before, Koch obviously fit that description. He would emphasize the point in his daily activities as mayor.[14]

Koch was clearly the underdog against Dinkins in the Democratic primary and against Giuliani in the general election as well. Despite the powers of incumbency the mayor's ability to mount a field operation was weaker than it had been in 1985. The Democratic party in Staten Island agreed to support him, but it was the smallest of the city's county organizations. The corruption scandals had created a fissure between Koch and the Democrats in Queens, where the new county leader, Congressman Thomas Manton, was just consolidating his power. The Queens organization endorsed Dick Ravitch in May. In Brooklyn, Borough President Howard Golden had replaced Meade Esposito as county leader. Golden and Koch had feuded publicly over Board of Estimate decisions and become bitter enemies. Golden threw his support to Comptroller Harrison Goldin, while many of his borough's district leaders, particularly those representing minority neighborhoods, backed Dinkins. Bronx County leader George Friedman added up the number of minority voters in his borough and decided that supporting Dinkins was the only safe decision he could make. Dinkins's home base in Manhattan rallied to his cause as well.[15]

Municipal unions were a second important source of potential campaign workers. Koch, of course, had battled most of them from the very start of his administration. Moreover, the shifts that had taken place in New York's population during his twelve years in office created a city workforce with more minorities than ever before. To a large degree the membership of the municipal unions reflected the change. By 1989 the heads of some of the most important labor organizations were minorities loyal to David Dinkins. Stanley Hill, a black man who succeeded Victor Gotbaum as president of District Council 37, the largest union in the city, announced his organization's support for Dinkins. Other unions had white leaders at serious odds with Koch over policies and tactics and the tone of the mayor's administration. And with so many blacks and

Hispanics among their rank and file the leaders could not prudently back a politician who had developed a reputation among minorities as a bigot. Teamster leader Barry Feinstein had endorsed Jesse Jackson in 1988 and answered back to Koch's dictum to Jews not to vote for the man, saying: "I'm as Jewish as anyone who ever lived, and I'm supporting Jackson." In 1989 he supported Dinkins. So did almost all of the city's major unions. After more than a decade out in the cold, municipal labor leaders saw David Dinkins as a chance to restore their influence over city policies that affected their wages and working conditions. The combined support of unions and the better part of the regular Democrats gave Dinkins the best field organization by far among the candidates.[16]

The Democratic primary turned into a contest between two coalitions. Dinkins was the candidate of the city's minorities and most liberal voters. Koch, Goldin, and Ravitch were Jewish candidates running on the claim of competence with their greatest appeal among the white middle-class. By July, when the candidates filed sufficient nominating petitions to secure ballot lines, it had already become clear that Comptroller Jay Goldin's campaign was losing momentum. Similarly, Dick Ravitch could claim only a sliver of support. Each man earned only single digits when newspapers took polls to gauge their standing. The battle for the Democratic nomination would be between Dinkins and Koch, and Koch's ratings, while low, had stabilized and begun to turn. Because his field operation was weak, Koch's campaign resorted to television ads earlier than usual. They emphasized that his competence was much more important than his style. "You don't like how he says it, but you like what he says," was Koch's description of the theme.[17]

The mayor knew blacks would not vote for him over Dinkins so he sought instead the backing of Jews, Catholics, and Hispanics. Among Jews, Koch campaigned as one of their own. He traveled to synagogues and Jewish community centers around the city and sought support from rabbis. A group of seventy orthodox organizations brought together in a Unity Coalition endorsed the mayor after he spoke to them at a candidates' forum in Borough Park, Brooklyn. Wealthier Jews from Manhattan, Riverdale, and Forest Hills—areas partially isolated from the poorer neighborhoods that often served as crucibles of racial fears— supported the mayor more tepidly. Koch campaigned actively in those areas in an effort to regain the confidence of the voters who lived there.

The mayor had fence mending to do with the Irish. In the past they had supported him strongly, but in one of the many political gaffes of his third term he praised the policies of British Prime Minister Margaret

Thatcher in Ireland. In response to the criticism that followed he retracted the statement, and throughout the campaign emphasized his past support for the Irish people and their causes, as well as the personal values he shared with them. He pitched his conservative values and sense of fiscal responsibility to Italian voters as well.[18]

Koch also sought favor among Hispanic voters who had backed him in past elections. Yet, the loyalty of Hispanic voters in a contest against David Dinkins was very uncertain because of competing visions of what Hispanics wanted from a candidate. On the one hand, many felt oppressed and believed they lived in a society that discriminated against them. For these voters a black man who could sympathize with their plight was more likely to give them a fair hearing than a white man who did not share their experience. Puerto Ricans in particular, the largest segment of the Hispanic population and its poorest, held this view strongly. On the other hand, traditional Catholic values and respect for the established order played an important role in the lives of many Hispanics, particularly Central American and South American immigrants. Koch appealed to these sentiments more strongly than Dinkins, and emphasized it in his Spanish-language communications.[19]

Not surprisingly, Dinkins's campaign was the mirror image of Koch's. Bill Lynch, Dinkins's chief aide, built an extensive field operation of ten thousand volunteers drawn from the city's political clubs and labor unions. Their role was to bring out the vote in black and Puerto Rican districts. In an effort to attract white liberals, particularly Jews, to their coalition, Dinkins's team aired television commercials that reinforced their candidate's image as a man who would bring harmony to the racially divided city. For the most part the campaign accepted the votes of white Catholics as lost.[20]

The Republican primary was on the one hand high farce and on the other serious drama. Ronald Lauder spent millions of dollars to hire an all-star team of Republican political consultants who then tripped over each other to tell him what to do, and who charged him a lot of money for the privilege. No message emerged; no image developed. The man became a laughing-stock. To some it looked like Alfonse D'Amato was using Lauder's checkbook to enrich his favorite advisers with the candidate's interests of secondary concern. D'Amato did deliver the Conservative party ballot line to his candidate in what would be Lauder's only success.[21]

Giuliani's victory in the Republican primary was never in doubt, but even so he paid a political price. Lauder's staff revealed that the law firm Giuliani joined after leaving his post as U.S. attorney had represented a Panamanian government agency during the regime of General Manuel Noriega. Associating the former prosecutor with a drug running dictator whom the United States would later oust from power by force hit at the center of Giuliani's reputation. It was a cheap shot to be sure, but typical of political campaigns. Giuliani, while media-wise, had no experience with the rough-and-tumble side of politics. He was simply unable to silence the charge.

Then the Supreme Court dented the *Roe vs. Wade* abortion decision by expanding the power of state governments to forbid women to terminate pregnancies. The other candidates immediately declared their support for a woman's right to choose. Giuliani waffled. He said he opposed abortion, but would obey the law. That did not answer the question of whether he favored a change in the state's statutes now that the court allowed it. Finally he declared he did not. The press made much of Giuliani's lack of conviction.

The former prosecutor's candidacy got a strong boost when Liberal party chief Ray Harding endorsed him. The boss's backing was tantamount to winning the Liberal ballot line. Then, to everyone's surprise, Donald Harrington, the former Liberal party chairman from whom Harding had wrested power, declared he would challenge Giuliani for the party's nomination in a primary. It was a last ditch effort by Harrington to punish Harding for taking over the party. After a brief flurry of activity the seventy-seven year old Harrington withdrew. Only modest publicity surrounded the episode, but it highlighted the Liberal party's lack of philosophical content with Harding at the helm.

Shortly after the controversy over abortion a *Daily News* poll asked voters how they would cast their ballots if Giuliani faced Dinkins in a November general election. It revealed that the former prosecutor's position among Jews had dropped seventeen percent compared to six months before, and his overall standing was a little bit softer among almost all groups. Giuliani remained formidable to be sure, but as a prosecutor he had developed an aura of invincibility. The primaries shattered that. He had become a candidate like all the rest.[22]

The Politics of Racial Murder

During the primaries the candidates skirted delicately around the issue of race. None wanted to exacerbate the tensions in the city, and none wanted to bear the political burden of running a nasty campaign against the first black candidate with a serious chance of becoming mayor.

Besides, Dinkins's political strength rested in part on his call for harmony, and his opponents understood that hostile rhetoric would simply make him stronger. Two episodes that under other circumstances might have hurt Dinkins, instead helped him.

On an April night, when the campaign was still in its early stages, a gang of young black teenagers went on a "wilding spree" in Central Park. After harassing a number of passers-by just for "kicks," they came across a young white woman jogging alone. They raped her repeatedly and beat her within a breath of her life with their fists and a pipe. Almost miraculously the strong willed woman, a vice president at a prominent investment bank, survived. The police caught the youths and brought them to the local precinct for booking where, in the presence of reporters, the young men joked uncaringly about their crime. Newspaper accounts of the event horrified the city. It was as if the youths did not understand that what they had shattered was a human being. It was the sort of event that boiled fear and rage into voters' blood.

David Dinkins responded rapidly by denouncing the band as "urban terrorists" and by talking with obvious sincerity about his concern for his own daughter's safety. His posture boosted his reputation as a man who would be able to respond to the deeply felt resentments that fueled minority hostility, but who also understood the importance of enforcing the law. "I'll be the toughest mayor on crime this city ever had," he declared in the neighborhoods where he campaigned. His staff and volunteers distributed pamphlets that called for enactment of an "anti-wilding" law. Dinkins's rhetoric seemed to offer a combination of social programs and police that appealed to many New Yorkers more than the blunt call for punishment that the other candidates mustered.[23]

The second event occurred in late August, just a few weeks before the primary. A sixteen-year-old black Brooklyn youth named Yusuf Hawkins traveled a few miles from East New York, where he lived, to Bensonhurst to look at a used car advertised in that day's newspaper. He crossed the path of some white teenagers who mistook him for a black man who had dated a white woman in their neighborhood. Without provocation the white men shot him to death. In the days that followed Al Sharpton and other militants marched in protest in Bensonhurst provoking vicious hostility from local residents that the media captured live on television. The name calling and spitting, the vulgarity and hideous gestures, once again brought the potential for racial calamity to the fore. The image burned sharply in people's minds as they went to the polls on September 12, 1989 to vote for candidates for mayor.[24]

In an unequivocal victory David Dinkins won fifty-one percent of the vote in the Democratic primary. Ed Koch took forty-two percent, Richard Ravitch just four percent and Jay Goldin three percent. For the first time in history the Democratic party in New York had chosen a black candidate for mayor. Dinkins's support from the city's blacks was virtually complete. Ninety-three percent cast their ballots for him. He won nearly seven Hispanic votes of ten, and thirty percent of white votes. New York's few white Protestants split their ballots equally between Koch and Dinkins. Three white Catholics in ten voted for Dinkins, and just under a quarter of the city's Jews voted for him as well.

Koch won more than sixty percent of white votes, with Ravitch and Goldin splitting about ten percent between them. Catholics cast sixty-three percent of their ballots and Jews sixty-eight percent for the three-term incumbent. The decline in support these groups gave Koch in comparison to his previous bids for reelection was significant. In 1981 and 1985 Koch had won more than three quarters of Catholic and Jewish votes. But the defections went to Ravitch and Goldin, not Dinkins. When the few percentage points won by those two candidates are added to Koch's totals, the decline in the white vote going to Jewish candidates campaigning on a claim of competence was modest indeed. The white voters who cast ballots for Dinkins in the Democratic primary were a hard core of liberals who almost certainly had voted against Koch in the past. The more important shift by far was the decline in support for Koch among Hispanics. Fewer than thirty percent of this group cast their ballots for the mayor, compared to seventy percent four years earlier. Koch ran somewhat better in non-Puerto Rican neighborhoods than in Puerto Rican ones, but suffered a precipitous decline overall.[25]

Dinkins's success with Hispanic voters, and the changed composition of the city's population, were at the root of his victory. The year after Koch's 1977 election a census bureau survey identified nearly fifty-five percent of New Yorkers as white, twenty-three percent as black, and fewer than sixteen percent as Hispanic. By 1987 a similar survey showed the proportion of whites had dropped to forty-six percent, the number of blacks had risen modestly to twenty-four percent, and the number of Hispanics had grown to more than twenty-three percent. Asians and others made up the difference. In short, the number of racial minorities exceeded the number of whites.

Virtually all blacks and Hispanics who registered to vote in New York City did so as members of the Democratic party. Whites split their affiliations between the Democratic and Republican organizations. Almost all of New York's Liberal and Conservative party members were white as well. This diluted the strength of white voters in a Democratic primary. A Democrat who could keep together a minority coalition was bound to beat a white candidate in a primary election. With the black vote firmly in his camp on the basis of ethnic pride, the key to Dinkins's Democratic primary success was the strong support he had received from Hispanic voters. When asked by pollsters why they cast ballots for David Dinkins, fully a third of Hispanics replied "because he cares about people like me." Koch, a white candidate appealing to Hispanic respect for tradition and authority, could not maintain his strength with the group against Dinkins, a black candidate who spoke for the city's disfranchised and who was endorsed by the city's leading Hispanic politicians.[26]

The Jewish Vote and Victory

Koch conceded defeat graciously. He declared Dinkins had run a clean campaign that beat him "fairly and squarely and by a large margin." He went on to announce that he was ready to "help David Dinkins become mayor," and to say that the city would overcome all of its problems, because "whites and blacks and Hispanics and Asians want a common, good life for all of us. And that desire and the need to root out the bigots in our society and to uplift the poor, that common agenda is what the next mayor, David Dinkins, will seek to implement." The next day, the four Democratic candidates stood on the steps of City Hall and with hands clasped together and raised high over their heads pledged to work together to win the general election in November against Rudolph Giuliani running on the Republican and Liberal lines.[27]

Dinkins appeared poised for an easy victory. He held the Democratic nomination in a city where five voters out of six were Democrats. His standing among blacks and Hispanics was solid. And despite a tough primary against three Jewish opponents, when asked on primary day who they would favor in the general election, Jewish voters who responded chose Dinkins over Giuliani by a margin of five to three. The Italian former prosecutor had won the Republican primary in a landslide, and he held the confidence of a majority of white Catholic voters. Typically more Catholics voted in the general election than in the primary, so he could expect a boost from their increased numbers. But even so, one analyst determined that if the Republican/Liberal won the votes of every Democrat who cast a ballot for Koch, when added to the total number of votes cast in the Republican primary, Giuliani would lose a general election to Dinkins by a little bit. Polls taken in the weeks following Dinkins's impressive primary victory showed the Democrat headed for City Hall in a landslide.[28]

Ronald Lauder remained on the ballot on the Conservative line, and the Right to Life party had a candidate on the ballot as well, but neither one was consequential. Giuliani would effectively face Dinkins in a head to head race. His campaign team knew it was hopeless to try to win black votes away from the first black Democratic candidate for mayor, so they had to try to eat into his support among whites and Hispanics. It would not be easy.[29]

To gain maximum advantage from his supporters and maintain the momentum of his campaign, Giuliani played to his strengths. The Police Department's Columbia Association of Italian officers endorsed him reemphasizing his law-and-order image. The candidate marched in the Columbus Day parade giving his fellow Italians a chance to cheer him heavily before TV cameras. President George Bush announced his support for the Republican candidate and implied Washington would work with New York City more effectively with a GOP mayor in office. Senator D'Amato ostensibly buried the hatchet with his rival, creating an aura of party unity; in practice, however, the Senator did little to help the campaign.[30]

Giuliani's campaign team gave special attention to Jewish voters. On the one hand, New York's Jews traditionally voted for Democrats. On the other, they were white and subject to the same racial fears as other whites in the city. In some ways the relationship between blacks and Jews was more complicated and subtle than the relationship between blacks and other whites. The mutual resentment between the two groups offered levers that a skillful politician could use to try and pry Jewish voters away from a black candidate.[31]

In one effort to appeal to Jews Giuliani's advisers invited Jackie Mason, New York's quintessential Jewish comedian, to join the campaign as an unofficial ambassador to the Jewish community. The entertainer was then enjoying tremendous popularity with a one-man show on Broadway in which he poked fun at the ethnic differences of all the city's people. The routine left his audiences in stitches. At first the celebrity attracted attention in a way that helped Giuliani. Then, in a long interview published in the *Village Voice*, Mason seemed to take his schtick seriously. "There is a sick Jewish problem of voting for a black man no matter how unfit he is for the job," the comedian philosophized. "They feel guilty for the black predicament as if the Jews caused it. . . . The Jews are constantly giving millions to the black people. Have you ever heard of a black person giving a quarter to a Jew?" He went on to declare Dinkins incompetent and insulted him personally. The uproar that ensued the day the weekly newspaper appeared on the stands was impressive. Mason resigned from Giuliani's campaign while the candidate announced, "the remarks do not reflect my views."[32]

Next Giuliani tried to scare Jewish voters away from his adversary by linking Dinkins to Jesse Jackson. He ran ads in a Yiddish weekly newspaper, *The Algemeiner Journal*, showing a picture of the two black men with their hands clasped together. Dinkins, the advertisement read, is a "Jesse Jackson Democrat." This appeal backfired too. A *Newsday* editorial implied that Giuliani had made "a sly appeal that exploits Jewish fears," and urged him to steer his campaign clear of "ugly low-road pitches." The *Jewish Daily Forward*, the city's largest Yiddish newspaper, responded by endorsing Dinkins. Their editorial pointed out that Dinkins had been "among the first to criticize his friend, the Rev. Jesse Jackson, when the latter characterized New York City as 'Hymie-town,' and he has consistently condemned Minister Louis Farrakhan for his anti-Semitic utterances." Democrats around the city denounced what one called Giuliani's "desperation game to get Jewish votes."[33]

Dinkins's campaign staff understood their candidate's potential vulnerability among Jewish Democrats and sought to anchor their support. Dinkins asked Koch and the other former Democratic contenders to campaign for him in Jewish communities. New York's senior Democratic politicians, prominent Jews among them, announced their support for Dinkins, as did most of the city's Jewish organizations. On just one well orchestrated day, in the morning Dinkins received "a double portion" of good luck from the Rabbi Menachem Mendel Schneerson, leader of Brooklyn's Lubavitcher Hasidic sect, and in the afternoon the endorsement of more than three dozen rabbis and Jewish lay leaders in the Pelham Parkway section of the Bronx.[34]

The Dinkins campaign hosted a kosher breakfast for 1,300 Jewish leaders to allow them to see the candidate for themselves. Aides passed out Hebrew "Dinkins for Mayor" buttons. The black candidate reaffirmed his unswerving support for Israel, reminded the crowd assembled that he had opposed the "Zionism is racism" resolution the United Nations had passed, and announced to the strongest applause of the day that "I am proud that in 1985 I denounced the anti-Semitic remarks of

Louis Farrakhan." Ed Koch rose to the podium to praise Dinkins for having denounced anti-Semitism his entire adult life. Abe Beame too spoke for Dinkins. "You know, when I first ran, there were people who worried I'd be a mayor for the Jews instead of a mayor for all the people. Now there are people who say Dave Dinkins will be mayor for black people. But I think I was a mayor for everybody, and Dave Dinkins will be a mayor for everyone too."[35]

In early October, with just a month to go before the election, Dinkins's standing with Jews remained strong. Almost half planned to vote for him, compared to a little over a third for Giuliani. The rest were undecided. It was a comfortable lead. But a few days before the breakfast with Jewish leaders took place the momentum began to change.[36]

Jitu Weusi was an unpaid adviser to Dinkins's campaign staff. Although his name had changed from Leslie Cambell, he was the man who at the time of the 1968 school strike read over the radio a viciously anti-Semitic poem scornfully dedicated to UFT president Albert Shanker. During the primary Weusi had helped to bring voters in Brooklyn neighborhoods to the polls, and he continued to work on behalf of Dinkins as the general election approached. The Giuliani campaign denounced the association and newspapers printed reminders of how nasty the verse he once broadcast had been. "How can you be sure who will work in a Dinkins's administration?" Giuliani's aides asked reporters in a question meant to raise fears in Jewish minds. Weusi denied he was an anti-Semite, but resigned from Dinkins's team. The candidate distanced himself from the unhelpful connection, but found himself forced to meet with Jewish leaders to explain the relationship.[37]

Then, reporters reviewing Dinkins's election finance filings, discovered that in August campaign chairman Bill Lynch had ordered almost ten thousand dollars worth of payments to Sonny Carson, a black militant from Brooklyn. Like Weusi, Carson had a fierce reputation for anti-Semitism dating back over twenty years to the school strike. The man was also a convicted kidnapper and an attempted murderer. As details of the payments emerged, it became apparent that after Yusuf Hawkins's killing in August, Carson had led hostile street protests in Bensonhurst. Dinkins's campaign staff had feared that an eruption of racial violence would scare white voters away from their candidate. The checks were "hush money" paid to buy peace. In an effort to hide the purpose the funds were channeled quietly through a phony organization called the Committee to Honor Black Heroes.[38]

The Giuliani team ran a campaign commercial that pointed out that the same David Dinkins who had failed to file income taxes "has paid a convicted kidnapper through a phony organization with no members, no receipts and no office," to work on his campaign. It was not lost on listeners that the man whose election staff had done that was asking for the power to control the city's finances. It was not lost on Jewish voters that the convicted kidnapper was a Jew hater. Carson did little to defuse the issue when he called a press conference to declare that he did not hate Jews in particular, but rather was anti-white. "Don't limit my anti-ing to just being one little group of people. I think you'd insult me if you tried to do that," the militant with enough hatred to go around told reporters.

Dinkins released a statement condemning the man. "Sonny Carson's comments represent the kind of bigotry and intolerance I utterly reject and have fought against my whole life. Had such comments come to my attention he would never have played any role in my campaign," the candidate declared. But the man had played a role, and a well paid one at that. And the same day that Giuliani's ads condemning Dinkins's connections to Carson began to appear, the former prosecutor's election team broke the stock sale scandal.[39]

In 1985 Dinkins bought a number of shares in Percy Sutton's Inner City Broadcasting Company. The corporation held lucrative cable TV franchises that astute New Yorkers knew were distributed by the city, typically on the basis of political connections. Dinkins initially reported that before assuming his position on the Board of Estimate as Manhattan borough president, he had given the stock to his son as a gift to avoid the potential for conflict of interest. But the candidate had filed no gift tax form as required. Dinkins then changed the story. He had not given the stock to his son, he now said, but had sold it to him for $58,000, so no gift tax filing was needed. Later it would become evident that another tax form was required for the transaction he described, but that had not been filed either.

Dinkins released a handwritten letter dated October 30, 1985 in which his son agreed to purchase the stock, but with no payments called for until January 1, 1991 when the entire principal amount was due, plus eight percent interest. The letter in turn implied a loan, which did not appear on Dinkins's city financial disclosure forms as required. Because a close family member still owned the stock, the city Ethics Commission had instructed Dinkins that it would be inappropriate for him to vote on matters affecting an affiliate of the company that held a cable TV franchise in Queens. Dinkins's staff, acting on behalf of the borough president, cast votes twice on such matters, through a lack of managerial oversight according to the candidate.

Then, information surfaced that three years before the supposed transaction with his son, Dinkins had valued the stock in excess of a million dollars on a New York State financial disclosure form. Dinkins had no answer for the discrepancy in the stated value of the stock other than to say that because the corporation was closely held it was hard to value it precisely. Percy Sutton, the head of Inner City Broadcasting, refused to release any documents that would clarify the matter. Dinkins's son took an extended vacation and could not be reached. The story itself strained credibility, and Dinkins's inability to respond adequately to basic questions about the transaction compounded public doubts.[40]

Faced with evidence of anti-Semites in his midst, and with a financial scandal that made the man appear both incompetent and dishonest, voters recoiled, especially Jews. One poll showed that Dinkins's position among Jews had deteriorated from a substantial lead over Giuliani to an eighteen point deficit. Others showed that the number of Jews who were undecided how to vote had risen. While it was among Jewish voters that the reaction was greatest, other whites too began to doubt that they could trust the Democratic party's first black nominee for mayor. Dinkins's overall lead over Giuliani, once as high as twenty-four percent, plummeted to four points in one survey. The momentum of the campaign had changed entirely. Dinkins's once inevitable victory was slipping away, with the changing attitude of Jewish voters the key factor in his decline.[41]

Dinkins stepped up his campaigning in orthodox Jewish communities where his support was least certain, but he found the response to his efforts mixed. On his way into a meeting with the Council of Jewish Organizations of Borough Park in Brooklyn, hecklers called him an anti-Semite. Inside, in response to tough questioning, Dinkins felt compelled to declare that his friend Jesse Jackson would have no influence in his administration if he were elected mayor. The group endorsed Dinkins, but on the same day, elsewhere in Brooklyn, a group of opponents hurled eggs at his podium while he spoke.[42]

The Dinkins campaign put Ed Koch on the air to ask voters to cast ballots for the Democrat because "he will fight for the people of this city." Dinkins paraded a succession of prominent rabbis before the news media to announce their endorsements. The candidate reminded Jewish voters at every opportunity that his opponent belonged to the Republican party while he, like them, was a Democrat. "My opponent campaigned with a man who was the only governor in America who refused to condemn the vile idea that Zionism is racism—White House Chief of

Staff John Sununu," Dinkins told one heavily Jewish breakfast gathering.[43]

In the final weeks of the election, the *New York Times*, the *Daily News*, and *Newsday* all endorsed Dinkins citing the need for racial comity. A poll taken a week before the final balloting showed that Dinkins's appeal to Jews was working. He had pulled even with Giuliani among Jewish voters with an opinion, although sixteen percent remained undecided. His support among Hispanics, which was solid until the damaging news appeared about his ethical practices and about the militants in his campaign, had eroded modestly while Giuliani had picked up support among the group. Still, a majority of Hispanic voters favored Dinkins compared to less than forty percent for Giuliani. The Republican's support among white Catholics remained solid, but overall, Dinkins appeared to be regaining his lost ground.[44]

Giuliani's campaign aired commercials that hit hard at Dinkins's tax troubles and made the man appear dishonest. And they also made much of his association with self-declared anti-whites that were sure to raise racial fears. During the last days of the campaign, while accepting the endorsement of the conservative United Jewish Coalition, Giuliani declared that the "naked truth is that David Dinkins will be the trusted servant of Jesse [Jackson] in City Hall." In the last two days of the campaign Giuliani shook hands in predominantly Jewish neighborhoods in Brooklyn and Queens "pleading with Democrats to abandon their party." According to a journalist who accompanied him on these last forays, "Jews . . . would be Giuliani's Little Big Horn." Dinkins, on the other hand, when asked on the Sunday before the election how Jews would vote, declared, "I am confident that the members of the Jewish community will be supportive of my candidacy." Polls showed his lead expanding.[45]

On November 7, 1989, almost one-and-three-quarter million New Yorkers went to the polls. They elected David Dinkins mayor by the smallest margin in the city's history. Fewer than fifty thousand votes separated the winner, who took just over half the ballots, from the loser, who took forty-eight percent. While the closeness of the race surprised political analysts it did nothing to dampen the euphoria among Dinkins's followers and all black New Yorkers. As midnight approached and the outcome became clear, the beaming mayor-elect stood before an ecstatic crowd accompanied by his elegant wife. First, he pledged to be mayor of all the people. Next, with his eighty-three year old father by his side, he declared that his election "forged a new link in the chain of memory" marking "another milestone on freedom's road." For the descendants of slaves the event evoked powerful emotions. Then Dinkins, a forty year veteran of New York City politics, who had studied the election returns district by district as they were reported to his campaign headquarters, offered "a special word" to New York's Jews. "That community is a light unto the nation tonight," he said. He owed his victory to them.

Nearly forty percent of the city's Jews voted for Dinkins. It was less than a majority to be sure, and far less than most polls had predicted, but dramatically higher than the twenty-three percent of white Catholics who voted for the black Democrat. If Dinkins had won no more support from white Jews than he did from white Catholics, Rudolph Giuliani would have been elected mayor. Dinkins's total support among whites was just over thirty percent. The rest of the balloting was unsurprising. Dinkins won ninety-seven percent of the votes cast by blacks, and seventy percent of Hispanic votes. These were essentially the same as the results in the Democratic primary. Giuliani won three quarters of the votes of white Catholics, sixty percent of Jewish ballots, and just thirty percent of the city's Hispanic votes. It was an impressive display for a non-Democrat in New York City, but by the slimmest of margins it was insufficient to elect him. Dinkins had kept his coalition together, and New York City, for the first time in its history, would have a black mayor.[46]

A New City Government

On election day 1989 New Yorkers also approved a new City Charter that changed the structure of municipal government. Late in 1981 the New York Civil Liberties Union had filed federal suit on behalf of three Brooklyn residents claiming that the Board of Estimate acted as a de facto legislative body and that its boroughwide basis of representation violated the constitutional norm of one person one vote. Brooklyn, with more than two million inhabitants, had just a single vote on the Board of Estimate, the same as Staten Island where only 350,000 New Yorkers lived. After a series of suits, in 1986 a federal appeals court justice ruled against the city. In response, Mayor Koch established a Charter Revision Commission, but the city continued to pursue the legal battle and the Supreme Court agreed to hear the case, so the commission's work lost its drama for a time.

On March 22, 1989 the highest court in the nation ruled that the structure New York City had used to govern itself for nearly a century violated the constitution of the United States. The Charter Revision Commission went back to work and ultimately developed a plan that reduced the Board of Estimate to ceremonial status. The new charter expanded the number of seats on the City Council from thirty-five to fifty-one with an express intent to draw district lines that would increase the number of minority representatives, and for the first time gave the City Council serious legislative and budgetary authority. At the same time, the power of the mayor and the operating agencies he controlled increased. In short, the City Council and the mayor divided between them the powers once held by the Board of Estimate. The proposal promised the most dramatic change in the structure of city government since consolidation in 1898. A ballot referendum allowed New Yorkers to declare their approval of the new charter, which they did by a margin of five to four.[47]

Another structural change received much attention during the 1989 campaign. It was the first conducted under a new law governing the size of contributions allowed in city elections. In return for limiting donations from a single source to $3,000, candidates received matching public funds. Participation was voluntary, but if one candidate did not join in, that candidate's opponent benefited from an even higher allotment of public money. It was hailed by good government groups as a great advance, while throughout the race candidates complained that the new law limited their ability to raise funds.

For two reasons the new law had little impact on election results in 1989. First, the high profile election for the city's first black mayor and the unusual circumstance of a colorful incumbent like Koch at risk of dethronement attracted enormous media attention. Serious candidates had little trouble getting heard. Second, the four major Democrats and two Republicans all spent large sums of money, certainly sufficient to send a message. Lauder spent more than $12 million in the Republican primary, by far the most money of any candidate; Giuliani laid out $2.5 million. Koch spent some $3.5 million dollars in the Democratic primary, Dinkins nearly $2.5 million, and Goldin and Ravitch $1.5 million each. There is no correlation between the money the candidates spent and the votes they won, nor any reason to believe that if any of the candidates had more money it would have changed the outcome. In each primary the richest candidate lost. Money certainly affects the ability of a candidate to wage a mayoralty campaign, but more than any other single factor, ethnic voting patterns continue to determine the outcomes of electoral races in New York City.[48]

THIRTEEN

To Be Mayor of New York

East Side, West Side, all around the town,
The kids play ring 'round-rosy, London Bridge
   is falling down.
Boys and girls together, me and Mamie Rourke
Tripped the life fantastic on the sidewalks
   of New York.

Me and Mamie Rourke were the lovers who tripped the life fantastic on New York's sidewalks in the days when Al Smith used *East Side, West Side* as his campaign theme song. It was a decidedly Irish pair and it symbolized the ethnic coloration of a long stretch of New York's political history. By 1977 Ed Koch and Bess Myerson, the nation's first Jewish Miss America, were the town's most glamorous couple. On January 1, 1990, Joyce Dinkins stood on the steps of City Hall by her husband David's side as he took the oath of office as New York's first black mayor. The Jews replaced the Irish as the dominant ethnic group in New York City politics, and then the blacks replaced the Jews. It happened in stages.

The Stages of Ethnic Succession

The Irish had created a powerful political machine by the time large-scale Jewish immigration began in 1881. For the next twenty years Jewish political development in New York City consisted principally of a process of arrival as East European Jews began to learn the political customs of the metropolis. Like other immigrants, Jews tended to vote in favor of the Irish dominated Democratic machine in return for the help they received from local district leaders. Yet, Jews were less rigid in their loyalty to the Democratic party than the other major ethnic groups that populated New York at the time. When confronted with excessive corruption, particularly scandals associated with criminal vice, Jewish voters abandoned the party of Tammany Hall in great numbers. During those first two decades, however, political organizing within the group was limited, and its voting pattern lacked coherence and force.

Organization dominated the second period of Jewish political development, from 1901 to about 1944. For many Jews, whose presence in the city continued to increase during this period, organizing simply meant joining the Democratic party. Some Jews joined the Republican party. But the strength of Jewish efforts to organize outside of the traditional two party system distinguished the group's politics from others.

Nontraditional organizing took place in a variety of ways. The fusion campaign of 1901, when the city's German Jewish elite descended into the slums of the Lower East Side in a conscious effort to convince Jewish voters to reject Tammany Hall, was one way. There was nothing new about fusion, but there was something new about a conscious effort to cast a fusion political campaign in ethnic terms. The organized response to Jewish concerns about anti-Semitism at home and abroad during the first decade of the twentieth century was another. From that time on the battle against anti-Semitism has been an enduring issue in New York's political campaigns. Also during the first decade of this century, the Socialist party matured. In New York City its development was inextricably linked to the Jewish labor movement. It was the Socialist party that gave force to the political demands of Jewish workers for improved factory conditions and better wages, and for a more just and more fair society. Political evolution transformed the Socialist party into the American Labor party, and then into the Liberal party. This last, which took form in the years between 1942 and 1944, was the final effort of a large segment of Jewish working-class immigrants to establish a distinct political voice outside of the Democratic party.

In the third period of Jewish political development in New York City, from 1945 to 1961, the group challenged barriers that prevented them from participating fully in the city's politics on the terms that they sought. The principal constraint Jews confronted was Irish Catholic domination of New York's majority political party. Even though by

1945 large numbers of Jews, and an increasing number of Italians, were participating actively in Democratic affairs, all five county leaders were still Irish. And the bosses continued to run a machine that jarred the cultural sensitivities of many Jews. The reform clubs emerged shortly after World War II, and their number increased throughout the 1950s. They consisted primarily of young, well-educated, Jewish activists who wanted to wield political power. These committed Democrats, unlike earlier generations of Jewish political organizers, had no thought of working outside of the city's majority party. They planned to control it.

In 1961, Herbert Lehman led the reform clubs on a crusade to topple the reigning party bosses. It was Lehman, along with Liberal party leader Alex Rose, who convinced Robert Wagner to break with the traditional Democratic organization. With that, Irish Catholic domination of the Democratic party in New York City effectively ended. Wagner was the city's last Irish Catholic mayor.

A fourth period in the political history of Jewish New Yorkers then began as control of the Democratic party shifted into the hands of Jewish politicians. Starting with Stanley Steingut's ascension as Brooklyn county leader in 1962, the process culminated with the election of Abe Beame, a Democratic party regular, in 1973, followed by Ed Koch, a product of a Democratic party reform club, in 1977. Koch endured until 1989. There is a certain chronological justice to the order in which the two men achieved New York's top office. Much of an earlier generation of Jewish Democrats followed Beame's path; much of a later one, Koch's. Jewish domination of the city's politics peaked in 1985. At the time of Koch's third election Jewish politicians held all three citywide offices, six of eight seats on the Board of Estimate, and nine of its eleven votes. Three of the city's five Democratic party county leaders were Jewish.

Black political development in New York City from the turn of the century until the present has taken place simultaneously on two different levels. One is ethnic, the other is racial. The first is characterized by accommodation and coalition building, the second by protest and confrontation.

The ethnic path clearly attracted some blacks as early as 1898 when the United Colored Democracy appealed to Tammany boss Richard Croker to award them jobs in accordance with their ability to deliver black votes. At first, such efforts generated few returns. Through the first three decades of the twentieth century blacks were modest in number in New York, tended to vote less than other ethnic groups, and typically cast ballots for Republicans, by far the city's weaker party. No clearer summary of the status of blacks in New York City politics in the 1930s need be offered than the simple but compelling reality that Democratic and Republican clubhouses remained segregated.

In 1936 the New Deal pulled blacks into the Democratic party at the national level, and by the mid-1940s, when Fiorello LaGuardia passed from the local scene, black New Yorkers were fiercely loyal Democratic voters. This concentrated their presence in the city's dominant party. Consistent migration expanded their numbers, making them more important in city elections, while changing social customs forced integration in political club houses and city government. In 1953, when Hulan Jack became the first black borough president of Manhattan, blacks made up about the same proportion of the county's population as Jews had a half-century earlier when the first member of their faith was chosen for the same post. In 1962 the Democrats nominated a black man as their candidate for the statewide office of attorney general, and in 1964 J. Raymond Jones became leader of the Democratic party in Manhattan. These were not insignificant posts, nor token exceptions. More important, they suggest that in spite of serious racial discrimination throughout American society at the time, blacks were on a path to political power in New York City similar to the one followed by the groups that had preceded them. Their successes depended on alliances and accommodation with other ethnic groups. The other groups happened to be white.

Blacks were also on a path to confrontation. The protest politics of Adam Clayton Powell began in the late 1930s and picked up speed in the 1940s and 1950s as Powell's stature as a leader of his race grew. The Civil Rights Movement of the 1950s combined protest and conciliation, but by the mid-1960s protest came to dominate the tone of the crusade. In New York, the 1966 controversy over the Civilian Review Board, and the 1968 school strike, followed by battles over the placement of low-income housing in Forest Hills and other middle-class neighborhoods, pushed racial politics to the fore. The intensity of the racial hostility that developed in the aftermath of these episodes made it impossible for blacks to create significant coalitions with whites in New York City. The forward momentum of black politicians abruptly halted. Percy Sutton's 1977 effort to energize non-blacks behind his campaign for mayor failed miserably, and for the next eight years no blacks sat on the board of estimate.

At first glance Dinkins's election to Manhattan's top post in 1985 was nothing more than a long overdue return to the established order that had begun with Hulan Jack more than thirty years before. A closer look reveals that it was very different. Jack was awarded his post as the junior member of an ethnic coalition. Dinkins won his as the senior partner in a racial one. Manhattan's demographics had changed so substantially that an alliance of blacks and Hispanics was able to elect a black borough president. The racial core of Dinkins's support is ironic. While he scarcely needed white votes to win the borough presidency in 1985, the small number of white voters who cast ballots for him in 1989 were crucial to his election as mayor. Dinkins won those votes because of his personal commitment to ethnic politics—a willingness to accommodate the interests of different groups. Because of the harsh racial tensions that persist in New York, expanding the nonminority part of his coalition will prove difficult despite Dinkins's personal style.

The Ties That Bind

For ethnic coalitions to endure the groups that compose them must benefit. Between 1901 and 1961 the Jews and the Irish had substantially different but marvelously complementary political priorities. The Irish wanted patronage, prestige, and power over the city and Democratic party bureaucracies. Jews, on the other hand, wanted protection against anti-Semitism, a liberal government that used its powers to improve the lives of the city's working-class and poor, and a relatively honest and scandal free administration of public affairs. The distinction between Irish and Jewish political desires was never quite so neat as a summary makes it sound. There were always Jewish job holders and political thieves, there were always high minded and dedicated Irish Catholic politicians. Yet, each group's center of gravity lay in a distinctly different place.

This reality generated a simple but powerful formula for winning citywide elections. To be mayor of New York during the first six decades of the twentieth century typically required a Democratic politician of Irish Catholic descent, sensitive to Jewish concerns about discrimination, liberal in social outlook, and substantially honest or at least perceived to be so. The Irish voted for the candidate on the basis of ethnic pride, and for the jobs and contracts that came to them with an Irish mayor in office. Jews voted for the candidate on the basis of their political priorities and philosophical commitments. The allegiance of the two groups—the two largest voting blocs in the city for most of the period—generally ensured victory. Irish loyalty was effectively determined the moment a candidate was chosen, so to an extraordinary degree New York mayoral campaigns were exercises in convincing Jewish voters that a candidate would respond to the constellation of issues that concerned them.

The Democrats applied the formula sporadically during the late nineteenth and the early twentieth centuries. Then, in fifteen of sixteen elections beginning in 1909 and continuing until 1961, the Democratic candidates for mayor fit the formula with great precision. They won eleven of the sixteen contests.

The 1950 special election was the one time during the period that the Democrats did not nominate an Irish politician. Vincent Impelliterri's surprise candidacy led the Democratic party bosses to choose an Italian to avoid accusations of bigotry. Impelliterri won, but he was an accident who did not meet the criteria for holding on to power. He did not last. John Purroy Mitchel beat Tammany in 1913 with a fusion campaign. Mitchel was himself a registered Democrat of Irish Catholic descent, perceived as liberal on important social issues at the time of his first campaign, and as more honest than what Tammany offered that year.

Fiorello LaGuardia, who New Yorkers elected mayor three times, is the only significant exception to the rule. He ran on the Republican and City Fusion tickets, and later the ALP ticket, rather than the Democratic line. He relied on Italians rather than the Irish to vote for him on the basis of ethnic pride. Yet, LaGuardia's popularity among Jewish voters was the key to his long tenure. In this respect he fits the formula well. LaGuardia had a strong reputation as an opponent of anti-Semitism, and had irrefutable liberal credentials. Furthermore, Tammany's arrogant plundering of the city in the years before LaGuardia's rise violated the implicit agreement between the Democrats and the Jews to keep corruption within acceptable bounds. This mistake provided LaGuardia with the wedge he needed to pry Jewish voters away from the Democratic coalition.

The Italians emerged as a weak third force within the Democratic party in New York beginning in the 1940s. Carmine DeSapio's success as a party leader, the sole Italian to achieve such prominence until Meade Esposito in the 1970s, is the exception that proves the rule. Italians wanted the same things out of politics that the Irish wanted, limiting the chance for an accommodation like the one that suited the Jews, and in head to head battles with the Irish the Italians faced disadvantages. To begin with, the Irish held firm control of the Democratic party bureaucracy when the rivalry began. Ostensibly the Italians had superior numbers on their side, but they diluted their strength by splitting their party registrations between the Republican and Democratic organizations, or by not registering at all. Irish New Yorkers registered to vote in greater proportions than the Italians and consistently registered Democratic until well into the 1960s, even though by then many had already begun to vote Republican in national elections. This gave their dwindling numbers maximum effect in Democratic primaries. Until 1961, when Jewish Democrats insisted on a role in running party affairs, the most bitter rivalries for party positions tended to be between Italian and Irish politicians. Christie Sullivan's refusal to seat Carmine DeSapio as district leader after he beat Battery Dan Finn in 1941 is a case in point.

The Italians never dominated the city's politics the way the Irish did for so long, and the way the Jews did more briefly. LaGuardia's rule was a spectacular one man show, but it was just that. The number of Italians holding important city posts did not rise during his three terms, nor did the number of Italians elected to municipal office increase noticeably during his administrations. LaGuardia, measured by the ethnic background of his major appointments, his liberal social convictions, and his sensitivity to anti-Semitism in New York and overseas, was more of a Jewish mayor than an Italian one. The Italians lacked the skill the Irish displayed for controlling the levers of party affairs and of city government, and they lacked the ideological consistency and special concerns of the Jews that allowed that group to determine the philosophical orientation of New York's politics throughout the twentieth century.

The one major concession that the Democratic party made to Italians was to include them in the ticket balancing equation for citywide offices. Between 1945 and 1961 the balanced ticket gave each of the city's three major ethnic groups a reason to support the Democratic slate. Assessing the effectiveness of the tactic is difficult. It may have had some direct effect on voters, but more important, it appeased the Democratic party workers from the various ethnic groups. It worked, in part, because by coincidence New York had three major ethnic groups at the time and three citywide elected offices. As the numbers of black and Puerto Rican voters in the city increased, it became tougher to offer something to everyone. In 1965, the Democratic candidates for primary ran on balanced tickets, and some effort was made again in 1969, but by then the practice had become obsolete. By 1973 it disappeared.

In 1961 the formula that kept Irish mayors and Jewish policies in power broke down. The Jews had reached a stage where they wanted to run the party, not just guide it philosophically. The Irish realized that the Democratic party's programs had become more liberal than they were, and by then the actual numbers and political presence of the Irish in New York had dwindled, making it harder to maintain control of party offices. Also, some of the most impcrtant benefits the Irish sought from politics had faded. The ability of local politicians to deliver attractive jobs had diminished because of civil service reform and the rise of municipal unions as the organizing vehicles of city workers. Irish demand for political patronage jobs had diminished by then because the Irish had achieved substantial success in business, the professions, and other arenas. Without a practical or philosophical reason to remain Democrats, some Irish began to leave the party. Resentment at their displacement led many Irish voters to cast their ballots in 1965 for the Irish Conservative, William Buckley, rather than the Jewish Democrat, Abe Beame.

That same year, a vague outline of a new coalition appeared. In addition to support from traditional Republican constituencies, John Lindsay won an unusually large numbers of votes from Jews and blacks. A common aversion to bigotry, and a shared belief that the government should use its power to help the weak and the impoverished, offered hope that these two groups could create an enduring alliance.

The racial turmoil of the mid-1960s, most emphatically the 1968 school strike, prevented such a coalition from forming. A wide segment of the Jewish population joined black and Puerto Rican voters to reelect John Lindsay in 1969, but that was because the fractured state of the Democratic party, and its primary rules, led to the selection of a candidate utterly unacceptable to Jewish liberals and moderates. Racial politics damaged the potential coalition of minorities and Jews before it ever really formed.

Beneath John Lindsay's electoral victories, the Democrats were responding to New York's changing political reality by inverting the formula that had obtained until 1961. Instead of a liberal Irish Catholic, a not-so-liberal Jew became the candidate of choice. That was the profile of the Democratic candidate for mayor in the six elections between 1965 and 1985, except for the debacle of 1969. It was the profile of the victor four times in succession between 1973 and 1985. Large numbers of Jews had emerged from the 1960s ill at ease with the political demands of racial minorities. This shift made it easy for Irish and Italian Catholics to vote for a Jewish mayor. It was a coalition held together by racial tensions, and whites had sufficient numbers to win.

In 1989 the same racially charged atmosphere prevailed, but New York's demographics had changed. Enough minorities now lived and voted in the city that a coalition of blacks and Hispanics could deliver the Democratic nomination to a black candidate almost without support from whites. In a general election the numbers were so close that a small number of white votes were still necessary to elect a black candidate. In 1989 enough liberal whites, principally Jews, cast ballots for David Dinkins to allow him to win. Jews continue to be New York City's swing voters; the ones who are most willing to shift their votes on the basis of issues, the ones whom electoral campaigns are designed to influence, and the ones who determine electoral outcomes.

David Dinkins's base among black voters is secure. His position among Hispanics, crucial to his victory in the Democratic primary, is uncertain, and his standing among Jews is similarly unclear.

Like blacks, Hispanics want tangible help from city government— jobs, better housing, and expanded resources on every level for their impoverished communities. The budget crisis that has harassed David Dinkins since he entered office has not allowed him to provide adequate benefits to those who demand them. Part of Dinkins's strength among Hispanics in 1989, according to polling data, was a belief by many that Dinkins was more likely than his opponents "to care about people like them." An inability to demonstrate his concern in a tangible way will diminish his standing among Hispanics. There is much evidence that this has already happened.

Hispanics also seek the prestige that goes with holding high office, but there is only one mayor, and if he is black he is not Hispanic. Still, racial solidarity—a common sense of oppression among people whose skin is dark in color—continues to bind many Hispanics to New York's first black mayor. Against a nonminority candidate, especially if that candidate appeals explicitly to the racial fears of middle-class whites, Dinkins will win a majority of Hispanic votes. But if a Hispanic runs in the Democratic primary the damage to Dinkins's coalition will be severe. The times do not yet favor a Hispanic candidate for mayor, but political analysts have already begun to view Bronx Borough President Fernando Ferrer as a potential citywide candidate. Rumors are circulating that Herman Badillo may again run for mayor. Mayor Dinkins must work hard to maintain the loyalty of Hispanic politicians to stay in office.

Holding onto Jewish votes presents another challenge for David Dinkins. In 1991 a tragic automobile accident in which a car forming part of a motorcade for Lubavitcher Rabbi Menachem Schneerson killed a black boy and sparked three days of race riots in the Crown Heights section of Brooklyn. Jews who voted for Dinkins in the hope that his election would ease tensions between blacks and Jews have been disappointed. Against Ed Koch, a Jewish Democrat, David Dinkins won less than a quarter of Jewish votes in the Democratic primary. The proportion rose to forty percent against a Republican Italian, Rudolph Giuliani, in the general election, providing the mayor with his margin of victory. If there were to be a rematch against Giuliani in 1993 it is unclear if Dinkins would fare as well. If a Jewish Democrat seeks and wins the Republican nomination and runs against Dinkins in 1993, the threat to the mayor will be real. White Catholics are almost certain to support such a candidate and Jewish Democrats are likely to do so as well. Rumors that City Council president Andrew Stein will seek Republican support for a mayoralty race began to circulate in 1991. Mayor Dinkins's coalition is vulnerable indeed.

New York and Beyond

Political analysts have long attributed much of the success of America's big city political machines during the late nineteenth and early twentieth centuries to the ability of local politicians to act as brokers among different ethnic groups. Little attention has been paid to the logical corollary that a political machine that fails to tame one of a city's significant tribes is vulnerable. In New York, the large number of Jews who acted independently of the local Democratic organization had a profound effect on the evolution of the machine. Democrats had to adjust not only their philosophical orientation, but their ethical practices as well, or else run the risk of losing large numbers of Jewish votes. This placed limits on the machine's ability to reward its members. Ultimately, in 1961, the successful movement to topple Carmine DeSapio was driven by Herbert Lehman, the largely Jewish reform clubs, and the Jewish dominated Liberal party. While the Jewish experience in New York is unique, in other cities, other ethnic groups may have provided the nucleus of the political coalitions that from time to time have toppled ruling regimes. In Chicago, for example, the Irish Catholic machine endured well into the 1970s. It collapsed ultimately only after a black mayor, Harold Washington, won election. The present mayor, Richard M. Daley, rules in a very different way than his father did twenty years ago.

The comparison with Chicago is instructive for another reason. That city signed its first formal collective bargaining contracts with municipal labor unions in 1985. This was after the machine had broken apart and almost thirty years after municipal unions existed in New York. It is telling that Victor Gotbaum, who enjoyed so successful a career organizing municipal workers in New York City, failed when he attempted to unionize municipal hospital workers in Chicago in the mid-1950s. Mayor Daley's political machine ran him out of town. Municipal unions and political machines depend to a great degree on the same resource—city government workers. One strengthens itself at the expense of the other. More than anything else, the rise of municipal unions as independent centers of power in New York ensures that a smoothly functioning, broadscale, citywide political machine will not revive. This change has had consequences for the city. Indirectly, and with clear limitations, party bosses and patronage workers ultimately responded to the general public through the political process. To stay in power, labor leaders need serve only the limited interests of their union members. It is impossible to imagine in the senior Richard Daley's Chicago the kind of behavior that DC 37 displayed in 1971 when it sabotaged traffic around New York and dumped raw sewage onto city beaches. In no small way, running against the municipal unions in 1977, which every candidate save Bella Abzug did, was comparable to running against the bosses in an earlier period. Municipal unions played an important role in helping elect David Dinkins mayor in 1989. As with other constituencies, however, the budget crisis has prevented Mayor Dinkins from rewarding them adequately. His standing with the group has been badly weakened as a result.

There is no question that the political machine in New York City has declined. It is now a shell of what it was in the 1920s under Charles Murphy and Al Smith, it is a fraction as powerful as it was in the 1950s under Carmine DeSapio and Robert Wagner. The Democratic organization in Manhattan never recovered from the 1961 split. Staten Island is small in citywide terms, and heavily Republican. The organizations in Queens, the Bronx, and Brooklyn were all battered by convictions of important leaders during the corruption scandals of the 1980s. The latter two are badly divided by racial rivalries as well.

The increasing significance of television advertising, and the use of the media in election campaigns, has mirrored the waning power of the machine. Still, a sense of balance must be maintained in assessing the relative importance of the mass media versus traditional political organizing in New York City mayoral contests.

John Lindsay is often considered a media product, yet in 1965 the force of his campaign came from more than one hundred store fronts opened throughout the city—an instant political organization. In 1969, his expensive and skillfully created television commercials had no effect in New York's Catholic community and limited impact upon Jews. The campaign also had all the trappings of a typical mayoralty race including an endless series of personal visits by Lindsay to synagogues and Jewish centers. Which technique was more important is hard to say. As an explanation of Lindsay's reelection, neither is as significant as Mario Procaccino's ineptness as a candidate and his unacceptability to New York's liberal Jews and to the city's minorities.

In 1973 the Bronx and Brooklyn Democratic organizations elected Abe Beame mayor. Pat Cunningham and Meade Esposito picked a candidate who fit the mood and the ethnic sensitivities of the time, just as Charles Murphy and Carmine DeSapio did when they ruled. Once the candidate was chosen, the two county leaders organized a typical block by block effort of the kind at which political machines excel. Beame shook hands in front of groceries and delicatessens, spoke to small gatherings and depended on local party workers to hand out pamphlets, stuff mail boxes with literature, and make telephone calls to voters. Certainly his campaign relied on television and radio commercials as well, but Abe Beame was no media star.

In 1977, Ed Koch and Mario Cuomo ran public relations campaigns to greater degrees than any previous mayoralty candidates. These were the two men who ran best in the first round of primary voting and who faced each other in the run-off and the general election. Yet, the closeness of the first-round victories—one percentage point of difference between each of the top four candidates—indicates that Beame's traditional campaign, and Bella Abzug's variation on one, were not anachronistic irrelevancies. Moreover, between the initial vote and the run-off, Ed Koch moved quickly to secure the support of Meade Esposito, the most powerful boss in the city at the time. Clearly Koch thought the Brooklyn machine, which had delivered the borough for Beame in the primary's first round, still had some strength. Less than it once did to be sure, but enough to make a difference in a tight contest. Mayor Koch's 1981 and 1985 reelections were by such huge margins, and against such weak opposition, that it is impossible to attribute his success to one aspect or another of his campaigns.

David Dinkins's 1989 campaign received widespread media attention. He was identified from the start as the man who could unseat a colorful, but by then unpopular, incumbent. He also promised to make history by becoming New York's first black mayor. Yet, the thrust of his campaign was a field operation staffed by Democratic party workers and union members whose main task was to bring out the vote in minority communities. Thus, while television and media attention have become terribly important in citywide campaigns in New York, traditional electioneering techniques remain important as well.

Between 1913, when New York State's primary law went into effect, and 1961 the Democratic party chose its candidate for mayor in a primary four times. The other eleven times a caucus of political bosses made the decision. Prior to 1961, the backing of the Democratic party leadership was by far the most important criterion for success in a New York City mayoralty campaign. Since then, money—for television and traditional campaign organizing—has replaced party support as the most scarce resource. On the one hand, the system allows more candidates to run. On the other, money now speaks so loudly that the individual voices of the citizenry are heard less and less in comparison to campaign financiers. The corruptions of the machine have not been ended so much as replaced. The 1989 effort to protect the electoral system from financing abuses is woefully inadequate. Unfortunately, incumbents elected by the current system control the legislative machinery that could enact meaningful election reform, so the prospects for change are doubtful.

The various candidates for mayor in New York have often taken nearly identical positions on local political matters. As a result, citizens cast their votes on the basis of the image the candidates present, not the policies they define. The vote is not a selection of a series of programs. It is a statement of the kind of world the voter would like to see. Some examples illustrate the point. In 1953 Vincent Impellitteri was the rare candidate who did not understand the right positions to take on local issues. He got trounced. On the other hand, virtually no policy differences separated Robert Wagner and Rudolph Halley. Wagner, the Democrat, was perceived as the truer representative of the New Deal, and more like the average New Yorker, so he won. In 1961 the issue of "bossism," the only one of the campaign, told little about how Wagner would run the rapidly changing city during the next four years. The mayor's declaration that he would be unbossed was a statement of philosophical conviction that Herbert Lehman had made important in the public mind. In 1917, 1941, and 1969, America was at war, or nearly so. The mayor of New York, of course, has no formal authority over foreign policy. Yet, the candidates' positions on the international conflicts of the day were critical in the campaigns of those years. In 1977 Ed Koch advocated the death penalty to define himself as less liberal than many might otherwise have thought, even though a mayor has no control over the legislation or the implementation of capital punishment.

The effective absence of issues during the campaigns helps explain why ethnic voting patterns are so strong. The kind of society each of us would like to see depends on the kind of person we are and what we value in life. These fundamental beliefs are determined in no small measure by the cultural values we grow up with. What those are has everything to do with ethnicity—a person's Irish, Jewish, Italian, black, Puerto Rican, or other experience in America. We vote for people who present an image of how we would like our society to be. For most of us, that image looks a lot like ourselves, our families, and our neighbors.

To be mayor of New York requires a leader who can reconcile the competing visions the city's ethnic groups hold of the metropolis, at least in sufficient measure to win the confidence of a majority. That has never been easy, and perhaps it has never been harder than today. It remains important. How well our democratic experiment succeeds in our greatest city in no small measure reflects the condition of the American way of life.

Ethnic Voting Statistics

Determining how many New Yorkers at any given moment were Irish, Jewish, Italian, black, Puerto Rican, or of some other heritage is a task that under the best of circumstances contains inherent imprecisions. Determining how the people who made up those groups voted permits less precision still. As a result, ethnic voting statistics are all approximations.

Throughout this study I have relied on three methods of measuring ethnic voting patterns. The most exact information comes from professional polls taken about the time of an election. Unlike the historian who examines an election long after it has been held, the pollster has the luxury of asking voters at the time of the event what their heritage is and how they voted. While statistical margin for error exists, it is less than the potential inaccuracies inherent in other methods of estimating voting patterns. Beginning in the mid-1950s such polls appear, sporadically and with differing levels of detail, in various archives pertaining to New York City's political history, as indicated in the chapter notes. By the 1960s summary results of political polls taken for New York

City mayoralty races were published regularly in local newspapers and national magazines.

For earlier periods, before polling became common, other methods must be used. The least exact is the examination of assembly districts that historical evidence indicates were heavily populated by a particular ethnic group. New York City assembly districts have always been too large for any one to have ever had a homogeneous population. Still, many have been heavily dominated by an ethnic group for a time, and therefore trends and tendencies can be discerned even if exact numbers cannot be determined.

A more refined technique, examination by electoral district rather than assembly district, allows more precise analysis. Electoral districts are typically just a few blocks big, and therefore many have contained reasonably homogeneous populations for a time. The difficulty lies in identifying which electoral districts contained which groups.

For blacks it is relatively easy. Census data rely on race as an identifying characteristic, and segregated residential patterns make finding contiguous census tracts where the population is eighty percent or more black a simple task. The researcher can then match these census tracts to electoral districts that fit inside them, and record the votes.

For other ethnic groups the task is more difficult. The census does not note ethnic heritage, but does register the nationalities of foreign-born residents. A researcher can therefore locate census tracts where twenty-five or thirty percent of the residents were born in Italy. The ratio of native-born Italians to foreign-born was about two to one at mid-century, so these districts were probably more than seventy-five percent Italian in composition. The electoral districts that corresponded to the census tracts can then be identified, and the names of the registered voters reviewed to ensure that they were in fact Italian. Care can be taken to eliminate any districts that have sizable concentrations of another ethnic group that might contaminate the results. Then the researcher can record the votes.

For Jews it is more complicated still. The census does not record religion, but some ninety percent of New York's Russian immigrants were Jewish, virtually one hundred percent of the Romanian immigrants, seventy percent of the Austrians, and sixty percent of the Poles. There were about three native-born Jews for every Jewish immigrant in New York City about mid-century. Therefore, any census tract where two of the nationalities that were heavily Jewish made up more than twenty percent of the population was probably well over fifty percent Jewish. As with the Italian voters, once these tracts are identified, the electoral districts that correspond can be located. Then the names of the registered voters can be checked to be certain that they were Jewish and to eliminate districts where a large proportion of the voters were from another group. Then the results can be recorded.

In theory the process could be repeated for other ethnic groups, but the small number of census tracts with large numbers of Irish immigrants by mid-century made identifying Irish districts by this method impossible.

For elections in 1949, 1950, 1953, 1956, and 1957, I used the electoral district technique described to identify the voting patterns of blacks, Italians, and Jews. The results of the sample I identified are included on the pages that follow.

For other elections sources of ethnic voting data are as cited.

Appendix

Ethnic Voting Patterns of New York City Voters
Blacks, Italians, and Jews

New York City Mayoralty Election, 1949

Party/Candidate	Blacks	Italians	Jews
Democrat: William O'Dwyer	42.1%	40.6%	41.1%
Republican: Newbold Morris	15.8	12.7	10.1
American Labor: Vito Marcantonio	32.9	40.6	19.7
Liberal: Newbold Morris	8.1	5.0	27.1
Other	1.2	1.1	3.0

New York State United States Senate Election, 1949

Party/Candidate	Blacks	Italian	Jews
Democratic: Herbert Lehman	64.9%	60.9%	60.2%
Republican: John Foster Dulles	21.4	30.7	7.2
Liberal: Herbert Lehman	12.8	6.1	32.2
Other	0.9	0.0	0.6

New York City Mayoralty Election, 1950

Party/Candidate	Blacks	Italians	Jews
Democrat: Ferdinand Pecora	37.4%	23.5%	44.9%
Republican: Edward Corsi	13.7	17.8	5.8
Experience: Vincent Impellitteri	37.0	48.6	21.2
Liberal: Ferdinand Pecora	5.0	2.3	17.2
Other	7.1	7.9	11.1

New York State United States Senate Election, 1950

Party/Candidate	Blacks	Italians	Jews
Democrat: Herbert Lehman	57.1%	48.8%	61.4%
Republican: Joseph Hanley	20.7	32.8	6.6
Liberal: Herbert Lehman	8.2	4.3	20.2
Other	14.3	13.3	12.0

New York State Gubernatorial Election, 1950

Party/Candidate	Blacks	Italians	Jews
Democrat: James Lynch	50.4%	36.6%	53.0%
Republican: Thomas Dewey	34.2	48.9	15.8
Liberal: James Lynch	5.9	2.9	18.3
Other	9.7	11.1	13.0

New York City Mayoralty Election, 1953

Party/Candidate	Blacks	Italians	Jews
Democrat: Robert F. Wagner	69.7%	60.1%	51.5%
Republican: Harold Riegleman	16.0	25.3	7.5
Liberal: Rudolph Halley	10.9	9.2	33.9
Other	3.3	5.3	7.0

New York State United States Senate Election, 1956

Party/Candidate	Blacks	Italians	Jews
Democrat: Robert F. Wagner	61.5%	44.9%	67.8%
Republican: Jacob K. Javits	30.5	51.1	18.5
Liberal: Robert F. Wagner	8.0	4.2	13.7

New York City Mayoralty Election, 1957

Party/Candidate	Blacks	Italians	Jews
Democrat: Robert F. Wagner	63.5%	60.1%	68.8%
Republican: Robert Christenberry	18.3	28.2	10.5
Liberal: Robert F. Wagner	13.8	6.6	17.7
Other	4.3	5.2	3.5

Notes

Introduction

1. A large body of empirical evidence suggests that in American elections in general, and in local elections especially, no factor offers as much insight into how voters cast their ballots as ethnocultural affiliation. Wealth, occupation or profession, educational achievement, union affiliation, age, and gender all can have an impact, but they appear to be secondary to ethnicity. Lee Benson, *The Concept of Jacksonian Democracy: New York as a Test Case* is a pathbreaking study of the development of ethnocultural voting in America. The pattern in New York City is apparent in Thomas M. Henderson, *Tammany Hall and the New Immigrants*, appendix; Robert Wesser, *A Response to Progressivism: The Democratic Party and New York Politics, 1902–1918*, appendix I; Arthur Mann, *LaGuardia Comes to Power, 1933*, 123–52; Ronald Bayor, *Neighbors in Conflict: The Irish, Germans, Jews and Italians of New York City, 1929–1941*, 30–56, 126–49; Nathan Glazer and Daniel Patrick Moynihan, *Beyond the Melting Pot: The Negroes, Puerto Ricans, Jews, Italians, and Irish of New York City*; Lawrence Fuchs, ed., *American Ethnic Politics* presents the ethnic component of American politics in a series of excellent articles. See Stephan Thernstrom, ed., *Harvard Encyclopedia of American Ethnic Groups* for a systematic assess-

ment of the meaning of ethnicity in the United States including an insightful essay on politics by Edward R. Kantowicz, 803–12. Arthur Mann, *The One and the Many* is a valuable reflection on ethnicity as a factor in creating the American identity. Complete bibliographical references to the works mentioned here can be found in the bibliography.

One: Ethnic Arithmetic

1. Kerby A. Miller, *Emigrants and Exiles: Ireland and the Irish Exodus to North America* (New York: Oxford University Press, 1985), 280, 291, 569; Robert Ernst, *Immigrant Life in New York City* (Port Washington, NY: Ira J. Friedman, 1949), 61; Ira Rosenwaike, *Population History of New York City* (Syracuse: Syracuse University Press, 1972), 67, 72–73.

2. Many of the fiercest legal restrictions, known collectively as the Penal Laws, were removed a few decades before the famine, but the effect on Irish attitudes toward the British was enduring. Miller, *Emigrants and Exiles*, 286; Marcus Lee Hansen, *The Atlantic Migration 1607–1860* (New York, Harper, 1940), 263–72; Andrew M. Greeley, *That Most Distressful Nation: The Taming of the American Irish* (Chicago: Quadrangle Books, 1972), 18.

3. Lee Benson, *The Concept of Jacksonian Democracy*, 64, 185; Miller, *Emigrants and Exiles*, 329; William V. Shannon, *The American Irish: A Political and Social Portrait* (New York: Macmillan, 1963), 50; Gustavus Myers, *The History of Tammany Hall* (New York: Dover, 1971), 56–59; Ernst, *Immigrant Life*, 162; Glazer and Moynihan, *Melting Pot*, 221.

4. Jerome Mushkat, *Tammany: The Evolution of a Political Machine, 1789–1865* (Syracuse: Syracuse University Press, 1971), *passim*; Myers, *History of Tammany Hall*, *passim*; Edward K. Spann, *The New Metropolis* (New York: Columbia University Press, 1981), 341–64; Alexander B. Callow, Jr. *The Tweed Ring* (New York: Oxford University Press, 1965), *passim*.

5. Spann, *The New Metropolis*, 358–60; Callow, *The Tweed Ring*, 66–67; Ernst, *Immigrant Life*, 166.

6. Until 1913 district leaders were also responsible for nominating their party's candidates to run for political office. Since then all candidates except those who run for statewide office have been subject to primaries in which all registered party members are eligible to vote. In practice, however, political support from the local district leader was often sufficient to determine the outcome. Statewide candidates were chosen in nominating conventions until 1970. Now any candidate who wins at least twenty-five percent of the state convention's votes is eligible to appear on the ballot in a primary.

7. Callow, *The Tweed Ring*, 103–7; Ernst, *Immigrant City*, 39–340, 165; Glazer and Moynihan, *Beyond the Melting Pot*, 223.

8. Edward M. Levine, *The Irish and Irish Politicians: A Study of Cultural and Social Alienation* (Notre Dame, Indiana: University of Notre Dame Press, 1966), 35–37, 45, 78; Glazer and Moynihan, *Melting Pot*, 221–30; Greeley,

That Most Distressful Nation, 203–6; Shannon, *The American Irish*, 14; George W. Potter, *To the Golden Door: The Story of the Irish in Ireland and America* (Boston: Little Brown, 1960), 229.

9. Arthur Mann, Introduction (hereafter Mann, "Plunkitt"), xii, in William Riordon, *Plunkitt of Tammany Hall* (New York: Dutton, 1963) and 12–13 for Plunkitt quote; Myers, *Tammany Hall*, 283; Morton Keller, *Affairs of State*, (Cambridge, MA: The Belknap Press, 1977), 239. One scholar has collected data from 1880, 1900, 1930 and 1970 that show a strong correlation between the numbers of Irish in a city and the numbers of municipal employees. Other immigrant groups used patronage to secure political power but they simply were not as skilled at it as the Irish. See Terry Nichols Clark, "The Irish Ethic and the Spirit of Patronage," *Ethnicity* 2 (1975), 305–59.

10. Riordon, *Plunkitt*, 25–29, 90–98; Lillian D. Wald, *The House on Henry Street* (1915; New York: Dover Publications, 1971), 257; Irving Howe, *World of Our Fathers* (New York: Harcourt, 1976), 386; Ernst, *Immigrant Life*, 67, 163; Miller, *Emigrants and Exiles*, 329–331.

11. Glazer and Moynihan, *Melting Pot*, 226; Ernst, *Immigrant Life*, 163; Nancy Joan Weiss, *Charles Francis Murphy, 1858–1924:* (Northampton, MA: Smith College, 1968), 18.

12. Ernst, *Immigrant Life*, 170; Miller, *Emigrants and Exiles*, 330; Myers, *Tammany Hall*, 270; Mark D. Hirsch, "Richard Croker: An Interim Report on the Early Career of a 'Boss' of Tammany Hall," in Irwin Yellowitz, ed. *Essays in the History of New York City* (Port Washington, New York: Kennikat Press, 1978), 101–31; Weiss, *Charles Francis Murphy*, 19; J. Joseph Huthmacher, "Charles Evans Hughes and Charles F. Murphy, The Metamorphosis of Progressivism," *New York History* 46 (January 1965), 28.

13. Riordon, *Plunkitt*, 7–8, 10; Mann, "Plunkitt," xvi, ix.

14. Myers, *Tammany Hall*, 288; Riordan, *Plunkitt*, 6.

15. Jon C. Teaford, *The Unheralded Triumph: City Government in America, 1870–1900* (Baltimore: Johns Hopkins University Press, 1984), 3–4, 8–10, 175; Callow, *The Tweed Ring*, 98.

16. Myers, *Tammany Hall*, 278–79; Glazer and Moynihan, *Beyond the Melting Pot*, 218; Wesser, *A Response to Progressivism*, 11–12; Edwin R. Lewinson, *John Purroy Mitchel: The Boy Mayor of New York* (New York: Astra Books, 1965), 47; Arthur Mann, *LaGuardia Comes to Power, 1933* (Chicago: University of Chicago Press, 1965), 37, 40–42; Martin Shefter, *Political Crisis/Fiscal Crisis* (New York: Basic Books, 1985), 21–26.

17. Callow, *The Tweed Ring*, 196; Shannon, *The American Irish*, 78.

18. Rosenwaike, *Population History*, 72. Foreign stock is a census counter's term meaning immigrants and the children of foreign born mothers.

19. The current borders of New York City were created in 1898 with the first elections for the expanded metropolis in 1897. The 1897 Charter extended the term of the mayor and certain other elected officials to four years from two.

A Charter reform in 1901 reverted to the two year terms, but beginning with 1905 the four year terms were reinstated and obtain to date.

20. Howe, *World of Our Fathers*, 366; Martin Shefter, "The Electoral Foundations of the Political Machine: New York City, 1884–1897," in Joel Silbey, et al., eds., *The History of American Electoral Behavior* (Princeton, New Jersey: Princeton University Press, 1978), 282.

21. Lucy S. Dawidowicz, *On Equal Terms* (New York: Holt, 1982), 13; Howe, *World of Our Fathers*, 5, indicates that 94% of Russia's Jews lived in the Pale of Settlement. The concentration resulted from laws that forbade Jews to live elsewhere in Russia, with certain limited exceptions. Moses Rischin, *The Promised City* (Cambridge: Harvard University Press, 1962), 23–24, 31–33.

22. Howe, *World of Our Fathers*, 27.

23. Howe, *World of Our Fathers*, 80; Kessner, *The Golden Door*, 37, 61–63, 168; Melvyn Dubofsky, *When Workers Organize: New York City in the Progressive Era* (Amherst, MA: The University of Amherst Press, 1968), 7; Will Herberg, "The Jewish labor Movement in the United States," *American Jewish Yearbook* 53 (1952), 14; Arthur Goren, *New York Jews and the Quest for Community* (New York: Columbia University Press, 1970), 20–21.

24. Nathan Glazer, *American Judaism* 2d ed. (Chicago, University of Chicago Press, 1972), 46. Naomi Wiener Cohen, *Encounter With Emancipation* (Philadelphia: The Jewish Publication Society, 1984), 162–3.

25. Naomi Wiener Cohen, *Not Free to Desist* (Philadelphia: Jewish Publication Society, 1972), 5–6; Goren, *New York Jews and the Quest for Community*, 12–7, 21; Rischin, *The Promised City*, 98 quoting *The American Hebrew*, no date.

26. Wald, *The House on Henry Street*, 255–66; Howe, *World of Our Fathers*, 90–94; Elisabeth Israels Perry, *Belle Moskowitz* (New York: Oxford University Press, 1987), 12–22; Allen F. Davis, *Spearheads for Reform* (New Brunswick: Rutgers University Press, 1967), 27.

27. Martin Shefter, "Electoral Foundations of the Political Machine," 280; M. R. Werner, *It Happened in New York* (New York: Coward McCann, 1957), 36–37, 64–66,; Myers, *Tammany Hall*, 276–7. The going price for a police captain's position was $12,000 to $15,000, a sound investment in view of the financial opportunities that went with the post.

28. David Hammack, *Power and Society: Greater New York at the Turn of the Century* (New York: Russell Sage Foundation, 1982), 67, 149–50; Werner, *It Happened in New York*, 89–90; Thomas M. Henderson, *Tammany Hall and the New Immigrants* (New York: Arno Press, 1976), 74. Between 1900 and 1910 the number of German immigrants living in New York declined from 322,000 to 278,000 and the second generation population from 659,000 to 328,000, as massive movement to suburban areas took place. Beginning in the late 1880s large numbers of Italian immigrants arrived in New York, but they were slow to adopt citizenship or register to vote. As a result, it was a long time before they cast ballots in proportion to their numbers. Furthermore, those who

did vote tended to respond to machine techniques and support Tammany loyally, so that Italians had only slight influence on the city's politics in the early years of the twentieth century. See Henderson, 48–50, 54, appendix, 297ff; Thomas Kessner, *The Golden Door* (New York: Oxford University Press, 1977), 26–31.

29. Riordan, *Plunkitt*, 48; Howe, *World of Our Fathers*, 372–76; S. L. Blumenson, "The Politicians," *Commentary* March 1956, 264.

30. Wesser, *A Response to Progressivism*, 30–31. The county names for the Bronx and Queens are the same as the borough names. Brooklyn is known as Kings County; Staten Island, Richmond County; and Manhattan, New York County. In 1900 the population of New York City consisted of: Manhattan, 1,850,093; Brooklyn, 1,166,582; Bronx, 200,507; Queens, 152,999; Staten Island, 67,021. Manhattan and Brooklyn held 88% of the total population and 71% of the foreign stock population. Rosenwaike, *Population History of New York City*, 58.

31. In 1937 the name of the Board of Aldermen was changed to the City Council and for its first eight years its members were elected by proportional representation of party instead of by district. In 1945 the City Council returned to the geographic district system. A 1988 Supreme Court decision ruled that the Board of Estimate structure violated the one man, one vote concept and was therefore unconstitutional. A new charter was approved by referendum in 1989 giving the City Council far more legislative power than it previously held. Neal Garelik, "The Board of Estimate," (Bachelor's Thesis, Columbia University, 1988), 41–46.

32. Hammack, *Power and Society*, 101.

33. Hammack, *Power and Society*, 152; Myers, *Tammany Hall*, 282–83.

34. Howe, *World of Our Fathers*, 97; Myers, *Tammany Hall*, 284–86.

35. Davis, *Spearheads For Reform*, 136, 148; Hammack, *Power and Society*, 155–56; Cohen, *Encounter With Emancipation*, 333. Emanuel Hertz, "Politics: New York," in Charles S. Bernheimer, ed., *The Russian Jew in the United States* (Philadelphia: John C. Winston, 1905), 257. The "brass checks" statement appears to refer to the buttons of a police captain's uniform.

36. Hertz, "Politics: New York," 257; Cohen, *Encounter With Emancipation*, 331–36 also reports a strong shift in voting among Jews on the Lower East Side in 1901 based on literary evidence.

37. Wald, *The House on Henry Street*, 258; Davis, *Spearheads for Reform*, 71–73, 136, 148, 182; Robert Wesser, *Charles Evans Hughes: Politics and Reform in New York, 1905–1910* (Ithaca, NY: Cornell University Press, 1967), 303; Lewinson, *John Purroy Mitchel*, 89, 93.

Two: Organized Religion

1. Weiss, *Charles Francis Murphy*, 18; Huthmacher, "Charles Evans Hughes and Charles Francis Murphy," 28; J. Joseph Huthmacher, *Senator Robert F.*

Wagner and the Rise of Urban Liberalism (New York: Atheneum, 1968), 24–27; M. R. Werner, *Tammany Hall* (Garden City, NY: Doubleday, 1928), 482–87; Alfred Connable and Edward Silberfarb, *Tigers of Tammany: Nine Men Who Ran New York* (New York: Holt, 1967), chapter 8.

2. Weiss, *Charles Francis Murphy*, 28; Huthmacher, *Senator Robert F. Wagner*, 24; Wesser, *A Response to Progressivism*, 23; Howe, *World of Our Fathers*, 375; Hammack, *Power and Society*, 156.

3. Cohen, *Not Free to Desist*, 4–8.

4. Goren, *New York Jews and the Quest for Community*, passim; John Higham, *Strangers in the Land: Patterns of American Nativism, 1860–1925* (New York: Atheneum, 1973), 159–165.

5. Jeffrey Gurock, "The 1913 New York State Civil Rights Act," *American Jewish Studies Review* 1 (1976), 102–3.

6. Rischin, *The Promised City*, 42–44; Will Herberg, "The Jewish Labor Movement in the United States," *American Jewish Yearbook* 53 (1952), 15–16; Dubofsky, *When Workers Organize*, 17, 48.

7. Herberg, "The Jewish Labor Movement," 6–23; Dubofsky, *When Workers Organize*, 52; Arthur Liebman, "The Ties That Bind: The Jewish Support for the Left in the United States," *American Jewish Historical Quarterly* 66 (December 1976), 293–94, 300.

8. Dubofsky, *When Workers Organize*, 16–18; Melvyn Dubofsky, "Success and Failure of Socialism in New York City, 1900–1918: A Case Study," *Labor History* 9 (1968), 365; Irving Howe, *Socialism and America* (New York: Harcourt, 1977), 8; Kessner, *The Golden Door*, 69–70.

9. Arthur Gorenstein, "A Portrait of Ethnic Politics: The Socialists and the 1908 and 1910 Congressional Elections on the East Side," *American Jewish Historical Quarterly*, formerly *Publications of the American Jewish Historical Society* 50 (March, 1961), 226; Dubofsky, "Success and Failure of Socialism in New York City," 366–67.

10. Dubofsky, "Success and Failure of Socialism in New York City," 362–63; Herberg, "The Jewish Labor Movement," 24–25.

11. Huthmacher, "Charles Evans Hughes and Charles Francis Murphy," 29; Hutchmacher, *Robert F. Wagner*, 28–37; Weiss, *Charles Francis Murphy*, 45–49, 88; Wesser, *A Response to Progressivism*, 27–30.

12. Henderson, *Tammany Hall and the New Immigrants*, appendix, 297 ff.

13. Henderson, *Tammany Hall and the New Immigrants*, 231; Arthur Mann, *LaGuardia: A Fighter Against His Times*, 94.

14. William E. Leuchtenberg, *The Perils of Prosperity* (Chicago: The University of Chicago Press, 1958), 79; Zosa Szajkowski, "The Jews and New York City's Mayoralty Election of 1917," *Jewish Social Studies* 32 (October 1970), 304; Herberg, "The Jewish Labor Movement," 38–43.

15. Marvin G. Weinbaum, "New York County Republican Politics, 1897–1922: The Quarter Century After Municipal Consolidation," *The New York Historical Society Quarterly* 50 (January 1966) 78–79; Wesser, *Charles Evans*

Hughes, 103–4, 112–13, 302–3; Huthmacher, "Charles Evans Hughes and Charles F. Murphy," 25–40.

16. Weinbaum, "New York County Republican Politics, 1897–1922," 79–83.

17. Weinbaum, ibid., 92; Cohen, *A Dual Heritage*, 210; Dubofsky, "Success and Failure of Socialism in New York City," 366; Henderson, *Tammany Hall and the New Immigrants*, 117.

18. Weinbaum, "New York County Republican Politics," 91–92; Stephen D. Isaacs, *Jews and American Politics* (Garden City, New York: Doubleday, 1974), 152; David Burner, *The Politics of Provincialism* (Cambridge: Harvard University Press, 1967), 71, 239–40.

19. Matthew and Hannah Josephson, *Al Smith: Hero of the Cities* (Boston: Houghton, Mifflin, 1969); Oscar Handlin, *Al Smith and His America* (Boston: Little Brown, 1958), 12, 20–27, 32–38, 52–60; Paula Eldot, *Governor Alfred E. Smith: The Politician as Reformer* (New York: Garland, 1983), 2–4; Robert Caro, *The Power Broker: Robert Moses and the Fall of New York* (New York: Vintage, 1975), 116–22.

20. Jeffrey Gurock, "The 1913 New York State Civil Rights Act," 103; Howe, *World of Our Fathers*, 389 for *Irisher mensch* term.

21. Josephson and Josephson, *Al Smith: Hero of the Cities* 184, 191–93; Handlin, *Al Smith and His America*, 71–72.

22. Perry, *Belle Moskowitz*; Robert Caro, *The Power Broker*, 91–94; Allan Nevins, *Herbert H. Lehman and His Era* (New York: Scribner's, 1963), 96–98; Howe, *World of Our Fathers*, 389; Josephson and Josephson, *Al Smith: Hero of the Cities*, 127–28, 187, 192–93, 302–04.

23. Josephson and Josephson, *Al Smith: Hero of the Cities*, 285.

24. Josephson and Josephson, *Al Smith: Hero of the Cities*, 444; David Burner, *The Politics of Provincialism*, 179–216; Henderson, *Tammany Hall and the New Immigrants*, appendix, 297 ff.

25. Herbert Mitgang, *The Man Who Rode the Tiger: The Life and Times of Judge Samuel Seabury* (New York: Lippincott, 1963), 159–202; 216–44; 245–65; 282–99; Edward J. Flynn, *You're the Boss* (New York: Viking, 1947), 56–59; Thomas Kessner, *Fiorello H. LaGuardia and the Making of Modern New York* (New York: McGraw-Hill, 1989), 222–32.

26. Mann, *LaGuardia Comes to Power*, 63–65.

27. Ibid., 67–87.

28. LaGuardia was so clearly identified as an Italian that his Jewish heritage rarely surfaced during political campaigns, although his ability to speak Yiddish helped him with Jewish voters. Once, when his Jewish heritage did become a public issue, he commented, "I never figured I had enough Jewish blood to brag about it." Kessner, *LaGuardia*, 247.

29. Ronald Bayor, *Neighbors in Conflict: The Irish, Germans, Jews and Italians of New York City*, (Baltimore: The Johns Hopkins University Press, 1978), 130 reports the total Italian vote for LaGuardia at 62% in 1933. Arthur

Mann offers weighty evidence that LaGuardia took between 80 and 90% of the Italian vote. Mann, *LaGuardia Comes to Power*, 133–34.

30. Bayor, *Neighbors in Conflict*, 130–33; Mann, *LaGuardia Comes to Power*, 138–52; Kessner, *LaGuardia*, 250–51.

31. Matthew Josephson, *Statesman of American Labor* (New York: Doubleday, 1952), 395.

32. About 60% of the dues-paying members of the ILGWU, about the same percentage of the Hatters Union's members, and more than half of Hillman's 160,000 Amalgamated Workers, were in New York.

33. William James Stewart, "A Political History of the American Labor Party, 1936–1944," (Masters Thesis, American University, Washington, DC, 1959), 4–6.

34. Stewart, "A Political History of the American Labor Party," 8–9.

35. The proportion of Jewish membership in the ILGWU, Amalgamated Clothing Workers, and other unions in 1936 is difficult to determine with certainty. About 80% of the workers in the men's clothing industry in New York were Jewish in 1913, but that figure had declined to about 30% by 1950 according to one estimate. The women's clothing industry was 65% Jewish in 1909, but it too underwent a substantial change by mid-century. See Herberg, "The Jewish Labor Movement," 54, 59. Straight interpolation suggests that more than half of the laborers in the men's industry and probably just under half in the women's industry were Jewish at the time the ALP was created. Convincing evidence, below, reveals that the ALP's voting strength, like its leadership, came from Jews.

36. Stewart, "A Political History of the American Labor Party," 12, 16.

37. *New York City Board of Elections Annual Report, 1937*, 122; Charles Garrett, *The LaGuardia Years: Machine and Reform Politics in New York City* (New Brunswick, NJ: Rutgers University Press, 1961), 275; Stewart, "A Political History of the American Labor Party, 1936–1944," 33–34.

38. Bayor, *Neighbors in Conflict*, 137.

39. Theodore Lowi, *At the Pleasure of the Mayor: Patronage and Power in New York City, 1898–1958*. (London: The Free Press, 1964), 38; Garrett, *The LaGuardia Years*, 138; Cohen, *Not Free to Desist*, 202; Bayor, *Neighbors in Conflict*, 25. Although LaGuardia aggressively implemented civil service regulations, it is clear that he also used patronage shrewdly to strengthen himself and weaken his opponents.

40. Mann, *LaGuardia Comes to Power*, 16; Bayor, *Neighbors in Conflict*, 136–39.

41. Bayor, *Neighbors in Conflict*, 143.

Three: The Machine Overhauled

1. Edward J. Flynn, "Bosses and Machines," *The Atlantic Monthly*, May, 1947, 34.

2. Edward J. Flynn, *You're the Boss* (New York: Viking, 1947), 3–37, *passim*.

3. Clifton D. Hood, "Underground Politics: A History of Mass Transit in New York City Since 1904," (PhD. diss., Columbia University, New York, 1986), 79, 93–4; Deborah Dash More, *At Home in America* (New York: Columbia University Press, 1981), 23; Jill Jonnes, *We're Still Here: The Rise Fall and Resurrection of the South Bronx* (New York: The Atlantic Monthly Press, 1986), 4. Brooklyn had more Jewish residents than the Bronx but a lower proportion as a percent of the total population.

4. Flynn, *You're the Boss*, 59; Warren Moscow, *Politics in the Empire State* (New York: Knopf, 1948), 89, explains that the so-called paving block scandal, the only one that marred Flynn's reputation, occurred when Flynn's wife tried to have some work done on their summer home in Mahopac while Flynn was out of town. She called the Bronx borough president's office to get the name of a contractor to lay down some stones, and an employee trying to be helpful sent a team of city workers to do the job. When Flynn discovered what had happened he called Mayor LaGuardia to arrange to pay for the work, and in the process of taking care of the paperwork a city employee hostile to Flynn got wind of the event and made it public. The irony is that the only reason the matter ever became known is because Flynn sought to make restitution for the minor task.

5. Flynn, *You're the Boss*, 132–38; Richard Rovere, "Profiles: Nothing Much To It," *The New Yorker*, September 8, 1946, 42; Haskell, *A Leader of the Garment Workers*, 257; Robert Williams and Peter J. McElroy, "The Flynn Machine—How the Bronx Is Ruled," *New York Post*, May 18, 19, 20, 21, 22, 1953. This series of articles makes it clear that Flynn could use machine tactics effectively even though he was honest and committed to responsible government.

6. Flynn, *You're the Boss*, 73, 84; James A. Farley, *Jim Farley's Story: The Roosevelt Years* (New York: McGraw-Hill, 1948), 347–58; William E. Leuchtenberg, *Franklin D. Roosevelt and the New Deal* (New York: Harper, 1963), 315–16.

7. James A. Farley, interview, Columbia University Oral History Project (hereafter, COH); The Reminiscences of Herbert H. Lehman, COH; Warren Moscow, *Politics in the Empire State*, 89–92; Nevins, *Herbert H. Lehman*, 220; Farley, *Jim Farley's Story*, 355.

8. Moscow, *Politics in the Empire State*, 108–13; David Dubinsky and A. H. Raskin, *David Dubinsky: A Life With Labor* (New York: Simon and Schuster, 1977), 271–76; Stewart, "The American Labor Party," 61–98 offers an extremely detailed account of the maneuvering between the two factions.

9. Jack Barbash, ed., "Special Supplement on David Dubinsky," *Labor History* 9 (Spring 1968), *passim*; Dubinsky and Raskin, *David Dubinsky*, *passim*; Max Danish, *The World of David Dubinsky* (New York: World, 1957), 15–21, 269 and *passim*; Harry Haskel, *A Leader of the Garment Workers: The Biography of Isidore Nagler* (New York: Shulsingers Brothers, 1950), 246.

10. Jerry Tallmer, "Alex Rose of the Liberal Party," *The New York Post,* October 25, 1966.

11. Alex Rose, Unpublished Diary, January 19, 21, 1919. Rose kept this diary between November 12, 1918 and February 1, 1919 while in the Jewish Foreign Legion. Apparently he was trying to improve his English because most entries appear twice, once in Yiddish and once in translation, both in Rose's hand. The diary is in the possession of Alex Rose's son, Herbert, in New York City, who kindly let me review the document and take extensive notes. Herbert Rose had previously confirmed that the Yiddish passages were the same as the English entries.

12. Alex Rose, Unpublished Diary, January 21, 1919.

13. Alex Rose, Unpublished Memoirs, in the possession of Herbert Rose, New York City. Alex Rose was writing a political memoir at the time of his death. He had completed the preface, from which the quote is taken, and two chapters, one on the gubernatorial election of Averell Harriman in 1954, and one on the gubernatorial election of Hugh Carey in 1974. Mr. Herbert Rose generously made these available to me.

14. Jerry Tallmer, "Alex Rose of the Liberal Party," *The New York Post,* October 25, 1966.

15. Rosenwaike, *Population History of New York City,* 94, 203–04; Kessner, *The Golden Door,* 26–30, 53; Henderson, *Tammany Hall and the New Immigrants,* 53–54; Riordan, *Plunkitt,* 62; Miller, *Emigrants and Exiles,* 526; Donald Tricarico, *The Italians of Greenwich Village: The Social Transformation of an Ethnic Community* (New York: The Center for Migration Studies, 1984), 57.

16. Henderson, *Tammany Hall and the New Immigrants,* 133; Warren Moscow, *The Last of the Big Time Bosses* (New York: Stein and Day, 1976), 45; Deborah Dash Moore, *At Home in America,* 217; George Combs, interview, COH.

17. Mann, *LaGuardia Comes to Power,* 129–38; Bayor, *Neighbors in Conflict,* 130, 137, 143.

18. Timothy Gilfoyle, *City of Eros: New York City, Prostitution and the Commercialization of Sex, 1790–1920* (New York: Norton, 1992), 243–47.

19. Goren, *New York Jews and the Quest for Community,* 139; Howe, *World of Our Fathers,* 99–100; Nevins, *Herbert H. Lehman,* 183; Daniel Bell, *The End of Ideology,* rev. ed. (New York: The Free Press, 1962), 133, 144–45; Glazer and Moynihan, *Beyond the Melting Pot,* 210; Caroline Ware, *Greenwich Village, 1920–1930* (New York: Harper, 1935), 59–62, 273–76.

20. George Walsh, *Public Enemies: The Mayor, the Mob and the Crime that Was* (New York: Norton, 1980), 102; Moscow, *The Last of the Big-Time Bosses.*

21. Robert Heilbroner, "Carmine G. DeSapio: The Smile on the Face of the Tiger," *Harper's Magazine* (July 1954), 26–27.

22. Alva Johnston, "Profiles: The Great Expurgator," *The New Yorker*

(March 29, 1947), 40–41. By 1940 over 95% of the urban homes in America had radio sets, Norbert Muhlen, "Radio: A Political Threat or Promise?" *Commentary* (March 1947), 201. Irving Foulds Luscombes, "WNYC: 1922–1940—The Early History of a Twentieth Century Urban Service," (Ph.D. diss., New York University, 1968) describes the extent to which politicians fought over control of New York City's municipal radio station. Democrats particularly objected to public broadcasts of City Council hearings after they learned from a survey that listeners were overwhelmingly sympathetic to the minority. John Cashmore, then majority leader, had the program taken off the air according to Councilmember Genevieve B. Earle. Genevieve B. Earle interview, COH.

23. Warren Moscow, "Exit the Boss, Enter the 'Leader,' " The *New York Times Magazine* (June 22, 1947), 16; Warren Moscow, "Political Machines Have Lost Their Grip," *Saturday Evening Post*, (April 12, 1947), 23; Irwin Ross, "Big City Machines and Liberal Voters," *Commentary* (October 1950), 303; Heilbroner, *The Smile on the Face of the Tiger*, 27.

24. Roger Biles, *Big City Boss in Depression and War: Mayor Edward J. Kelly of Chicago* (Dekalb: Northern Illinois University Press, 1984), 33–36, 40–43, 75–76, 156; Frank S. Robinson, *Machine Politics: A Study of Albany's O'Connells* (New Brunswick, NJ: Transaction Books, 1977), 51, 121; Garrett, *The LaGuardia Years*, 275; Moscow, "Political Machines," 23, 149. Ross, "Big City Machines and Liberal Voters," 303.

25. Garrett, *The LaGuardia Years*, 285; Howard Brubacker, "Of All Things," *The New Yorker*, May 12, 1945, 42.

26. Garrett, *The LaGuardia Years*, 282; Philip Hamburger, "That Great Big New York Up There," *The New Yorker* (May 28, 1957), 82; Robert Caro, *The Power Broker* (New York: Vintage Books, 1975), 699.

27. William O'Dwyer, *Beyond the Golden Door* (New York: St. John's University Press, 1987), *passim*; Walsh, *Public Enemies*, 1–3; Milton McKaye, "The Ex-Cop Who Runs New York," *The Saturday Evening Post* (May 31, 1947), 81.

28. Richard Norton Smith, *Thomas E. Dewey and His Times* (New York: Simon and Schuster), 262–63, 285; O'Dwyer, *Beyond the Golden Door*, 161–69, 209–16; *The New York Times*, (hereafter, *NYT*), June 2, 1945.

29. Bayor, *Neighbors in Conflict*, 143:O'Dwyer, *Beyond the Golden Door*, 210.

30. *NYT*, June 6, 8, 1945; Moscow, *The Last of the Big Time Bosses*, 63. Robert Caro in *The Power Broker*, 788, reports that as incredulous as Bert Stand's story sounds, he interviewed four Tammany Democrats who participated in the decision and who insist that Stand's comment was not a joke but the way the nomination was made. However, it is not believable that the Democrats would have dumped candidates chosen by Ed Flynn and Tammany leader Ed Loughlin without more reason than the need for a long Italian name. Lawrence Gerosa, the original Italian on the ticket, was a well respected member of the Italian community and would have served as a perfectly acceptable

political representative of that group, as he did in 1953 and 1957 when he was the successful Democratic candidate for comptroller. Irwin Davidson was also an acceptable candidate. Caro does not comment on the ticket switch in his account. The story that follows, as reported by Warren Moscow, makes more sense and is consistent with the other information available.

31. "Vito Marcantonio: New York's Leftist Laborite," in Richard H. Luthin, *American Demogogues: Twentieth Century* (Gloucester, MA: Peter Smith, 1957): 209–33; Gerald Meyer, *Vito Marcantonio: Radical Politician, 1902–1954* (Albany: State University of New York Press, 1989), *passim*.

32. Warren Moscow, interview with author, New York City, May 4, 1987. Moscow was a political reporter for many years, first with the Hearst newspapers beginning in 1922, and later with the *New York Times*. He also worked for Robert F. Wagner in the Manhattan borough president's office after 1949 and in the mayor's office after 1953. George Combs, interview, COH, confirms the close relationship between Impellitteri and Lucchese. Combs was an active member of Tammany Hall and served on the Democratic party campaign committee in 1949 and other years.

33. O'Dwyer, *Beyond the Golden Door*, 219; *NYT*, June 13, 1945.

34. Flynn, *You're the Boss*, 222; Robert Spivack, "New York's Mayoralty Race," *The New Republic* (July 9, 1945), 43; *NYT*, November 3, 1945.

35. Richard S. Childs, "Introducing Jonah J. Goldstein," *The Searchlight*, Published by the Citizens Union of the City of New York, (July 1945), 1–2; *NYT*, October 4, 1945.

36. Howard Brubacker, "Of All Things," *The New Yorker* (September 22, 1945), 52; Spivack, "New York's Mayoralty Race," 43.

37. The Liberal Party, *For Our City: 1945 Municipal Program* (New York: The Liberal Party of New York State, 1945), *passim*.

38. When O'Dwyer asked Moses to agree to stay on, the city building expert made it clear that he planned to vote for Morris. "Hell, I don't care who you vote for, just stick around," the confident O'Dwyer replied. *NYT* November 2, 1945.

39. David Dubinsky, *Liberal Party News*, October 15, 1945; *NYT* June 3, 1945.

40. *NYT*, June 9, 1945; Howard Brubacker, "Of All Things," *The New Yorker*, August 11, 1945, 56 and August 18, 1945, 38; Moscow interview, May 4, 1987.

41. "Campaign Ephemera, 1945," New York Public Library (hereafter NYPL); "New York City Politics, 1945," Vertical Files of the Municipal Reference and Research Library of New York City (hereafter MRRL); *NYT* August 8, October 13, November 2, 1945.

42. Howard Brubacker, "Of All Things," *The New Yorker*, (August 11, 1945), 56; ibid. (August 18, 1945), 38.

43. *NYT* November 2, 1945 reporting radio broadcast of November 1, 1945;

Jonah J. Goldstein, "The Jewish Vote," *American Hebrew* 98 (November 22, 1912), 99.

44. Printed text of radio address delivered by William O'Dwyer on September 13, 1945, in "Campaign Ephemera, 1945," NYPL; Printed text of radio address delivered by William O'Dwyer, November 5, 1945, in "New York City Politics, 1945," Vertical Files, MRRL.

45. McKaye, "The Ex-Cop Who Runs New York," 81; Spivack, "New York's Mayoralty Race, 43.

46. Walsh, *Public Enemies*, 121–24; O'Dwyer, *Beyond the Golden Door*, 222–26.

47. Ethnic electoral data for the 1945 mayoralty race are based on William Spinrad, "New Yorkers Cast Their Ballots" (Ph.D. diss., Columbia University, 1955). Spinrad correlated voting returns for the 1941 and 1945 mayoralty elections in New York City with census tract ethnic data and the socioeconomic information provided in the New York City Health Survey. The survey divides the city into 257 districts which Spinrad used as his unit of analysis. The study is comparative. It describes the characteristics of the districts where O'Dwyer ran better in 1945 than in 1941 rather than the percentage vote he took of each category of voter. The study is very useful, but its method makes comparison with data from other elections difficult.

48. Spinrad, "New Yorkers Cast Their Ballots," 108–13. The ALP also had a slight concentration of black voters. Robert Bower, "How New York City Labor Votes," *Public Opinion Quarterly* (Winter, 1947–48): 614–15 confirms that neither the American Labor nor Liberal parties had extra strength in areas with a high concentration of workers.

49. Spinrad, "New Yorkers Cast Their Ballots," 110.

50. Ethnicity of New York City county party leaders and Board of Estimate members was determined from the information available in "Biography Notebooks," maintained at MRRL. The leaders in 1945 were Edward J. Flynn (Bronx); Frank V. Kelly (Kings); Edward V. Loughlin (New York); James A. Roe (Queens); and Jeremiah Sullivan (Richmond). The five borough presidents elected in 1945 were James J. Lyons (Bronx); John Cashmore (Brooklyn); Hugo Rogers (Manhattan); J. A. Burke (Queens); and Cornelius A. Hall (Richmond). Rogers was Jewish. Hall was Scotch Irish and Protestant. All of the others were Irish Catholic.

Four: The Machine Breaks Down

1. *NYT*, November 7, 1945.

2. "Talk of the Town," *The New Yorker* (April 13, 1946), 24; Woolf, "O'Dwyer Tells Why It's Tough," 14.

3. Unidentified press clipping dated February 2, 1946 and July 24, 1947 in "The Public Career of William O'Dwyer," compiled for use of campaign workers, Summer 1949, on file at MRRL; "Talk of the Town," *The New Yorker*

(April 13, 1946), 24; Ross, "Big City Machines and Liberal Voters," 301 for quote on O'Dwyer's labor policies.

4. *The New York Daily News* (hereafter *DN*), November 24, 1947; *NYT*, November 26, 1947; Lillian Ross, "A Reporter at Large," *The New Yorker* (July 12, 1947), 27; Philip Hamburger, "Some People Watch Birds," *The New Yorker* (December 26, 1953), 48.

5. Unidentified press clipping dated February 2, 1946 in "The Public Career of William O'Dwyer."

6. McKaye, "The Ex-Cop Who Runs New York," 19; *The New York Herald Tribune* (hereafter *HT*), March 4, 1947; *NYT*, March 5, 1947.

7. Moscow, *Last of the Big Time Bosses*, 67–68.

8. *HT*, July 2, 1948; Walsh, *Public Enemies*, 158; Some fifty letters and post cards from citizens supporting the mayor in his contest with Tammany can be found in The Papers of Mayor William O'Dwyer, New York City Municipal Archives, box 149 (hereafter WOD Papers).

9. New York City Board of Elections, *Annual Report*, 1948; Max Frankel, "Robert B. Blaikie and His Irregular Democratic Club" (Master's thesis, Columbia University, 1953), 105, 146.

10. Correspondence indicating O'Dwyer support for an open Democratic National Convention in 1948, WOD Papers, box 83; *HT*, August 28, 30, 1948; Undated press clipping from the *New York Post* (hereafter *NYP*) in David Dubinsky Papers, ILGWU Archives, box 136, file 2b (hereafter DD Papers); Combs, interview, COH; John Cooney, *The American Pope: The Life and Times of Francis Cardinal Spellman* (New York: Times Books, 1984), 173. Strom Thurmond also ran for president in 1948 on a segregationist platform, but he had little support in New York City.

11. Warren Moscow, *Last of the Big Time Bosses*, 74; George Combs indicated that Bert Stand often tried to push Tammany in a liberal direction, but exercised caution because he rarely got much support. Combs, interview, COH.

12. Frankel, "Robert B. Blaikie," 151; *HT*, May 4, 1949; *NYT*, May 16, 17, 1949; Heilbroner, "The Smile on the Face of the Tiger," 30.

13. Heilbroner, "The Smile on the Face of the Tiger," 30–31; Max Frankel, "Robert B. Blaikie and His Irregular Democratic Club," 94–96; Seymour B. Forman, " 'Silk Stocking' Politics: A Study of Two Political Clubs in a New York County Assembly District," (Master's thesis, Columbia University, 1954), 51–54; James S. Ottenberg, *The Lexington Democratic Club Story* (New York: Lexington Democratic Club, 1959), 7.

14. James Q. Wilson, *The Amateur Democrat* (Chicago: University of Chicago Press, 1962), 14–15, 28; Elmer E. Cornwell, Jr., "Bosses, Machines, and Ethnic Groups," in Lawrence H. Fuchs, *American Ethnic Politics* (New York: Harper, 1968), 213. Where available a review of the names of the participants in the clubs further suggests their heavily Jewish composition, for instance Ottenberg, *Lexington Democratic Club*, 40–42 lists the Executive Committee,

Advisory Council, and Standing Committees, 40–42. Surveys confirm the point more definitively for later periods.

15. McKaye, "The Ex-Cop Who Runs New York," 84; Hamburger, "That Great Big New York Up There," *The New Yorker* (May 28, 1957), 62; *NYT* February 13, 23, 1948; *NYT* May 27, 1949; Telegram dated June 7, 1949, WOD Papers, box 83.

16. Various telegrams dated June 9 through June 14, 1949, WOD Papers, box 83; Hutchmacher, *Senator Robert F. Wagner*, 22.

17. Combs, interview, COH; Robert F. Wagner, interview with author, New York City, March 28, 1988.

18. *Berle Diary*, June 1, 1949, Roll 6, Frame 823; July 21, 1949, Roll 6, Frame 832; Moscow, interview, May 4, 1987; Walsh, *Public Enemies*, 162; Harry Uviller, interview, COH. Uviller was the Republican-Liberal candidate for Comptroller in 1949.

19. *NYP*, April 14, 1949; Minutes of Meeting dated October 21, 1949, DD Papers, box 136, file 2b; "New York Mayoralty Campaign" Sixth Quarterly Meeting, GEB, November 14–16, 1949, DD Papers, box 136, file 2a. *Berle Diary*, "Memorandum: The Liberal Party: 1948–1949 Position," December 1, 1948, Roll 6, Frame 799.

20. *Berle Diaries*, July 7, 1949, Roll 6, Frame 829.

21. Vito Marcantonio, interview, COH; Paul Ross, interview, COH. Ross managed Marcantonio's 1949 mayoralty campaign and ran as the ALP candidate for Governor in the 1950 election.

22. Nevins, *Herbert H. Lehman*, 303, 308.

23. Moscow, *Last of the Big Time Bosses*, 76–78.

24. Ibid., 82; *NYT* August 4, 1949; *Berle Diary*, August 4, 1949, Roll 6, Frame 838; Wagner interview, March 28, 1988.

25. Address by Mayor William O'Dwyer at Carnegie Hall, October 24, 1949, and Address at Hunts Point Palace, November 1, 1949 broadcast over WOR radio, WOD Papers, box 83. Speech by Herbert H. Lehman delivered at Columbia University, November 2, 1949, COH.

26. Newbold Morris, interview, COH; "Campaign Ephemera, 1949," NYPL. Morris's effort to portray himself as LaGuardia's replacement was a touch monotonous. In one satirical piece of campaign literature the Democrats included a picture of a tiny Newbold Morris running out of control along the edge of a phonograph disk bearing the label "LaGuardia's Record." Underneath appear the lyrics," . . . me too . . . me too . . . me too." "Campaign Ephemera, 1949," NYPL.

27. Labor's Round-Up Rally AFL-CIO, November 3, 1949, broadcast on WJZ, WINS, WMCA radio and WCBS television, and Joint Broadcast with Mrs. Franklin D. Roosevelt, November 7, 1949, heard on WNBC radio, WOD Papers, box 83.

28. Combs interview, COH.

29. "Campaign Ephemera, 1949," NYPL; Harry Uviller, interview, COH.

Paul O'Dwyer, *Counsel for the Defense*; Conversation with Seymour Gross, New York City, Summer 1987. A mutual acquaintance, Robert Zenilman, introduced me to Mr. Gross, born in New York City of Jewish immigrant parents. He and members of his family were politically active in New York City in the 1940s and 1950s.

30. Cooney, *The American Pope*, 176–85; Combs interview, COH; O'Dwyer, *Beyond the Golden Door*, 312–13.

31. Nevins, *Herbert H. Lehman*, 310.

32. Recording by Mayor William O'Dwyer for Herbert H. Lehman, November 4, 1949, WOD Papers, box 83; "Campaign Ephemera, 1949," NYPL.

33. "Campaign Ephemera, 1949," NYPL; "New York City Politics-1949–1950," Vertical Files, MRRL; Vincent Impellitteri Speech, November 2, 1949 broadcast on WNBC radio, WOD Papers, box 83; Combs, interview, COH.

34. Harry Uviller, interview, COH; George Combs, interview, COH; Letter dated September 27, 1949 from Gus Tyler, Director, ILGWU political department to Jacob Javits, Campaign Chairman for Newbold Morris, DD Papers, box 136, file 2c.

35. Houston Irvine Flournoy, "The Liberal Party in New York State" (Ph.D. diss., Princeton University, 1956), 163. "Excerpts from a speech delivered by President Dubinsky to a meeting of local managers, October 2, 1949 on the question of endorsing Newbold Morris," and Letter dated November 9, 1949 from Lester B. Stone to David Dubinsky, and "New York City Mayoralty Campaign," Sixth Quarterly Meeting, GEB, November 14–16, 1949, DD Papers, box 136, file 2a.

36. Ethnic voting data for the 1949 election were developed by the author as described in the appendix. For 1941 see Bayor, *Neighbors in Conflict*, 143 and for 1945 see Spinrad, "New Yorkers Cast Their Ballots."

37. NYT, June 20, 1949; Luthin, "Vito Marcantonio," 232–33.

38. Will Herberg, "From Marxism to Judaism: Jewish Belief as a Dynamic of Social Action," *Commentary* (January 1947), 25–32; Alexander Bloom, *Prodigal Sons: The New York Intellectuals and Their World* (New York: Oxford University Press, 1986), 50–55, 95.

39. See entries for "Soviet Union," in the years 1948 to 1954 by Joseph Gorden, in *American Jewish Yearbook* (Philadelphia: Jewish Publication Society of America).

40. Nathan Glazer, *American Judaism* 2d ed., rev. (Chicago: University of Chicago Press, 1972), 115–16.

41. Wesley and Beverly Allinsmith, "Religious Affiliation and Politico-Economic Attitude: A Study of Eight Major US Religious Groups," *Public Opinion Quarterly* (Fall 1948): 377–89.

42. Hamburger, "That Great Big New York," 61–62; Warren Moscow, interview with author, May 4, 1987 reports that O'Dwyer's hospital bedroom curtain caught on fire because of Moran's melodramatic reaction to the mayor's

decision. Only because of this accident, which attracted others to the room, did anyone other than the mayor and his assistant find out about the episode.

43. "Talk of the Town," *The New Yorker* (April 13, 1946), 24; Walsh, *Public Enemies*, 174–76.

44. Walsh, *Public Enemies*, 174–76; *The New York World Telegram & Sun* (hereafter *WTS*), March 31, 1950.

45. Warren Moscow reports that Charles Buckley, a congressman and the successor to Edward J. Flynn as Bronx Democratic county leader, told him that O'Dwyer's exit involved a deal worked out in 1949 between the mayor and Edward Flynn. The Bronx boss wanted his party to regain the governor's seat in 1950 and thought that only by offsetting the Republican majority upstate with an exceptionally high voter turnout in the city could a Democrat be successful. If the mayor won reelection, and resigned the next year in time for a special contest, then city voters would come to the polls in great numbers to choose a new chief executive and add to Democratic chances to capture the Governor's Mansion. In return for O'Dwyer's commitment to run and serve until the fall, Flynn negotiated with President Truman to secure the retirement spot in Mexico for the mayor. Moscow interview, May 4, 1987.

46. Joseph A. Gavagan, interview, COH. Impellitteri was Gavagan's law secretary when Gavagan was city magistrate. Genevieve B. Earle, interview, COH; Combs, interview, COH; Moscow interview, May 4, 1987.

47. Combs, interview, COH.

48. Letter dated November 10, 1950 from Ben Davidson, Executive Director of the New York State Liberal Party to James Wechsler, Editor, *NYP*, DD Papers, box 135, file 2b; *Berle Diary* June 13, 1949, Roll 6, Frame 827; Karl Shriftgiesser, "A Frantic Day With Our Next Mayor," *The New York Times Magazine*, October 22, 1950, 15; "New York City Politics, 1949–1950," Vertical Files, MRRL.

49. Frankel, "Robert Blaikie," 77.

50. Moscow interview, May 4, 1987.

51. Speech by Sydney S. Baron, Campaign Coordinator for Vincent R. Impellitteri, broadcast over WINS radio, October 20, 1950, and Speech by Vincent R. Impellitteri broadcast over WNBC radio, October 28, 1950, The Papers of Mayor Vincent R. Impellitteri, New York City Municipal Archives, box 48 (hereafter, VRI Papers).

52. "This is New York," Bill Leonard Reporting, Transcript of WCBS Profile of Candidates, VRI Papers box 48, and Radio Address by Acting Mayor V. R. Impellitteri delivered November 6, 1950, VRI Papers, box 49.

53. Combs, interview, COH.

54. Combs, interview, COH; *WTS* October 27, 1950. Impellitteri won 1,161,175 votes, Pecora 935,351 and Corsi only 382,372. In 1949 Newbold Morris won 570,713 on the Republican ticket. New York City Board of Elections, *Annual Report*, 1949 and 1950. Ethnic voting data for the 1950 election were developed by the author as described in the appendix.

55. Frankel, "Robert Blaikie," 124.

56. Unidentified news clipping, "New York City Politics, 1949–1950," Vertical Files, MRRL; Letter dated November 10, 1950 from Ben Davidson, Executive Director of the New York State Liberal Party to James Wechsler, Editor, *NYP*, DD Papers, box 135, file 2b; *Berle Diary*, July 18, 1951, Roll 6, Frame 975.

57. Walsh, *Public Enemies* 187; *Berle Diary*, July 18, 1951, Roll 6, Frame 975.

58. Letter dated November 5, 1951 from Ben Davidson to Nat Kanner, LPP, box 19; Telegram from David Dubinsky to Local Managers, dated November 7, 1951, DD Papers, box 135, file 1a.

59. Heilbroner, "The Smile on the Face of the Tiger," 31; Ottenberg, *Lexington Democratic Club*, 14–15.

60. Herbert S. Parmet, *The Democrats: The Years After FDR* (New York: Oxford University Press, 1976), 95–98; Wilson, *The Amateur Democrat*, 52–58; Moscow, *The Last of the Big-Time Bosses*, 137–38; Hamlen Hunt, "New Deal Wake: Boston Massachusetts," *Commentary* (December 1952), 592.

61. Ottenberg, *The Lexington Democratic Club*, 15; Heilbroner, "The Smile on the Face of the Tiger," 31.

Five: Robert F. Wagner

1. Report of the Mayor's Committee on Management Survey, *Modern Management for the City of New York*, vol. 1, 1953 reported on page 1, "The management studies under our direction have given instance after instance of departments in which things have gone wrong, where there is evidence of waste and mismanagement, or where matters have been handled badly or without adequate supervision." Edgar M. Hoover and Raymond Vernon, *Anatomy of a Metropolis* (Cambridge: Harvard University Press, 1959), 16, 202; *WT&S*, January 2, March 6, 1953.

2. U.S. Census Office, *U.S. Census of Population, 1950: Population and Housing Characteristics* (Washington: U.S. Government Printing Office, 1953–54), summary pages for each of the five counties of New York City; *WT&S*, March 6, 1953; *The Brooklyn Eagle* (hereafter, *BE*), March 16, 1953; Hood, "Underground Politics," 411–17.

3. *BE*, March 15, 26, 30, 1953; Citizens Union, "Press Release: Citizens Union Announces Program for City's Fiscal Crisis" March 10, 1953.

4. Philip Hamburger, *Mayor Watching and Other Pleasures* (New York: Rinehart, 1958), 9, 21.

5. Editorial, *NYT*, January 1, 1952; *HT*, May 15, 1953; Moscow interview, December 7, 1987.

6. *BE*, January 21, February 20, March 23, 1953; *HT*, March 3, May 21, 1953; *WT&S*, January 1, 1953.

7. Moscow, *Last of the Big-Time Bosses*, 98–99; Israel Glasser, "An Analy-

sis of Differential Voting Participation in the 1953 Democratic Mayoralty Primary Election in New York City" (Ph.D. diss., New York University, 1957), 21; *HT*, March 13, 1953; *BE*, May 15, 1953; *WT&S*, March 6, March 15, 1953.

8. Moscow interview, December 7, 1987; *BE*, February 22, 1953.

9. Jacob K. Javits with Rafael Steinberg, *Javits: The Autobiography of a Public Man* (Boston: Houghton Mifflin, 1981), 191, 195–97; *HT*, February 15, April 13, May 22, 1953; *Berle Diaries*, Roll 6, frames 1281, 1288, 1309, 1324; *WT&S*, May 26, 1953; *BE*, March 23, June 15, 17, 1953; *The New York Daily News* (hereafter *DN*), May 3, 1953; *NYT*, July 14, 1953.

10. *BE*, May 25, June 24, 1953. According to Warren Moscow, after Dewey became governor he picked Frank Hogan to run for Manhattan District Attorney on a joint ticket after several Republican candidates he proposed proved unacceptable to the Democrats. Hogan remained linked to Dewey in the eyes of many Democrats for years afterward. Moscow interview, December 7, 1987. Richard Norton Smith, *Thomas E. Dewey and His Times* (New York: Simon & Schuster, 1982), 340 offers a slightly different interpretation.

11. *WT&S*, May 22, 1953; Moscow interview, December 7, 1987.

12. *Berle Diaries*, roll 6, frame 1318; Javits, *Autobiography*, 197; *BE*, June 12, 1953; *HT*, June 18, June 30, 1953; *WT&S*, April 10, 1953.

13. *WT&S*, May 2, 1953; *BE*, July 22, 1953.

14. Citizens Union, "Press Release: DeSapio Tells 'Citizens Union Searchlight' He Will Abide By Poll of Party Even If It Favors Impellitteri," March 30, 1953; *HT*, June 12, 1953; *WT&S*, June 17, 1953.

15. Citizens Union, "Press Release: Wagner Tells Citizens Union He Does Not Object to Mention for Mayoralty," March 16, 1953; *BE*, May 5, May 15, 1953; *WT&S*, May 19, 1953; *HT*, May 3, 1953; Moscow interview, December 7, 1987.

16. Citizens Union, "Press Release: Wagner Willing to Enter Primary Fight," June 29, 1953.

17. Glasser, "Analysis of Differential Voting Participation," 17–18; Wallace S. Sayre and Herbert Kaufman, *Governing New York City*, 141–45.

18. *DN*, May 10, 1953; *BE*, July 22, 1953; Moscow interview, December 7, 1987.

19. *HT*, July 21, 1953; Moscow interview, December 7, 1987.

20. Wagner interview, March 28, 1988; *NYT*, July 18, 1953; *HT*, July 18, 1953; *DN*, July 19, 1953; *BE*, July 19, 1953.

21. *HT*, July 24, 1953; Statement by hon. HH Lehman, and Statement by W. Averell Harriman, box 2208, The Papers of Mayor Robert F. Wagner (hereafter, RFW Papers).

22. Wagner interview, March 28, 1988; Huthmacher, *Senator Robert F. Wagner and the Rise of Urban Liberalism*, 22.

23. *HT*, July 21, July 22, 1953; *NYT*, July 23, 1953.

24. *WT&S*, September 14, 1953.

25. John Albert Morsell, "The Political Behavior of Negroes in New York

City," (Ph.D. diss., Columbia University, 1950), 8–11; Gilbert Osofsky, *Harlem: The Making of a Ghetto*, 2nd ed. (New York: Harper & Row, 1971), 45.

26. Morsell, "The Political Behavior of Negroes," 26–31; Edwin R. Lewinson, *Black Politics in New York City* (New York: Twayne Publishers, Inc, 1974), 44.

27. Osofsky, *Harlem*, 18–28, 89–91.

28. Lewinson, *Black Politics*, 144; Nancy J. Weiss, *Farewell to the Party of Lincoln: Black Politics in the Age of FDR* (Princeton: Princeton University Press, 1983), 209 and *passim*.

29. Spinrad, "New Yorkers Cast Their Ballots," 50–51; U.S. Census Office, *Census of the Population*, Vol. I, 85.

30. *HT* July 28, 1953; *NYT*, August 15, 1953; *WT&S*, September 14, 1953.

31. Moscow interview, December 7, 1987.

32. *NYT*, August 10, 1953.

33. Liberal Party News, "Biographical Sketch of Robert F. Wagner, Liberal Party Candidate for U.S. Senate," LP Papers, box 26.

34. *WT&S*, August 19, 1953; *NYT*, August 19, 1953; *HT*, August 21, September 9, 1953.

35. *BE*, July 30, September 4, 1953; *WT&S* August 18, 1953.

36. *BE*,, July 14, 1953; *WT&S*, July 14, 1953.

37. Hamburger, *Mayor Watching*, 48; *WT&S*, July 14, 1953; *HT*, August 15, 1953.

38. *WT&S* August 25, 1953; *HT*, September 8, September 15, October 14, 1953; Moscow interview, May 4, 1987.

39. *BE*, September 6, 9, 14, 1953.

40. *HT*, September 13, 1953.

41. Hamburger, *Mayor Watching*, 48; *BE*, October 10, 1953; *HT*, September 13, 1953.

42. *HT*, September 17, 1953.

43. *HT*, October 20, 1953; *WT&S*, October 21, 22, 1953; *BE*, October 29, 1953.

44. *WT&S*, September 24, 1953; *HT*, October 3, 1953.

45. *BE*, October 8, 1953.

46. *WT&S*, September 26, 1953; *HT*, September 23, September 28, 1953; *BE*, September 23, 1953; *Berle Diaries*, roll 6, frame 1216.

47. *HT*, August 20, 1953; *WT&S*, September 3, 1953.

48. *HT*, September 29, October 3, 29, 1953.

49. All ethnic voting statistics, unless otherwise referenced, were compiled by the author according to the method outlined in the appendix.

50. Warren Moscow, *What Have You Done For Me Lately?* (Englewood Cliffs, NJ: Prentice Hall 1967), 141.

51. Jonathan B. Bingham to Robert F. Wagner, November 10, 1953, RFW Papers, box 1856; Moscow, *What Have You Done For Me Lately?*, 40; Lowi, *At the Pleasure of the Mayor*, 38.

52. Citizens Union, "Press Release: Citizens Union Recommends in Five Leadership Fights," September 11, 12, 1953; Ottenberg, *The Lexington Democratic Club*, 15.

53. Heilbroner, "Smile on the Face of the Tiger," 31; *HT*, June 6, 9, 10, 1954; *BE*, June 8, 9, 1954.

54. *Berle Diaries*, roll 7, frame 120; Moscow, *Last of the Big-Time Bosses*, 121–24.

55. E. J. Kahn, Jr., "Plenipotentiary I: Profile of W. Averell Harriman," *The New Yorker* (May 3, 1952), 41ff; Kahn, "Plenipotentiary II," ibid., May 10, 1952, 36ff.

56. Combs, interview, COH.

57. *Berle Diaries*, roll 6, frame 1368; Rose, Unpublished Memoirs; Moscow interview, December 7, 1987; Author's interview with Louis Harris, New York City, November 28, 1988. Harris, then a fledgling pollster, managed much of the negotiations for FDR, Jr.'s candidacy in 1954.

58. Javits, *Autobiography*, 203; Smith, *Dewey*, 618.

59. Kahn, "Plenipotentiary I," 41, 44; Kahn, "Plenipotentiary II," 37, 40; Campaign Literature, LP Papers, box 13; Text of Harriman Campaign Speeches, LP Papers, box 23; Smith, *Dewey*, 618–19.

60. Javits, *Autobiography*, 205–09.

61. Rose, Unpublished Memoirs.

62. Heilbroner, "Smile on the Face of the Tiger," 28; Moscow, *Last of the Big-Time Bosses*, 120–21.

63. Moscow, ibid., 130–31.

64. Ibid.

65. Parmet, *The Democrats*, 130–41.

66. Javits, *Autobiography*, 289; Moscow interview, December 7, 1987; Wagner interview, May 2, 1988.

67. Mrs. Irwin Forster, *née* Marilyn Landberg, to Ben Davidson, October 6, 1956, LP Papers, box 24; Wilson, *The Amateur Democrat*, 52.

68. Wilson, ibid., 46, 301–12, 336–37; Vernon M. Goetchus, "The Village Independent Democrats: A Study in the Politics of the New Reformers," (B.A. Thesis, Wesleyan University, 1963), 111; Elmer E. Cornwell, Jr. "Bosses, Machines, and Ethnic Groups," in Lawrence Fuchs, ed., *American Ethnic Politics* (New York: Harper, 1968), 213; Daniel Patrick Moynihan, " 'Bosses' and 'Reformers': A Profile of the New York Democrats," *Commentary* (June 1961), 462.

69. Javits, *Autobiography*, 248–50; Ethnic voting data compiled by the author. See appendix.

70. Wilson, *The Amateur Democrat*, 52–58; Goetchus, "Village Independent Democrats," 33–37; Ottenberg, *Lexington Democratic Club*, 17–18; Edward N. Costikyan, *Behind Closed Doors* (New York: Harcourt, 1966), 19; Dan Wakefield, "Greenwich Village Challenges Tammany: Ethnic Politics and the New Reformers," *Commentary* (October 1959), 307–12; Robert Lekachman,

"How We Beat the Machine: Challenging Tammany at the District Level," *Commentary* (April 1958), 290–97.

71. The Wagner Administration Major Accomplishments, RFW Papers, box 1856; The City Club of New York, "The Wagner Record: One Year Later," January 1955; E. W. Kenworthy, "The Emergence of Mayor Wagner," *New York Times Magazine* (August 20, 1955), 20; "New York," *Time*, October 1, 1956, 23; Charles Morris, *The Cost of Good Intentions* (New York: McGraw-Hill, 1980), 16.

72. Mr. and Mrs. Joseph A. Gott to Robert F. Wagner, March 8, 1957, RFW Papers, box 1855.

73. Extract From Address by David Dubinsky at Luncheon Honoring Wagner/Gerosa/Stark, October 19, 1957, and Press Release: Speech by Alex Rose delivered at Bronx County Committee Meeting of the Liberal Party, October 7, 1957, LP Papers, box 26.

74. *Berle Diaries*, May 28, 1954, roll 7, frame 77, June 11, 1954, roll 7, frame 90; Dorothy Rabinowitz, "The Case of the ILGWU," *Dissent* (Winter 1972), 87; Flournoy, "The Liberal Party," 56–57, 85–86, 110, 149, 234; Letter from Albert C. Ney to Ben Davidson, September 10, 1953, LP Papers, box 20; Letter from Ben Davidson to Angelo Cordaro, December 3, 1963, LP Papers; Flier circulated December, 1952, LP Papers, box 20; Letter from Lewis Silverman to Ben Davidson, about December 9, 1968, LP Papers, box 33; "Analysis of Enrollments of ILGWU Locals—Kings County, September 1956, LP Papers, box 2; *NYP*, June 29, 1961; Author's interview with Rev. Donald Harrington, former Chairman of the New York State Liberal party, New York City, September 28, 1988.

75. *Berle Diaries*, May 28, 1954, roll 7, frame 77, June 11, 1954, roll 7, frame 90; Letter dated July 20, 1954 from David Dubinsky to Adolph Berle, LP Papers, box 21; Letter dated April 27, 1954, from Ben Davidson to John L. Childs, LP Papers, box 21; Harrington interview, September 28, 1988; Rose argued in favor of dissolving the Liberal party in 1961, see Dubinsky and Raskin, *David Dubinsky*, 317.

76. *NYP*, July 21, 1957; Various letters and post cards from members of the Liberal party to Ben Davidson, LP Papers, box 26.

77. *NYP*, July 31, 1957.

78. "A Survey for the Race for Mayor of New York," August 1957, and "A Survey for the Race for Mayor, Early October 1957," Prepared by Louis Harris and Associates, RFW Papers, box 1856.

79. "Survey," Early October 1957, 5–6; "Survey," August 1957, vi-vii.

80. Nathan Straus to Julius C. C. Edelstein, November 30, 1953, RFW Papers, box 2207; Moscow interview, December 7, 1987; Citizens Union, "Voters Directory," November 5, 1957.

81. Ethnic voting data compiled by the author for blacks, Italians and Jews show that these groups voted for Wagner in even greater proportions than the Harris survey projected.

82. Ottenberg, *Lexington Democratic Club*, 17; Costikyan, *Behind Closed Doors*, 25–27; Lekachman, "How We Beat the Machine," 290; Goetchus, "Village Independent Democrats," 68.

83. Goetchus, "Village Independent Democrats," 80; Meg Greenfield, "Tammany in Search of a Boss," *The Reporter* (April 13, 1961), 28–31; Frances H. Costikyan, "The Captain in the Election District," ir Costikyan, *Behind Closed Doors*, 57–84.

84. Lekachman, "How We Beat the Machine," 290–93.

85. Ibid., 294.

Six: Boss Blow-Out

1. The events leading up to the 1958 Democratic Nominating Convention held in Buffalo, and what happened there, are described in ample detail and with essential consistency in Robert Bendiner, "DeSapio's Big Moment, or the Rout of the Innocents," *The Reporter* (October 16, 1958), 23–27; Moynihan, " 'Bosses' and 'Reformers,' " 461–70; Moscow, *The Last of the Big-Time Bosses*, 139–59; Costikyan, *Behind Closed Doors*, 159–63; Wilson, *The Amateur Democrat*, 58–64. The summary that appears on the next several pages is taken from these sources unless otherwise referenced.

2. *NYT*, August 28, 1958; Leo Egan, "The How and Why of DeSapio," *The New York Times Magazine* (September, 14, 1958), 25; Wagner interview, May 2, 1988; Moscow, interview, December 7, 1987.

3. Arthur Schlesinger, Jr., "Death Wish of the Democrats," *The New Republic* (September 15, 1958), 7–8.

4. Various letters and post cards to Ben Davidson, LP Papers, box 68; Berle Diaries, roll 7, frames 841, 843, 844.

5. Circular to All Liberal Party Clubs and County Organizations, September 10, 1958, LP Papers, box 16.

6. Ben Davidson to Angelo Cordaro, Liberal party official in Erie County, July 1, 1955, box 12; Ben Davidson to Angelo Cordaro, August 1, 1957, box 16; Ben Davidson to Alex Rose, March 5, 1958, box 16; Ben Davidson to Angelo Cordaro, September 17, 1958, box 16; all in LP Papers. In the September 17, 1958 communication Davidson wrote, "I have been receiving, steadily, and continuously, letters attacking Crotty—of his contempt and ill-treatment of the Liberal Party, that he is a hack type and real machine leader and boss . . . that our attitude was one of opposition to him."

7. Moynihan, " 'Bosses' and 'Reformers,' " 468–69. Rumors circulated that Rose and Dubinsky chose to run an independent candidate in order to ensure the election of Lefkowitz. I find no evidence to support the assertion, but it is logical that because the Liberals perceived a Lefkowitz victory as unthreatening it made the decision not to support Crotty easier. Transcript of "Let's Find Out," WCBS Radio Program, November 2, 1958, box 16, LP Papers, discusses the rumors.

8. *Berle Diaries*, roll 7, frames 845, 865–68; Transcript of "Let's Find Out" radio program, November 2, 1958, LP Papers, box 16; James Desmond, *Nelson Rockefeller: A Political Biography* (New York: Macmillan, 1964), 184–86; Editorial, *NYP*, November 3, 1958.

9. Statement by Governor Harriman, undated, LP Papers, box 112; *NYP*, November 3, 1958, front page; Moscow interview, December 7, 1988.

10. Data for 1950 compiled by the author. Data for 1958 in James Coleman, Ernest Heau, Robert Peabody and Leo Rigsby, "Computers and Election Analysis: The *New York Times* Project," *Public Opinion Quarterly* (1963), 435.

11. Moscow interview, December 7, 1987.

12. Neil Hickey and Ed Edwin, *Adam Clayton Powell and the Politics of Race* (New York: Fleet, 1965); Adam Clayton Powell, Jr. *Adam By Adam* (New York: Dial, 1971); Edward Lewinson, *Black Politics in New York City*, 109–43; Charles V. Hamilton, *Adam Clayton Powell, Jr.: The Political Biography of an American Dilemma* (New York: Atheneum, 1991), *passim* for biographical information on Adam Clayton Powell.

13. David Hapgood, "The Purge That Failed: Tammany v. Powell," *Case Studies in Practical Politics* (New York: Holt, 1959), 2–3.

14. Moscow interview, December 7, 1987; Hapgood, "The Purge That Failed," 1–14, and Will Chasan, "Congressman Powell's Downhill Fight in Harlem," *The Reporter* July 10, 1958, 24–28, describe the purge attempt. The summary on the pages that follow is from those sources unless otherwise referenced.

15. Lewinson, *Black Politics in New York City*, 144–59; John C. Walter, *The Harlem Fox*, (Albany: State University of New York Press, 1989), *passim*.

16. Nevins, *Lehman and His Era, passim*.

17. Arthur Schlesinger, Jr., "Herbert H. Lehman: the Conservative as Radical," address at Hunter College in the Bronx, December 18, 1967, in Herbert H. Lehman Collection, Columbia University, hereafter HHL Papers; Press Release: "Floor Remarks of Senator Herbert H. Lehman Commenting on Senator McCarthy's Charges of 'Anti-Semitism' Against Senator Monroney and Others," July 20, 1953, RFW Papers, Senator Lehman File, box 2207.

18. Herbert H. Lehman, "Liberalism and Judaism," *Jewish Heritage* Spring 1958, 5–10.

19. Barbara Ward, "Lehman at 80: Young Elder Statesman," *The New York Times Magazine* (March 23, 1958). Robert F. Wagner, Jr., son of the former mayor, remembered that liberal Jews thought of Lehman as "practically God" in a conversation with the author, New York City, December 6, 1988.

20. Various communications between Herbert Lehman and Carmine De-Sapio, 1949 through 1958, Special Correspondence File: Carmine DeSapio, HHL Papers; Herbert Lehman to Julius Edelstein, August 17, 1958 and August 30, 1958, and Julius Edelstein memorandum to Herbert Lehman, August 29, 1958, in HHL Papers; Moscow interview, March 7, 1988; Julius C. C. Edelstein, interview with author, New York City, March 9, 1988. Mr. Edelstein was

Herbert Lehman's chief of staff from 1949 through 1956 while Lehman was Senator, and continued to work for him afterward. In 1961 he became executive assistant to Mayor Robert Wagner.

21. Edelstein interview, March 9, 1988; Moscow interview, March 7, 1988.

22. Edelstein interview, March 9, 1988.

23. Moscow, *The Last of the Big-Time Bosses*, 124; Edelstein interview, March 9, 1988; Julius Edelstein, memorandum to Herbert Lehman, Jan 30— Friday, apparently 1959, and undated "Memorandum to the Senator," both in Special Subject Files, NYC Reform Politics, 1957–Jan. 1959, HHL Papers; Julius Edelstein to Herbert Lehman, January 29, 1959, HHL Papers.

24. Press Release: "Joint Statement by Mrs. Franklin D. Roosevelt, Senator Herbert H. Lehman and Thomas K. Finletter," January 22, 1959, HHL Papers.

25. *NYT*, January 23, 1959.

26. James T. Maher, memorandum to the Executive Committee, March 19, 1959, Special Subject File, New York City Reform Politics, HHL Papers; Edelstein interview, March 9, 1988.

27. Herbert Lehman to Julius Edelstein, May 9, 1959, HHL Papers; *NYT*, February 22, 1959.

28. Editorial, *NYT*, January 24, 1959.

29. Herbert Lehman, to Thomas K. Finletter, April 2, 1959, HHL Papers.

30. Wagner interview, March 28, 1988. During the interview former Mayor Wagner emphasized his growing resentment of DeSapio's influence and high public profile beginning even before the 1958 convention, but he did not actually break with him until 1961.

31. Moscow interview, March 7, 1988. The "delicate sense of self-preservation" term is Moscow's. *NYT*, February 10, April 17, 1959.

32. Moscow, *The Last of the Big-Time Bosses*, 51, 101–2, 132–34, 194–95.

33. Julius Edelstein memorandum to Senator Lehman, March 10, 1961, HHL Papers; Wilson, *The Amateur Democrat*, 302.

34. Julius Edelstein to Herbert Lehman, Jan 30—Friday, apparently 1959, in Special Subject Files, New York City Reform Politics, 1957–Jan. 1959, HHL Papers.

35. Julius Edelstein, undated "Memorandum to the Senator," Special Subject Files, New York City Reform Politics, 1957–Jan. 1959, HHL Papers.

36. Herbert Lehman to Thomas K. Finletter, April 2, 1959, and Herbert Lehman to Julius Edelstein, May 9, 1959, HHL Papers.

37. Author's interview with Patrick Cunningham, New York City, September 28, 1988 for the comment that Jews made up the largest part of the regular party organization in some districts. Mr. Cunningham was a member of the regular party organization during the 1950s, and ultimately served as Bronx County Leader between 1967 and 1979. He was also New York State Democratic Party Chairman in 1975 and 1976.

38. *NYT*, August 3, 1959; *NYP*, August 31, 1959.

39. Moscow interview, March 7, 1988; Edelstein interview, March 9, 1988.

40. Vernon M. Goetchus, "The Village Independent Democrats," 47; *NYT*, September 9, 1959.

41. *NYT*, June 18, 1959.

42. Theodore H. White, *The Making of the President, 1960* (New York: Atheneum, 1961), 163–64.

43. *NYT*, June 17, 1960; Edelstein interview, March 9, 1988.

44. Daniel Patrick Moynihan, " 'Bosses'and 'Reformers,' " 466; *NYT*, June 24, 1960; Moscow, *Last of the Big-Time Bosses*, 165.

45. Arthur Schlesinger, Jr., *Robert Kennedy and His Times* (New York: Ballantine Books, 1978), 228.

46. Moynihan, " 'Bosses' and 'Reformers,' " 466–67.

47. Moscow, *Last of the Big-Time Bosses*, 168.

48. Wilson, *The Amateur Democrat*, 337; Moscow, *Last of the Big-Time Bosses*, 170.

49. Moscow interview, March 7, 1988; Moscow, *Last of the Big-Time Bosses*, 170.

Seven: The Destruction of Tammany Hall

1. Philip Hamburger, *Mayor Watching and Other Pleasures* (New York: Rinehart, 1958), 53; Edelstein interview, March 9, 1988. *Time*, October 1, 1956, 23.

2. Hamburger, *Mayor Watching*, 58; Moscow interview, March 7, 1988.

3. Fred J. Cook and Gene Gleason, "The Shame of New York," *The Nation* (October 31, 1959), 264, 275, and *passim*.

4. Louis Harris & Associates, "A Survey of Voter Attitude Toward New York City and Its Government," May, 1959, in possession of the author.

5. Moscow interview, December 7, 1987.

6. *NYT*, December 29, 31, 1960, February 15, 1961; Moscow interview, March 7, 1988.

7. *NYT*, February 4, 1961.

8. *NYT*, February 4, 1961.

9. *NYT*, February 13, 1961.

10. Wagner interview, March 28, 1988.

11. *NYT*, January 6, 1961; Edelstein interview, March 9, 1988.

12. Louis Harris and Associates, Inc. "A Study of Where Robert F. Wagner Stands in the 1961 Race for Mayor of New York and What New Yorkers Think of His Incumbent Administration," March 29, 1961, in the possession of the author; Ira Rosenwaike, *Population History of New York City* (Syracuse, NY: Syracuse University Press, 1972), 135; *NYT*, June 26, July 25, 1961. One program designed to improve the mayor's standing in minority communities sent mobile vans into distressed neighborhoods to listen to people's complaints and to help them with their problems. The vehicles, irreverently called "bitch

buggies" by the mayor's staff, generated a lot of good will toward the man in City Hall. In a way, they played one of the roles once held by the district leaders and revealed how unsuccessful the political machine had been in integrating racial minorities into its organization. Warren Moscow, *What Have You Done for Me Lately?* (Englewood Cliffs, NJ: Prentice Hall, 1967), 40.

13. Harris "A Study of Where Robert F. Wagner Stands in the 1961 Race of Mayor," March 29, 1961.

14. *NYP*, April 16, 1961; Moscow interview, March 7, 1988; Edelstein interview, March 9, 1988.

15. Wallace S. Sayre and Herbert Kaufman, *Governing New York City* (New York: Norton, 1965), 662; William Kaufman, "The New York City Board of Estimate," (Master's Thesis, City College of New York, 1963), 97; Garelik, "The Board of Estimate" (Bachelor's Thesis, Columbia University, 1988),11–41; Arthur Mann, "When LaGuardia Took Over," *The New York Times Sunday Magazine*, January 2, 1966, 42.

16. Robert F. Wagner, "Inaugural Speech," January 1, 1958, RFW Papers; Kaufman, "The New York City Board of Estimate," 46–52.

17. Mann, *LaGuardia Comes to Power*, 91.

18. Charles Garrett, *The LaGuardia Years* (New Brunswick, NJ: Rutgers University Press, 1961), 275–76.

19. Raymond D. Horton, *Municipal Labor Relations in New York City: Lessons of the Lindsay-Wagner Years* (New York: Praeger Publishers), 24–26, 30–31; Mark H. Maier, *City Unions: Managing Discontent in New York City* (New Brunswick, NJ: Rutgers University Press, 1987), 44–50.

20. Horton, *Municipal Labor Relations*, 36–37.

21. Theodore Lowi, "Old Machines for New," *The Public Interest* (Fall 1967), 89–90; Charles R. Morris, *The Cost of Good Intentions*, 17.

22. *NYT*, January 1, January 30, 1961; *HT*, February 15, 1961; *JA*, February 26, 1961; Wagner interview, May 2, 1988.

23. *JA*, June 21, 1961; Jacob K. Javits, with Rafael Steinberg, *Javits: Autobiography of a Public Man*, 242; Moscow interview, March 7, 1988.

24. Wilson, *The Amateur Democrat*, 50–51; Moscow, *Last of the Big-Time Bosses*, 176; Wagner interview, May 2, 1988.

25. *NYP*, June 18, 1961; *HT*, June 19, 1961; Wagner interview, May 2, 1988; Dubinsky and Raskin, *David Dubinsky*, 308.

26. *JA*, June 23, 1961.

27. *NYT*, June 23, 30, 1961; Moscow interview, March 7, 1988.

28. *NYT*, July 2, 1961; *HT* July 7, 1961.

29. *NYP*, June 29, 1961.

30. *NYP*, June 29, 1961; Program Transcript, New York Forum—WCBS TV News, May 14, 1961, HHL Papers.

31. "Lehman Statements on Wagner," HHL Papers.

32. Edelstein interview, March 9, 1988; Julius Edelstein, undated memorandum to Senator Lehman, in Special Subjects File, New York City Reform

Politics, Jan.–April 1961; "Thought Fragments," apparently written by Edelstein, May 3, 1961; "Club Meetings on Wagner Endorsement;" all in HHL. The last document shows that many of the reform club votes to support Wagner were not unanimous. Marcia Allina, a member of the Lenox Hill Democratic Club in 1961, recalls that it was quite clear to reform club members that Lehman's financial support was dependent on endorsing Wagner.

33. Cunningham interview, September 29, 1988.

34. *NYT*, July 1, 1961; Wagner interview, March 28, 1988; Louis Lefkowitz, interview, and John Jay Feeney, interview, both in Arthur Levitt Project, Columbia University Oral History Project (hereafter, Levitt Project, COH). Lefkowitz, of course, was Attorney General and the Republican candidate for mayor in 1961. John Jay Feeney was deputy controller of New York State in 1961 and had a close personal relationship with Arthur Levitt. As late as the day before Levitt announced he would run, Feeney and some other close Levitt aides thought he would decline.

35. *NYP*, July 2, 1961; *NYT*, July 6, 7, 1961; *HT*, July 6, 8, 1961.

36. Lefkowitz interview, Arthur Levitt Project, COH; *NYT* May 11, 29, 1961; *HT* February 20, 1961; Javits, *Autobiography*, 372.

37. Lefkowitz interview, Arthur Levitt Project, COH; Moscow interview, March 7, 1988.

38. *NYT*, May 15, 1961.

39. *NYT*, June 30, September 12, 1961; unidentified press clipping, August 14, 1961, Vertical Files, "New York City Politics, 1961," MRRL; *NYP*, October 22, 1961.

40. Moscow interview, March 7, 1988; *NYT*, June 23, 28, 1961; Julius Edelstein, memorandum to Senator Lehman, May 21, 1961, Special Subject Files, New York City Reform Politics, HHL Papers.

41. *NYT*, August 9, 1961.

42. Concern over the significance of the great discrepancy in the signature count among Wagner's top staff began to subside after about a week. To determine the depth of support for Levitt Louis Harris conducted a survey of the people who had signed his petitions. It turned out that a large number of the supposed signatures were fraudulent, and that many of those who signed did so to avoid conflict with the local district leader even though they had not yet decided for whom to vote. Wagner interview, May 2, 1988; Harris interview, November 28, 1988.

43. Louis Harris and Associates, Inc. , "A Study of the Election for Mayor of New York With Special Focus on the Democratic Primary," August 4, 1961, in the possession of the author.

44. Harris Poll, August 4, 1961.

45. Various letters, RFW Paper, box 5547.

46. Harris Poll, August 4, 1961.

47. Press Release, September 4, 1961, RFW papers, box 2154.

48. Press Release: "Summary of Report from Commissioner of Investiga-

tion Louis I. Kaplan Concerning the Activities of Frank Kenna and a Real Estate Group With Which He Was Associated," August 7, 1961, and Press Release, August 27, 1961, both in RFW papers, box 2117; *NYT* August 12, 1961.

49. "Remarks by Herbert H. Lehman At a Public Rally Sponsored by the New Chelsea Club," Special Subject Files, New York City Reform Politics, May–July 1960, HHL Papers.

50. *NYT* August 9, 1961; *HT* August 9, 1961; Richard Wade, "The Withering Away of the Party System," 280 in Jewell Bellush and Dick Netzer, eds. *Urban Politics, New York Style* (Armonk, N.Y.: M. E. Sharpe, 1990).

51. *NYT*, August 3, 1961.

52. *NYT*, July 28, August 14, 1961. Although J. Raymond Jones was working with Wagner, and Jones and Powell were political allies at the time, Powell supported Levitt, who was of course backed by the same Carmine DeSapio who had tried to punish Powell for party disloyalty in 1958. Warren Moscow claims that Powell and Jones had an arrangement where each would take a different side on any important issue so that one of the two would always be on the winning team, and benefits would always accrue to the partnership.

53. *NYT*, August 14, 22, 1961.

54. *NYT*, August 11, 18, 28 1961; Editorial, *The Jewish Daily Forward*, August 31, 1961, translation in HHL Papers.

55. *NYT*, July 31, August 16, 28, 1961.

56. Wagner interview, March 28, 1961; RFW Papers, box 5547; *NYT*, September 1, 2, 1961; Interim Report Re: Printing and Distribution of Anonymous Campaign Literature in 1961 Mayoralty Primary, From John G. Bonomi, Special Assistant Attorney General and Counsel, New York Fair Campaign Practices Committee, To Attorney General Louis Lefkowitz. The interim report is undated, but is included as part of the final report dated November 3, 1961.

57. *NYT*, September 1, 2, 1961; Press Release, September 1, 1961, RFW Papers, box 2154; Wagner interview, May 2, 1988.

58. Wagner interview, March 28, 1961; Bonomi, "Interim Report," Lefkowitz interview, Arthur Levitt Project, COH; *NYT*, September 9, 1961.

59. Wagner interview, May 2, 1988. Wagner says that Buckley told him this story some years after the primary election.

60. *NYT*, September 8, 1961.

61. *NYT*, July 31, 1961.

62. *NYP* September 8, 1961; Moscow, *Last of the Big-Time Bosses*, 185–86; Costikyan, *Behind Closed Doors*, 215–18;

63. *NYT*, September 11, 1961; *NYP* September 13, 1961.

64. *NYT*, October 6, 11, November 5, 1961; "Gerosa for Mayor," Letter in MRRL, Vertical Files, New York City Politics 1961.

65. New York City Board of Elections, *Annual Report*, 1961.

66. Jerry Tallmer, "Alex Rose of the Liberal Party," *New York Post*, October 24, 1966; Wagner interview, May 2, 1988. Wagner also relied heavily on Louis Harris during the 1961 campaign.

67. *NYT*, September 12, 1961.

68. Moscow interview, December 7, 1987; *NYT* September 30, October, 1, 1961; *HT* November 28, 1961.

Eight: The Ambitions of John V. Lindsay

1. Off the record interview with a high-level government official who participated in the meeting.

2. Moscow interview, May 4, 1987; Author's interview with Meade Esposito, October 6, 1988, New York City. Esposito, ultimately elected Kings County Democratic party leader, was a district leader in 1961 who sided with Steingut in the battle with Wagner over control of Brooklyn's Democratic party. According to one minor political figure of the time, Esposito, who represented Brooklyn's Italian Democratic faction and Steingut, who represented the Jewish faction, decided to put an end to Irish control of the party leadership. With respect to Alex Rose's role in the episode, Esposito offered an emphatic if uninformative, "Alex Rose was full of shit!" He did not elaborate. *JA*, November 20, 1963; *NYT*, December 3, 1963; Alex Rose, Unpublished Memoirs, confirms Rose's friendship and respect for Jacoby. Mayor Wagner had little comment on the nature of the conflict.

3. *NYP*, May 10, 1964; *NYT* January 23, 1967; Cunningham interview, September 29, 1988.

4. Sean Keating File, RFW Papers for patronage lists; Costikyan, *Behind Closed Doors*, 38–39; Herbert Lehman, undated letter to Irving Engle, General Campaign File, 1961 and Mrs. Joseph P. Lash to Manfred Ohrenstein, May 31, 1960, HHL Papers. Edward N. Costikyan Papers (hereafter ENC Papers) have patronage requests from reform leaders for the period 1962 to 1964.

5. Costikyan, *Behind Closed Doors*, 30–34; Wagner interview, May 2, 1988.

6. Wagner interview, May 2, 1988.

7. Julius Edelstein, undated memorandum to Senator Lehman, Special Subject Files, New York City Reform Politics, May 1961, and Julius Edelstein to Herbert Lehman, September 10, 1961, in HHL Papers.

8. Wagner interview, May 2, 1988; Moscow interview 4,1988; Edelstein interview, March 9, 1988; *NYT*, September 19, November 7, 1962.

9. Moscow interview, May 4, 1988; *NYT* November 5, 6, 7, 1962.

10. Coleman et al., "Computers and Election Analysis: The *New York Times* Project," 435; *NYT* November 6, 1962.

11. J. Daniel Mahoney, *Actions Speak Louder* (New York: Arlington House, 1968), 17, 31, 34, 37 and *passim*.

12. Oliver Pilat, *Lindsay's Campaign: A Behind the Scenes Diary* (Boston: Bacon Press, 1968), 95; Mark Goret, "A History of the Bronx Conservative Party," *The Bronx County Historical Society Journal* 23(1) (Spring 1986), 8–12.

13. *HT*, January 19, 1965.

14. *HT*, January 19, 1965; *American Jewish Year Book* (New York: American Jewish Committee), 1940 and 1961 demographic data estimates.

15. Sayre and Kaufman, *Governing New York City*, 195–96.

16. Deborah Dash Moore, *At Home in America*, 23; *American Jewish Year Book*, 1961.

17. Javits with Steinberg, *Javits*, 372–74.

18. Nat Hentoff, *A Political Life: The Education of John V. Lindsay* (New York: Knopf, 1969), 51; Daniel Button, *Lindsay: A Man for Tomorrow* (New York: Random House, 1965), 18–19.

19. Hentoff, *A Political Life*, 54; Button, *A Man for Tomorrow*, 15–17.

20. Button, *A Man for Tomorrow*, 16, 21, 42–55; John V. Lindsay, *Journey into Politics* (New York: Dodd Mead,1967), 4–5; Casper Citron, *John V. Lindsay and the Silk Stocking Story* (New York: Fleet, 1965), 60–61.

21. Hentoff, *A Political Life*, 36–39; Citron, *Silk Stocking*, 2–4.

22. Calvin B. T. Lee, *One Man, One Vote* (New York: Scribner's, 1967), 96–103; Mark I. Gelfand, *A Nation of Cities* (New York: Oxford University Press, 1975), 369–70; Barbara Carter, *The Road to City Hall: How John Lindsay Became Mayor* (Englewood Cliffs, NJ: Prentice-Hall, 1967), 20; Oliver Pilat, *Lindsay's Campaign*, 8–9.

23. Hentoff, *A Political Life*, 47; Javits with Steinberg, *Autobiography*, 373; *NYP*, January 17, 1965; Elisabeth A. Griffith, "John Lindsay: Candidate and Campaign" (Bachelor of Arts Thesis, Wellesley College), 1969, 20–21. Griffith interviewed a number of Lindsay's 1965 campaign assistants, including Robert Price, the campaign manager, in great detail, when preparing her study. Price shared his copy of the thesis with me and told me that the information in it is accurate. Because my own conversation with Price was brief, I rely on Griffith's work for certain details where they fit the pattern suggested by other evidence.

24. *HT*, July 19, August 28, 1963; *JA*, August 7, 1963; *NYT* August 26, 1963; Carter, *The Road to City Hall*, 40–43; Javits with Steinberg, *Javits*, 373; Wagner Interview, May 2, 1988.

25. Maas and Thimmesch, "The Fight for City Hall,"; *NYT* April 26, 1965; *HT*, June 3, 1965.

26. Pilat, *Lindsay's Campaign*, 14–16; Carter, *Road to City Hall*, 118–22; Citron, *Silk Stocking*, 62.

27. Maas and Thimmesch, "The Fight for City Hall," 7; *NYT* May 12, 1965.

28. *HT*, May 14, 1965.

29. Moscow interview, May 4, 1988; Arthur M. Schlesinger, *Robert Kennedy and His Times* (New York: Ballantine Books, 1978), 719–20.

30. Fred C. Shapiro and James W. Sullivan, *Race Riots: New York 1964*, (New York: Thomas Crowell, 1964), *passim*; Nathan Glazer, "Is New York City Ungovernable?" *Commentary* (September 1961), 185–193; Jane Jacobs,

The Death and Life of Great American Cities (New York: Vintage, 1961), 3, *passim; NYT* February 1, 1965.

31. *HT*, May 18, 1965; *NYT*, May 28, 1965; Carter, *The Road to City Hall*, 45; Pilat, *Lindsay's Campaign*, 63.

32. *NYT*, June 11, 1965; *NYP*, March 22, 1964; *HT* June 11, 1965.

33. *NYT* June 11, 1965; *HT* June 11, 1965.

34. Griffith, "John Lindsay: Candidate and Campaign, 1965," 51.

35. Wagner interview, March 28, 1988; *WT&S*, January 31, 1964; April 10, 1964. The other members of Wagner's advisory council were Louis Harris, the pollster; John Coleman, a member of the New York Stock Exchange; Norman Winston, a businessman and long-time friend of the mayor; and Anna Rosenberg Hoffman, an old friend of the mayor's father who ran the Social Security Offices in New York City. Harris, who had done polling for President John F. Kennedy, often served as intermediary between Wagner and the President between 1960 and 1963.

36. Harrington interview, September 28, 1988; Moscow interview, May 4, 1987; *HT*, June 12, 1965.

37. *HT* June 12, 1965; Carter, *The Road to City Hall*, 66.

38. *HT*, June 20, 1965.

39. William F. Buckley, Jr., *The Unmaking of a Mayor* (New York: Viking, 1966), 104–5.

40. Ibid., 110–11; 120.

41. *NYT* June 13, 15, 17, 23 1965; *HT*, July 25, 1965. The City Charter amendments that went into effect in 1963 created two councilmen-at-large positions in each borough. Elections for the offices were borough-wide, each voter was allowed to cast only one ballot even though there were two posts, and each political party was allowed to nominate only one person for the office. The provision was designed to ensure minority party representation on the council.

42. Author's interview with Abraham D. Beame, September 28, 1988, New York City; *JA*, May 8, 1964; *NYT* June 29, 1965; Pilat, *Lindsay's Campaign*, 24–26.

43. Carter, *The Road to City Hall*, 47.

44. *NYT* June 29, 1965; Speech by Alex Rose, June 28, 1965, Liberal Party Papers, box 80. The delegate vote was 800 to 50.

45. Maas and Thimmesch, "The Fight for City Hall," 13; Pilat, *Lindsay's Campaign*, 138.

46. Author's Interview with Sid Davidoff, September 14, 1988, New York City. Davidoff served as John Lindsay's advance man throughout the campaign. Carter, *The Road to City Hall*, 188–21; *Newsweek*, November 15, 1965; *NYT* May 25, 1965; *WT&S*, August 16, 1965; Griffith, "John Lindsay: Candidate and Campaign, 1965," 57–59.

47. Author's conversation with Robert Price, May 23, 1988, New York City.

48. *NYT*, August 1, 1965; Conversation with Robert Price, May 23, 1988.

49. Maas and Thimmesch, "The Fight for City Hall," 47; "Lindsay Campaign Election District Handbook," explains the work of the Lindsay volunteers. A copy is in Liberal Party Papers, Box 40; *JA* August 14, 1965; Pilat, *Campaign Diary*, 163.

50. Memo—Subject: Beame and Screvane Recognition and Images, August 4, 1965, Edward N. Costikyan Papers, (hereafter ENC Papers), Beame Folder, box 8; *NYT*, July 13, 1965; *HT* July 13, 1965; Douglas Schoen, *Pat: A Biography of Daniel Patrick Moynihan* (New York: Harper, 1979), 97–99. Moynihan, as it happened, was the worst campaigner of the three in 1965. He learned.

51. Maas and Thimmesch, "The Fight for City Hall," 10; *NYP*, August 31, 1965.

52. *NYT* July 9, 1965; *JA* November 3, 1965; *HT* July 20, 1965.

53. *NYT* September 16, 1965; *WT&S*, September 15, 1965.

54. *NYT*, September 16, 1965; Conversation with Robert Price, May 23, 1988.

55. Conversation with Robert Price, May 23, 1988; *JA* October 18, 1965; *HT* July 2, 1965; Pilat, *Campaign Diary*, 95.

56. Davidoff interview, September 14, 1988; Griffith, "John Lindsay: Candidate and Campaign, 1965," 64.

57. Edward N. Costikyan to J. Raymond Jones, September 22, 1965, ENC Papers, box 8; O'Brien-Sherwood Associates, Inc. "New York City Voters Attitudes and Opinion Study Regarding the 1965 Mayoralty Elections Phase I—September 20–25, 1965," in ENC Papers, box 10; Maas and Thimmesch, "The Fight for City Hall," 15.

58. Press Release: John V. Lindsay for Mayor, October 9, 1965, Press Release: John V. Lindsay for Mayor, October 3, 1965, John V. Lindsay Papers, (hereafter JVL Papers); Griffith, "John Lindsay: Candidate and Campaign, 1965," 67.

59. O'Brien-Sherwood Associates, Inc., "New York City Attitudes and Opinion Study Regarding the 1965 Mayoralty Elections," ENC Papers, box 10; Maas and Thimmesch, "The Fight for City Hall," 16. Few white New Yorkers trusted Powell, and Beame feels that more Jews were concerned with the implication that by helping to elect a Jewish mayor the Harlem congressman would advance his own ambitions than were offended by Powell's appeal to their ethnic pride. Beame interview, September 28, 1988.

60. *NYT*, October 19, 1965; Maas and Thimmesch, "The Fight for City Hall," 16; Undated Memorandum, "Additional Themes," ENC Papers, Beame Folder, box 8.

61. Buckley, *The Unmaking of a Mayor*, 122–29, 157–58; *NYT* September 25, 1965.

62. *DN*, October 18, November 2, 1965. Beame feels that the debates were very important, and that he made a tactical error when he accused Lindsay of lying during the broadcasts. Because Lindsay's image was of a charming young

man, Beame's comments offended "the little old ladies who thought Lindsay was a nice boy, even though he was lying." Beame interview, September 28, 1988.

63. *NYT*, October 28, 29, 1965; Pilat, *Lindsay's Campaign*, 330–33.

64. Maas and Thimmesch, "The Fight for City Hall," 48.

65. *NYT*, November 3, 1965.

66. New York City Board of Election, *Annual Report, 1969*.

67. Ethnic voting data was compiled by Louis Harris and Associates at the time of the election and appeared in *Newsweek* November 15, 1965, 34.

68. Griffith, "John Lindsay: Candidate and Campaign, 1965," 59.

Nine: The Politics of Polarization

1. Woody Klein, *Lindsay's Promise* (New York: Macmillan, 1970), 44.

2. L. H. Whittemore, *The Man Who Ran the Subways: The Story of Mike Quill* (New York: Holt, Rinehart and Winston, 1968), prologue xi, *passim*.

3. Whittemore, *Quill*, 226; Mark H. Maier, *City Unions* (New Brunswick, NJ: Rutgers University Press, 1987) 33–40; Thomas R. Brooks, "Lindsay, Quill and the Transit Strike," *Commentary* (March 1966), 50.

4. Whittemore, *Quill*, 257–61. Whittemore estimates that at the time Quill began working for the Interborough Rapid Transit Company in 1926 about 80% of its employees were Irish, page 12. Maier, *City Unions*, 40–41; Joshua B. Freeman, "Catholics, Communists and Republicans: Irish Workers and the Organization of the Transport Workers Union," in Michael H. Frisch and Daniel J. Walkowitz, *Working Class America* (Urbana: University of Illinois Press, 1983) *passim*.

5. Whittemore, *Quill*, 265; Klein, *Lindsay's Promise*, 95.

6. Whittemore, *Quill*, 279, 284; Klein, *Lindsay's Promise*, 45–47.

7. Whittemore, *Quill*, 284; *NYT*, January 11, 1969.

8. *NYT*, March 1, 1966. Two weeks after the strike, Quill's heart gave out and he died. He became something of a martyr among segments of the Irish and TWU workers.

9. *NYT*, June 9, 1967; "A City Building Bridges to Its People: A Report on Mayor John V. Lindsay's Neighborhood City Halls Program," Municipal Reference and Research Library Vertical Files, New York City Politics, 1968; Morris, *The Cost of Good Intentions*, 28.

10. Richard Reeves, " 'A Great Mayor,' 'That Bum' " *The New York Times Magazine*, January 1, 1967; Author's interview with Sanford Garelik, September 9, 1988, New York City. Garelik, who is married to an Irish Catholic, displayed no animosity when making his comment. It was simply a statement of fact.

11. While the creation of a Civilian Review Board was an important issue, polling data gathered for Abe Beame's 1965 mayoralty campaign revealed that two-thirds of the voters did not wish to see one created. O'Brien-Sherwood

Associates, Inc., "New York City Voters Attitude and Opinion Study Regarding the 1965 Mayoralty Elections," in ENC Papers, box 10.

12. David W. Abbott, Louis H. Gold and Edward T. Rogowsky, *Police, Politics and Race: The New York City Referendum on Civilian Review* (New York: American Jewish Committee and The Joint Center for Urban Studies of the Massachusetts Institute of Technology and Harvard University, 1969) gives a thorough summary of the event and provides the voting data. *HT*, May 16, 1965 for the issue in the mayoralty campaign; Klein, *Lindsay's Promise*, 110, 117, 125, 155.

13. Morris, *The Cost of Good Intentions*, 74–77.

14. Hentoff, *A Political Life*, 289; Richard Reeves, "The Impossible Takes a Little Longer," *The New York Times Magazine*, January 28, 1968.

15. Morris, *The Cost of Good Intentions*, 104.

16. Kenneth B. Clark, *Dark Ghetto: Dilemmas of Social Power* (New York: Harper, 1965), 111–53.

17. Naomi Levine, *Ocean Hill-Brownsville: A Case History of Schools in Crisis* (New York: Popular Library, 1969), and Martin Mayer, *The Teachers Strike: New York 1968* (New York: Harper, 1968) are detailed treatments of the school strike. Marilyn Gittell, "Education: The Decentralization-Community Control Controversy," in Jewel Bellush and Stephen M. David, eds. *Race and Politics in New York City* (New York: Praeger, 1971) offers an excellent, shorter summary. Diane Ravitch, *The Great School Wars: New York City 1805–1973* (New York: Basic Books, 1974) places the event in the context of periodic struggles by different ethnic groups for control of the New York City Public School system. All of these accounts agree on the basic details, including the interpretation that McCoy and the Ocean Hill-Brownsville governing board deliberately sought a confrontation. The poem Cambell read appears in Levine, *Ocean Hill-Brownsville*, 94. Louis Harris and Bert E. Swanson, *Black-Jewish Relations in New York City* (New York: Praeger, 1970), 131–158 provides the results of surveys taken after the school strike that reveal the damaging effect the event had on black-Jewish relations.

18. *NYT*, February 11, 1969.

19. Author's interview with Richard Aurelio New York City, June 17, 1988.

20. Ibid.; *NYT*, March 27, 1969.

21. *NYP*, June 20, 1966; *NYT*, June 1, August 2, 1966; Schlesinger, *Robert Kennedy*, 808–13. Kennedy thought that the reformers were "divided between opportunists trying to get into the organization and emotionalists" who were virtually committed to losing, even though Kennedy worked with the reformers during the surrogate's contest.

22. Mitchel Levitan, "Rise Fall and . . . of FDR, Jr., " *The New York Times Magazine*, October 23, 1966; *NYT*, August 19, September 8, 1966; *NYP*, August 18, September 14, October 24, 25 1966.

23. *WT&S*, September 25, 1966; *NYP*, October 27, 1966; Harrington interview, September 28, 1988; Various Letters throughout October and November

1968, LP Papers, box 33. A typical example, undated, from Mrs. M. Altschuler of Flushing, Queens, reads: "I and the rest of my family, have voted for the Liberal party line since its inception. Because of your prejudiced and your irrational espousal of Ocean-Hill Brownsville against the UFT, we are voting Dem. or Rep. this year—no more Liberal."

24. *NYP*, October 28, 1966, April 15, 1969. Author's interview with John V. Lindsay, New York City, October 25, 1988. Lindsay confirmed the strong respect he had for Alex Rose. He did not discuss matters of patronage. Donald Harrington recounted the horse story, interview, September 28, 1988.

25. Author's interview with Sid Davidoff, New York City, September 14, 1988. LP Papers, box 33, has correspondence between Sid Davidoff and Ben Davidson regarding Liberal party patronage positions.

26. *NYP* November 1, 1969; Aurelio interview, June 17, 1988.

27. Aurelio interview, June 17, 1988. Author's interview with Louis Harris New York City, November 28, 1988.

28. Aurelio interview, June 17, 1988.

29. *DN*, June 3, 1969; *NYP*, March 12, May 14, June 13, 1969; *NYT*, February 27, April 3, 1969.

30. Aurelio interview, June 17, 1988; *NYT*, April 3, 1969; E.J. Kahn, *Jock: The Life and Times of John Hay Whitney* (Garden City, NY: Doubleday, 1981).

31. This story is Aurelio's account. Garelik remembers being very reluctant to run and confirms that Aurelio and Albano made persistent efforts to convince him. He does not deny the Roosevelt Hotel meeting, but does not recall the event with the detail that Aurelio offered. About five o'clock in the morning after he finally agreed to run, John Lindsay called Garelik to make the formal request that he join the ticket, and Garelik confirmed his decision. When Garelik's wife woke up and learned what he had done, she talked him out of it again, but when he called the mayor's office to bow out, Aurelio told him that news of his candidacy had already been "leaked" to the press and that he had to run, so he did.

32. *NYP*, June 9, 1969. Other estimates ranged between 35 and 45%.

33. *NYP*, June 5, 1969; Author's interview with Herman Badillo, New York City, September 20, 1988. Badillo emphasized that although both his running mates were Jewish he ran with a broader coalition by supporting Italian, Irish, and black candidates for City Council positions and other offices. He also indicated that some Italians assumed he was Italian because his last name ended in "o," and that he won some votes on that basis.

34. Badillo interview, September 20, 1988; *DN*, June 1, 1969; Peter Manso, ed., *Running Against the Machine* (Garden City, NY: Doubleday, 1969), 241–42; Joe Flaherty, *Managing Mailer* (New York: Coward McCann, 1969) for a book length treatment by Mailer's campaign manager.

35. *NYT*, May 13, 1969; *NYP*, October 27, 1969;

36. *NYP*, April 16, 1969; *NYT*, April 17, 1969; *DN*, June 11, June 13, 1969; Manso, *Running Against the Machine*, 85.

37. *NYT*, April 12, 17, 1969; Aurelio interview, June 17, 1988.

38. *NYT*, June 19, 1969 reports these results based on polling done for WCBS-TV and WNBC-TV. Badillo attributes his loss not to the split vote between him and Wagner, but to Mailer's candidacy. Mailer took more than 41,000 votes, which Badillo argues would have gone to him had Mailer not been in the race. With them, he would have beat Procaccino by a few thousand votes. It is a very believable, but of course unprovable, scenario. Badillo interview, September 20, 1988. The vote count was Procaccino: 252,283; Wagner: 221,585; Badillo: 215,291; Mailer: 41,136; Scheuer: 38,631.

39. Frank O'Connor resigned his City Council presidency on January 1, 1969 after winning a New York State Supreme Court Judgeship. Francis X. Smith, Sr., a long-time City Councilman from Queens, resigned his seat, and his son, Francis X. Smith, Jr., was installed in his place and promptly elected City Council president. He was thus the incumbent when the primary was held.

40. *NYT*, June 19, 1969. As Republican party leader, Governor Rockefeller felt obliged to abide by the results of the primary, but he did not actively campaign for Marchi.

41. *NYT*, June 19, 1969; Aurelio interview, June 17, 1988.

42. *NYP*, June 30, 1969; *NYT*, July 8, 1969, October 20, 1969; *Manhattan Tribune* August 9, 1969; Aurelio interview, June 17, 1969.

43. *NYT*, June 19, 1969.

44. *NYP*, November 6, 1969; Cunningham interview, September 29, 1988; Author's interview with Meade Esposito, New York City, October 6, 1969. Dick Aurelio claims that Esposito periodically called him to share information about Procaccino's campaign plans, Aurelio interview, June 17, 1988. Esposito did not recall having conversations with Aurelio until after Lindsay's election. Virtually all of the people interviewed who participated in the 1969 election, Democrats and Lindsay supporters alike, were unimpressed with Procaccino as a candidate.

45. Transcript of "Let's find Out," WCBS Radio, Interview with Mario Procaccino, August 17, 1969, JVL Papers, box 110714.

46. Press Conference Notes, unidentified news clippings, June 4, September 14, 1969, JVL Papers, box 110633; *NYT* July 20, August 25, 26, 1969. The registration drive, as it turned out, was not very successful. In order to gain maximum turnout on election day, Sid Davidoff arranged for numbers runners in Harlem and Brooklyn to bring voters to the polls. Davidoff interview, September 14, 1988.

47. Morris, *The Cost of Good Intentions*, 125; Davidoff confirmed that a number of municipal unions were important sources of workers, particularly for some of the more difficult logistical tasks. Davidoff interview, September 20, 1988.

48. *Newsweek*, November 3, 1969; Aurelio interview, June 17, 1988. Aurelio reports that several of Young & Rubicam's senior staff members were considered exceptionally able political advertising experts, but that the firm did not want to get involved in the New York City political campaign and risk being

on the losing side. After Aurelio and others made several unsuccessful efforts to get the firm to work with Lindsay's media team, Goldman Sachs partner Gustave Levy asked Aurelio to secure for him a list of Young & Rubicam's most important corporate accounts, which Aurelio did. Over the next few weeks, at Levy's request, the top officers of the Madison Avenue firm's largest clients called to urge it to accept the Lindsay assignment, which ultimately it did.

49. *NYT*, September 15, 1969.

50. Various neighborhood reports, JVL Papers, box 110714; Aurelio interview, June 17, 1988; *Newsweek*, November 3, 1969.

51. Davidoff interview, September 20, 1988; Press Release, September 11, 1969, JVL Papers, box 110633. The complicated arrangements that went into hosting the affair forced Davidoff to negotiate compromises between reform, conservative, and orthodox Jews. For example, one orthodox sect insisted that they would come to the dinner and protest because Israel allowed autopsies to be performed, a practice forbidden by their interpretation of Jewish law. Davidoff promised that Mayor Lindsay would express the group's concern to Prime Minister Meir, in return for a commitment by the protesters to stay several blocks away from the succah, far from the television cameras.

52. Aurelio interview, June 17, 1988; Davidoff interview, September 14, 1988.

53. Aurelio interview, June 17, 1988.

54. *DN*, October 23, 1969; *NYT*, October 21, 28, November 3, 1969. Lindsay's campaign team did everything it could to excite Procaccino and make him look bad on television. For instance, Davidoff went to the television studios before the debates and arranged to have the candidates sit on very high chairs. Lindsay, six feet three inches tall, looked comfortable. Marchi, of average height, managed to sit straight. The diminutive Procaccino, however, could not reach the floor with his feet, so he looked like a child. "It used to drive him crazy," Davidoff recalled with a mischievous smile. Davidoff interview, September 14, 1988.

55. *Newsweek*, November 3, 1969.

56. *NYT*, November 6, 1969 reports the ethnic breakdown based on polling data prepared by CBS-TV and WNBC-TV. There are slight differences with the latter giving Procaccino a slightly higher proportion of the Jewish vote, and Lindsay and Marchi both slightly less.

Ten: The Jewish Assumption

1. Aurelio, interview, June 17, 1988; David K. Shipler, "The Two John Lindsay's," *New Republic* (May 1, 1971); Nicholas Pileggi, "Inside Lindsay's Head," *New York Magazine,* January 19, 1971.

2. Aurelio interview, June 17, 1988; Richard Aurelio, "Memo to Messrs. Beame, Marchi, Blumenthal, Biaggi: How to Run Your Campaign," *New York*

Times Magazine, September 16, 1973; Author's interview with Jay Kreigel, New York City, July 15, 1988; *NYT*, December 31, 1973.

3. New York State Committee on Crime and Correction, "The Tombs Disturbances," October 5, 1970; Jewel Bellush, "Housing: The Scattered Site Controversy," 96–133, in Bellush and David, eds., *Race and Politics in New York City*; Mario Cuomo, *Forest Hills Diary: The Crisis of Low-Income Housing* (New York: Random House, 1974), *passim*.

4. Jewel and Bernard Bellush, *Union Power and New York: Victor Gotbaum and District Council 37* (New York: Praeger, 1984), 193; Morris, *Good Intentions*, 156; Maier, *City Unions*, 88.

5. Morris, *Good Intentions*, 136–39, 156–59; Martin Shefter, *Political Crisis/Fiscal Crisis* (New York: Basic Books, 1985), 106, 115–19; Ken Auletta, *The Streets Were Paved With Gold* (New York: Vintage, 1980), 205–07.

6. Tom Buckley, "Running for the Unrunnable," *New York Times Magazine*, June 3, 1973, 60; Aurelio interview, June 17, 1988; Harris interview, November 28, 1988.

7. *NYT*, January 26, February 19, 22, 26, March 4, 8, 1973.

8. Peter D. Hart Research Associates, "A Survey of the Attitudes of Voters in New York City, January 1973," in The Papers of Mayor Abraham D. Beame, New York City Municipal Archives (hereafter Beame Papers) box 117352.

9. Harris and Swanson, *Black-Jewish Relations in New York City*, 123, 231.

10. Tom Buckley, "Running for the Unrunnable," 61.

11. Ibid., 61; *NYT* March 19, 1973.

12. *NYT* February 2, March 12, 13, 1973.

13. *NYT*, March 13, 14, 16, 20, April 12, 1973.

14. *NYT*, January 26, February 19, 20, 22, 1973.

15. *NYT*, March 3, 1973; Paul O'Dwyer, *For the Defense*, 241–42.

16. *NYT*, March 3, 1973; Buckley, "Running for the Unrunnable," 61.

17. *NYT*, March 4, 1973; Badillo interview, September 28, 1988.

18. *NYT*, March 4, 5, April 13, 1973; Badillo interview, September 20, 1988.

19. Garelik interview, September 9, 1988; Beame interview, 28, 1988.

20. Hart Research Associates, "Voter Survey January 1973," ADB Papers.

21. Ibid.; Esposito interview, October 6, 1988; Cunningham interview, September 29, 1988.

22. *NYT*, February 23, March 9, May 18, November 2, 1973; Herman Badillo and Meade Esposito both insist that the story of a deal between Sutton and Beame is true. Beame called it "nonsense." I have not spoken with Sutton. Badillo interview, September 20, 1988; Esposito interview, October 6, 1988; Beame interview, September 28, 1988.

23. *NYT*, January 26, March 14, 19, 22, April 4, 1973.

24. *NYT*, April 9, 1973.

25. *NYT*, April 2, 1973.

26. *NYT*, April 18, 1973.

27. *NYT* April 20, 21, 22, 26, 27, May 1, 2, 3, 5, 8, 11, 1973.

28. *NYT*, May 11, 23, 1973; Campaign Ephemera, 1973, NYPL.

29. *NYT*, May 18, 1973.

30. *NYT*, May 15, 18, 20, 21, 23, 25, 26, 1973.

31. *NYT*, May 23, 28, 29, 1973; Badillo interview, September 28, 1988.

32. *NYT*, June 5, 1973; I supplemented newspaper analysis of the voting results with a sample of results in twenty-one assembly districts. The sample included districts where each of the candidates ran well in the initial primary, and districts that Beame and Badillo did not win in the initial primary but won in the run-off. I relied on newspaper accounts and interview comments for information regarding the ethnic composition of these districts.

33. *NYT*, June 6, 9, 1973; Badillo interview, September 20, 1988.

34. *NYT*, June 9, 21, 1973.

35. *NYT*, June 19, 1973.

36. ADB Papers, box 117352; Campaign Ephemera, 1973, NYPL; *NYT*, June 24, August 30, 1973.

37. *NYT*, June 25, 1973; News Release, Friday, June 8, 1973, "Beame Demands Badillo Explain Use of Numbers Runners," ADB Papers.

38. *NYT*, June 27, 1973.

39. *NYT*, June 27, July 18, 25, October 26, 1973; *DN*, July 2, 1973.

40. Beame interview, September 28, 1988. A fundraising dinner held for Beame on October 25, 1973 showed "a rare display of unity [with] party regulars and Reform members gathered . . . last night at the Americana Hotel." *NYT*, October 26, 1973.

41. *NYT*, October 3, 1973; *DN*, October 15, 31 1973; *NYP*, October 31, 1973. Quayle Poll, Week Ending September 23, 1973, ADB Papers, box 117352.

42. Beame interview, September 28, 1988; Robert Daley, "The Realism of Abe Beame," *The New York Times Magazine* (November 18, 1973), 38.

43. *NYT*, October 3, 1973; *DN*, October 15, 1973; *NYP*, October 31, 1973; Quayle Poll, Week Ending September 23, 1973, ADB Papers, box 117352.

44. Beame interview, September 28, 1988; Cunningham interview, September 29, 1988; Esposito interview, October 6, 1988; Badillo interview, September 20, 1988.

45. *NYT*, November 8, 1973; *Transition Papers Covering the Change of City Administration, 1973–74* Vol. 1 (Fund for the City of New York, 1974), 20.

46. Auletta, *Paved With Gold*, 97–103; *Transition Papers, 1973–74*, 20; Beame asserts that he had opposed all of these techniques during the second Lindsay term, and objected to some of the practices Mayor Robert Wagner used during Beame's first term as comptroller. Beame interview, September 28, 1988.

47. Auletta, *Paved With Gold*, 223–24; Shefter, *Political Crisis/Fiscal Crisis*, 149–51.

48. *DN,* January 3, 1977.

49. *NYT,* September 28, 1976; *Soho Weekly News,* June 10, 1976; Badillo interview, September 20, 1988; Beame interview, September 28, 1988.

50. Kreigel interview, July 15, 1988; Davidoff interview, September 20, 1988.

51. *DN,* January 4, 1977; *NYT,* May 16, June 2, 22, 1977; *The Soho Weekly News,* July 28, 1977; Geoffrey Stokes, "What Makes Bella Run Cautious?" *Village Voice,* August 22, 1977.

52. Arthur Browne et al., *I, Koch* (New York: Dodd, Mead, 1985), 83, 88.

53. *NYT,* May 12, 1977; *Soho Weekly News,* May 12, 1977; *DN,* September 21, 1977.

54. *NYT,* January 8, June 10, 1977; *New York Post,* January 26, 1977; Doug Ireland, "The Wizard of Ooze," *New York,* January 31, 1977.

55. *DN,* April 25, 1977; *NYT,* April 15, May 7, 8, 1977.

56. Steven Marcus, "Cuomo and the Liberal Party: A Double Crap Shoot," *New York* May 23, 1977, 8; Alex Rose, Unpublished Memoirs, in the possession of Herbert Rose; *NYT,* May 7, 1977.

57. *DN,* February 10, 1977; *Wall Street Journal,* August 26, 1977.

58. *NYT,* February 19, May 28, 1977; Nat Hentoff, "The Political Education of Mario Cuomo," *Village Voice,* August 15, 1977, 31–32

59. Robert S. McElvaine, *Mario Cuomo: A Biography* (New York: Scribner's, 1988) 238–41.

60. *NYP,* April 7, 1977; Maurice Carroll, "Beame's Scenario: How to Beat Bella," *The New York Times Magazine* (June 26, 1977), 32–34.

61. *NYT,* July 14, 1977; United States Securities and Exchange Commission, *Staff Report on Transacting Securities of the City of New York,* August 26, 1977, Vol. 1, 3. Beame attributes the timing of the report's release to politics, and remains bitter about it to this day. Beame interview, September 20, 1988.

62. *NYT,* July 13, 1977; *DN,* August 29, 1977.

63. *DN,* May 15, 1977; *Time* July 18, 1977; *West Sider* July 21, 1977; *Soho Weekly News* July 28, 1977: Anna Mayo, "Why Men Fear Bella," *Village Voice,* July 4, 1977.

64. Doug Ireland, "Democratic Dogfight: A Hopeless Welter of Nonissues," *New York* September 5, 1977; John Corry, "The Koch Story," *The New York Times Sunday Magazine,* October 30, 1977.

65. *NYT,* March 5, September 21, 1977; *West Sider,* April 28, 1977; Denis Hamill, "Hi, I'm for Capital Punishment. Are You?" *Village Voice,* September 5, 1977.

66. Denis Hamill, "Hi, I'm for Capital Punishment," 11; *Village Voice,* September 19, 1977, 35.

67. Denis Hamill, "Hi, I'm for Capital Punishment," 11; Campaign Ephemera, 1977, NYPL.

68. *NYT* March 5, May 12, August 6, 1977; *Wall Street Journal,* November 1, 1977; Denis Hamill, "Hi, I'm for Capital Punishment," 13.

69. Denis Hamill, "Hi, I'm for Capital Punishment," 13; Browne, et al., *I, Koch*, 119–62 gives a detailed account of Koch's 1977 election campaign. Edward I. Koch, with William Rauch, *Mayor: An Autobiography*, (New York: Warner Books, 1984), 21–39 gives Koch's description of the campaign.

70. *DN*, August 24, 1977; *NYP*, August 19, 1977. Apparently at Murdoch's direction, the *Post* began reporting campaign news in a biased way that favored Koch. Ultimately, a number of reporters protested, and some resigned over the issue. McElvaine, *Mario Cuomo*, 244–45; Browne, et al., *I, Koch*, 152–53.

71. *NYT*, May 13, June 10, 1977; Campaign Ephemera, 1977, NYPL.

72. Hentoff, "The Political Education of Mario Cuomo," 31; *NYT*, August 25, 1977.

73. *NYT*, July 25, August 24, 1977.

74. *NYT*, September 9, 10, 1977.

75. *NYT*, September 10, 1988. I followed a process for the 1977 primary and run-off similar to that described for the 1973 race in footnote 40.

76. Browne, et al., *I, Koch*, 155–56; Esposito interview, October 6, 1988.

77. *NYT*, September 14, 1977.

78. *NYT*, September 9, 1977.

79. *NYT*, September 14, 19, 1977.

80. *NYT*, September 21, 1977.

81. *NYT*, September 22, 27, 1977.

Eleven: The Chutzpah of Edward I. Koch

1. *NYT*, January 1, 3, 24, February 27, 1978; Koch, *Mayor*, 44.

2. Shefter, *Political Crisis, Fiscal Crisis*, 128–37; Dick Netzer, "The Economy and Governing of the City," 41–53 in Jewel Bellush and Dick Netzer, eds. *Urban Politics: New York Style*.

3. Shefter, *Political Crisis, Fiscal Crisis*, 172–74; Browne, et al., *I, Koch*, 182–83.

4. Shefter, *Political Crisis, Fiscal Crisis*, 128; Auletta, *The Streets Were Paved With Gold*, 145–46.

5. *NYT*, January 2, 1978.

6. Browne, et al., *I, Koch*, 162–67; Koch, *Mayor*, 63.

7. Browne, et al., *I, Koch*, 185; Koch, *Politics*, 18; Edward I. Koch, interview with author, New York City, September 24, 1991; Shefter, *Political Crisis, Fiscal Crisis*, 174–76.

8. Koch, *Mayor*, 159; *NYT*, August 2, 4, 1979.

9. Koch, *Mayor*, 182–88; *NYT*, April 6, 1980.

10. Browne, Collin & Goodwin, *I, Koch*, 207.

11. Davidoff interview, September 14, 1988; Koch interview, September 24, 1991; Morris, *The Cost of Good Intentions*, 61–67.

12. Browne, et al., *I, Koch*, 197; Koch interview, September 24, 1991.

13. Ken Auletta, "Profiles: E. I. Koch," *The New Yorker,* September 10, 1979, 54ff.; September 17, 1979, 50ff.

14. Koch, "How'd I do?," 27; Koch interview, September 24, 1991; Charles V. Hamilton, "The Black Experience," 374 in Bellush and Netzer, eds., *Urban Politics: New York Style.*

15. *NYT,* September 3, 1981.

16. Browne, et al., *I, Koch,* 229–37; Koch, *Mayor,* 313–15.

17. *NYT,* September 24, 1981

18. Ibid.

19. *NYT,* September 11, 12, 1981; Kevin Flynn and Ellis Henican, "The Steady Rise of David Dinkins: Lessons from Harlem's Politics," *New York Newsday,* October 29, 1989, 21.

20. Koch interview, September 24, 1991; Browne, et al., *I, Koch,* 248; Robert F. Wagner, Jr., interview with author, New York City, September 11, 1991.

21. McElvaine, *Mario Cuomo,* 283–86.

22. McElvaine, *Mario Cuomo,* 288–302; Koch, *Mayor,* 347–54.

23. Sam Roberts, "Koch Against Koch," *The New York Times Magazine* (June 11, 1989), 32.

24. Koch, *Mayor, passim.*

25. New York City Human Resources Administration, "Homeless Shelter Population Statistics," 1986–1988.

26. *NYT,* July 19, 27, 29, November 8, 15, December 16, 1983.

27. Browne, et al., *I, Koch,* 292–93.

28. *NYT,* October 30, 1984, February 5, 1985.

29. *NYT,* April 5, 1984.

30. *NYT,* September 29, 1984, February 1, 1985; *NYP,* February 11, 1985; Wayne Barrett, "Denny Farrell Betrays the Coalition," *The Village Voice,* February 19, 1985; Badillo interview, September 20, 1988.

31. Koch, *Politics,* 222–25; Koch interview, September 24, 1991.

32. *NYT,* September 11, 12, 1985.

33. *NYT,* November 6, 7, 1985.

34. Jack Newfield and Wayne Barrett, *City for Sale: Ed Koch and the Betrayal of New York* (New York: Harper, 1988), *passim.*

35. Newfield & Barrett, *City for Sale, passim.*

36. *NYT,* June 16, 1988.

37. Koch, "How'd I do?," 47; *NYT,* October 4, December 22, 1988.

38. James B. Stewart, *Den of Thieves* (New York: Simon & Schuster), 1991, *passim.*

39. Jim Sleeper, *The Closest of Strangers: Liberalism and the Politics of Race in New York,* (New York: Norton, 1990) 138–40, 184–88.

40. Robert D. McFadden, et al., *Outrage: The Story Behind the Tawana Brawley Hoax,* (New York: Bantam Books, 1990), *passim.*

41. *NYT*, April 12, 1988.

42. *NYT*, April 21, 1988.

Twelve: A City in Search of Harmony

1. Flynn and Henican, "The Steady Rise of David Dinkins," 10; Joe Klein "The Friends of David Dinkins," *New York Magazine*, October 30, 1989, 14; Sleeper, *The Closest of Strangers*, 269–73.

2. Flynn and Henican, "The Steady Rise of David Dinkins"; Joe Klein, "Mr. Softy," *New York Magazine*, January 16, 1989; Sleeper, *The Closest of Strangers*, 272–74.

3. Klein, "Mr. Softy," 20; Peter Wilkinson, "Who'll Stop the Reign?" *7 Days*, 14; *NYT*, December 8, 1988; January 29, February 15, September 17, 1989.

4. Joe Klein, "Koch's Last Stand?," *New York Magazine*, December 5, 1988, 54ff.

5. Ibid.

6. Klein, "Koch's Last Stand?," 55; Author's interview with Richard Ravitch, New York City, September 9, 1991.

7. Joe Klein, "Great Man Theory," *New York Magazine*, February 13, 1989, 16; *NYT*, January 5, 1989.

8. Joe Klein, "Ready for Rudy," *New York Magazine*, March 6, 1989, 31; Newfield & Barrett, *City for Sale*, 18.

9. *NYT*, August 12, 1968; Author's interview with FBI official, name withheld, 1986.

10. Klein, "Great-Man Theory," 19; *NYT*, January 5, 1989.

11. Klein, "Great-Man Theory," 16; Klein, "Ready for Rudy," 31; *NYT*, January 5, 1989.

12. *NYT*, January 11, 1989.

13. Andy Logan, "Around City Hall," *The New Yorker*, January 2, February 13, 1989; *Newsday*, July 14, 1989; Koch interview, September 24, 1991; Wagner, Jr. interview, September 9, 1991.

14. Joe Klein, "Been Down So Long It Looks Like Up To Me," *New York Magazine* (February 20, 1989), 35; Koch interview, September 24, 1991; Wagner, Jr. interview, September 9, 1991.

15. Andy Logan, "Around City Hall," *The New Yorker* (April 17, 1989), 123. Just days before the Democratic primary the Queens Democratic organization realized that Ravitch had no chance to win and switched their endorsement to Koch.

16. Klein, "The Friends of David Dinkins," October 30, 1989, 14; Blanche Blank, "Bureaucracy: Power in Details," 124–25, in Bellush and Netzer, eds. *Urban Politics New York Style*.

17. *Newsday*, July 7, 19, 1989.

18. *Newsday*, July 8, 21, 1989.

19. *NYT*, May 2, 1989.

20. *Newsday*, July 21, 23, 24, 1989; Joe Klein, "Can Dinkins Do It?," *New York Magazine*, July 31, 1989, 31ff.

21. *Newsday*, July 8, 9, 1989.

22. *DN*, July 14, 1989; Joe Klein, "Rudy's Fall from Grace," *New York Magazine*, August 21, 1989.

23. *NYT*, April 21–29, November 4, 1989; Campaign paraphernalia paid for by the Committee for David Dinkins, in the possession of the author.

24. *NYT*, August 23–29, September 1, 1989; Joe Klein, "Brotherhood Week," *New York Magazine*, September 11, 1989, 36ff.; Sleeper, *The Closest of Strangers*, 193.

25. *Newsday*, September 14, 1989; *NYT*, September 14, 1989.

26. *Newsday*, September 13, 14, 1989; *NYT*, September 14, 1989. Both newspapers report the election results broken down by ethnic group and other demographic characteristics according to information gathered in exit polls on primary day. The two sets of data are consistent except for how the Hispanic vote split. *Newsday*, relying on a poll commissioned in conjunction with WNBC-TV, reports the breakdown of the Hispanic vote as 68% in favor of Dinkins and 27% for Koch. In this poll Hispanics are presented as an independent category separate from whites and blacks. *The New York Times*, relying on a poll commissioned in conjunction with CBS-TV News, did not offer Hispanic as a separate category, but makes the following statement in a footnote: "Not shown are 160 respondents who indicated they were Hispanic and 35 who indicated other races. Of Hispanics, 41 percent said they voted for Koch; 54 percent said they voted for Dinkins. " I have cited the *Newsday* figure in the text because it appeared to gather the information in a more direct and therefore more reliable manner. The figures are sufficiently different that the nuance of the analysis would change, but the basic point still holds even with the more even split reported in *The New York Times*.

27. *NYT*, September 13, 14, 1989; *Newsday*, September 14, 1989.

28. *Newsday*, September 14, 1989;

29. *Newsday*, September 13, 1989; *NYT*, October 9, 1989.

30. *Newsday*, October 7, 1989.

31. Jonathan Rieder, *Canarsie: The Jews and Italians of Brooklyn Against Liberalism* (Cambridge: Harvard University Press, 1985) offers an insightful analysis of the ways that Jewish attitudes toward race compare and differ with the attitudes of Italians even when the two groups live in the same neighborhood and are therefore faced with the same environmental circumstances. Sleeper, *The Closest of Strangers*, examines the peculiar relationship between New York's white liberals, predominantly Jews, and blacks.

32. *Village Voice* September 27, 1989; *Newsday*, September 28, 1989; Jeanie Kasindorf, "Jackie Mason Tries to Talk Himself Out of Trouble," *New York Magazine*, October 16, 1989, 36ff.

33. *Newsday*, September 29, October 2, 3, 10, 1989.

34. *Newsday*, September 28, October 10, 1989.
35. *Newsday*, October 13, 1989.
36. *Newsday*, October 8, 1989.
37. *Newsday*, October 13, 1989.
38. *Newsday*, October 12, 1989.
39. *Newsday*, October 13, 20, 1989.
40. *Newsday*, October 12, 13, 14, 15, 16, 17, 18, 19, 20, 21, 1989. Subsequent to his election, formal investigations into the mayor's sale of Inner City Broadcasting stock concluded that no charges were warranted.
41. *Newsday*, October 24, 1989.
42. *Newsday*, October 30, 1989.
43. *Newsday*, October 30, November 1, 1989.
44. *Newsday*, November 2, 1989.
45. *Newsday*, November 3, 5, 6, 1989.
46. *NYT*, November 9, 1989; *Newsday*, November 9, 1989.
47. *NYT*, March 23, November 8, 1989.
48. *NYT*, September 9, 1989.

Bibliography

Archives and Manuscripts

Adolph A. Berle Diaries. Columbia University, Microfilm Collection.

Campaign Ephemera Files, various years. The New York Public Library (NYPL).

David Dubinsky Papers (DD Papers). International Ladies Garment Workers Union Archives. Cornell University School of Industrial and Labor Relations, Ithaca, New York.

Edward N. Costikyan Papers (ENC Papers). Columbia University, New York City.

Herbert H. Lehman Papers (HHL Papers). Columbia University, New York City.

Liberal Party Papers (LP Papers). New York Public Library.

New York City Municipal Archives, Mayoral Papers:

Abraham D. Beame Papers (ADB Papers)

Vincent R. Impellitteri Papers (VRI Papers)

John V. Lindsay Papers (JVL Papers)

William O'Dwyer Papers (WOD Papers)

Robert F. Wagner Papers (RFW Papers)

Bibliography

New York City Politics Vertical Files, various years. The Municipal Reference and Research Library of New York City (MRRL).

Rose, Alex. Unpublished Diary, November 12, 1918 to February 1, 1919. In the possession of Herbert Rose, New York City.

Rose, Alex. Unpublished Memoirs. In the possession of Herbert Rose, New York City.

Newspapers and Periodiocals

Brooklyn Eagle, (BE)
Commentary
Jewish Daily Forward
Liberal Party News
Manhattan Tribune
New York
New York Daily News, (DN)
New York Herald Tribune,(HT)
New York Journal American, (JA)
New York Post, (NYP)
New York Times, (NYT)
New York World Telegram & Sun, (WT&S)
New Yorker
Newsweek
Soho Weekly News
Time
Village Voice
Wall Street Journal
West Sider

Author's Interviews, New York City

Richard Aurelio, June 17, 1988.
Herman Badillo, September 20, 1988.
Abraham D. Beame, September 28, 1988.
Patrick Cunningham, September 27, 1988.
Sid Davidoff, September 14, 1988.
Julius C. C. Edelstein, March 9, 1988.
Meade Esposito, October 6, 1988.
Sanford Garelik, September 9, 1988.
Rudolf W. Giuliani, July 28, 1992.
Seymour Gross, August, 1987.
Donald S. Harrington, September 28, 1988.
Louis Harris, November 28, 1988.
Raymond L. Jones, May 7, 1991.

Edward I. Koch, September 24, 1991.
Jay Kriegel, July 15, 1988.
John V. Lindsay, October 25, 1988.
Warren Moscow, May 4, December 7, 1987, March 7, 1988.
Robert Price, May 23, 1988.
Robert F. Wagner, Sr., March 28, May 2, 1988.
Robert F. Wagner, Jr., December 6, 1986.

Columbia University Oral Histories

George Combs, 1949, 1950, 1951
Genevieve B. Earle, 1949
Julius Edelstein, 1958, 1963
James A. Farley, 1957
John Jay Feeney, 1983
Joseph A. Gavagan, 1950
Louis Lefkowitz, 1983
Herbert H. Lehman, 1949, 1957, 1959
Vito Marcantonio, 1949
Newbold Morris, 1949
Eleanor Roosevelt, 1957
Paul Ross, 1949
Harry Uviller, 1949

Books, Articles, and Miscellaneous Publications

Abbott, David W., Louis H. Gold and Edward T. Rogowsky. "Police, Politics and Race: The New York City Referendum on Civilian Review," New York; American Jewish Committee and the Joint Center for Urban Studies of the Massachusetts Institute of Technology and Harvard University, 1969

Allinsmith, Wesley and Beverly. "Religious Affiliation and Politico-Economic Attitude: A Study of Eight Major U.S. Religious Groups." *Public Opinion Quarterly* (Fall 1948), 377–89.

Auletta, Ken. *The Streets Were Paved With Gold: The Decline of New York— An American Tragedy*. New York: Vintage Books, 1980.

Aurelio, Richard. "Memo to Messrs. Beame, Marchi, Blumenthal, Biaggi: How to Run Your Campaign." *The New York Times Sunday Magazine*, September 16, 1973.

Barbash, Jack, ed. "Special Supplement on David Dubinsky." *Labor History* 9 (Spring 1968).

Bayor, Ronald. *Neighbors in Conflict: The Irish, Germans, Jews and Italians of New York City, 1929–1941*. Baltimore: Johns Hopkins University Press, 1978.

Bell, Daniel. *The End of Ideology*. rev. ed. New York: the Free Press, 1962.

Bibliography

Bellush, Jewel and Bernard. *Union Power and New York: Victor Gotbaum and District Council 37*. New York: Praeger, 1984.

Bellush, Jewel. "Housing: The Scattered Site Controversy." In Jewel Bellush and Stephen M. David, eds. *Race and Politics in New York City*. New York: Praeger, 1971.

Bellush, Jewel and Dick Netzer, *Urban Politics: New York Style*. Armonk, N.Y.: M. F. Sharp, 1990.

Bendiner, Robert. "DeSapio's Big Moment, or the Rout of the Innocents." *The Reporter*, October 16, 1958.

Benson, Lee. *The Concept of Jacksonian Democracy: New York as a Test Case*. Princeton: Princeton University Press, 1961.

Biles, Roger. *Big City Boss in Depression and War: Mayor Edward J. Kelly of Chicago*. Dekalb: Northern Illinois University Press, 1984.

Bloom, Alexander. *Prodigal Sons: The New York Intellectuals and Their World*. New York: Oxford University Press, 1986.

Blumenson, S.L. "The Politicians." *Commentary*, March, 1956.

Bower, Robert. "How New York City Labor Votes." *Public Opinion Quarterly* (Winter, 1947–48), 614–15.

Brooks, Thomas R. "Lindsay, Quill and the Transit Strike." *Commentary*, March 1966.

Browne, Arthur, Dan Collins and Michael Goodwin. *I, Koch: A Decidedly Unauthorized Biography of the Mayor of New York City, Edward I. Koch*. New York: Dodd Mead, 1985.

Buckley, Tom. "Running for the Unrunnable." *The New York Times Magazine*, June 3, 1973.

Buckley, William F. *The Unmaking of a Mayor*. New York: Viking, 1966.

Burner, David. *The Politics of Provincialism: The Democratic Party in Transition, 1918–1932*. Cambridge: Harvard University Press, 1967.

Button, Daniel. *Lindsay: A Man for Tomorrow*. New York: Random House, 1965.

Callow, Alexander B., Jr., *The Tweed Ring*. New York: Oxford University Press, 1965.

Caro, Robert. *The Power Broker: Robert Moses and the Fall of New York*. New York: Vintage, 1975.

Carroll, Maurice. "Beame's Scenario: How to Beat Bella." *The New York Times Magazine*, June 26, 1977.

Carter, Barbara. *The Road to City Hall: How John Lindsay Became Mayor*. Englewood Cliffs, NJ: Prentice Hall, 1967.

Chasan, Will. "Congressman Powell's Downhill Fight in Harlem." *The Reporter*, July 10, 1958.

Chern, Kenneth S. "The Politics of Patriotism: War, Ethnicity, and the New York Mayoral Campaign, 1917." *New York Historical Society Quarterly* (1979): 291–313.

Childs, Richard S. "Introducing Jonah J. Goldstein." *The Searchlight*, Published by the Citizens Union of the City of New York, July, 1945.

Citizen's Union Press Releases, various dates, MRRL.

Citron, Casper. *John V. Lindsay and the Silk Stocking Story*. New York: Fleet, 1965.

Clark, Kenneth B. *Dark Ghetto: Dilemmas of Social Power*. New York: Harper, 1965.

Clark, Terry Nichols. "The Irish Ethic and the Spirit of Patronage," *Ethnicity* 2 (1975), 305–59.

Cohen, Naomi Wiener. *A Dual Heritage: The Public Career of Oscar Straus*. Philadelphia: Jewish Publication Society, 1969.

Cohen, Naomi Wiener. *Encounter With Emancipation*. Philadelphia: Jewish Publication Society, 1984.

Cohen, Naomi Wiener. *Not Free to Desist: The American Jewish Committee, 1906–1966*. Philadelphia: Jewish Publication Society, 1972.

Coleman, James, Ernest Heau, Robert Peabody, and Leo Rigsby. "Computers and Election Analysis: *The New York Times* Project." *Public Opinion Quarterly* (1963), 418–46.

Connable, Alfred and Edward Silberfarb. *Tigers of Tammany: Nine Men Who Ran New York*. New York: Holt, 1967.

Cook, Fred J. and Gene Gleason. "The Shame of New York." *The Nation*, October 31, 1959.

Cooney, John. *The American Pope: The Life and Times of Francis Cardinal Spellman*. New York: Times Books, 1984.

Cornwall, Elmer J., Jr. "Bosses, Machines and Ethnic Groups." In *American Ethnic Politics*. Edited by Lawrence H. Fuchs, New York: Harper, 1968.

Corry, John. "The Koch Story." *The New York Times Sunday Magazine*, October 30, 1977.

Costikyan, Edward N. *Behind Closed Doors: Politics in the Public Interest*. New York: Harcourt, 1966.

Cuomo, Mario. *Forest Hills Diary: The Crisis of Low-Income Housing*. New York: Random House, 1974.

Danish, Max. *The World of David Dubinsky*. New York: World, 1957.

Davis, Allen F. *Spearheads for Reform: The Social Settlements and the Progressive Movement, 1890–1914*. New Brunswick, NJ: Rutgers University Press, 1967.

Dawidowicz, Lucy S. *On Equal Terms: Jews in America, 1881–1981*. New York: Holt, 1982.

Desmond, James. *Nelson Rockefeller: A Political Biography*. New York: Macmillan, 1964.

Dubofsky, Melvyn. "Success and Failure of Socialism in New York City, 1900–1918: A Case Study." *Labor History* 9 (1968), 361–75.

Dubofsky, Melvyn. *When Workers Organize: New York City in the Progressive Era*. Amherst, MA: The University of Amherst Press, 1968.

Bibliography

Egan, Leo. "The How and Why of DeSapio." *The New York Times Magazine*, September 14, 1958.

Eldot, Paula. *Governor Alfred E. Smith: The Politician as Reformer*. New York: Garland Publishers, 1983.

Erie, Steven P. *Rainbow's End: Irish Americans and the Dilemmas of Urban Machine Politics, 1840–1985*. Berkeley, CA: University of California Press, 1988.

Ernst, Robert. *Immigrant Life in New York City*. Port Washington, NY: Ira J. Friedman, 1949.

Farley, James A. *Jim Farley's Story: The Roosevelt Years*. New York: McGraw-Hill, 1948.

Flaherty, Joe. *Managing Mailer*. New York: Coward McCann, 1969.

Flournoy, Houston Irvine. "The Liberal Party in New York State." Ph.D. diss., Princeton University, 1956.

Flynn, Edward J. "Bosses and Machines." *The Atlantic Monthly*. May, 1947.

Flynn, Edward J. *You're the Boss*. New York: Viking, 1947.

Forman, Seymour B. " 'Silk Stocking' Politics: A Study of Two Political Clubs in a New York County Assembly District." Master's Thesis, Columbia University, 1954.

Frankel, Max. "Robert B. Blaikie and His Irregular Democratic Club." Master's Thesis, Columbia University, 1953.

Freeman, Joshua B. "Catholics, Communists and Republicans: Irish Workers and the Organization of the Transport Workers Union." In Michael H. Frisch and Daniel J. Walkowitz, eds. *Working Class America*. Urbana, IL: University of Illinois Press, 1983.

Friedman, Jacob A. *The Impeachment of Governor William Sulzer*. New York: Columbia University Press, 1939.

Fuchs, Ester R. *Mayors and Money: Fiscal Policy in New York and Chicago*. Chicago: University of Chicago Press, 1992.

Fuchs, Lawrence, ed. *American Ethnic Politics*. New York: Harper, 1968.

Garelik, Neal. "The Board of Estimate." Bachelor's Thesis, Columbia University, 1988.

Garrett, Charles. *The LaGuardia Years: Machine and Reform Politics in New York City*. New Brunswick, NJ: Rutgers University Press, 1961.

Gelfand, Mark. I. *A Nation of Cities*. New York: Oxford Univesity Press, 1975.

Gilfoyle, Timothy. *City of Eros: New York City, Prostitution and the Commercialization of Sex, 1790–1920*. New York: Norton, 1992.

Gittell, Marilyn. "Education: The Decentralization–Community Control Controversy." In Jewel Bellush and Stephen M. David, eds. *Race and Politics in New York City*. New York: Praeger, 1971.

Glasser, Israel. "An Analysis of Differential Voting Participation in the 1953 Mayoralty Primary Election in New York City." Ph.D. diss., New York University, 1957.

Glazer, Nathan. *American Judaism.* 2d ed. Chicago: The University of Chicago Press, 1972.

Glazer, Nathan and Daniel Patrick Moynihan. *Beyond the Melting Pot: The Negroes, Puerto Ricans, Jews, Italians and Irish of New York City.* 2d ed. Cambridge: MIT. Press, 1970.

Glazer, Nathan. "Is New York City Ungovernable?" *Commentary,* September 1961.

Goetchus, Vernon M. "The Village Independent Democrats: A Study in the Politics of the New Reformers." Bachelor's Thesis, Weslayan University, 1963.

Goldstein, Jonah J. "The Jewish Vote." *The American Hebrew,* November 22, 1912.

Goren, Arthur. *New York Jews and the Quest for Community: The Kehillah Experiment, 1908–1922.* New York: Columbia University Press, 1970.

Gorenstein, Arthur. "A Portrait of Ethnic Politics: the Socialists and the 1908 and 1910 Congressional Elections on the East Side." *American Jewish Historical Quarterly,* formerly *Publications of the American Jewish Historical Society* 50 (March, 1961), 202–38.

Goret, Mark. "A History of the Bronx Conservative Party." *The Bronx County Historical Society Journal* (Spring 1986), 8–12.

Greeley, Andrew M. *That Most Distressful Nation: The Taming of the American Irish.* Chicago: Quadrangle Books, 1972.

Greenfield, Meg. "Tammany in Search of a Boss." *The Reporter,* April 13, 1961.

Griffith, Elisabeth A. "John Lindsay: Candidate and Campaign: An Analysis of the New Politics." Bachelor's Thesis, Wellesley College, 1969.

Gurock, Jeffrey. "The 1913 New York State Civil Rights Act." *American Jewish Studies Review* 1 (1976), 93–121.

Hamburger, Philip. *Mayor Watching and Other Pleasures.* New York: Rinehart, 1958.

Hamburger, Philip. "Some People Watch Birds." *The New Yorker,* December 26, 1953.

Hamburger, Philip. "That Great Big New York Up There." *The New Yorker,* May 28, 1957.

Hamill, Denis. "Hi. I'm For Capital Punishment. Are You?" *The Village Voice,* September 5, 1977.

Hamilton, Charles V. *Adam Clayton Powell, Jr.: The Political Biography of an American Dilemma.* New York: Atheneum, 1991.

Hammack, David. *Power and Society: Greater New York at the Turn of the Century.* New York: Russell Sage Foundation, 1982.

Handlin, Oscar. *Al Smith and His America.* Boston: Little, Brown, 1958.

Hansen, Marcus Lee. *The Atlantic Migration, 1607–1860.* New York: Harper, 1940.

Bibliography

Hapgood, David. "The Purge That Failed: Tammany v. Powell." *Case Studies in Practical Politics*. New York: Holt, 1959.

Harris, Louis and Associates. "A Study of the Election for Mayor of New York With Special Focus on the Democratic Primary, August 4, 1961." In the possession of the author.

Harris, Louis and Associates. "A Study of Where Robert F. Wagner Stands in the 1961 Race for Mayor of New York and What New Yorkers Think of His Incumbent Administration, March 29, 1961." In the possession of the author.

Harris, Louis and Associates. "A Survey for the Race for Mayor of New York, August, 1957," and "A Survey for the Race for Mayor, Early October, 1957." In RFW Papers.

Harris, Louis and Associates. "A Survey of Voter Attitude Toward New York City and Its Government, May 1959." In the possession of the author.

Harris, Louis and Bert E. Swanson. *Black-Jewish Relations in New York City*. New York: Praeger, 1970.

Hart, Peter D. and Research Associates. "A Survey of the Attitudes of Voters in New York City, January 1973." In ADB Papers.

Haskel, Harry. *A Leader of the Garment Workers: The Biography of Isidore Nagler*. New York: Shulsingers Brothers, 1950.

Heilbroner, Robert. "Carmine G. DeSapio: The Smile on the Face of the Tiger." *Harper's Magazine*, July, 1954.

Henderson, Thomas M. *Tammany Hall and the New Immigrants*. New York: Arno Press, 1976.

Hentoff, Nat. *A Political Life: The Education of John V. Lindsay*. New York: Knopf, 1969.

Hentoff, Nat. "The Political Education of Mario Cuomo." *Village Voice*, August 15, 1977.

Herberg, Will. "From Marxism to Judaism: Jewish Belief as a Dynamic of Social Action." *Commentary*, January, 1947.

Herberg, Will. "The Jewish Labor Movement in the United States." *The American Jewish Yearbook* (53) 1952.

Hertz, Emanuel. "Politics: New York." In Charles S. Bernheimer, ed. *The Russian Jew in the United States*. Philadelphia: The John C. Winston Company, 1905.

Hickey, Neil and Ed Edwin. *Adam Clayton Powell and the Politics of Race*. New York: Fleet, 1965.

Higham, John. *Strangers in the Land: Patterns of American Nativism, 1860–1925*. New York: Atheneum, 1973.

Hirsch, Mark D. "Richard Croker: An Interim Report on the Early Career of a 'Boss' of Tammany Hall." In Irwin Yellowitz, ed. *Essays in the History of New York City*. Port Washington, NY: Kennikat Press, 1978.

Hood, Clifton D. "Underground Politics: A History of Mass Transit in New York City Since 1904." Ph.D. diss., Columbia University, 1986.

Hoover, Edgar M. and Raymond Vernon. *Anatomy of a Metropolis.* Cambridge: Harvard Univesity Press, 1959.

Horton, Raymond D. *Municipal Labor Relations in New York City: Lessons of the Lindsay-Wagner Years.* New York: Praeger, 1972.

Howe, Irving. *Socialism and America.* New York: Harcourt, 1977.

Howe, Irving. *World of Our Fathers: The Journey of the East European Jews to America and the Life They Found and Made.* New York: Harcourt, 1976.

Hunt, Hamlen. "New Deal Wake: Boston Massachussetts." *Commentary*, December 1952.

Hutchmacher, Joseph J. *Senator Robert F. Wagner and the Rise of Urban Liberalism.* New York: Atheneum, 1968.

Huthmacher, Joseph J. "Charles Evans Hughes and Charles F. Murphy, the Metamorphosis of Progressivism," *New York History* 46 (January 1965), 25–40.

Interim Report Re: Printing and Distribution of Anonymous Campaign Literature in 1961 Mayoralty Primary, From John G. Bonomi, Special Assistant Attorney General and Counsel, New York Fair Campaign Practices Committee, To Attorney General Louis Lefkowitz. Final report dated November 3, 1961.

Ireland, Doug. "Democratic Dogfight: A Hopeless Welter of Nonissues." *New York*, September 5, 1977.

Ireland, Doug. "The Wizard of Ooze." *New York*, January 31, 1977.

Isaacs, Stephen D. *Jews and American Politics.* Garden City, NY: Doubleday, 1974.

Jacobs, Jane. *The Death and Life of Great American Cities.* New York: Vintage, 1961.

Javits, Jacob K. with Rafael Steinberg. *Javits: The Autobiography of a Public Man.* Boston: Houghton Mifflin, 1981.

Johnston, Alva. "Profiles: The Great Expurgator." *The New Yorker*, March 29, 1947.

Jonnes, Jill. *We're Still Here: The Rise Fall and Resurrection of the South Bronx.* New York: The Atlantic Monthly Press, 1986.

Josephson, Matthew and Hannah. *Al Smith: Hero of the Cities.* Boston: Houghton Mifflin, 1969.

Josephson, Matthew. *Statesman of American Labor.* New York: Doubleday, 1952.

Kahn, E. J. *Jock: The Life and Times of John Hay Whitney.* Garden City, NY: Doubleday, 1981.

Kahn, E. J. "Plenipotentiary I: Profile of W. Averell Harriman," and "Plenipotentiary II: Profile of W. Averell Harriman." *The New Yorker*, May 3, 10, 1952.

Kantrowitz, Nathan. *Ethnic and Racial Segregation in the New York Metropolis: Residential Patterns Among White Ethnic Groups, Blacks and Puerto Ricans.* New York: Praeger, 1973.

Bibliography

Kaufman, William. "The New York City Board of Estimate." Master's Thesis, City College of New York, 1963.

Keller, Morton. *Affairs of State: Public Life in Late Nineteenth Century America.* Cambridge, MA: The Belknap Press, 1977.

Kenworthy, E. W. "The Emergence of Mayor Wagner." *The New York Times Magazine,* August 20, 1955.

Kessner, Thomas. *Fiorello H. LaGuardia and the Making of Modern New York.* New York: McGraw-Hill, 1989.

Kessner, Thomas. *The Golden Door: Italian and Jewish Immigrant Mobility in New York City, 1880–1915.* New York: Oxford University Press, 1977.

Klein, Woody. *Lindsay's Promise: The Dream That Failed.* New York: Macmillan, 1970.

Koch, Edward I., with William Rauch. *Mayor: An Autobiography.* New York: Warner Books, 1984.

Koch, Edward I., with William Rauch. *Politics.* New York: Simon and Schuster, 1985.

Lee, Calvin B. T. *One Man, One Vote.* New York: Scribner's, 1967.

Lehman, Herbert H. "Liberalism and Judaism." *Jewish Heritage* (Spring 1958), 5–10.

Lekachman, Robert. "How We Beat the Machine: Challenging Tammany at the District Level." *Commentary,* April 1958.

Leuchtenberg, William E. *Franklin D. Roosevelt and the New Deal.* New York: Harper, 1963.

Leuchtenberg, William E. *The Perils of Prosperity, 1914–1932.* Chicago: The University of Chicago Press, 1958.

Levine, Edward M. *The Irish and Irish Politicians: A Study of Cultural and Social Alienation.* Notre Dame, Indiana: University of Notre Dame Press, 1966.

Levine, Naomi. *Ocean Hill-Brownsville: A Case History of Schools in Crisis.* New York: Popular Library, 1969.

Levitan, Mitchel. "Rise Fall and . . . of FDR, Jr." *The New York Times Magazine,* October 23, 1966.

Lewinson, Edwin R. *Black Politics in New York City.* New York: Twayne, 1974.

Lewinson, Edwin R. *John Purroy Mitchel: The Boy Mayor of New York.* New York: Astra Books, 1965.

Liebman, Arthur. "The Ties That Bind: The Jewish Support for the Left in the United States." *American Jewish Historical Quarterly* 66 (December 1976), 285–321.

Lindsay, John V. *Journey into Politics: Some Informal Observations.* New York: Dodd Mead, 1967.

Lowi, Theodore. *At the Pleasure of the Mayor: Patronage and Power in New York City, 1898–1958.* London: The Free Press, 1964.

Lowi, Theodore. "Old Machines for New." *The Public Interest* (Fall 1967), 83–92.

Luscombes, Irving Foulds. "WYNC: 1922–1940: The Early History of Twentieth Century Urban Service." Ph.D. diss., New York University, 1968.

Luthin, Richard H. *American Demogogues: Twentieth Century.* Gloucester, MA: Peter Smith, 1957.

Maas, Peter and Nick Thimmesch. "The Fight for City Hall." *The New York Herald Tribune Magazine,* January 2, 1966.

Mahoney, J. Daniel. *Actions Speak Louder.* New York: Arlington House, 1968.

Maier, Mark H. *City Unions: Managing Discontent in New York City.* New Brunswick, NJ: Rutgers University Press, 1987.

Mann, Arthur. *LaGuardia: A Fighter Against His Times, 1882–1933.* Chicago: University of Chicago Press, 1959.

Mann, Arthur. *LaGuardia Comes to Power, 1933.* Chicago: University of Chicago Press, 1965.

Mann, Arthur. *The One and the Many.* Chicago: The University of Chicago Press, 1979.

Mann, Arthur. "When LaGuardia Took Over." *The New York Times Magazine,* January 2, 1966.

Manso, Peter, ed. *Running Against the Machine.* Garden City, NY: Doubleday, 1969.

Marcus, Steven. "Cuomo and the Liberal Party: A Double Crap Shoot." *New York,* May 23, 1977.

Mayer, Martin. *The Teachers Strike: New York 1968.* New York: Harper, 1968.

Mayor's Committee on Management Survey, *Modern Management for the City of New York,* vol. 1, 1953.

McElvaine, Robert S. *Mario Cuomo: A Biography.* New York: Scribner's, 1988.

McFadden, Robert D., Ralph Blumenthal, M. A. Farber, E. R. Shipp, Charles Strum and Craig Wolf. *Outrage: The Story Behind the Tawana Brawley Hoax.* New York: Bantam Books, 1990.

McKaye, Milton. "The Ex-Cop Who Runs New York." *The Saturday Evening Post,* May 31, 1947.

Meyer, Gerald. *Vito Marcantonio: Radical Politician, 1902–1954.* Albany, NY: State University of New York Press, 1989.

Miller, Kerby A. *Emigrants and Exiles: Ireland and the Irish Exodus to North America.* New York: Oxford University Press, 1985.

Mitgang, Herbert. *The Man Who Rode the Tiger: The Life and Times of Judge Samuel Seabury.* New York: Lippincott, 1963.

Moore, Deborah Dash. *At Home in America: Second Generation New York Jews.* New York: Columbia University Press, 1981.

Morris, Charles. *The Cost of Good Intentions: New York City and the Liberal Experiment, 1960–1975.* New York: McGraw-Hill, 1980.

Bibliography

Morsell, John Albert. "The Political Behavior of Negroes in New York City." Ph.D. diss., Columbia University, 1950.

Moscow, Warren. "Exit the Boss, Enter the 'Leader.'" *The New York Times Magazine*, June 22, 1947.

Moscow, Warren. "Political Machines Have Lost Their Grip," *Saturday Evening Post*, April 12, 1947.

Moscow, Warren. *Politics in the Empire State*. New York: Knopf, 1948.

Moscow, Warren. *The Last of the Big-Time Bosses: The Life and Times of Carmine DeSapio and the Rise and Fall of Tammany Hall*. New York: Stein and Day, 1976.

Moscow, Warren. *What Have You Done For Me Lately?* Englewood Cliffs, NJ: Prentice Hall, 1967.

Moynihan, Daniel Patrick. "'Bosses' and 'Reformers': A Profile of the New York Democrats." *Commentary*, June 1961.

Muhlen, Norbert. "Radio: A Political Threat or Promise?" *Commentary*, March, 1947.

Mushkat, Jerome. *Tammany: The Evolution of a Political Machine, 1789–1865*. Syracuse: Syracuse University Press, 1971.

Myers, Gustavus. *The History of Tammany Hall*. 1901. New York: Dover, 1971.

Nevins, Allan. *Herbert H. Lehman and His Era*. New York: Scribner's, 1963.

New York City Board of Elections Annual Report, various years.

New York State Committee on Crime and Correction. "The Tombs Disturbances," October 5, 1970.

O'Brien-Sherwood Associates, Inc. "New York City Attitudes and Opinion Study Regarding the 1965 Mayoralty Elections." In ENC Papers, Columbia University.

O'Dwyer, Paul, *Counsel for the Defense*. New York: Simon & Schuster, 1979.

O'Dwyer, William. *Beyond the Golden Door*. New York: St. John's University Press, 1987.

Osofsky, Gilbert. *Harlem: The Making of a Ghetto*. 2nd ed. New York: Harper, 1971.

Ottenberg, James S. *The Lexington Democratic Club Story*. New York: Lexington Democratic Club, 1959.

Parmet, Herbert S. *The Democrats: The Years After FDR*. New York: Oxford University Press, 1976.

Perry, Elizabeth Israels. *Belle Moskowitz: Feminine Politics and the Exercise of Power in the Age of Alfred E. Smith*. New York: Oxford University Press, 1987.

Pilat, Oliver. *Lindsay's Campaign: A Behind the Scenes Diary*. Boston: Bacon Press, 1968.

Pileggi, Nicholas. "Inside Lindsay's Head." *New York Magazine*, January 19, 1971.

Potter, George W. *To the Golden Door: The Story of the Irish in Ireland and America.* Boston: Little, Brown, 1960.

Powell, Adam Clayton. *Adam By Adam.* New York: Dial, 1971.

Rabinowitz, Dorothy. "The Case of the ILGWU." *Dissent* (Winter 1972), 83–90.

Raskin, A. H. *David Dubinsky: A Life With Labor.* New York: Simon and Schuster, 1977.

Ravitch, Diane. *The Great School Wars, New York City, 1805– 1973.* New York: Basic Books, 1974.

Reeves, Richard. " 'A Great Mayor,' 'That Bum' " *The New York Times Magazine,* January 1, 1967.

Reeves, Richard. "The Impossible Takes a Little Longer." *The New York Times Magazine,* January 28, 1968.

Rieder, Jonathan. *Canarsie: The Jews and Italians of Brooklyn Against Liberalism.* Cambridge: Harvard University Press, 1985.

Riordon, William L. *Plunkitt of Tammany Hall.* Paperback ed., New York: E. P. Dutton, 1963.

Rischin, Moses. *The Promised City: New York's Jews, 1870– 1914.* Cambridge: Harvard University Press, 1962.

Robinson, Frank S. *Machine Politics: A Study of Albany's O'Connells.* New Brunswick, NJ: Transaction Books, 1977.

Rosenwaike, Ira. *Population History of New York City.* Syracuse: Syracuse University Press, 1972.

Ross, Irwin. "Big City Machines and Liberal Voters." *Commentary,* October, 1950.

Rovere, Richard. "Profiles: Nothing Much To It." *The New Yorker,* September 8, 1946.

Sayre, Wallace S. and Herbert Kaufman, *Governing New York City: Politics in the Metropolis.* 1960. New York: Norton, 1965.

Schlesinger, Arthur, Jr. "Death Wish of the Democrats." *The New Republic,* September 15, 1958.

Schlesinger, Arthur Jr. "Herbert H. Lehman: the Conservative as Radical." Address at Hunter College in the Bronx, December 18, 1967. Text in Herbert H. Lehman Collection, Columbia University.

Schlesinger, Arthur, Jr. *Robert Kennedy and His Times.* New York: Ballantine Books, 1978.

Schoen, Douglas. *Pat: A Biography of Daniel Patrick Moynihan.* New York: Harper, 1979.

Shannon, William V. *The American Irish: A Political and Social Portrait.* New York: Macmillan, 1963.

Shapiro, Fred C. and James W. Sullivan. *Race Riots: New York, 1964.* New York: Thomas Crowell, 1964.

Shefter, Martin. *Political Crisis/Fiscal Crisis.* New York: Basic Books, 1985.

Shefter, Martin, "The Electoral Foundations of the Political Machine: New

York City, 1884–1897." In Joel Silbey, Allan Bogue, and William Flanagan, eds. *The History of American Electoral Behavior*. Princeton: Princeton University Press, 1978.

Shipler, David K. "The Two John Lindsay's." *New Republic*, May 1, 1971.

Shriftgiesser, Karl. "A Frantic Day With Our Next Mayor." *The New York Times Magazine*, October 22, 1950.

Sleeper, Jim. *The Closest of Strangers: Liberalism and the Politics of Race in New York*. New York: Norton, 1990.

Smith, Mortimer. *William Jay Gaynor: Mayor of New York*. Chicago: Henry Regnery, 1951.

Smith, Richard Norton. *Thomas E. Dewey and His Times*. New York: Simon and Schuster, 1982.

Spann, Edward K. *The New Metropolis*. New York: Columbia University Press, 1981.

Spinrad, William. "New Yorkers Cast Their Ballots." Ph.D. diss., Columbia University, 1955.

Spivack, Robert. "New York's Mayoralty Race." *The New Republic*. July 9, 1945.

Stewart, James B. *Den of Thieves*. New York: Simon and Schuster, 1991.

Stewart, William James. "A Political History of the American Labor Party, 1936–1944." Master's Thesis, American University, 1959.

Swanberg, W. A. *Citizen Hearst: A Biography of William Randolph Hearst*. New York: Scribner's, 1961.

Szajkowski, Zosa. "The Jews and New York City's Mayoralty Election of 1917," *Jewish Social Studies* 32 (October 1970), 286–306.

Tallmer, Jerry. "Alex Rose of the Liberal Party," *The New York Post*, October 25, 1966.

Teaford, Jon C. *The Unheralded Triumph: City Government in America, 1870–1900*. Baltimore: Johns Hopkins University Press, 1984.

The Liberal Party. "For Our City; 1945 Municipal Program." In New York City Politics Vertical Files, 1945 at MRRL.

"The Public Career of William O'Dwyer." Press clippings compiled for use of campaign workers, Summer, 1949, at MRRL.

Thernstrom, Stephan, ed. *Harvard Encyclopedia of American Ethnic Groups*. Cambridge, MA: Belknap Press, 1980.

Transition Papers Covering the Change of City Administration, 1973–74. New York: Fund for the City of New York, 1974.

Tricarico, Donald. *The Italians of Greenwich Village: The Social Transformation of an Ethnic Community*. New York: The Center for Migration Studies, 1984.

U.S. Census Office. *U.S. Census of the Population, 1950: Population and Housing Characteristics*. Washington, DC: US Government Printing Office, 1953–54.

U.S. Securities and Exchange Commmission. *Staff Report on Transacting Securities of the City of New York*. August 26, 1977.

Wakefield, Dan. "Greenwich Village Challenges Tammany: Ethnic Politics and the New Reformers." *Commentary*, October 1959.

Wald, Lillian D. *The House on Henry Street*. 1915. New York: Dover, 1971.

Walsh, George. *Public Enemies: The Mayor, the Mob and the Crime That Was*. New York: Norton, 1980.

Walter, Jon C. *The Harlem Fox*. Albany: State University of New York Press, 1989.

Ward, Barbara. "Lehman at 80: Young Elder Statesman." *The New York Times Magazine*, March 23, 1958.

Ware, Caroline. *Greenwich Village, 1920–1930: A Comment on American Civilization in the Post-War Years*. New York: Harper, 1935.

Weinbaum, Marvin G. "New York County Republican Politics, 1897–1922: The Quarter Century After Municipal Consolidation." *The New York Historical Society Quarterly* 50 (January 1966), 63–94.

Weiss, Nancy Joan. *Charles Francis Murphy, 1858–1924: Respectability and Responsibility in Tammany Politics*. Northhampton, MA: Smith College, 1968.

Weiss, Nancy Joan. *Farewell to the Party of Lincoln: Black Politics in the Age of FDR*. Princeton: Princeton University Press, 1983.

Welles, Sam. "The Jewish Elan." *Fortune*, February 1960.

Werner, M. R. *It Happened in New York*. New York: Coward McCann, 1957.

Werner, M. R. *Tammany Hall*. Garden City, NY: Doubleday, 1928.

Wesser, Robert. *A Response to Progressivism: The Democratic Party and New York Politics, 1902–1918*. New York: NYU Press, 1986.

Wesser, Robert. *Charles Evans Hughes: Politics and Reform in New York, 1905–1910*. Ithaca: Cornell University Press, 1967.

White, Theodore H. *The Making of the President, 1960*. New York: Atheneum, 1961.

Whittemore, L.H. *The Man Who Ran the Subways: The Story of Mike Quill*. New York: Holt, 1968.

Williams, Robert and Peter J. McElroy, "The Flynn Machine—How the Bronx is Ruled." *The New York Post*, May 18–22, 1953.

Wilson, James Q. *The Amateur Democrat: Club Politics in Three Cities*. Chicago: The University of Chicago Press, 1962.

Woolf, S. J. "It's a Friendly Town, Says the Mayor." *The New York Times Magazine*, April 6, 1947.

Woolf, S. J. "O'Dwyer Tells Why It's Tough." *The New York Times Magazine*, March 21, 1948.

Index

397

Index

Index